A Chicago Tradition Begins

The name of Chicago's pioneer thief is now unknown, but a record of his wickedness remains—he stole thirty-four dollars from a fellow-boarder, one Hatch, at the Wolf Tavern, and was arrested by Constable Reed on a warrant issued by Justice Russell E. Heacock. He was taken at once to Reed's carpenter shop for examination, and the Justice held court sitting on the workbench. Since there was no state's Attorney to handle the prosecution, Hatch engaged John Dean Caton, afterward a noted judge, and the defendant employed Caton's partner, Giles Spring, who likewise became a well-known jurist and City Attorney as well. Despite Spring's objections, Caton compelled his partner's client to strip, and at length the stolen money was found wadded in the toe of the accused man's sock. The defendant was held for trial, which got under way next morning in the Wolf Tavern, "where the public could hear the young lawyers to the best advantage." After much argument and speech-making by counsel, the prisoner was found guilty, but was released on nominal bail pending action on a motion for a new trial. He promptly disappeared, thus establishing a precedent which has been followed more or less regularly in Chicago ever since.

The Gangs of
Chicago

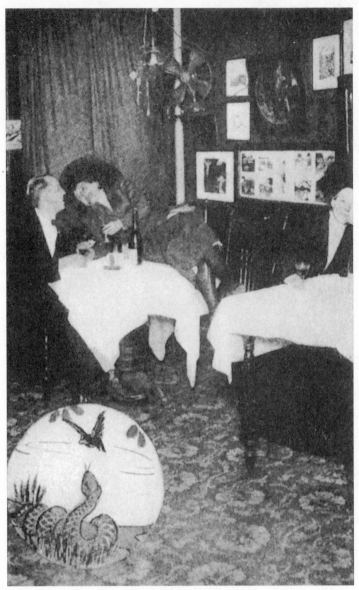

THE FATAL WINE ROOM

And there with drugged potations at her hand,
She soon will be "Another" on the Strand.

The Gangs of
Chicago

AN INFORMAL HISTORY OF THE
CHICAGO UNDERWORLD

Herbert Asbury

THUNDER'S MOUTH PRESS

NEW YORK

THE GANGS OF CHICAGO: *An Informal History of the Chicago Underworld*

©1940 by Alfred A. Knopf, Inc.
©1986 by Northern Illinois University Press

Published by Thunder's Mouth Press
An Imprint of Avalon Publishing Group Incorporated
161 William Street, 16th Floor
New York, NY 10038

Library of Congress Cataloging-in-Publication Data is available.

ISBN 1-56025-454-8

9 8 7 6 5 4 3 2 1

Printed in the United States of America
Distributed by Publishers Group West

TO SVEND AND LIS

FOREWORD

LIMITATIONS OF space have prevented the inclusion in this book of a really comprehensive survey of the Chicago underworld during the prohibition epoch. For more detailed accounts of the activities of Johnny Torrio, Al Capone, Dion O'Banion and other ornaments of gangland the reader is referred to Part Three of the *Illinois Crime Survey*, by John Landesco; *The One-Way Ride*, by Walter Noble Burns; *Al Capone*, by Fred D. Pasley; and *King Crime*, by Collinson Owen, which presents an Englishman's point of view.

I am grateful to many Chicagoans for advice and assistance in gathering material for this book. I wish particularly to express my thanks to Mitchell Dawson; Miss Mildred Bruder of the Chicago Public Library; Colonel Henry Barrett Chamberlin of the Chicago Crime Commission; and L. E. Dicke of Evanston, Illinois.

H. A.

INTRODUCTION

Perry R. Duis

ONE OF THE marks of a great city is that some of the more insightful descriptions and interpretations of its character or personality come from out-of-towners. While they are sometimes naive and ignorant of things known only by natives, the visitors are usually unencumbered by local feuds and prejudices; and they also manage to breathe meaning into things that residents take for granted. So it was with Chicago. Upton Sinclair spent only a few weeks in the city before he wrote *The Jungle*. *If Christ Came to Chicago!*, the vitriolic exposé of 1894, was the result of a British journalist's visit of a few months. Further, Bessie Pierce found nearly fifty other travelers' accounts for her *As Others See Chicago;* and in the half-century since her book was published, numerous other out-of-towners have tried to discover what is both unique and commonly American about Chicago. Even A. J. Liebling, whose *Chicago: The Second City* coined the now-famous nickname of the same words, was an easterner. It is thus not surprising that *Gem of the Prairie*, the most complete story of Chicago crime, came from a New York writer and editor.[1]

Herbert Asbury's work, like that of all authors—especially the popular ones who make no pretense of scholarly detachment—reflects the prejudices of his background. Born in 1891 in Farmington, Missouri, a small town near St. Louis, Asbury had ambition and an interest in journalism that pushed him through the ranks of newspapers from Quincy, Illinois, to Atlanta and by the early 1920s to the *New York Tribune*. Like many other reporters, he also dreamed of a literary career and submitted short pieces to magazines; and it was one of these articles that brought young Asbury instant notoriety. In its April 1926 issue, the *American Mercury* published his "Hatrack," the sympathetic description of Farmington's only prostitute. She is depicted as sad, lonely, and exploited by a town of hymn-singing hypocrites. As perhaps symbolic of the town's moral decay, she services Protestant clients in the Catholic cemetery and Catholics in the Protestant.[2]

The shock and indignation in Farmington was to be expected; the national reaction was a surprise. When the Farmington postmaster refused to deliver the issue, Postmaster General Harry S. New quickly extended the ban nationwide. When the New England Watch and Ward Society pressured the Boston police to stop sales, the *Mercury*'s publisher, Henry L. Mencken, decided to challenge censorship personally. Already regarded as America's leading iconoclast, Mencken arranged to buy a copy from a dealer on Boston Common, where he was promptly arrested. That case was quickly dismissed, but weeks of litigation followed before a permanent federal injunction lifted the nationwide postal ban.[3]

The controversy, one of the most famous in the struggle over the censorship issue, suddenly launched Asbury's career as a commentator on American morals. "Hatrack" became a chapter in his first book, *Up from Methodism* (1926). Its title, a play on that of Booker T. Washington's autobiography, revealed its cynical tone; and a second book, *Methodist Saint* (1927), attacked early American intolerance. Ironically, its central figure was the author's early ancestor, Francis Asbury, America's first Methodist bishop.[4]

These two volumes were the first of sixteen that Herbert Asbury wrote over the next quarter century. While there was some variety in the topics, which included a post-Prohibition bartender's guide and a history of the nation's first oil gusher, the bulk of his life's work focused on the question of how a nation that claimed its morality so fervently could support such an extensive industry of gambling, prostitution, illegal liquor, and other crimes. Two volumes, *Carry Nation* (1929) and *The Great Illusion* (1950), criticized the temperance movement; and another, *Sucker's Progress* (1938), was one of the earliest chronicles of gambling in America. But Asbury became most famous for studies of the underworlds of four cities: San Francisco (*The Barbary Coast*, 1933), New York (*The Gangs of New York*, 1928), New Orleans (*The French Quarter*, 1936), and Chicago (*Gem of the Prairie*, 1940). Taken together, the latter four volumes constitute our greatest compendium of information about American urban lowlife.[5]

The last of these books, *Gem of the Prairie*, deserves reading and rereading for at least a pair of reasons. It remains, first of all, an important work in the historiography of the city. When Asbury's book was published in 1940, accounts of Chicago's past were still largely dominated by booster history, the celebration of the deeds of merchants and industrial barons. Everything from the pioneer fur trade to the Great Fire of 1871 to the opening of every new bank was subjugated to the story of progress. Booster history had little room for the story of such social developments as the growth of ethnic neighborhoods, the struggle for food and shelter, the transformation of work, and, especially, the growth of crime. By 1940 Bessie Louise Pierce's pioneering academic history of the city had just begun to appear; and even her work was predominantly economic and devoted only a few pages to crime. In 1929, *Chicago: A History of Its Reputation*, by local newsmen Lloyd Lewis and Henry Justin Smith, had taken the first tentative steps toward providing Chicago with a glimpse of the people and events that the booster histories ignored. It was up to Asbury, however, to provide what is still the most detailed, reliable, and readable account of the nether side of Chicago's first century.[6]

Gem of the Prairie also provides detailed sketches of those who helped give rise to Chicago's long-standing image problem. Probably no other city in America has labored more than Chicago under a worldwide impression that it was filled with violence and crime. A frontier town during its infancy (the 1830s and 1840s), its population was predominantly young, male, and easily amused by gambling, prostitution, and physical violence. As Chicago developed, the world viewed it as a glimpse into the future of industrial society; and the shocking poverty, social conflict, and tolerance for the so-called victimless crimes reinforced the negative image. Al Capone and his cohorts only perpetuated a problem that was already nearly a century old. Chicagoans liked to think that the violent image was a plot that had been hatched and rehashed for each generation by easterners who were jealous of midwestern growth. More likely, as Anselm Strauss explains it, cities, like minorities, become the victims of stereotyping because the human mind prefers simplicity to complexity and tries to generalize from a limited number of characteristics or people. Since cities attract very diverse populations and activities, it is easier to think quickly of a single image than to try to conceptualize an encyclopedia of human variety. It is clear from the reviews that a major part of Asbury's reading audience consisted of those who were curious about Chicago's unsavory reputation, and *Gem of the Prairie* provided the chronicle that helped answer their questions.[7]

This book is more about people than processes. Like the booster histories it undermined, Asbury's study enshrined innovators. He clearly believed that the inventive criminal mind deserved historical recognition, much in the same way that commercial and industrial leaders were lionized. Thus, while Field, Pullman, and Armour inhabited one pantheon, such characters as Roger Plant, Mickey Finn, Big Jim O'Leary, and Mike McDonald deserved recognition because they introduced new ideas and became the best at what they did. Thus, Asbury credits Johnny Torrio with being the organizational genius who turned bootlegging into a massively profitable business, while dismissing Al Capone as a ruffian who substituted brutal force for intelligence.[8]

Asbury's emphasis on personalities was rooted in part in his choice of sources. He made heavy use of self-important autobiographical material generated by Mayor "Long John" Wentworth and Detective Clifton Wooldridge, but Asbury's press credentials and reputation also gave him access to old clipping files, a considerable advantage in a city where printed newspaper indexes are virtually nonexistent. Those nineteenth-century stories and features were not only much more detailed than today's counterparts, but they were seldom reluctant to publish the kind of embarrassing detail usually associated with modern supermarket tabloids.[9]

Gem of the Prairie could not have been written without the newspapers, but their use presented clear difficulties. Besides errors introduced by sloppy journalism, Asbury had to deal with the perpetual problem of sensationalism. Flashy stories sold papers. By pushing routine stories to the front page and trying to link unrelated wrongdoing, often under headlines that implied conspiracy, editors could generate the notions of crime waves or epidemic corruption. The way a paper handled a crime often depended on whether the candidate it supported was in power. In the case of postbellum crime, the *Tribune* surmised that the Civil War had created the modern newspaper reporter and that peacetime had freed this new giant to unleash investigatorial talents on urban wrongdoing. Thus, although the actual level of crime and corruption had not increased, the newly intensified press coverage created an impression that it had. Furthermore, the press emphasized the deeds of specific people, rather than larger transitions or generalizations. Balanced against these flaws was the fact that newspapers were always quick to criticize the competition's mistakes and that a rag that clouded its reputation with inaccuracy would lose readers. Chicago's intense journalistic rivalry also meant that reporters tried, sometimes creatively, to best each other in uncovering detail.[10]

Another major problem in *Gem of the Prairie* arises from Asbury's biographical approach. History built on the deeds of a series of individuals tends to be episodic and to ignore long-term trends and similarities in different time periods; Asbury's innovators, then, generated change—not industrialization, immigration, communication, or a host of other social forces. Thus, while the book remains an excellent acount for the popular reader, it is for the historian a detailed compilation of information on which to base interpretive ideas.

The information in *Gem of the Prairie* suggests several themes. One is the impact on crime of Chicago's function as the nation's crossroads. Initially, this role grew out of the city's position at the end of the water route to the West; but as the rail network emerged during the last three decades of the nineteenth century, the proportion of host to travelers significantly increased. Tens of thousands of conventioneers, passengers changing trains, vacationers, farmers selling their pigs and wheat in the agricultural markets, salesmen, and others guaranteed an abundance of strangers at any time. This plenitude, in turn, helped shape some of the types of locally based crime that thrived in the city. Pickpockets worked the endless crowds, confident that visitors would never recognize them. Evil cabbies delivered loads of the innocent to their doom: immigrants to exploitive hotels, young women to brothel recruiters, and prosperous-looking marks to thieves. The booming hotel business provided rich opportunities for hotel thieves, while con men cruised the lobbies, bars, dining rooms, and barbershops in search of potential victims. And the fact that so many of the sojourners were men traveling alone contributed to the thriving armies of gamblers and prostitutes and the burgeoning ranks of concert saloons, massage parlors, and other illicit entertainments for the man who left his wife in Keokuk or Kalamazoo.[11]

Furthermore, the crossroads function tended to intensify the city's image problem. As early as 1859, books with such titles as *Tricks and Traps of Chicago* and *Chicago after Dark* warned travelers to beware of Chicagoans, especially those who tried to be friendly. Montgomery Ward, which worried about the welfare of the company's customers, warned farmers not to talk to strangers but to come directly to its offices when visiting town. Many travelers who changed trains and bought newspapers carried back to their homes column after column of detail that appeared to prove the evils of the city. When Chicagoans made a sustained effort in the first decade of this century to attack white slavery and prostitution, the crusade itself damaged the city's reputation. The rail hub was also a major interchange for brothel inductees and, as a consequence, the target of federal enforcement of the Mann Act. Meanwhile, the city's efforts to purge itself of organized vice generated even more sensational publicity than parallel efforts in New York City. Such titles as *The Black Hole, Chicago's Dark Places,* and *From the Dance Hall to White Slavery,* which were often little more than rehashed versions of newspaper features or the Chicago Vice Commission's report, *The Social Evil in Chicago,* were peddled in rural areas by subscription book salesmen. Countless readers who had never visited the city undoubtedly formed negative opinions from these accounts.[12]

A second, and only implicit, theme in Asbury's work is the geographical distribution of vice. He notes the rise and fall of such vice areas as the Sands, Conley's Patch, and the Levee without attempting to generalize about the segregation of sin. It is clear that there were strong community objections to the presence of gambling and prostitution near the business center at midcentury. Not only did it damage the image of the city among visitors, but it threatened upper-class housing areas just south of downtown along Michigan Avenue. Ethnic and racial prejudice may also have been a motivation to squeeze vice into the Sands and the Patch, both Irish neighborhoods, and later into the Levee that partially overlapped the city's emerging black neighborhood. In general, this process of forced concentration, which never became a part of officially stated public policy, represented a geographical compromise between those who were opposed to vice and those who thought it inevitable. The solution was to allow it to thrive, but in a restricted area, where its damage to neighborhoods could be confined.[13]

While these external pressures were part of the rationale for segregated vice, economic forces also favored centralization. Viewed as part of the larger pattern of emerging land use, the Levee and Gamblers' Row on Clark Street were only two of several areas in which such specialized functions as warehousing, culture, theater, department store retailing, and stock trading and banking were concentrated. Moreover, the Levee was conveniently adjacent to several rail terminals that supplied customers, while Gamblers' Row was next to the financial district. Many monied men inhabited the latter area during the workday, and critics were quick to point out that there was a narrow distinction between stock speculation and the roulette wheel. Bucketshops, a specialized form of gambling, grew out of wagering on fluctuations in grain prices.[14]

The geographical distribution of vice was related to a third theme that remains only implicit in *Gem of the Prairie*. Concentration made collaboration convenient, and primordial forms of organized crime were much more prevalent than Asbury's admiration of brilliant individuals would allow us to believe. As more recent historians have noted, the complicated nature of the games that became popular at midcentury encouraged partnerships, while the need to avoid losses in raids grew with the volume of money handled by the gambling houses. These factors helped create a close relationship between gamblers, police, and the politicians who controlled law enforcement. Similarly, as bordellos grew in size and splendor, they also sought immunity from prosecution. The organizers of both forms of vice thus found it more convenient to operate as part of clustered districts, and such prominent politicians as Cook County Democratic Chairman Mike McDonald and Aldermen "Bathhouse John" Coughlin and Michael "Hinky Dink" Kenna exploited the situation for financial and political gain.[15]

Asbury also chronicles the downfall of the era of segregated vice without explaining the broad forces responsible for its demise. The severe depression of the 1890s destroyed decades of financial stability, particularly among gamblers, while the waning political star of Mike McDonald and the assassination of Mayor Carter Harrison I introduced an element of unpredictability into the political side of the relationship. The public revulsion against crime, especially the reaction to William T. Stead's damning exposé *If Christ Came to Chicago*, had prompted businessmen to create the Civic Federation, which envisioned itself a department store of reform that would right a number of Chicago's wrongs. It was no accident, however, that Gamblers' Row became the Federation's first successful target. It was adjacent to the financial district and attracted young clerks and businessmen whose noonhour gaming tarnished the image of respectable firms and fostered rumors of thefts to pay gambling debts and manipulation of market prices whose fluctuations were the subject of wagering. Finally, Gamblers' Row, which occupied the two blocks of Clark Street north of Madison, was in the heart of downtown and in the shadow of City Hall, hardly an aid to the civic booster's efforts to improve Chicago's image.[16]

Another factor in the dispersal of gambling that is also only implicit in *Gem of the Prairie* is the role of technology. The use of telephone and telegraph equipment allowed wagering on races to move to more secluded neighborhood locations; and an old lake ship, *The City of Traverse*, was outfitted with one of the earliest wireless radios in Chicago. Boatloads of gamblers could play the ponies while floating safely outside local police jurisdiction. Thus, electronic communication fostered forms of gambling that were less vulnerable to harassment by reformers and law enforcement officials than the large Clark Street halls with their roulette wheels and dice tables.[17]

Technology was also an important factor in the dispersal of the Levee. Asbury provides a good chronological portrait of the growing anti-vice crusade and the roles of such important individuals as evangelist Gipsy Smith, States Attorney John Wayman, and Mayor Carter Harrison II in shutting down the infamous district. But by the time the Levee lost its unofficial status as a protected district in 1912, the telephone and the automobile were already encouraging the outward dispersal of organized vice. Instant and relatively private communication put "call flats," scattered bordello apartments in the neighborhoods, in contact with saloons and cabbies that supplied customers. Meanwhile, the auto gave criminals speed, anonymity, and, eventually, the protection of armor-plated doors that allowed the geographic expansion of their operations. In retrospect, it is difficult to imagine Al Capone, machinegun in hand, emerging from a horsedrawn buggy or a streetcar![18]

The demise of the Levee was also part of another trend that was only implicit in Asbury's study. This was the declining tolerance of the more public forms of vice. Chicago did not become more morally pure during the first two decades of the century; but it did decide that streetwalking, red lights over doors, anatomical window displays, and brochures issued by the luxurious Everleigh Club were so brazenly obvious that they tarnished the city's already-smudged reputation. This desire to privatize even such minor vices as drinking led to the rapid rise of home delivery of beer and liquor and the proliferation of private clubs among the respectable classes, many of whom lived in the large outlying expanse of all-dry neighborhoods created after the enactment of the local option law of 1907. There was a growing belief that what people did in private was their own business, but what happened in public was everyone's concern. That attitude, along with an extensive tradition of semisecret unlicensed barrooms, paved the way for the world of speakeasies and enormous profits from liquor sales that characterized national Prohibition.[19]

The changes wrought by technology, dispersal, and privatization forced a reorganization of crime. The demise of the Levee stripped Bathhouse John Coughlin and Hinky Dink Kenna of most of their power, in large part because Chicago's fragmented political structure prevented an extension of their influence beyond the borders of the First Ward. Asbury correctly notes that a new organization, Italian rather than Irish in leadership, evolved out of the ruins of the old. Originating under Big Jim Colosimo, it expanded quickly under protégé and successor Johnny Torrio. Other criminal organizations evolved from youth gangs, burglary rings, and other minor outfits into more sophisticated regional forms that clashed over territorial hegemony and ethnic hatreds. The domestication of weaponry developed during the First World War, and the relative youth of the combatants may also have contributed to the amount of bloodshed.[20]

It was appropriate that Asbury ended *Gem of the Prairie* with Capone's 1931 incarceration for income tax evasion. An era had passed, and the Great Depression had ended the age of bouyant optimism. It is also clear that the author developed an increasing distaste for the post–World War years of his subject. The gang wars of the twenties do not sparkle with the witty stories and admiration for innovators that characterized the earlier portions of the book. It may also be that when such major figures as Torrio, Capone, and Moran had departed the scene, Asbury realized the limitations of his biographical approach. A new, more analytical approach to the subject was beginning to appear. The *Illinois Crime Survey,* to which Asbury refers his readers for further information about the 1920s, also based its findings heavily on newspapers; but it asked far broader questions about causation, symbolic events, and the relationship between organized wrongdoing and such contributory factors as juvenile delinquency and a poorly operated criminal justice system. Sociologists were also beginning to answer questions at a level of generalization that was much more sophisticated than Asbury's popular biographical approach allowed. Although *Gem of the Prairie* would certainly not be the last popular book on Chicago crime, those that followed would represent an increasing division between academic studies and those intended for mass audiences.[21]

Despite the lack of a modern interpretive framework, *Gem of the Prairie* remains a valuable contribution to the literature. For the professional historian, it is a mine that never ceases yielding details that grow into ideas. As a document of its time, the book reflected the popular fascination with the *enfant terrible* of cities. The gangster and *film noir* movie genres had created a visual picture of Windy City violence, and pulp detective magazines grew to great popularity during the 1930s, in part because of the frequent Chicago stories. Asbury told the world how the nether side of the city had evolved. For today's reader, *Gem of the Prairie* is a remarkably lively and informative introduction to a slice of the story of one of the world's truly fascinating places.

NOTES

1. The outstanding source on visitors' accounts is Bessie Louise Pierce, *As Others See Chicago* (Chicago: University of Chicago Press, 1933). A. J. Liebling's *Chicago: The Second City* (New York: Alfred A. Knopf, 1952) began as a series of

articles in the *New Yorker*. See also William T. Stead, *If Christ Came to Chicago!* (Chicago: Laird and Lee, 1894); Joseph O. Baylen, "A Victorian's Crusade in Chicago, 1893–94," *Journal of American History* 51 (December 1964): 418–34. The classic description by a Chicagoan remains Nelson Algren, *Chicago: City on the Make* (Garden City, N.Y.: Doubleday, 1951).

2. *Chicago Tribune*, 25 February 1963; *New York Times*, 25 February 1963; Herbert Asbury, "Hatrack," *American Mercury* 7 (April 1926): 479–83.

3. The events are chronicled in the *New York Times*, 5–10, 15, 16, 29, and 30 April; 12 May 1926. On the importance of the case, see Paul Boyer, *Purity in Print* (New York: Charles Scribner's Sons, 1968), 176–81.

4. Herbert Asbury, *Up from Methodism* (New York: Alfred A. Knopf, 1926); and *A Methodist Saint: The Life of Bishop Asbury* (New York: A. A. Knopf, 1927). The divine lived from 1745 to 1816. For a time during the late 1920s Asbury was regarded as an expert on the current status of American religion. See "An Asbury Tries to Toll Protestantism's Knell," *Literary Digest* 96 (3 March 1928): 28–29; and "The Gossip Shop," *Bookman* 64 (October 1926): 246–47.

5. Herbert Asbury, *Ye Olde Fire Laddies* (New York: A. A. Knopf, 1930); Jerry Thomas, *The Bon Vivant's Companion; or, How to Mix Drinks*, ed. Herbert Asbury (New York: Grosset & Dunlap, 1934); his other noncrime works include *The Devil of Pei-Ling* (New York: Burt, 1927); *The Golden Flood: An Informal History of America's First Oil Field* (New York: A. A. Knopf, 1942); *The Tick of the Clock* (New York: Burt, 1928); and an edited work, *Not at Night* (New York: Macy-Macius, 1928). The books on the underworld include *The Barbary Coast: An Informal History of the San Francisco Underworld* (New York: A. A. Knopf, 1933); *The French Quarter: An Informal History of the New Orleans Underworld* (New York: A. A. Knopf, 1936); *The Gangs of New York: An Informal History of the Underworld* (New York: A. A. Knopf, 1928); *Sucker's Progress: An Informal History of Gambling in America from the Colonies to Canfield* (New York: Dodd, Mead & Company, 1938). His temperance studies include: *Carry Nation* (New York: A. A. Knopf, 1929); and his last book, *The Great Illusion: An Informal History of Prohibition* (Garden City, N.Y.: Doubleday, 1950). His *All around the Town* (New York: A. A. Knopf, 1934) includes crime subjects among its varied sketches of New York. Asbury also wrote an introduction and captions to Philip Van Doren Stern, comp., *The Breathless Moment: The World's Most Sensational News Photos* (New York: A. A. Knopf, 1935).

6. Booster histories include, for example, A. T. Andreas, *History of Chicago*, 3 vols. (Chicago: A. T. Andreas Publishing Company, 1884–1886). The best scholarly history is Bessie Louise Pierce, *A History of Chicago*, 3 vols. (New York: Alfred A. Knopf, 1937–1957). The most useful popular studies include Lloyd Lewis and Henry Justin Smith, *Chicago: The History of Its Reputation* (New York: Harcourt, Brace and Company, 1929). Other popular studies include Lloyd

Wendt and Herman Kogan, *Lords of the Levee: The Story of Bathhouse John and Hinky Dink* (Indianapolis: Bobbs Merrill, 1943) and *Big Bill of Chicago* (Indianapolis: Bobbs Merrill, 1953) and Emmett Dedmon, *Fabulous Chicago* (New York: Random House, 1953, 1981).

7. On the city's image, see Pierce, *As Others See Chicago*. The best piece on image-making is Anselm Strauss, *Images of the American City* (New York: Free Press of Glencoe, 1961), esp. pp. 33−51. On the early social structure and crime, see Pierce, *History of Chicago*, I: 172−73, 215−17, 255, 267, 351−52; and II: 431−44. On the gangland image, see John Kobler, *Capone: The Life and World of Al Capone* (New York: G. P. Putnam's Sons, 1971): 306−15. Chicago's reputation colored such reviews as *New Yorker* 16 (12 October 1940): 104 and *Time* 36 (14 October 1940): 124.

8. The best example of booster history based on biography is Paul Gilbert and Charles Bryson, *Chicago and Its Makers* (Chicago: Felix Mendelsohn, Publisher, 1929).

9. John Wentworth Scrapbooks and Harpel Scrapbooks, Chicago Historical Society, contain hundreds of clippings recording interviews with Wentworth about early Chicago. The destruction of early primary sources have left historians greatly dependent on such reminiscences. Clifton R. Wooldridge, *Hands Up! In the World of Crime* (Chicago: Stanton and Van Vliet, 1901); and *The Devil and the Grafter, and How They Work Together to Deceive, Swindle and Destroy Men, Women, Society and Religion* (Chicago: n.p., n.d.) provided Asbury with most of his illustrations. Besides a manuscript index of 1855 newspapers at the Chicago Historical Society, the only early index is of the *Chicago Record-Herald*, 1904−1912. Contemporary newspapers have been indexed since 1972.

10. The best description of newspaper coverage of crime can be found in Justin E. Walsh, *To Print the News and Raise Hell: A Biography of Wilbur F. Storey* (Chapel Hill: University of North Carolina Press, 1968), which describes the *Chicago Times*, a major Asbury source, and its reputation. On the *Tribune* and the impact of war, see *Chicago Tribune*, 21 July 1865.

11. Perry R. Duis, *The Saloon: Public Drinking in Chicago and Boston, 1880−1920* (Urbana: University of Illinois Press, 1983): 233. Ironically, Asbury never mentions one of America's leading con men, Yellow Kid Weil, who resided in the city. See Joseph Weil, *"Yellow Kid" Weil* (Chicago: Ziff-Davis Publishing Company, 1948).

12. *Tricks and Traps of Chicago* (New York: Dinsmore, 1859); A. C. Anderson, *Chicago after Dark* (Chicago: n.p., 1868); Henry B. Leonard, "The Immigrants' Protective League of Chicago, 1908−21," *Journal of the Illinois State Historical Society* 66 (Autumn 1973): 271−84; Perry R. Duis, "Chicago As It Was: Life of a Salesman," *Chicago* 34 (May 1985): 110−13; Vivia Divers, *The Black Hole* (n.p., [1892]); Chicago Vice Commission, *The Social Evil in Chicago* (Chi-

cago: Gunthorp-Warren Printing Company, 1911); *Chicago's Dark Places* (Chicago: Craig Press and Woman's Temperance Publishing Association, 1891); W. H. Lytle and John Dillon, *From the Dance Hall to White Slavery* (Chicago: Charles C. Thompson Company, 1912).

13. On early vice districts, see John J. Flinn, *History of the Chicago Police* (Chicago: Police Book Fund, 1887): 82–83; and Duis, *The Saloon*, 205–73. There are also rough parallels between Detroit during the middle decades of the century. Both cities went through anti-prostitution disorders (although Mayor Wentworth's raid on the Sands was hardly a riot) and ethnic disorders. Both cities also segregated vice into districts to protect the business and high-class residential areas. See John C. Schneider, *Detroit and the Problem of Order, 1830–1880* (Lincoln: University of Nebraska Press, 1980).

14. On the economic land-use question, see Homer Hoyt, *One Hundred Years of Land Values in Chicago* (Chicago: University of Chicago Press, 1933): 97, 103, 201–2; on bucketshops, see Johnathan Lurie, *The Chicago Board of Trade, 1859–1905* (Urbana: University of Illinois Press, 1979): 77–87, 96–104, 138–51, 161–67, 176–81, 185–96.

15. The most useful explanation of the interrelationship of midcentury gamblers and police can be found in David R. Johnson, "A Sinful Business: The Origins of Gambling Syndicates in the United States, 1840–1887," in David H. Bayley, ed., *Police and Society* (Beverly Hills: Sage Publications, 1977): 17–47; and Mark Haller, "Bootleggers and American Gambling, 1920–1950," in United States Commission on the Review of the National Policy toward Gambling, *Report*, Appendix I: 102–43, esp. 104–8. See also Duis, *The Saloon*, 240–44.

16. For essential background information on public morality, see Robert Riegel, "Changing American Attitudes toward prostitution, 1800–1920," *Journal of the History of Ideas* 29 (July–September 1968): 437–52; and Paul Boyer, *Urban Masses and Moral Order in America, 1820–1920* (Cambridge: Harvard University Press, 1968). Duis, *The Saloon*, 246–49; and Eric Anderson, "Prostitution and Social Justice: Chicago, 1910–15," *American Journal of Sociology* 44 (June 1974): 203–28 provide additional insight.

17. Perry Duis and Glen Holt, "Chicago As It Was: Playing the Ponies on Lake Michigan," *Chicago* 30 (August 1981): 108–10, 112.

18. Duis, *The Saloon*, 110; Chicago Vice Commission, *Social Evil in Chicago*, 79–82.

19. Duis, *The Saloon*, 275–303; it should be noted that national Prohibition, through the constitutional amendment and the Volsted Act which enforced it, allowed both the private possession and consumption of liquor; only the manufacture, sale, and transportation of it was banned.

20. On the elaborate structural evolution of the underworld, see Haller, "Bootleggers"; and Humbert Nelli, *The Business of Crime: Italians and Syndicate*

Crime in the United States (New York: Oxford University Press, 1976): 111–77; Kobler, *Capone*, remains the best popular study of crime during the 1920s in Chicago, while John Landesco, *Organized Crime in Chicago* (Chicago: University of Chicago Press, 1968), excerpted from *The Illinois Crime Survey* (Chicago: Illinois Association for Criminal Justice, 1929), contains an excellent introduction by Mark Haller. David R. Johnson, "Crime-Fighting Reform in Chicago: An Analysis of Its Leadership, 1919–1927" (M.A. thesis, University of Chicago, 1966), is also very useful in delineating the activities of the Crime Commission and other anti-mob groups.

21. *Illinois Crime Survey*. Pioneer urban sociologists at the University of Chicago emphasized the social pathologies of the city in many of their studies, including Frederic Thrasher, *The Gang: A Study of 1,313 Gangs in Chicago* (Chicago: University of Chicago Press, 1927, 1938); Walter C. Reckless, *Vice in Chicago* (Chicago: University of Chicago Press, 1933); Clifford Shaw, *The Natural History of a Delinquent Career* (Chicago: University of Chicago Press, 1931); Clifford Shaw and Henry D. McKay, *Juvenile Delinquency and Urban Areas* (Chicago: University of Chicago Press, 1942).

CONTENTS

ILLUSTRATIONS

ILLUSTRATIONS

The Gangs of
Chicago

CHAPTER I

THE EVOLUTION OF SLAB TOWN

MOST OF America's great cities were founded by organized companies of adventurers, who selected sites with some care and proceeded more or less according to definite plan. But nobody planned Chicago, and the area upon which stubborn mankind built the second largest city of the Western Hemisphere would have presented few attractions to a band of ambitious colonists. The country on both sides of the main stream of the Chicago River was very low and wet, a depressing expanse of bogs and sloughs; while what is now the city's principal business section, the famous Loop district, was only a few inches higher than the level of Lake Michigan, and in consequence was under water for several months of the year. The mouth of the river was choked with sand, preventing the passage of any vessel larger than a canoe or rowboat; the stream itself was filled with wild rice except for a narrow channel, and its banks were covered by a rank and noisome growth of skunk cabbage or wild onion, which gave shelter and sustenance to a large and resentful colony of polecats. To the Indians both the river and the vegetation were known as *Chickagou,* or *Checagou,* of which Chicago is a corruption. The word was also in general use among the savages to indicate a bad smell, a symbolism which is still kept alive by the politicians and the stockyards.

2

THERE were really two settlements in early Chicago. One was at the junction of the north and south branches of the

Chicago River, commonly known as the Forks or Wolf Point, where the city's first permanent settler, a Santo Domingan Negro named Baptiste Point De Saible, built a cabin in 1779. The other was at a place called Hardscrabble, four miles south of the Forks, where in 1803 one Charles Lee cleared and began to cultivate a farm. That the town eventually grew up at the Forks and not at Hardscrabble was due principally to the natural advantages of the site and its nearness to Fort Dearborn, which was erected in the summer and fall of 1803 on the south bank of the main river near the approach to the present Michigan Avenue bridge. But it was due partly to the presence of John Kinzie, a silversmith and Indian trader. He had operated successfully in Detroit and along the St. Joseph River in Michigan before he came to Chicago in the spring of 1804 and bought De Saible's cabin and land from a French-Canadian named Le Mai, who had owned it since 1796. Before Kinzie's arrival three or four other traders had built shelters near the Forks. One of them, Antoine Ouilmette, later gave his name to the North Shore village of Wilmette.

Kinzie was the real founder of Chicago — his widespread activities made the place one of the most important trading posts in the Northwest, and he was the first settler to construct anything better than a rude shack of logs and bark. Within a year Kinzie had transformed De Saible's old shanty into a commodious and, by frontier standards, luxurious home. In a historical novel called *Wau-bun, or the Early Days in the Northwest,* Kinzie's daughter-in-law described the house as " a long, low building with a piazza extending along its front, a range of four or five rooms. A broad green space was enclosed between it and the river, and shaded by a row of Lombardy poplars. Two immense cottonwood trees stood in the rear of the building. A fine, well-cultivated garden extended to the north of the dwelling, and surrounding it were various buildings appertaining to

4

the establishment — dairy, bake-house, lodging houses for the Frenchmen, and stables."[1] Kinzie and his family fled from their wilderness estate in 1812, when the Indians burned the fort and massacred twenty-six soldiers, two women and twelve children, and twelve trappers and settlers who had been sworn in as militiamen, among them Captain Billy Wells,[2] a famous Indian fighter of the time. Because of his influence with the savages, Kinzie's property was not damaged, and he returned to Chicago in 1816, when Fort Dearborn was rebuilt. About the same time there came to the settlement another notable of the early days — Jean Baptiste Beaubien, sometimes called Squawman Beaubien, who had for several years operated trading posts at Green Bay and Milwaukee. Beaubien is especially recalled in the annals of Chicago as the president and organizer of the town's first debating society, the first colonel of the Cook County militia, and the father of twenty children, most of them half-breeds. His brother, Jolly Mark Beaubien, who exceeded this production of progeny by three, was Chicago's first ferry-man, a famous tavern-keeper, and a fiddler of rare renown.

3

IN 1814 President James Madison asked Congress to authorize the construction of a ship canal from the Chicago River to the Des Plaines and the Illinois, and thus connect Lake Michigan and the Mississippi River, a project which was first advocated by the French explorer Joliet in 1683. Madison's recommendations were ignored as visionary, but the scheme was kept alive in Congress for thirteen years,

---

[1] The house was the show-place of the village until Kinzie died in 1828, but it deteriorated rapidly thereafter, and was finally abandoned in 1833. Most of the logs of which it had been built were used by the Indians as fuel.

[2] For whom Wells Street was named.

mainly through the efforts of Nathaniel Pope, Territorial Delegate from Illinois, who "stole" Chicago from Wisconsin when Illinois was admitted into the Union as a state in 1818; and Representative Daniel P. Cook, for whom Cook County was named, and who introduced the custom of stump-speaking into Illinois politics. In 1827 Congress finally authorized the canal, and agreed to give the State of Illinois every alternate section in a belt of land six miles wide on either side of the chosen route. Two years later the Illinois Legislature appointed the Illinois and Michigan Canal Commission and empowered it to finance and build the canal, to select the state lands, to lay out towns, and to sell town lots.

To facilitate the use of the projected canal, Congress in 1833 appropriated $25,000 to build a suitable harbor at or near Chicago. The work was begun on July 1 of that year, the delay being due to a controversy between Stephen A. Douglas, the Little Giant of Illinois politics, and Jefferson Davis, then a young officer of the Army. Douglas insisted that the harbor should be constructed at the mouth of the Calumet River, fourteen miles south of Chicago, while Davis contended that the logical and most practicable place for the development was at the mouth of the Chicago River. Davis's recommendations were at length adopted, and by the spring of 1834 two five-hundred-foot piers had been built, creating a new channel for the river. Nature assisted the engineers with a timely freshet, and on July 11, 1834 the first large vessel to enter the Chicago River, the schooner *Illinois,* sailed triumphantly into the harbor.

Actual construction work on the ship canal was delayed until 1836, but the Commissioners immediately set about their other duties. The ink was scarcely dry on the enabling act before a surveyor, James Thompson, had been instructed to survey and plat a town at Chicago. This work was completed on August 4, 1830, and soon afterward the lots, each

6

eighty by one hundred feet, were sold at auction for from forty to seventy dollars. Thompson's map, the first ever made of Chicago, embraced an area of about three-eighths of one square mile, bounded by Madison, Desplaines, Kinzie, and State Streets. This included the settlement at the Forks, but not the little colony at Hardscrabble, which remained a separate community for several years. These were the limits when Chicago was incorporated as a town on August 5, 1833 and when, five days later, its twenty-eight voters elected a Board of Trustees with power " to abate nuisances, gambling and disorderly conduct; to prevent fast driving and enforce police regulations; to license shows, control markets, take charge of the streets and sidewalks, and to protect the town against fire." On November 6, 1833, Chicago's population having increased to approximately a hundred and fifty, the Board of Trustees extended the corporate boundaries to Jackson Street on the south, Jefferson and Cook Streets on the west, and Ohio Street on the north. State Street remained the eastern boundary from Jackson Street to the Chicago River; north of the river the limits ran eastward to the lake. In 1835 the Illinois Legislature gave to the town all of the land east of State Street except the strip from Madison Street to the river, which was held by the United States government as a military reservation. This tract became a part of Chicago soon after Fort Dearborn was abandoned by the Army on December 29, 1836.

4

IN 1831, a year after the town had been platted by the surveyor Thompson, Chicago was detached from Peoria County, of which it had been a part since 1825, and became the county seat of the new county of Cook, which embraced, besides its present limits, all of the territory from which the counties of Will, McHenry, and Du Page were afterward formed. The government of Cook County was placed in the hands of a Court of County Commissioners, two of the three members of which were Chicagoans. At the first meeting of the Court, on April 13, 1831, Chicago's first tax was levied, one-half of one per cent " on town lots; on pleasure carriages; on distilleries; on all horses, mules, and neat cattle above the age of three years; on watches, with their appurtenances; and on all clocks." The Court also bought a scow from Samuel Miller, one of the Commissioners, for sixty-five dollars, and the right to operate a ferry across the Chicago River was sold to Mark Beaubien for fifty dollars a year. Residents of Cook County, "with their travelling apparatus," were entitled to free passage; all others were charged according to rates fixed by the Court. Tavern licenses were granted to Elijah Wentworth, at seven dollars a year; to Samuel Miller, at five dollars; and to Russell E. Heacock, "to keep a tavern at his residence." At that time Heacock lived one mile south of Hardscrabble, but a year or so later he moved into town and became Chicago's first lawyer and a justice of the peace. The tavern-keepers were ordered to make the following charges for their goods and services:

Each half pint of rum, wine or brandy	$.25
Each pint do.	.37½
Each half pint of gin	.18¾
Each pint do.	.31¼
Each gill of whisky	.06¼
Each half pint do.	.12½
Each pint do.	.18¾
For each breakfast and supper	.25
For each dinner	.37½
For each horse fed	.25
Keeping horse one night	.50
Lodging for each man per night	.12½
For cider or beer, one pint	.06¼
For cider or beer, one quart	.12½

Miller's tavern was on the east side of the north branch of the Chicago River, near the Forks, where he and his brother had lived and kept a small store since 1829. He operated the house for a year or so, but sold the property when his wife died in 1832, and left Chicago. Thereafter the building was used as a dwelling. Wentworth's place, on

From an old print

CHICAGO IN 1833

the west side of the river opposite Miller's, was Chicago's first hotel, and was originally a one-room log cabin chinked with clay. It was built in 1828 by Archibald Caldwell and John Kinzie's son James, and Caldwell opened it as a tavern on December 8 of that year, with a license issued by the Commissioners of Peoria County. Caldwell ran the place, to which several rooms had been added, until 1830, when he sold his interest to Kinzie and removed to Green Bay; he was convinced that Chicago would never amount to anything and that the Wisconsin village would become the metropolis of the Northwest.

Elijah Wentworth, better known as Old Geese because of his habit of prefacing his remarks with " By Geese! "

9

came to Chicago in the late fall of 1829 with his wife and three children, three yoke of oxen, and all of his worldly goods in two covered wagons. He was en route to his old home in Maine, but was compelled to winter in Chicago because early snowstorms had blocked the overland route and he was unable to obtain passage on a boat. When Caldwell went to Green Bay, Old Geese rented the hotel from James Kinzie for three hundred dollars a year. In Caldwell's time the house was called the Fork Tavern, but Wentworth changed the name to Wolf Tavern after he had found a wolf in his meat-room and had killed the animal with an ax.[1] Old Geese sold his lease on the tavern to Charles Taylor late in 1831, and after a few months Taylor in turn transferred the property to William Wattles. While Wattles was landlord, a crude painting of a wolf hung above the door, but it came down when Chester Ingersoll took over the place in November 1833 and called it Traveller's Rest. Ingersoll operated the house for about a year, part of the time as the Western Stage House. According to the historian A. T. Andreas, the tavern passed out of existence as a hotel late in 1834, but Edwin O. Gale, in his *Reminiscences of Early Chicago and Vicinity,* wrote that the house was still being run, as the Wolf Tavern with the sign again in place, when he arrived in Chicago in May 1835.

The most famous of Chicago's early hotels were the Green Tavern and the Sauganash, both of which were near the Forks and fronted on the ox-cart road and footpath which afterward became Lake Street. The Green Tree was built in 1833 by James Kinzie and was opened for business that same year under the management of David Clock. Improvements were made in the Green Tree from time to

---

[1] Some Chicago historians say that the Forks was not known as Wolf Point until after Wentworth had performed this feat. In fact, however, the locality was so called by the savages many years before, when it was the home of an Indian chief whose name, in English, meant the Wolf.

time as other taverns were opened and provided competition, but in the early days its accommodations were very primitive. The bedrooms, as a traveler complained, were "altogether too dirty for the comfort of persons unaccustomed to such surroundings," and as a place of rest and refreshment the establishment apparently left much to be desired. Edwin O. Gale thus described the public room of the Green Tree as it appeared in 1835:

"On the east and west sides of the seemingly prehistoric whitewashed walls and board partitions were the inevitable puncheon benches. Scattered around in a more informal manner was an assortment of wooden chairs. Near the north end was a bar counter useful not only to receive the drinks, but umbrellas, overcoats, whips and parcels. The west end of the bar was adorned with a large inkstand placed in a cigar box filled with No. 8 shot, in which were sticking two quill pens — steel being unknown here, though invented in 1830. . . . At the other end of the counter were a dozen or more short pieces of tallow candles, each placed in a hole bored in a 2x4 block, fortified by six-penny nails, standing like mourners around the circular graves in which they had seen so many flickering lights pass away into utter darkness.

"Hanging in a row against the wall were large cloth and leather slippers, which the guests were expected to put on at night, that mud might not be tracked to every part of the house. Under the counter was a large wooden bootjack and a box containing two old-fashioned boot brushes and several pieces of hard, raw tallow, black from application to stogas. There was also a collection of old-fashioned, perforated tin lanterns. . . . There was also to be seen the indispensable tinder box, used fifty times a day, at least, for lighting pipes, when the old, rusty bar stove was taking its summer vacation. Above the tinder box was one of the old-fashioned, square, cherry, veneered clocks. . . . The ablutionary arrangements were exceedingly primitive, consisting of tin wash basins, soiled towels, small mirrors and toothless combs. Several dishes of soft soap were arranged along the back of the water trough. Though pretty strong for washing the hands of a ' tenderfoot,' it was in great demand after greasing the boots or applying tar to wagon axles.

"In the middle of the room, standing in a low box filled with lake sand, was a large stove used in winter to good advantage, not only for the warmth imparted to the room, but for furnishing hot water for toddies, shaving and washing as well. . . . We were called to supper by a large bell, which was rung by our host in a manner which required no explanation as to its meaning. In the dining room were two tables, the length of the room, covered with green checked oil cloth, loaded with roasted wild duck, fricassee of prairie chicken, wild pigeon pot pie, tea and coffee, creamless, but sweetened with granulated maple sugar procured from our red brethren. These furnished a banquet that rendered us oblivious to chipped dishes, flies buzzing or tangled in the butter, creeping beetles and the music of the Mosquito Band."

Under various names, among them the Chicago, the Noyes, the Rail-Road House, the Atlantic and the West Lake Street House, the old Green Tree was operated continuously as a hotel until 1859, when it was converted into tenements. In 1880 the building was removed to Nos. 33–37 Milwaukee Avenue, where it stood for many years as a landmark of old Chicago.

The Sauganash Hotel, the first frame building erected

in Chicago, was built early in 1831 by Mark Beaubien, and was a two-story addition to the one-room log shack in which he had lived since his arrival from Detroit in 1826. It was named in honor of a famous Potawatomi chief known as Billy Caldwell, whose Indian name was Sauganash. Except for a brief period in the fall of 1837, when Harry Isherwood and Alexander McKenzie converted it into Chicago's first theater and gave a successful season of six weeks, the Sauganash remained open as a hotel until March 4, 1851, when it was destroyed by fire. On the site of the building, the southeast corner of Lake and Market Streets, was erected the Republican Wigwam in which Abraham Lincoln was nominated for the Presidency on May 16, 1860.

The accommodations of the Sauganash in its early days were certainly no better than those of the Green Tree, and were probably much worse. Patrick Shirreff, a Scotch agriculturist who visited Chicago in 1833, wrote that Jolly Mark's tavern was "dirty in the extreme, and confusion reigned throughout." The English traveler and author Charles Joseph Latrobe, also a Chicago visitor in 1833, described the Sauganash as a "vile two-storied barrack," and declared that "all was in a state of most appalling confusion, filth and racket. The public table was such a scene of confusion, that we avoided it from necessity. The French landlord was a sporting character, and everything was left to chance, who, in the shape of a fat housekeeper, fumed and toiled round the premises from morning to night." Beaubien, whose stocky figure, "with ruddy face and closely trimmed side whiskers, wearing a brass-buttoned, swallow-tailed blue coat," was a familiar sight in Chicago for many years, spent most of his time racing his horses, shooting ducks and other wildfowl from the front porch of his tavern, and gossiping with his cronies.

Despite its manifold shortcomings, the Sauganash during the first half-dozen years of its existence was the gayest tavern on the Northwestern frontier and the social center of Chicago — it was the scene of nightly dances at which Jolly Mark played the fiddle, or the weekly meetings of the debating society, and of most of the public balls, meetings, and entertainments. It was also Chicago's most popular drinking place until the summer of 1835, when Solomon Lincoln, the "Prairie Tailor," abandoned his efforts to clothe the pioneers in genteel garments and opened the city's first saloon, which he called Lincoln's Coffee House, on the northeast corner of Lake and La Salle Streets. Lincoln was also a noted wolf-hunter. "Many a time," wrote an old-time Chicagoan, "I have seen Mr. Lincoln mount his horse when a wolf was in sight on the prairie toward Bridgeport, and within an hour's time come in with the wolf, having run him down with his horse and taken his life with a hatchet or other weapon."

The popularity of the Sauganash began to decline in 1835, when a syndicate of business men built the Lake House, an imposing three-story and basement structure of brick, at Kinzie and Rush Streets. The Lake House was the first hotel in Chicago to employ a French chef and use printed menus, but despite these innovations it was never a great financial success, and was finally turned into residence flats in 1858. Two years after the Lake House was completed Francis Sherman, who began his career in Chicago as a boarding-house keeper and afterward served two terms as Mayor, built the first Sherman House, which was called the City Hotel until 1844. This was the finest hotel in the Northwest until 1850, when Ira and James Couch, who had operated taverns in Chicago since 1834, erected the famous Tremont House, the third of that name, at Lake and Dearborn Streets. Five and one-half stories high and magnificently furnished, the Tremont was known at first as "Couch's Folly"; few Chicagoans believed that the city would ever be large enough to support such an establishment.

14

But time more than vindicated the brothers' judgment. The Tremont was enlarged twice within the next twenty years, and when it burned in the great fire of 1871, it had three hundred rooms, an elegant Ladies' Parlor, a cuisine " unsurpassed in bounty and excellence," and " Atwood's celebrated improved passenger elevator." Its principal rival before the fire was the Briggs House at Wells and Randolph Streets, which was Abraham Lincoln's headquarters during his first campaign for the Presidency. William Briggs, who built the house about a year after the Tremont was opened, boasted that it was the largest hotel west of the Alleghenies. Both Briggs and the various landlords who operated the place were extremely proud of their elaborately decorated menu cards, which in 1856, according to a traveler, featured a fancy dessert printed as " Glass E. Jenny Lind."

5

WILLIAM H. KEATING, a noted historian and geologist, who was in Chicago in 1823 as a member of an exploring expedition, reported that the village presented " no cheering prospect," and that the habitations of the settlers were " low, filthy and disgusting, displaying not the least trace of comfort." He might have said the same thing ten years later, even after Chicago had entered upon its new dignity as an incorporated town. Almost all of the hundred or so buildings, described by a New York lawyer, Charles Butler, as " of the cheapest and most primitive character for human habitation," were strung out along the south bank of the main stream of the Chicago River between Lake Michigan and the Forks. " There were scattered shanties over the prairie south," wrote Andreas, " and a few rough, unpainted buildings had been improvised on the north side between the old Kinzie home and what is now Clark Street. All together it . . . represented a most woebegone appearance, even as a frontier town of the lowest class. It did not show a single steeple nor a chimney four feet above any roof. . . . The buildings of the fort were low posted and none of them exceeding two low stories in height. Approaching the village by land from the south, one would see on emerging from the oak woods . . . a good stretch of level grass, the lake on the right, woods along the borders of the main river, and, lying on the background of the green woods, only a thin cloud of smoke from the shanty chimneys, a line of almost indefinable structures, and the flag over the fort, if perchance it was flying. A brown path, where the grass had been trodden out, led to the fort, and another, better trodden and wider, led across the prairie towards the Forks, where the Sauganash Hotel then flourished." [1]

Most of the stores and dwellings in the Chicago of this period were of logs. Those that weren't, and a majority of those put up during the next fifteen years, were built in the "balloon fashion," a method of construction first used in Chicago. "Posts were placed in the ground at the corners," wrote William Bross, a noted Chicago editor and historian, "and at proper distances between them blocks were laid down singly or in cob-house fashion. On these foundations were laid, and to these were spiked, standing on end, 3x4 scantling. On these sheathboards were nailed, and weatherboards on the outside of them; and lath and plaster inside with the roof completed the store or dwelling."

It was because of this unique system of building that Chicago received the nickname of Slab Town, by which it was generally known throughout the country except when it was being ridiculed as the Mud Hole of the Prairies. The latter was really more appropriate, for early Chicago's middle name was Mud — mucilage-like mud that stuck to

---

[1] *History of Chicago*, by A. T. Andreas; three volumes; Chicago, 1884; Volume I, page 128.

the memory as well as to the feet. There were few side-walks, and no paving of any description, and the heavy traffic and frequent rains transformed the roads and foot-paths into quagmires through which travel was frequently dangerous and often impossible. William Bross said that at different times he had seen " empty wagons and drays stuck in every block on Lake and Water Streets between Wabash Avenue and the river." Charles Cleaver, a pioneer Chicago manufacturer, recalled that he had often seen teams mired in the mud. " I remember once," he said, " a stage-coach got mired on Clark Street, where it remained several days, with a board driven in the mud at the side of it bear-ing this inscription, ' No bottom here.' " A pedestrian be-ing pulled out of the mud was a commonplace spectacle, and wags adorned the street crossings with signs reading: " To the lower regions," and " The shortest road to China." A classic story of mud-times in Chicago is that of the citizen who saw a man's head and shoulders sticking out of the mire and asked if he could be of assistance. " No, thanks," the man replied. " I have a horse under me."

In 1849 planking was laid on half a dozen downtown streets, and an experiment in grading was made by digging Lake Street down to the level of the lake and planking it. " It was supposed," said William Bross, " that the sewage would settle in the gutters and be carried off, but the ex-periment was a disastrous failure, for the stench at once became intolerable." Engineers then advised the City Coun-cil that the only way Chicago could be properly drained, and the mud overcome, was to raise the grade of the streets twelve feet. This gigantic task, which necessitated filling twelve hundred acres and jacking up virtually every build-ing in the city, was begun in 1855 and completed during the middle 1860's. But while the work was in progress pedestrian travel in Chicago was a curious and sometimes hazardous business. " For ten years," wrote Lloyd Lewis,

17

"the sidewalks ran on erratic levels. In front of one row of houses, pedestrians would walk high in the air, looking down upon carriages and teams; in front of another they would be walking six feet lower. Between the various levels, steps went up and down. The town was a giant jack-in-the-box, with crowds popping up, scurrying, dropping down." [1] In his history of the great fire, Elias Colbert wondered "how the drunken men of that epoch managed to stumble home without breaking their necks." It was commonly said that "when the genuine Chicagoan visited New York he found himself unable to walk on a level surface; he was obliged to turn into the adjacent buildings, every half block or so, and run up and down a stairway, for the sake of variety."

Most of Chicago's buildings were raised without any great difficulty, but the biggest structure in town, the Tremont Hotel, five stories high and covering an area of 180 by 60 feet, had the engineers biting their lips for months. Meanwhile, the streets being filled in all about it, the hotel looked as if it were slowly sinking into the mud, and rumors began to spread that this was true. Finally the engineers reported that the building could not be raised because it had been built of brick, and the owners of the Tremont resigned themselves to abandoning the structure. But a brash young newcomer named George M. Pullman, whose sleeping cars were to revolutionize railroad travel, did the job. With twelve hundred men operating five thousand jackscrews, Pullman lifted the Tremont eight feet, inch by inch, without breaking a single pane of glass and without any of the hotel's guests knowing what was going on.

---

[1] *Chicago, the History of Its Reputation*, by Lloyd Lewis and Henry Justin Smith; Chicago, 1929; page 67.

ANDREAS declared that the muddy and malodorous waste which was Chicago in the early 1830's "had all the required elements of civilization within itself," but another Illinois historian, Rufus Blanchard, was more nearly correct when he said that Chicago was "yet essentially an Indian town. Peltries and furs, guns, blankets, kettles, knives, hatchets, vermillion and whisky were its stock in trade, and Indians were its suppliers and consumers. Quiet reigned because no one had occasion to offend the Indians, and when they became intoxicated the squaws took care to keep sober in order to restrain them." So important were the savages in the life of Chicago that in 1832 the Potawatomi contributed $200 of the $486.20 expended in the construction of the first bridge, "suitable for teams and loaded wagons," over the Chicago River — a dangerous contraption of logs on the south branch just north of the present Randolph Street. Both this structure and a rude foot-bridge over the north branch near the Forks were reported at a meeting of the town's Trustees in December 1833 as being badly in need of repair. A Chicago historian remarked that this was probably because "their bulk had been lessened for the building of fires; the said bridges being nothing more nor less than piles of rough wood thrown into the channel." But they sufficed until 1834, when the first drawbridge, forerunner of Chicago's present magnificent system of bridges, was built over the main stream at Dearborn Street.

The final steps toward making Chicago a white man's town were taken in 1833. During the summer some eight thousand Chippewa, Ottowa, and Potawatomi Indians assembled on the outskirts of the village, and on September 28 their chiefs signed a treaty with United States Commissioners by which they relinquished all claim to their land east

19

of the Mississippi, amounting to approximately five million acres. In return the government agreed to pay the savages $1,000,000 in money and supplies over a period of twenty-five years, and to transport them, within two years, to an area of equal size in Kansas and northern Missouri. A down payment of about $150,000, mostly in goods, was made. "It is reported," wrote Elias Colbert, "that not less than twenty thousand dollars' worth of the goods were stolen by the Indian traders during the first two nights, after the owners had been liberally saturated with whisky, for which they paid out a large proportion of the articles furnished. A letter from a traveller, who witnessed the scene, was unearthed and published in the *Tribune* in 1869. The description there given of the disgusting revels of the red men, and the rapacity of the whites, was almost enough to make one lose faith in human nature."[1] Another payment of thirty thousand dollars in goods was made to four thousand savages in October 1834. "The scene was simply disgusting," wrote Colbert, "and several of the Indians were killed in a drunken brawl." While the distribution of the goods was in progress, on October 6, a black bear was killed at Jackson and Market Streets, and a hunting party killed forty wolves in the same neighborhood.

The Indians said their final good-bys to Chicago with much ceremony in August 1835, and with them, by their own choice, when they set out for the West, went several half-breeds who had become citizens of considerable prominence. One was Madore B. Beaubien, son of John B. Beaubien and a member of Chicago's first Board of Trustees.

---

[1] *Chicago and the Great Conflagration*, by Elias Colbert and Everett Chamberlin; Cincinnati and New York, 1872; page 34.

7

WITH the Indian menace removed, hordes of immigrants from the East swarmed into the Northwest to claim the vast territory opened for occupation by the treaty with the savages. Chicago was the gateway to the promised land, and the stream of immigration poured into and through the little town almost without cessation. The vanguard began to arrive in the spring of 1834, and by midsummer, at which time some two hundred and fifty west-bound wagons were leaving Buffalo every day, Chicago was literally overflowing with land-hungry settlers. "The hotels and boarding houses were always full," wrote Andreas, " and full meant three in a bed sometimes, with the floor covered besides. Many of the emigrants coming in their own covered wagons had only them or a rude camp, hastily built, for home or shelter. All about the outskirts of the settlement was a cordon of prairie schooners, with tethered horses between, interspersed with camp fires at which the busy house-wives were ever preparing meals for the voracious pioneers." [1] In its issue of June 11, 1834, the Chicago *Democrat* thus noted the immigration:

> " Hardly a vessel arrives that is not crowded with emigrants, and the stage that now runs twice a week from the East is thronged with travelers. The steamboat *Pioneer,* which now performs her regular trips to St. Joseph, is also a great accommodation to the traveling community. Loaded teams and covered wagons, laden with families and goods, are daily arriving and settling upon the country back."

[1] *History of Chicago,* Volume I, page 134.

Most of the "voracious pioneers" pushed on into the wilderness, but enough remained in Chicago to transform the village from an Indian trading post into a lively city, and to provide the incentive and help form the sucker list for Chicago's first boom, which was marked by the wildest speculation in land that America had ever seen. The boom actually began in the spring and summer of 1833 with the erection of more than a hundred and fifty buildings and the recording of an unusually large number of legitimate real-estate deals, transactions in which the purchasers bought, for cash, lots upon which they proposed to build stores or dwellings. As prices naturally rose, speculators invaded the field, and land agents appeared and opened offices and auction rooms, some of which were "equal to any in New York or Philadelphia." As Andreas said, "It did not take long to develop a strong speculative fever, which infected every resident of the town and was caught by every new-comer. At the close of the year 1834, the disease had become fairly seated. Whatever might be the business of a Chicagoan, or however profitable, it was not considered a full success except it showed an outside profit on lots bought and sold."[1]

The excitement increased throughout 1835 and reached its peak in 1836, when impetus was given the boom by the breaking of ground, on July 4, for the Lake Michigan–Illinois River Canal. The English writer Harriet Martineau, who visited the town in the summer of 1836, wrote that she had never seen a "busier place than Chicago was at the time of our arrival. The streets were crowded with land speculators, hurrying from one sale to another. A negro, dressed up in scarlet, bearing a scarlet flag, and riding a white horse with housings of scarlet, announced the times of sale. At every street-corner where he stopped, the crowd flocked round him; and it seemed as if some

---

[1] Ibid.

prevalent mania infected the whole people. The rage for speculation might fairly be so regarded. As the gentlemen of our party walked the streets, storekeepers hailed them from their doors, with offers of farms, and all manner of land lots, advising them to speculate before the price of land rose higher." [1]

The turnover of property was enormous. One young lawyer realized five hundred dollars a day for five days by merely making out titles to land; another earned in two years ten times the amount he had estimated would provide him with a competence for life. In four months the United States Land Office sold almost half a million dollars' worth of public lands; in ten months real estate valued at $1,800,-000 passed through the hands of a single agent, while half a dozen others each sold lots and farm acreage valued at more than a million dollars. Additions to Chicago were hurriedly surveyed, staked, platted and thrown on the market, where the lots changed hands a dozen times within a month. "As the interior became settled," wrote Andreas, "the mania for land speculating spread throughout the newly-settled country, and Chicago became the mart where were sold and resold monthly an incredible number of acres of land and land-claims outside the city, purporting to be located in all parts of the Northwest. It embraced farming lands, timber lands, town sites, town lots, water lots, and every variety of land-claim or land title known to man. . . . Town lots were platted, often without any survey, all over Wisconsin and Illinois, wherever it was hoped that a town might eventually spring up." [2] Another Chicago historian, Joseph Balestier, said that "the prairies of Illinois, the forests of Wisconsin, and the sand hills of Michigan, presented a chain almost unbroken of supposititious

[1] Quoted in *As Others See Chicago*, compiled and edited by Bessie Louise Pierce; Chicago, 1933; page 83.

[2] *History of Chicago*, Volume I, page 134.

villages and cities. The whole land seemed staked out and peopled on paper." The Chicago *American,* on July 2, 1836, remarked that "the rapidity with which towns are thrown into market is astonishing."

Under the impact of heavy speculative buying, the prices of land, especially that in or near Chicago, soared to heights not legitimately reached for another thirty years. A tract comprising one-fourth of Kinzie's Addition, offered in 1833 for $5,500, sold in 1836 for $100,000. Forty acres of Chicago lots, which went begging at $400 for the tract in 1833, brought $200,000 three years later. Another large parcel sold for $20,000 in 1835, and for $100,000 within three months; in 1836 the owners refused $500,000, to their subsequent regret. Land on Lake Street near State, for which $300 was considered too high a price early in 1834, was cheap at $60,000 in 1836; while $96,700 was paid for a tract of a few lots which had sold at $62 in 1830. Gurdon S. Hubbard, a pioneer Indian trader, famous in early Chicago for his feats of walking, — he once covered seventy-five miles in a single day — bought two lots on La Salle Street in 1830 for $66.66. In 1836 he sold them for $80,000. In 1835 he and two partners paid $5,000 for eighty acres on the outskirts of the town. Three months later Eastern buyers paid $80,000 for one-half of the tract.

William B. Ogden, a young lawyer, a native of upstate New York, and for one term a member of the New York Legislature, arrived in Chicago in the spring of 1835 to inspect a piece of land which a kinsman had bought for $100,-000, sight unseen. He found most of the property ankle-deep in water, and the remainder an apparently useless waste of bogs and sloughs. "You have been guilty of the grossest folly," he wrote to the purchaser. "There is no such value in the land and won't be for a generation." Nevertheless, he surveyed and platted the tract, and within three months the speculators whom he had derided as lunatics had

24

bought one-third of the acreage for as much as the kinsman had paid for the entire parcel. And by that time Ogden
had become so convinced of the future greatness of the
Northwest that he severed his Eastern business connections and settled in Chicago. He was the city's first Mayor,
and for many years its leading real-estate operator and its
wealthiest and most forward-looking citizen.

8

C H I C A G O was still riding the crest of the boom when the
Illinois Legislature, on March 4, 1837, passed an act in-
corporating the town as a city and extending its corporate
limits to include a total area of about ten square miles. The
first city election was held on May 2, and Ogden was chosen
as Mayor by a two-to-one vote over John H. Kinzie, son of
the " Father of Chicago." A census taken two months later
showed that the city had a population of 4,170, and contained more than five hundred buildings, including a court
house, a jail, a fire-engine house, almost four hundred
dwellings, eighty-odd stores and warehouses, ten taverns,
and five churches. It also supported two newspapers — the
Democrat, established by John Calhoun on November 26,
1833, and the *American,* founded by T. O. Davis and first
printed on June 8, 1835. In one of its early issues the *American* published this unusual announcement:

NOTICE

My wife, Mary Bumley, left my house and bed
on Saturday, 8th instant, without any just cause, and
is supposed to have went away with another Hoosier,
who probably knew her better than I did. They will
be handsomely rewarded for keeping her forever.
                                        Jacob Reichter.
Chicago, August 8, 1835.

When Chicago became a city most of the business houses, and the residences of the most important families, were on Lake and Water Streets between State and Franklin, and on a few streets running north and south from the river. Andreas wrote that the city "lay low down on the marshy ground and was, to the sight of the newcomer, a most unsightly place to live, or even die in." But the people of Chicago, contemplating the achievements of half a dozen years, were convinced that nothing could stop them; they boasted that within another two decades, or even one, their miraculous city would have crowded St. Louis and Cincinnati off the industrial map, and would be hot on the trail of New York and Philadelphia.

But the banking panic and depression which struck the United States in the spring of 1837 brought Chicago's dream to a sudden and painful end. By the first of May the boom had collapsed, and by the first of June the ruin was complete. Lots for which speculators had fought but a few months before were unsalable at any price, while men who owned titles to huge tracts of land were too poor to pay their board bills. The State of Illinois went bankrupt, and only Mayor Ogden, himself on the verge of financial disaster, kept Chicago from doing likewise. The Mayor declared that for Chicago to start its career as a city by repudiating its obligations would be shameful; he suppressed a widespread demand for a moratorium on debts, with appeals to civic pride and the stentorian cry of "Do not tarnish the honor of our infant city!" Backed by the bankers and business men, Ogden induced the City Council to issue $5,000 in scrip, receivable for taxes and carrying interest of one per cent a month. With this illegal paper money, personal I.O.U.'s, certificates issued by the banks against deposits, and trade tickets issued by the stores, Chicago transacted what little business there was and kept the city's credit unimpaired. And virtually every citizen planted a garden, to raise at least a part of the food he. could no longer afford to buy. Within a year Chicago had taken on the appearance of a vast vegetable patch; whole blocks were covered by cabbages and potato hills, beans, onions, peas, and corn. Thus did the town acquire the nickname of "the Garden City," by which it was called, locally at least, for many years. But to the remainder of the country Chicago was still Slab Town and the Mud Hole of the Prairies.

For more than half a decade Chicago was flat on its back, and business and industry were as stagnant as one of its own mud puddles. Thousands of immigrants continued to pass through en route to the farm lands of the Northwest, but Chicago held no attraction for them; from 1837 to 1840 the population increased by only three hundred. But in the early 1840's the city began to stir. Real-estate prices slowly rose, a few new factories and stores were established, and between 1840 and 1845 the population tripled. About the middle of the decade another boom slowly got under way. John Wentworth, editor of the Chicago *Democrat* and a member of Congress, started it in 1847 by bringing to Chicago the first River and Harbor Convention, which served to impress three thousand delegates from eighteen states with Chicago's natural advantages and potential greatness. That same year Cyrus H. McCormick, with the financial support of William B. Ogden, erected the largest factory in Chicago and began to manufacture his famous grain reapers, with which he revolutionized not only American farming but American business methods as well; he was the first manufacturer to guarantee his product, to sell at a fixed price, and to give his customers time in which to pay. Ogden, absorbed for several years in refinancing the Lake Michigan–Illinois River Canal and in raising money for a railroad, saw both projects come to fruition in 1848. In April the first vessel was locked through the canal, and on April 10 it was floating in Lake Michigan. On the 16th the canal was officially opened with great public rejoicing. On October 26 the *Democrat* announced that on the day before "The locomotive, with the tender and two cars, took its first start and run out a distance of about five miles upon the road — the Galena and Chicago Union Road." On November 20 the train chugged ten miles out to the Des Plaines River and chugged back to Chicago with a load of grain.

Two years after these historic events the Galena and Chicago had been completed as far as Elgin, forty miles away, and in 1854 the first train rolled into Galena. Meanwhile great gangs of workmen were pushing up from the south with the tracks of the Illinois Central, and from the east came the Michigan Southern, running its first train into Chicago on February 20, 1852, while the citizens celebrated by cheering, ringing bells, and shooting cannon. Three months later the Michigan Central arrived, and by the end of the year the tracks of the Chicago, Rock Island and Pacific had been laid as far as Quincy, on the Mississippi River. By 1855 Chicago was the terminus of ten railroad trunk lines and eleven branch lines, and was the country's second greatest meat-packing center and the world's greatest grain port, shipping from three to five million bushels a year more than New York. With a population of 80,000, humming factories, hundreds of fine buildings in course of erection, with sixty miles of sewers and four miles of wharves, with sidewalks and planked streets illuminated by gas, and with a land boom fully as spectacular as that of 1836, but this time based on solid value, Chicago could no longer be jeered at as Slab Town and the Mud Hole of the Prairies.

As Lloyd Lewis put it, Chicago had become Chicago.

CHAPTER II

"FIRST THE BLADE..."

THE CHICAGO underworld developed according to the traditional American pattern, and in time attained unique proportions and a viciousness equaled in this country only by San Francisco's Barbary Coast. But its early growth was remarkably slow, despite the fact that the first white man known to have built a shelter on the site of the city was, by modern standards, a criminal — a French trapper and trader named Pierre Moreau, better known to the Indians as the Mole, who sold liquor and other illegal goods to the savages with the blessing and protection of his friend and patron Count Frontenac, Governor of New France. This pioneer bootlegger flourished as early as the middle 1670's, but he vanished a hundred years before Baptiste De Saible appeared upon the scene, and scarcely anything is known of him. He is little more than a phantom of rascality, of interest mainly because he was the prototype of the beer barons and alky princes who transformed Chicago into a gangsters' paradise some two and a half centuries after he had watered his last bottle of booze.

The handful of colonists who followed De Saible during the next fifty years may have been, as the geologist Keating said in 1823, " a miserable race of men, scarcely equal to the Indians from whom they are descended." But they certainly were law-abiding; probably no other American town was so free from crime or harbored so few really undesirable characters during its formative years as a frontier settlement. There is no record of criminal activity in Chicago until the first elements of the underworld began to appear in the summer of 1833, attracted by the rumble of the incipient boom and the extensive preparations which had been made for the treaty with the Indians. The English traveler Latrobe, who was in Chicago at that time, reported that the village was " one chaos of mud, rubbish and confusion . . . in an uproar from morning to night, and from night to morning . . . crowded to excess . . . immigrants and land speculators as numerous as the sand . . . horse-dealers, and horse-stealers, — rogues of every description, white, black, brown and red — half-breeds, quarter-breeds, and men of no breed at all: — dealers in pigs, poultry and potatoes . . . sharpers of every degree; peddlers, grog-sellers, Indian agents and Indian traders of every description . . . betting and gambling were the order of the day."

In this heterogeneous mob were Chicago's first thief, or at least the first to get caught; and an unfortunate wanderer named Harper, who appears to have been the first person lodged in Chicago's first jail, which was built of " logs firmly bolted together " soon after the village had been incorporated as a town. There is almost no record of Harper's career; one Chicago historian says that he was a young loafer from Maryland, another that he had once been a respectable citizen of some education, who had been reduced to a low estate by frontier whisky. In any event, Harper was arrested as a vagrant, and in the early fall of 1833 was offered for sale under the Illinois vagrancy law, with Constable Reed acting as auctioneer. Public sentiment was opposed to the sale of a white man, and although a large crowd attended the auction, the only bid was that of George White, the Negro Town Crier. Harper was finally knocked down to White for a quarter, and the Negro led the vagrant away at the end of a chain. What became of Harper after that is not clear. John J. Flinn, historian of the Chicago police, says that the vagrant escaped into the woods that same night and " never was seen in these parts again "; but it is interesting to note that when Chicago's first directory was published in 1839, it contained this listing: " Harper, Richard, called ' Old Vagrant.' "

The name of Chicago's pioneer thief is now unknown, but a record of his wickedness remains — he stole thirty-four dollars from a fellow-boarder, one Hatch, at the Wolf Tavern, and was arrested by Constable Reed on a warrant issued by Justice Russell E. Heacock. He was taken at once to Reed's carpenter shop for examination, and the Justice held court sitting on the work-bench. Since there was no state's Attorney to handle the prosecution, Hatch engaged John Dean Caton, afterward a noted judge, and the defendant employed Caton's partner, Giles Spring, who likewise became a well-known jurist and City Attorney as well.[1] Despite Spring's objections, Caton compelled his partner's client to strip, and at length the stolen money was found wadded in the toe of the accused man's sock. The defendant was held for trial, which got under way next morning in the Wolf Tavern, " where the public could hear the young lawyers to the best advantage." After much argument and speechmaking by counsel, the prisoner was found guilty, but was released on nominal bail pending action on a motion for a new trial. He promptly disappeared, thus establishing a precedent which has been followed more or less regularly in Chicago ever since.

2

M o s t of the gambling in early Chicago was betting on the frequent horseraces promoted by Jolly Mark Beaubien and

[1] In December 1833 Caton opened Chicago's first law office in the Temple Building on Lake Street, but at this time he and Spring kept office " on the head of the barrel at the corner of Lake and Wells."

other Slab Town sports; and friendly card-playing in the taverns and stores and in private homes. But there were also a few games conducted by professionals who had drifted into the settlement from Cincinnati and St. Louis. Little is known of these tricksters, but their activities were extensive enough to incur the wrath of the godly element of the population, which in those early days was a majority, and make them the object of Chicago's first moral crusade.

This valiant attempt to drive out or destroy the gamblers was led by the Reverend Jeremiah Porter, founder of Chicago's first regularly organized church, the First Presbyterian, and the town's first resident preacher. The Reverend Mr. Porter spread the gospel in New Jersey for a brief period after leaving Princeton Theological Seminary, and came to the Western country late in 1831 as chaplain to the garrison at Fort Brady, Sault Ste. Marie, Michigan. He labored in this fruitful field for about a year and a half with conspicuous success; he stopped the dancing with which the soldiers and settlers had been accustomed to relieve the tedium of the winter months, and converted to religion and to temperance every person in the fort and the settlement except a young lieutenant and his wife. This unfortunate couple remained outside the fold despite almost constant prayer and objurgation. Early in 1833, when the troops at Fort Brady were sent to Chicago to relieve the Fort Dearborn garrison, the Reverend Mr. Porter accompanied them. He arrived in Chicago on May 13, 1833, and was thus welcomed by John Wright, a merchant, described by Andreas as " one of the praying men of the village ":

" Well, I do rejoice, for yesterday was the darkest day I ever saw. I have been talking about and writing for a minister for months in vain, and yesterday as we prayed with the Christians about to leave us, I was almost ready to despair, as I feared the troops coming

32

in would all be utterly careless about religion. The fact that you and a little church were, at the hour of our meeting, riding at anchor within gunshot of the fort, is like the bursting out of the sun from behind the darkest clouds." [1]

On Sunday, May 19, the Reverend Mr. Porter delivered his first sermon, from John vi, 8, in the carpenter shop of Fort Dearborn. That night he made this entry in his journal:

" The first dreadful spectacle that met my eyes on going to church was a group of Indians sitting on the ground before a miserable French dram house, playing cards, and as many trifling white men standing around to witness the game."

The Reverend Mr. Porter organized his congregation, with twenty-six members, on June 26, 1833, and on July 7 held the first communion service ever celebrated in Chicago. " Many witnessed the solemn scene," he wrote in his journal, " but a majority were females, as two vessels were unloading in the harbor, causing a wanton abuse of the holy day by many who sin against clear light, and abuse divine compassion and love." Plans were now made to build a church, and a lot was purchased at Clark and Lake Streets, in those times " a lonely spot, almost inaccessible on account of surrounding sloughs and bogs." Materials for the edifice were assembled, but before actual work could begin, squatters started to erect a building on the Lake Street frontage of the property. They refused to leave, and instead of turning the other cheek and giving them the Clark Street frontage also, the outraged Presbyterians went to the scene at night, attached heavy chains to the sills of the building, hitched a yoke of oxen to the chains, and dragged the structure two

---

[1] *History of Chicago*, Volume I, page 299.

hundred yards down Lake Street. The members of the congregation then set to work with hammer and ax and saw, and " the timbers were at length hewed and squared and set up on the prairie." The church was completed in the early

THE REV. JEREMIAH PORTER, CHICAGO'S
FIRST REFORMER

fall of 1833, and was dedicated on January 4, 1834, with the temperature at twenty-four below zero. There was no competition on this occasion, and many men were present.

With construction well under way, the Reverend Mr. Porter turned his attention to the gamblers, against whom an increasingly large number of complaints had been made, chiefly on the ground that they were luring young men to perdition. Several powerful sermons so aroused the authorities that two " nests " were raided and two card-players put in jail for a few days, while others were warned that they must obey the law and close their resorts. The evil was thus abated, but only for a short time; in a letter to the editor of the *Democrat* in December 1833, a citizen declared that gambling was more prevalent than ever. The Reverend Mr. Porter returned to the attack in 1834, and in October of that year a mass meeting of the anti-gambling faction appointed a Committee of Nine to devise measures for the extirpation of gambling and the punishment of all gamblers. Resolutions adopted by this committee pledged its members to withhold the hand of friendship from card-players and to wage unrelenting warfare upon sharpers and blacklegs. "Cost what it may," said the committee's report, "we are determined to root out this vice, and to hunt down those who gain by it an infamous substance." The Reverend Mr. Porter launched another campaign in the summer of 1835, and during a rousing "season of prayer" many young men were converted and two gamblers imprisoned.

In the long run the gamblers were not greatly disturbed by the Reverend Mr. Porter's fulminations or the pronouncements of the Committee of Nine, especially since the former abandoned the fight soon after the "season of prayer" and resigned his pastorate to accept a call to Peoria. The sharpers knew that words, however imposingly strung together in resolutions, could never hurt them; and with the boom approaching its peak the city officials were too busy counting their paper profits on lots and trying to keep up with the growth of the town to worry about the few dollars that foolish citizens lost at the gaming tables. Consequently the games became larger and the gamblers increased in numbers and boldness; one even identified himself as "Gambler" in the City Directory for 1839, and another, in the same volume, was listed as "Generous Sport."

By the early 1840's, despite the collapse of the boom and the complete stagnation of the city's commercial life,

Chicago harbored more gambling-houses than either Cincinnati or St. Louis, and was the most important gaming center north of New Orleans and west of the Allegheny Mountains. Short card games, such as brag, poker, and seven-up, were principally played, with an occasional faro bank and sometimes a session of chess, checkers, and backgammon. Roulette, keno, and chuck-a-luck appear to have been almost unknown until after 1850. Betting on horseraces had been one of Chicago's favorite pastimes since the arrival of Mark Beaubien, but bookmaking appears not to have been introduced until 1844, when W. F. Myrick laid out Chicago's first race-track on the prairie between Twenty-sixth and Thirty-first Streets and Vincennes and Indiana Avenues. Bill McGraw, Dutch House, and Little Dan Brown are said to have been the first gamblers to make a business of handling racing bets, and are also believed to have operated the first roulette wheel and chuck-a-luck cage ever seen in Chicago.

Some of the Slab Town gamblers of the 1840's were kicked out of Natchez and Vicksburg during the uprising against the sharpers which swept through the Mississippi Valley in 1835; and virtually all had learned their trade on the Mississippi River steamboats. Among them were such noted sporting men as John Sears, George Rhodes, Walt Winchester; Cole Martin and King Cole Conant, who afterward kept a famous house in St. Paul; and the Smith brothers — Charles, Montague, and George, the last-named better known as One-Lung. The dean of this group, and the outstanding figure of early Chicago gambling, was John Sears, a soft-voiced Southerner of French descent, who was one of the most expert poker-players of his time. But even more than for his skill at cards Sears was noted for his love of poetry, especially that of Burns and Shakespeare, for his gifts as a story-teller, and for his good looks and elaborate wardrobe. For years he was considered the best-dressed man in Chicago. " He was a singularly handsome man," wrote an old-time gambler, " of jovial and generous temperament, and with faultless manners. He enjoyed the reputation of being a thoroughly ' square ' player, and though he died poor, his demise was widely and sincerely lamented."

3

As in other American frontier towns, the gamblers were followed by the prostitutes and their pimps. As early as 1835 the town's Board of Trustees adopted an ordinance which imposed a fine of twenty-five dollars upon any person convicted of keeping a house of ill fame, and less than three years later, in February 1838, another ordinance provided still higher fines. At the same time complaint was made to the authorities that brothels were in open operation on Wells Street between Jackson and First — shabby, unpretentious dives, but the beginnings of the largest red-light district that the United States has ever seen. They were also the first of the resorts which were to make Wells Street such a sink of vileness that in 1870 the Board of Aldermen changed the name of the thoroughfare to Fifth Avenue, that it might no longer dishonor the name of Captain Billy Wells. It was not changed back to Wells until after the turn of the twentieth century.

Close upon the heels of the gamblers and harlots, the fundamental props of the underworld, came the ragtag and bobtail, filtering into Slab Town throughout the boom of the 1830's and the subsequent depression — hoodlums and rowdies, con men and pickpockets, burglars and footpads, gunmen and garroters, sneak thieves and horse-thieves; there was even a gang of counterfeiters, which flourished in the early 1840's under the leadership of the notorious " General " Jim Brown. To satisfy the demand created by these agents of iniquity, more saloons were opened, " tippling houses " began to appear, and " liquor groceries " which sold more liquor in the back rooms than groceries over the counters. Resorts of this character became so numerous and disposed of such huge quantities of bad whisky that before the city was out of its municipal swaddling-clothes it had acquired a nation-wide reputation for toughness and inebriety. John Hawkins, head of the Washingtonian temperance movement, observed the guzzling and said that he " could frankly state that in all his tours of the United States he had never seen a town which seemed so like the universal grog-shop as did Chicago."

By 1840 the Chicago newspapers were publishing increasingly numerous accounts of thievery, hold-ups, disturbances by drunken men, brawls, street fights, and minor riots, and were complaining that the liquor groceries and tippling houses were frequented by " rowdies, blacklegs and other species of loafers." In the summer of 1839 a newspaper of Jackson, Michigan, jeeringly remarked that " the population of Chicago is said to be principally composed of dogs and loafers." That same year, on April 25, the Chicago *American* published this warning:

> " The scoundrel who set fire the other night to the old postoffice building is suspected. He and all other suspicious loafers about the city had better, as soon as possible, make themselves scarce, or the city watch will be at their heels."

One of the loafers against whom the *American* directed its dark hints of reprisal was a young Irishman named John Stone, who arrived in the United States when he was thirteen years old, and at the age of thirty-four expiated his crimes on the gallows in the first legal execution in Chicago's history. Stone came to Chicago late in 1838, after having served prison sentences in Canada for robbery and murder, and in New York for horse-stealing. He worked desultorily as a wood-chopper, but spent most of his time loafing in the liquor groceries and in Chicago's first billiard hall, which was opened in 1836 on the second floor of Couch's tavern, the first Tremont House, at Lake and Dearborn Streets. In the spring of 1840 Stone was arrested for the rape and murder of Mrs. Lucretia Thompson, wife of a Cook County farmer, and in May was tried and convicted, upon circumstantial evidence which was thus summarized by Andreas:

"A bit of flannel torn from a shirt which was proved to have belonged to the accused and which was found near the body of the victim, the burning by him of the clothes worn in the earlier part of the day of her disappearance, the club used as the instrument of killing to which still adhered, when found, a bunch of her hair, and a remembered threat by him against her virtue, sworn to by a single witness, in the absence of any circumstances pointing toward any other neighbor, were deemed sufficient to warrant a verdict of murder in the first degree. Nor has there been any doubt of its justice, although John Stone stolidly asserted his innocence to the last." [1]

On Friday, July 10, 1840, chained and handcuffed, Stone was placed in a wagon and, escorted by two hundred mounted citizens and sixty armed militiamen under the command of Colonel Seth Johnson, who " appeared in full uniform," was conveyed to a spot on the lake shore three miles south of the Court House. There he was hanged in the presence of a large and interested crowd of spectators. This account of the execution was published in the *American* of July 17:

"The execution took place about a quarter after three. The prisoner ascended the scaffold, dressed in a

---

[1] Ibid., page 445.

loose white gown, and with a white cap upon his head, as is usual in such cases. He evinced much firmness upon the gallows, under the circumstances, and in the presence of the spectators (among whom we regretted to see women enjoying the sight) he persisted to the last in the assertion of his innocence — which declaration was publicly made in his behalf by the Sheriff, together with his acknowledgement, as requested, of the satisfactory manner in which he was treated in the jail. He stated that he was never in the house of Mrs. Thompson, and did not see her on the day she was murdered. He also stated that he believed two individuals were engaged in the murder, but on being asked if he knew them, he replied in substance, that if he did he would swing before their blood should be upon him. The Rev. Mr. Hallam, Isaac R. Gavin, Sheriff, and Messrs. Davis and Lowe, deputies, attended the prisoner on the scaffold. The Sheriff seemed particularly affected, even unto tears. After the·beautiful, solemn and impressive services of the Episcopal Church for such occasions had been performed by Mr. Hallam, and the appropriate admonitions bestowed, the death warrant was read by Mr. Lowe, the knot adjusted, the cap pulled over the face of the prisoner, and he was swung into another world. After he was hung until he was ' dead, dead,' a wagon containing a coffin received his body, which was delivered by Drs. Boone and Dyer, pursuant to the order of the court, for dissection. It is supposed that he died from strangulation and that his neck was not broken in the fall, which was about four feet."

4

CHICAGO had no peace officer of any description until the fall of 1825, when Archibald Clybourne, a native of Virginia and one of the founders of the city's meat-packing industry, was appointed Constable of the first precinct of Peoria County, a vast wilderness which comprised virtually all of northeastern Illinois. It could not possibly have been patrolled efficiently by one man, or for that matter, a score of men; but since the white population of the precinct was considerably less than a hundred, a patrol was scarcely necessary. So far as the records show, Clybourne never made an arrest; his official duties consisted in attending the frontier courts and serving the extraordinary documents produced by the justices of the peace, who were not remarkable for either intelligence or book-learning. It was a Peoria County justice, in Clybourne's time, who issued this classic marriage certificate:

State of Illenois Peoria County ss

To all the world Greeting. Know ye that John Smith and Peggy Myres is hereby certified to go together and do as old folks does, anywhere inside coperas precinct, and when my commission comes I am to marry em good and date em back to kivver accidents.

In the annals of early Chicago no mention is made of a police officer in the list of town officials chosen at the first municipal election in 1833; and there is no evidence to indicate that the town had a police force of any sort for another two years. The peace of the settlement during this period appears to have been kept by Constable Reed, a Cook County official, and a mysterious personage referred to briefly by Andreas and other historians as "Officer Beach," to whom the keys of the jail were entrusted. Crimes and disorder were further discouraged by large placards, posted at prominent street corners, which notified all citizens that violations of law were punishable by fines, and that one-half of any fine collected would be paid to the informer. Until the Bridewell at Polk and Wells Streets was completed in

41

1851, prisoners who couldn't pay were laden with ball and chain and worked on the streets in gangs.

Chicago's first policeman was O. Morrison, of whom nothing seems to be known except that he was elected Constable in 1835 and again in 1836. In 1837 John Shrigley was elected High Constable, an office created by the charter under which Chicago was incorporated as a city. The charter also authorized the City Council to appoint one assistant constable from each of the six wards into which the city was divided, but only two were named. In 1839 Samuel J. Low was elected City Marshal — he was also called High Constable and Chief of the City Watch — and three assistants were appointed. During the next fifteen years the same organization was maintained, and Chicago's police force never numbered more than nine men, although in that time the population increased from about 4,500 to more than 80,000.

It was manifestly impossible for such a small body of men to control crime and rowdyism in so large and turbulent a city, and throughout the early 1850's there was much complaint about the size of the city watch and its lack of efficiency, and of the manner in which the men were appointed. On May 3, 1850, commenting on a robbery, one of the newspapers said: " The city watch knew nothing of it, of course. They were probably regaling themselves in pleasant quarters at the time." A few months later, in August, a letter from a taxpayer declared that in choosing watchmen " bad material was selected," that the " force was composed of strangers instead of respectable citizens," and that " sailors, of unknown character, were preferred to well-known residents." That same year, however, the watchmen were highly commended for their promptness in suppressing a bloody brawl between two groups of soldiers at the Farmers' Home, a low tavern at La Salle and Water Streets. Two constables who " interfered in the interest of good order " were thrown into the street, and one was knocked down with a club " which cut his head open frightfully." But three other watchmen came up and forced their way into the tavern, and " once inside, they assaulted the soldiers, knocked them down with their clubs, and dragged them bleeding to the calaboose."

Despite the obvious shortcomings of the system of constables and watchmen, Chicago had nothing better until early in 1855, when the City Council adopted ordinances creating a Police Department. Cyrus P. Bradley, a prominent volunteer fireman and afterward a noted private detective and a member of the Secret Service, was appointed first Chief of Police. Three precinct organizations were formed and stations established, and about eighty policemen were enrolled. Some authorities say that these men wore stars, but the best evidence is that the Chicago police had no distinguishing insignia until 1857, when Mayor John Wentworth issued leather stars and allowed the cops to carry heavy canes in the daytime and batons at night. Each man was also equipped with a " creaker," a sort of rattle, which was eventually superseded by the police whistle. In 1858 Mayor John C. Haines changed the leather star to one of brass and introduced the first uniform — a short blue frock coat, and a blue navy cap with a gold band. Mayor Haines also increased the department to slightly more than a hundred men.

Chicago's new police force received its baptism of fire in the famous Lager Beer Riot of 1855, which was the city's first serious disturbance. The immediate cause of the trouble was an attempt to enforce the Sunday closing law and increase saloon license fees. But there were two basic causes. One was the aggressiveness of the prohibition movement, which had made great progress everywhere in the country and, in the winter of 1854–5, had forced through the Illinois Legislature a drastic prohibition law which was to be submitted to the voters in June of 1855. The other

43

was the wave of anti-foreign sentiment which swept over the United States in the late 1840's and the early 1850's, and culminated in the formation of the Native American or Know-Nothing Party, which was both anti-foreign and anti-Catholic.[1] In Chicago the excitement over the foreign and liquor questions reached a peak of intensity early in 1855, at which time about sixty per cent of the city's population was foreign-born, and the animosity of both factions was largely directed against the Germans, who had settled in large numbers on the North Side. There they kept their own language, maintained their own schools and newspapers, and made little or no effort to adopt the customs or speech of the country in which they had sought refuge. But more to the point, in the eyes of the prohibitionists, they maintained several hundred schools and beer gardens, and were the darlings of the liquor interests.

5

IN 1855 the Native Americans elected as Mayor of Chicago Dr. Levi D. Boone, a grand-nephew of Daniel Boone and a well-known physician. They also controlled the City Council by a large majority, and when the new police force was appointed, every man was a native-born citizen. Dr. Boone's first action as Mayor was to recommend to the City Council that the fee for saloon licenses be increased from fifty to three hundred dollars a year, and that no license be issued for more than three months. An ordinance embodying this suggestion was immediately passed. In later years Dr. Boone said that at the time he firmly believed that the prohibition law would be ratified by the voters, and that his purpose in advocating higher license fees was to

---

[1] Antipathy toward the foreign elements of the population was evident in Chicago as early as 1840, when the *Democrat* published a petition urging Congress to deny the right of suffrage to all foreigners not already enfranchised.

" root out all the lower classes of dives, and leave the business in the hands of the better class of saloon-keepers, who, when the temperance law should go into force, could be rationally dealt with." But the Germans, especially the saloon-keepers, saw the ordinance as an attempt to deprive them of their rights. " The excitement throughout the city ran high," wrote John J. Flinn, " but the *Nord Seite* was in a perfect ferment. Meetings were held, speeches made, resolutions adopted, and pledges registered that the Germans of Chicago would die, if need be, rather than submit to this outrage upon their rights."[1] The Irish and Scandinavian residents, equally affected by the ordinance, made common cause with the Germans " against the fanatical party."

A week or so after the passage of the higher-license ordinance, Mayor Boone ordered the police to enforce the Sunday closing law, to which no attention had been paid for a dozen years. The German beer gardens and saloons were immediately closed tight, but the bars on the South Side, owned by Americans, were permitted to open their back and side doors. There is no evidence that this discrimination was by the express order of Mayor Boone; more likely it was due to the natural sympathy of the police for men of their own race. But the Germans felt that it savored of persecution; they flatly refused either to close on Sunday or to pay a higher fee for licenses, and some two hundred arrests were made. All were released on bail, and their lawyer agreed with the City Attorney that a test case should be tried, the decision to be binding upon all defendants and upon the city. The trial was begun on the morning of April 21, 1855, before Police Magistrate Henry L. Rucker in the Court House, but before the proceedings had more than begun a terrific uproar was heard outside. Wrote Flinn:

---

[1] *History of the Chicago Police*, by John J. Flinn; Chicago, 1887; pages 73–4.

45

"The liberated saloon-keepers had collected their friends on the North Side, and, preceded by a fife and drum, the mob, about five hundred strong, had marched in solid phalanx upon the justice shop, as many as could entering the sacred precincts. After making themselves understood that the decision of the court must be in their favor if the town didn't want a taste of war, they retired and formed at the intersection of Clark and Randolph Streets, and held possession of these thoroughfares to the exclusion of all traffic. Crowds gathered from all sections of the city, friends and enemies, and the uproar was deafening."[1]

After half an hour of noise and turmoil Mayor Boone ordered Luther Nichols, Captain of Police, to clear the streets and disperse the mob. Nichols attacked at the head of a score of policemen armed with clubs, and after a brief but bloody fight the mob broke and fled northward, leaving nine prisoners in the hands of the police. Several shots were fired, but no one was wounded, although the *Democrat* reported that Allan Pinkerton, who had founded his famous detective agency five years before, narrowly escaped "being shot by a policeman who had become crazy with the excitement of the scene." The South Side was quiet during the remainder of the afternoon, but on the North Side the Germans were holding more mass meetings and preparing for another attempt. In preparation for the battle, the Mayor summoned every policeman in town to the Public Square, and enrolled a hundred and fifty special deputies.

About three o'clock in the afternoon a mob of about a thousand men, armed with shotguns, rifles, knives, clubs, and every other variety of weapon, marched down Clark Street in two detachments. The first swarmed across the bridge, whereupon, under orders from the Mayor, the

_____

[1] Ibid., pages 74–5.

bridge-tender swung the draw and prevented the second detachment from following. "As soon as the rioters realized how neatly they had been tricked," said Flinn, "a howl went up that was heard in the Court House Square. They demanded that the bridge-tender close the draw at once. They threatened him with death. They coaxed him with honeyed words. They offered bribes. Some talked of shooting him. The parley went on for some time, till at length the Mayor, having perfected his arrangements, ordered the bridge opened, and the rioters swarmed across." They were met by more than two hundred policemen, formed in a solid line across Clark Street between Lake and Randolph.

With cries of "Shoot the police!" the mob attacked, firing guns and brandishing knives and clubs. The police returned the fire and then met the assault of the rioters with swinging bludgeons. The battle raged for more than an hour before the rioters turned and fled across the bridge into the North Side. A score of men were more or less seriously wounded, but despite the fierceness of the fighting and the large number of shots fired, only one man was known to have been killed — a German named Peter Martin, who was shot by a deputy after he had blown Patrolman George W. Hunt's arm off with a shotgun. "A few days later," said the Chicago *Times,* "there were several mysterious funerals on the North Side, and it was generally believed that the rioters gave certain victims secret burial." The deputy who had killed Martin was arrested on complaint of several saloon-keepers, but was released when the Sheriff said that the shot had been fired at his express order. For several days the Public Square was guarded by two companies of militia, with their artillery, but there were no further disturbances. At its first meeting after the riot the City Council voted Patrolman Hunt "the snug sum of $3,000," and for more than twenty-five

47

years Hunt kept the money out at interest, with Dr. Boone as his financial adviser.

Sixty prisoners were taken by the police at the battle of the Clark Street bridge, and fourteen were tried for rioting. Two, Irishmen named Farrell and Halleman, were convicted, but were granted new trials, which were never held. As Andreas wrote, " It seemed little less than a travesty on justice that in a sedition notoriously German, the only victims should be two Irishmen."

6

THE campaign for and against the prohibition measure, which was voted upon at a special election held on the first Monday in June 1855, was one of the most exciting contests in the history of Illinois. "Temperance workers stumped the state," said an Illinois historian, "copies of their organs were strewn broadcast, their organizations conducted a systematic campaign with the support of a majority of the regular newspapers, but the opposition revealed strength that was scarcely in accordance with calculations. . . . Anti-prohibitionist papers were started in Chicago and Belleville, and the liquor dealers of Chicago subscribed to a large fund with which to fight ratification. As a result, the returns of the heaviest vote ever cast in the state shattered the hopes of the over-confident temperance forces." The prohibition law was defeated by a majority of 14,447, and the Chicago saloon-keepers were subjected to no further annoyance of a really serious nature until nation-wide prohibition was instituted sixty-four years later.

CHAPTER III

"WE ARE BESET ON EVERY SIDE!"

IN 1857, celebrating the twentieth anniversary of its in-
corporation as a city, Chicago could boast of almost
fifteen hundred business establishments, a dozen banks of
issue; eleven railroad trunk lines and seventeen branch lines,
with more than a hundred trains arriving or departing every
day; a million and a half tons of shipping and nearly two
million dollars' worth of imports and exports annually; sixty
hotels, of which at least ten were first-class, comparable in
every way to the great houses of the East; forty newspapers
and periodicals, half a dozen theaters, enough bar-rooms
for five cities; eighty ballrooms, where "bands played from
morning to night, waltzing continuing without intermis-
sion"; and a population of ninety-three thousand — it was
the largest city in the Northwest and the metropolis of an
area larger than that of the original thirteen states. "The
first two decades of Chicago's city life," wrote Andreas,
"showed the most marvelous advance ever shown in the
development of a community or the aggregation of a resident population ever known in the history of the world."

But not all of Chicago's accomplishments could be written in black ink; there was a plenitude of entries on the debit
side of the ledger. Crime of every description had increased,
and it continued to increase as 1857 wore on to its dismal
close, and the city felt the full force of the money panic
which began in the great financial centers of the East and

spread throughout the country, causing widespread business demoralization and unemployment. Burglaries, shootings, stabbings, holdups, sneak thievery, and rowdyism became commonplace; many such crimes were committed by bands of boys, and by men who had once been respectable laborers and mechanics, now " driven from sheer want and by the sufferings of their families, to try their fortunes as garroters, highwaymen, burglars and thieves." One gang of twenty-seven young thugs, all armed with pistols, knives, and bludgeons, was led by an eighteen-year-old boy, who calmly told the police of a hundred robberies. The rendezvous of this gang was the Limerick House, a disreputable tavern near the Michigan Southern depot, kept by Jerry Shine, " a desperate character." Another band, composed of youthful sneaks and pickpockets, was loyal to a noted thief known to the police as John the Baptist; he dressed in ministerial black, with a red handkerchief about his throat, but no shirt. He carried a pocketful of religious tracts, and customarily left one at the scene of a crime.

Daily the newspapers published accounts of the doings of these and other criminals, with almost hysterical warnings of worse to come. " The people became almost panic-stricken," wrote John J. Flinn, " and honest citizens returning to their homes or visiting friends after dark, ran the risk of being mistaken for criminals and shot. . . . Life and property were in constant danger from mobs of criminals." Noting that fifty-three burglaries had been reported in one week, the *Tribune* declared that Chicago was " at the mercy of the criminal classes," and advocated a mass meeting of citizens to employ Allan Pinkerton to clean up the city. This was not done, but a group of business men did hire Pinkerton to stop the depredations of a gang of ghouls and vandals who were raiding the Old Catholic Burying Ground north of the city, desecrating the graves and digging up bodies to sell to medical students. Eight operatives

50

under the command of Timothy Webster, one of Pinkerton's famous early detectives, guarded the cemetery for weeks.

The little nest of gamblers dominated by the patrician John Sears had become, in 1857, a large and discordant colony of deadfalls and skinning joints, with a few square houses struggling desperately for survival. The liquor groceries had given way to cheap lodging-houses and low grogshops with back rooms, more than ever the resort of thieves and hoodlums. The few dingy brothels of Wells Street had spawned a score of such establishments. Most of them were two-bit houses catering exclusively to the riffraff, but two or three charged from fifty cents to a dollar, had carpets on the floor and melodeons in the parlors, and advertised with red lights and red window curtains. The most pretentious, though in no way equal to the luxurious parlor-houses of a later day, were Julia Davenport's Green House, on State Street; and the Prairie Queen, on the same thoroughfare, which was kept by Eleanor Herrick, better known as Mother Herrick, who was a familiar figure in Chicago's red-light district for thirty years. The Prairie Queen was noted for the variety and nature of its entertainment; there was dancing every night, an erotic show once a week, and a monthly prize-fight between two bruisers who fought with bare knuckles for a purse of two dollars and a night with one of Mother Herrick's cyprians. The police ignored the dancing and the erotic shows, but they finally stopped the prize-fighting, raiding the Prairie Queen on the afternoon of June 3, 1857, and arresting Billy Fagan, a local tough, and Con McCarthy, a ruffian from Rochester, New York.

In addition to those on Wells and State Streets, brothels of varying degrees of viciousness had appeared on Blue Island Avenue, and on Madison, Monroe, and Green Streets. There was also a dive of singular depravity on the second floor of a brick warehouse at No. 109 South Water

Street, which housed a large resident population of harlots and had a row of cubicles which were rented to streetwalkers. The police had frequently invaded this den to quell drunken orgies, but on the night of October 19, 1857 they were too late. A playful strumpet kicked over a lighted lamp, and in the holocaust that followed twenty-three persons lost their lives and property valued at almost $500,-000 was destroyed. But all of the harlots escaped.

2

EVEN the worst of the Wells Street dives was a veritable Sunday school compared with those in the Sands, a stretch of lake shore just north of the Chicago River, approximately where the Wrigley and *Tribune* buildings now stand. Originally the Sands was the site of a few lodging-houses and grog-shops which catered to sailors and canal men, but it was gradually enlarged, and in 1857 contained between twenty and thirty ramshackle buildings and a dozen shanties, each housing gambling dens, saloons, and bordellos in which the service charge ranged from twenty-five to fifty cents. To the volunteer firemen the Sands was a source of sport and entertainment; whenever a fire started there, they wielded axes with great vigor but no discrimination, gleefully knocked down shanties with streams of water, and sprinkled the enraged jezebels as freely as they did the fire. But to the respectable element the Sands was an abomination and a sink-hole flaunting sin and corruption. The *Tribune* declared that it was " decidedly the vilest and most dangerous place in Chicago. For some years past it has been the resort or hiding place of all sorts of criminals, while the most wretched and degraded women and their miserable pimps congregated there in large numbers. A large number of persons, mostly strangers in the city, have been enticed into the dens there and robbed, and there is but little doubt that a number of murders have been committed by the desperate characters who have made these dens their homes. The most beastly sensuality and darkest crimes had their homes in the Sands. . . ."

The king-pins of this unsavory community in the days of its evil glory were Dutch Frank, Freddy Webster, Anna Wilson; Mike O'Brien and his son Mike, Senior a gifted burglar and a noted fighter, and Junior a pickpocket and a pimp for his four sisters; and John Hill and his wife Mary, who are said to have been the first persons in Chicago to work the badger game. Unfortunately, John Hill possessed a wide streak of jealousy; after a successful coup he always tried to kill his wife for encouraging the victim of their racket. Dutch Frank owned a kennel of fighting dogs, a gambling-house, and a saloon presided over by a gargoyle of a bartender whose nose and ears had been chewed off in brawls. Freddy Webster's place, a groggery and twenty-five-cent bagnio, was a dump of exceptional viciousness even for the Sands. One of his inmates, Margaret McGuinness, was said to have been neither sober nor out of the house for five years, and not to have had her clothes on for three. She customarily entertained from ten to forty men a night. She died on March 8, 1857, and the Coroner said the cause was "intemperance." It was the seventh unnatural death in the Sands in one week.

Anna Wilson's house, the only fifty-cent brothel in the Sands, was enlivened by the presence of a belligerent young strumpet named Annie Stafford, better known as Gentle Annie. Despite the terrific competition, Gentle Annie had won renown as a fighter, and she was Madame Wilson's main reliance in her war against Mother Herrick of the Prairie Queen, which began early in 1857 when Mother Herrick lured away one of Madame Wilson's fairest flowers by offering her a clean dress and more money. The madames and their loyal henchwomen fought several indecisive street battles, but the war remained a stalemate until the night of April 3, when Gentle Annie, with three more of Madame Wilson's girls and supported by a detachment of pimps, made a surprise attack upon the Prairie Queen. They broke down the front door with clubs, smashed the furniture, chased away the customers, and administered sound beatings to Madame Herrick and half a dozen of her girls. Then Gentle Annie returned in triumph to the Sands, driving before her not only the stolen strumpet but the pick of Mother Herrick's flock as well.

3

ABOVE the turmoil of crime and panic that was Chicago in 1857 loomed the gargantuan figure of Long John Wentworth — three hundred pounds on the hoof and six feet and seven inches in his socks — who walked barefoot into Chicago soon after his graduation from Dartmouth College in 1836, became editor of the *Democrat* at twenty-one, a member of Congress at twenty-eight, and was now in 1857 in his first term as Mayor. Long John was one of the famous characters of early Chicago, at once a shrewd politician of whom Abraham Lincoln said "he knows more than most men," and an eccentric official of unbounded self-esteem, who scorned advice and bitterly resented criticism. He made no secret of the fact that he regarded himself as the greatest man Chicago had produced or was likely to produce; once when an author asked his opinion of a new history of Chicago, Long John calmly scratched out everything that did not refer to himself, and said: "There, young man, is a correct history of the city!" When the Prince of Wales, later Edward VII, visited Chicago in 1860, the Mayor welcomed him in the breezy and informal manner characteristic of the American politician of the period.

54

He thus introduced the royal guest from a hotel balcony to a crowd gathered in the street:

" Boys, this is the Prince of Wales. He's come to see the city and I'm going to show him around. Prince, these are the boys."

As Mayor, Long John Wentworth strove mightily to keep the city's credit unimpaired and to restore business confidence, and led the police on several spectacular but largely futile forays against the underworld. As editor of the *Democrat,* he denied vehemently that criminals were unduly active, accused the other newspapers of exaggeration and misrepresentation, and insisted that the police were valiantly performing their duties. He printed column after column lauding his administration and proclaiming loudly that God was in His heaven and all was right with Chicago. Throughout the summer of 1857 he carried on a violent controversy with the *Tribune,* with an occasional blast at the *Journal,* which politely referred to him as " His Highness the Mayor." The issue was himself. " Neither paper spared abusive language," wrote John J. Flinn, " nor epithets of questionable decency, and sometimes, during the most violent stage of the warfare, careful fathers and husbands hesitated before introducing the sheets into their families." [1]

Long John was elected Mayor in a blaze of violence — there were rioting and disorder at the polls on March 3, 1857, in which one man was killed and several wounded — and violent actions marked the whole of his executive career. He introduced the first successful steam fire-engine into Chicago, and when the volunteer firemen demonstrated against the newfangled machine, he ordered two hundred members of half a dozen companies arrested for disorderly

---

[1] The *Democrat* was absorbed by the *Tribune* in 1861, the final issue being published on July 24 of that year. The *Tribune* was first issued on June 10, 1847.

conduct. Policemen guarded the engine until the excitement had subsided. In June 1857 the Mayor announced in the *Democrat* that he intended to enforce the ordinance, long ignored, which prohibited the obstruction of streets and sidewalks by signs, awnings, posts, and displays of merchandise. No attention was paid to the warning, and on the night of June 18 Long John assembled a large force of policemen with drays and wagons and superintended the removal of every obstruction on all of the principal streets. They were piled in a heap at the north end of Market Hall, on State Street, and police placed on guard. Next morning owners of the articles were notified in the *Democrat* that their property would be restored to them upon payment of fines.

Several times during the early summer of 1857 Mayor Wentworth warned the gamblers to close their resorts, but they refused to profit by the experience of the merchants who had obstructed the sidewalks. On July 17 a detachment of police headed by the Mayor in person broke into Dave Burrough's place in Randolph Street, one of the largest gaming resorts in the city, and arrested eighteen men. Long John saw to it that each prisoner was properly booked at the calaboose, and announced that if any person doing business under a city license attempted to furnish bail, his license would be forthwith revoked. This, as the Mayor intended, prevented the saloon-keepers from assisting the gamblers, and the distressed sharpers remained in jail all night. When they paid their fines next day and returned to the gambling-house, they found the place bare — the police had hauled away everything that could be moved. Burroughs never reopened his resort, and many other gamblers quit when Long John notified them that instead of making arrests he would simply confiscate all furniture and apparatus.

Long before Wentworth was elected Mayor there had

LONG JOHN WENTWORTH

been talk about demolishing the rookeries in the Sands, but the land on which they stood was in litigation in the United States courts, and, as the *Tribune* explained, " in view of the uncertainty of the law, the litigants were disinclined to take any violent measures to eject the occupants." About the first of April 1857 William B. Ogden bought the interests of several of the litigants, and his agents notified the denizens of the Sands to vacate the buildings, and at the same time, to avoid trouble, offered to buy the structures of " such of the owners as would sell them for a reasonable price." A few sold, but most of the squatters vowed that they would die a thousand deaths rather than leave their homes. This was reported to the Mayor, who promised to take action as soon as he could without risking bloodshed. The opportunity came when a fight was arranged between one of Dutch Frank's dogs and an animal owned by Bill Gallagher, a Market Street butcher, for a purse of two hundred and fifty dollars.

April 20 was decided upon as the date of the combat, and on the early morning of that day every able-bodied man in the Sands accompanied Dutch Frank to the Brighton racetrack. Chicago legend has it that Long John himself arranged the fight and caused it to be advertised, but there is no evidence to support the story. There is ample evidence, however, that he took advantage of it. Dutch Frank and his cohorts had scarcely left the Sands when Long John Wentworth marched across the Clark Street bridge, followed by Ogden's agent, a Deputy Sheriff bearing writs of ejectment, thirty-odd policemen, a team of horses drawing a wagon loaded with hooks and chains, and a curious crowd of several hundred citizens. The occupants of five houses and four shanties were permitted to remove their belongings, and then " hooks and chains were attached to the buildings, one after another, and down they came." Meanwhile the crowd had swarmed into the other houses, where it stole whatever caught its fancy, smashed furniture and bottles, and dragged the inmates into the streets. At the height of the excitement a fire company rattled into the Sands, knocked down two or three shanties, and with streams of water sent the denizens of the dives scurrying into their holes. They scurried out again a few hours later, after the Mayor and the mob had gone, when three of the remaining houses caught fire. The flames spread to three others, and all six, " houses of the worst character," were destroyed. " As the fire broke out in three of the buildings simultaneously," said the *Tribune,* " it is probable that they were set on fire by the inmates, out of spite." When the male inhabitants of the Sands returned from the dog-fight late in the afternoon, little remained of their sinful colony but ashes. Said the *Tribune* of April 21, 1857:

> " Thus this congregation of the vilest haunts of the most depraved and degraded creatures in our city has been literally ' wiped out,' and the miserable beings who swarmed there driven away. Hereafter, we hope the Sands will be the abode of the honest and industrious, and that efficient measures will be taken to prevent any other portion of the city from becoming the abode of another such gathering of vile and vicious persons."

But the result of Long John Wentworth's dramatic invasion of the Sands was not what had been hoped and expected. Several hundred " miserable beings " had been driven from the district, but they had simply crossed the Chicago River and, instead of being more or less confined to one small area, were soon scattered throughout the city.

4

DURING the four years that followed the panic and depression of 1857, Chicago remained almost stationary;

there was only a slight increase in the volume of business and in population, and in one year, 1858, the number of inhabitants actually decreased by ten thousand, because of the exodus of unemployed workmen. But as the historian Elias Colbert said, " Chicago neither lost faith nor energy." On the contrary, the city as a whole conducted itself " like the individual merchant who employs his spare time in taking account of stocks, noting deficiencies, and putting his store in order, so that he can attend to business all the better when it does come." While waiting for more and better customers, Chicago completed the raising of its big buildings to the new street grade; laid the rails of the first horse-car line on State Street from Lake south to the city limits; built sixteen churches and a new Post Office and Custom House; and permitted women, for the first time, to become " head assistants in the public schools."

Prosperity returned with a rush at the beginning of the Civil War, and the decade which elapsed between the outbreak of this conflict and the great fire of 1871 was another of those periods in the history of Chicago which can only be measured in astonishment and described in hyperbole. While the world gaped and gawked, the wonder city of the prairies increased in population to 300,000, in area to thirty-six square miles, in assessed property valuation to almost three hundred million dollars, in number of buildings to sixty thousand and of churches to one hundred and fifty-six; and in first-class hotels to twenty, including the magnificent Palmer House.[1] The mighty men of Chicago drove a tunnel two miles long under the bed of Lake Michigan to ensure a bountiful supply of water, reversed the current of the Chicago River, erected seventeen grain elevators with a total

---

[1] It was destroyed in the great fire of 1871. The second Palmer House, opened in 1873, was especially famous for the two hundred and twenty-five silver dollars embedded in the floor of the barbershop. They were put there by William S. Eaton, lessee of the shop.

capacity of nearly twelve million bushels, opened the great Union Stock Yards and superseded Cincinnati as the meat-packing center of the world, built the University of Chicago and installed therein the "largest and best refracting-telescope in the world," saw George M. Pullman construct the first sleeping-car and Marshall Field forge to the front as one of America's foremost merchants, and confounded the critics who deplored the lack of culture by supporting a symphony orchestra and an annual season of grand opera.

But one vitally important factor of municipal great-ness was neglected — the development of a police force capable of suppressing crime and providing adequate pro-tection to life and property. A start had been made when Mayor Boone reorganized the department in 1855, but scarcely anything calculated to increase the efficiency of the force was accomplished by Mayors Thomas Dyer and John C. Haines, or by Long John Wentworth in his first admin-istration. During his second term as Mayor, which began in 1860, Long John demoralized the department by constant interference in the most trivial details of management, and by dismissing without cause both patrolmen and high-ranking officers. "While reducing the numerical strength of the force," wrote John J. Flinn, "he left large districts of the rapidly-growing city at the mercy of the criminals who in-fested Chicago in shoals. . . . The force under Went-worth toward the close of his administration had been re-duced to a captain, six lieutenants and about fifty patrolmen, and it proved to be entirely inadequate to meet the demands made upon it." [1]

Innumerable complaints were made of the eccentric manner in which Long John ruled the police, and finally, in 1861, the Illinois Legislature enacted a law which took from the Mayor all control over the department and vested it in a Board of Police Commissioners. Angered by the af-

---

[1] *History of the Chicago Police*, page 93.

front to his dignity, Mayor Wentworth summoned every policeman in Chicago to the City Hall on the night of March 21, 1861, and at two o'clock next morning summarily discharged them. The Police Board reorganized the force as quickly as possible, but for almost twenty-four hours Chicago was without police protection of any sort. Great improvement was expected under the rule of the Board, but authority had simply been transferred from one politician to a group of politicians, and the new force was little better than the old. A few capable and famous officers appeared in the ranks, in particular Captain Jack Nelson, noted handler of bad men, and Simon O'Donnell, Chicago's first traffic policeman and the " dandy copper " of the Lake Street crossings; but except for a brief period when Cyrus P. Bradley was Superintendent, the force as a whole continued to be weak in numbers, badly organized, poorly disciplined, and notorious among criminals and decent folk alike for venality and inefficiency.

It was largely because of the helplessness of the police that Chicago acquired, during the Civil War decade, worldwide renown as "the wickedest city in the United States," a distinction which it has never relinquished. For with no proper law-enforcement agency to prevent it, the growth of the underworld was no less remarkable than Chicago's expansion in other directions. Attracted by the easy money of a boom town, by thousands of soldiers on the loose with thousands of dollars from Army payrolls, by the bounties of from three hundred to five hundred dollars paid for enlistments, and by the knowledge that there was nothing to fear from the police, the human scum of a hundred cities swarmed into Chicago from all over the country. There were literally thousands of them, from the lowly streetwalker and the cringing sneak thief to the elegant confidence man and the lordly gambler. They overflowed into the suburbs, particularly into Lemont, where a collection of dives known as Smoky Row was a municipal canker for almost forty years; and into Cicero, notorious in later years as the headquarters of Al Capone. Throughout the early 1860's the *Tribune* repeatedly called attention to the wickedness of Cicero, and especially to the numerous shooting and stabbing affrays that occurred in the Dutch Gardens, a resort kept by Pete Schlapp. "A more lawless, uncivilized, uncontrollable settlement does not exist in the whole country," said the *Tribune*. "It would seem as if the greater portion was peopled by a set of riotous, untamable, half-savage rowdies."

In Chicago proper the newcomers took over and enlarged the isolated criminal outposts which had been formed by the "vile and vicious persons" driven from the Sands. Within a year after the Civil War began, there was scarcely a downtown street that didn't have its row of brothels, groggeries, gambling dens and cheap lodging-houses, all open day and night seven days a week. The South Side below Madison Street, and from the lake to the river, was almost wholly occupied by criminals, and was "untenable for decent folk for years"; not even the great fire could cleanse it. The Chicago *Journal* summed up the situation when it cried: "We are beset on every side by a gang of desperate villains!"

The "very core of this corruption," as a noted journalist of the period phrased it, was Roger Plant's resort on the northeast corner of Wells and Monroe Streets. Originally this dive was confined to a single two-story house, but one adjoining rookery after another was added, and by the middle 1860's the establishment extended half-way down the block on both streets. The police knew the place as "Roger's Barracks," but with a delicate touch of sentimentality Plant called it "Under the Willow," because a lone willow tree drooped languidly over a corner of the main building. The physical appearance of the dive was further distinguished by a bright blue shade at each of the windows, upon which was lettered in gilt: "Why Not?" It became a favorite catch-phrase throughout the country.

Roger's Barracks was described by Frederick Francis Cook as "one of the most talked about if not actually one of the wickedest places on the continent," and as "a refuge for the very nethermost strata of the underworld — the refuse of the Bridewell."[1] It was popularly believed that a tunnel ran from the resort under Wells Street to the underworld colonies that filled the district between that thoroughfare and the south branch of the Chicago River. There were at least sixty rooms in the various shacks which made up Roger Plant's domain, and in them was practiced virtually every sort of vice and criminality known to man. There was a saloon; two or three brothels where men were often robbed, stripped, and thrown into the alleys; rooms for assignation; procuresses' dens where young girls were raped by half a dozen men and then sold to the bordellos; cubicles which were rented to streetwalkers and male degenerates; and hidden rooms used as hide-aways by every species of crook. One of Plant's tenants in the war era was Mary Hodges, a noted shoplifter and pickpocket who drove a cart into the shopping district several times a week and drove it away loaded with plunder; another was Mary Brennan, called by the *Tribune* an "audacious old sinner," who ran a thieves' school for little girls, with two of her own daughters as prize pupils and tutors. The children picked pockets, snatched purses, and stole from store counters, and brought their loot to the old lady, who rewarded them with a few pennies to spend for candy. A third ornament of Under the Willow was Speckled Jimmy Calwell, a burglar and safe-robber, who is said to have been the first to gag and bind his victims with plaster and tape. He was also be-

---

[1] *Bygone Days in Chicago,* by Frederick Francis Cook; Chicago, 1910; page 160. Cook was a member of the editorial staff of the Chicago *Times*.

lieved to have been implicated in the manufacture of Chicago's first bomb, which was found on the tracks of the Blue Island horse-car line late in December 1870. " Such a discovery in a civilized community," said the *Times,* " seems almost incredible, but there is not the slightest doubt of its truth."

The landlord of Under the Willow, Roger Plant, was a diminutive Englishman, a native of Yorkshire, who measured about five feet one inch in height and never weighed more than a hundred pounds. Despite his lack of brawn, however, he was a famous fighter, being very agile, and adept in the use of all weapons, especially his teeth. Ordinarily Roger carried a knife and a pistol in his pocket and a bludgeon in his hand, but when he got drunk, which was often, he laid aside his armament, filled a bucket with a mixture of water and whisky, and with the assistance of his cronies ceremoniously drenched the roots of his willow tree. Roger succeeded in dominating the unruly customers of his saloon, but he was in turn dominated by his wife, who tipped the scales at two hundred and fifty pounds. She could — and frequently did — hold her squirming spouse at arm's length with one hand and spank him with the other. Mrs. Plant's special province was that portion of Under the Willow which was devoted to vice, and when she wasn't busy at congenial tasks in connection with the brothels and street-walkers' dens, she was producing children. No outsider ever knew the exact number of her progeny, but it was generally believed to be about fifteen, cunning little rascals who could pick a pocket almost before they could crawl.

This happy family flourished at Under the Willow for some ten years with virtually no interference. " The police seldom troubled the place during the war years," wrote Cook. " Roger paid his toll with exemplary regularity." [1] But about 1868, having made more money than he could

---

[1] Ibid., page 159.

ever spend, Plant suddenly closed his resort, bought a house in the country, and "became a patron of the turf and otherwise blossomed into a pattern of respectability." Several of his children, however, continued to carry on the family tradition, Roger, Jr., first coming into public notice at the age of fifteen, when he and another boy were arrested for tapping the till of a Monroe Street saloon. In 1894, when the English journalist William T. Stead published a Black List of Chicago property used for immoral purposes, Roger Plant, Jr., was listed as the keeper of three saloons and two brothels, while Kitty and Daisy Plant ran adjoining bordellos in South Clark Street.

Scarcely less vicious than Under the Willow were John Ryan's Concert Saloon in South Clark Street, which advertised "elegant and chaste performances" and instead presented immoral shows and was a hangout of hoodlums; George Clark's New York Saloon and Ben Sabin's bar, both in Wells Street; the Clark Street grog-shops of Tim Reagan and Andy Routzong, noted for "the desperate character of both proprietors and their patrons"; a group of Negro dives in Shinbone Alley, between Adams and Quincy Streets near Wells; a huddle of dilapidated shacks on Chicago Avenue, known as the Chicago Patch, where an old harridan called Mother Klein reigned supreme; and Mother Conley's Patch, a collection of rookeries at Adams and Franklin Streets. The boss of Conley's Patch was a gigantic black woman known as the Bengal Tigress, who has become a legendary character of the underworld. Her business was procuring young girls for sailors, but her avocations were fighting, drinking, and raising hell generally. When she went on a rampage the denizens of Conley's Patch barricaded their doors and windows and waited in fear and trembling for the worst to happen; on at least two occasions the Bengal Tigress tore down, single-handed, shanties whose occupants had angered her. The police seldom bothered her, but when they did they came in force; no fewer than four cops were required to drag her to the lockup.

The saloons run by Andy Routzong and Tim Reagan, and Ben Sabin's place in Wells Street, were the favored rendezvous of the bounty-jumpers, thugs and rowdies who enlisted for the war, deserted as soon as they had collected the bounty, and then re-enlisted under a different name in another regiment, repeating the process until the hue and cry drove them to cover. Some operated through bounty-brokers, agents who, for a commission, furnished information as to what regiments most urgently needed men to fill their quotas and would pay the highest prices. Many of these patriotic hoodlums, among them Big Denny O'Brien; Black Jack Yattaw, who was a bumboat pirate in times of peace; and the notorious cop-fighter Mike Garrity, enlisted in as many as a dozen regiments, collecting from three hundred to four hundred dollars for each enlistment. But the prince of bounty-jumpers was Con Brown, horse-thief and all-around bad man; a vicious and brutal fighter when drunk, but remarkably kind and generous when sober. Once, after wantonly beating a young mechanic, Brown paid his victim's medical bills and gave him a large sum of money besides. During the first three years of the war Con Brown got himself on the rolls of no fewer than twenty military organizations and collected about eight thousand dollars in bounties. In 1864, while serving a month's sentence in the Bridewell, he escaped five times, with the connivance of his jailers, and enlisted in three different regiments. His crimes finally caught up with him in 1865, and he was sent to the state prison at Joliet, from which he escaped six times in less than three years. The prison authorities and the police finally quit worrying about him on the night of December 26, 1868, when he was killed by Pete Boyle in a Smoky Row saloon in Lemont, after he had tried to cut Boyle's throat with a butcher knife.

66

THE aristocrats of the Chicago underworld during the war decade were the so-called "big gamblers," swaggering, roistering, devil-may-care rascals with ready trigger-fingers, who were by far the best-dressed and most picturesque figures in the life of the city; they were extravagantly admired by scatterbrained youths who copied their clothing and mannerisms and listened in open-mouthed awe to their boastings. Many of them had come to Chicago from New Orleans, Natchez, Vicksburg, and the Mississippi River steamboats, and their sympathies remained with the South, even though their aversion to the rigors and perils of war was obvious. They were more than free with their opinions, and, according to Frederick Francis Cook, " not only worked up a good deal of Southern sympathy among the unthinking younger generation about town, but went far in giving the impression that Chicago was a hotbed of disaffection. Indeed, so far did this Southern gambling influence extend, that of all the resorts for men-about-town, the Tremont House was about the only place where one invariably heard outspoken Union sentiment. And while there was among all classes (the German element excepted) a goodly number with more or less avowed Southern sympathies, it was the gambler who above all gave an extraordinarily aggressive tone to the local opposition to the war, and was the moving spirit in the organization of lodges of Knights of the Golden Circle." [1]

This is a somewhat exaggerated estimate of the gamblers' influence, for Southern sentiment was mainly fostered in Chicago by the *Times,* one of the leading Copperhead newspapers of the country. Founded in 1854 to further the political fortunes of Senator Stephen A. Douglas, the

[1] Ibid., page 171.

Times was the principal organ of the Douglas faction until 1860, when it was bought by Cyrus H. McCormick, the reaper-manufacturer, who already owned the Chicago *Herald*. In 1861 McCormick sold the Times to Wilbur F. Storey, a Vermonter who had owned the Detroit *Free Press* since 1853. The *Times* became violently anti-war as soon as Abraham Lincoln had signed the Emancipation Proclamation; in common with other Douglas adherents, Storey held that Lincoln had deceived the people by switching war aims. So inflammatory were Storey's articles that on June 3, 1863 General Ambrose E. Burnside of the United States Army ordered the *Times* suppressed, thus precipitating greater excitement than Chicago had seen since the Lager-Beer Riot of 1855. Scarcely had a squad of soldiers marched into the *Times* office before two mobs began to form, one composed of anti-war Democrats, and the other of Union sympathizers, mostly Republicans; by nightfall it was estimated that twenty thousand angry men were on the streets. Armed guards were posted about the *Tribune* office, which the Copperheads threatened to burn if the *Times* were not allowed to publish. Meanwhile leaders of both factions were meeting in an effort to prevent rioting, and at length a joint telegram was sent to President Lincoln asking him to revoke General Burnside's order of suppression. The revocation arrived on June 4, and the excitement subsided. On June 5 the *Times* resumed publication. Thereafter Storey's editorials were much milder in tone.

After the Civil War the *Times,* under Storey's able editorship, became not only one of Chicago's most valuable newspaper properties, but one of America's great crusading journals. For almost fifteen years the *Times* carried on a continuous campaign against political corruption and the underworld, exposing the city's plague spots, pointing out the growing intimacy between criminals and politicians, publishing lists of unsolved crimes, and frequently naming

68

persons who permitted their property to be used for immoral purposes. Storey's philosophy of journalism was summed up in his observation that " it is a newspaper's duty to print the news and raise hell." On one occasion, however, he raised a little hell that backfired. Lydia Thompson, noted burlesque actress of the period, brought her troupe of English Blondes to Crosby's Opera House, and the *Times'* account of the performance accused the young ladies of " capering lasciviously and uttering gross indecencies." As for Miss Thompson, the *Times* said that she was little better than a strumpet and should be run out of town. When Storey refused to retract or apologize, Miss Thompson intercepted him in front of his home on Wabash Avenue and thrashed him soundly with a horsewhip.

In journalistic circles Storey's methods of handling his editorial staff were regarded as extremely peculiar. His reporters were never told what or how to write, and in preparing their articles they were encouraged to make free use of the vernacular. As early as 1876 the *Times* was using the word " racket " in the sense which is now considered modern; on October 24 of that year Storey's paper said: " big thieves are boldly traversing our streets by day, planning their racket." On November 3, 1877 the hell-raising editor anticipated the modern gossip-columnist by some fifty years by putting the single word " WELDED " over the story of a wedding. Another typical Storey headline appeared in the *Times* on September 10, 1872, when Christopher Rafferty, a well-known hoodlum, was found guilty of the murder of Patrolman Patrick O'Meara:

SHUT OFF HIS WIND

A Satisfactory Job for Jack Ketch at Last.

The Hangman's Rope Awarded to
Christopher Rafferty.

Now, Do Not Reprieve Nor Pardon Him,
Nor Give Him a New Trial.

And, in the Name of All That's Decent,
Don't Commute His Sentence.

The Jury Concludes, in Just Twenty Minutes,
To String the Ruffian Up.

Of all the *Times'* headlines, the most startling, and one that is still talked about by newspaper men, was printed on November 27, 1875:

JERKED TO JESUS

Four Senegambian Butchers Were
Wafted to Heaven on Yes-
terday from Scaffolds.

Two of Them, in Louisiana, Died with
the Sweet Confidence of
Pious People.

While Yet Two Others, in Mississippi, Expired
Exhorting the Public to Beware of
Sisters-In-Law.

The troublesome tricksters from the South, and the local crop of sharpers as well, probably prospered to a greater extent in war-time Chicago than did the purveyors of any other form of underworld entertainment, even though, or perhaps because, they regularly paid huge sums for police protection. The city was alive with suckers — Army officers and paymasters, soldiers back from the front with the accumulated pay of months, men grown rich on

Army contracts, young men earning more money than ever before — and they supported hundreds of gaming places, from the palatial skinning house to the hovel where the only equipment was a plank and a greasy deck of cards. They were scattered all over the city, but the biggest and fanciest were on Randolph Street between Clark and State, better known as Hairtrigger Block; and on Gamblers' Row — Clark Street from Randolph to Monroe — where they clustered so thickly as to exclude all other business except saloons and a few brothels. The *Tribune* called Randolph and Dearborn Streets " a thieves' corner," and the *Times* said that both Clark and Randolph Streets, and Dearborn south of Madison, had " become so contaminated by these execrable vagabonds that respectable persons avoid them as they would a cesspool."

The best-known gamblers of Hairtrigger Block and the Row were George Trussell, Cap Hyman, John Brown, Evander Morris, Watt Robbins; Frank Connelly, whose Senate was one of the show-places of the city and the most elaborately equipped gaming resort east of New York; Johnny Lawler, who, when he bucked another man's game and lost, would scream, butt his head against a wall, and try to pull off his ears; Colonel Wat Cameron, a courtly Virginian who ran a square game until he was forced out by Gabe Foster and Ben Burnish, skin artists from St. Louis; Jere Dunn, who vanished after killing Jim Elliott, a pugilist; James Watson, also called Sir James, who was shot by White Pine Russell, a faro dealer; John Sutton, killed in a Clark Street saloon; Dave Stanley, described by the *Tribune* as " a garroter, a burglar, anything that will bring money, a professional thief and pimp of the worst character, gambling being one of the best traits in his fiendish character "; and Theodore Cameron, whose two houses were famous for bird suppers and wine, all free to the sucker. Cameron made a million dollars in Chicago in eight years,

71

JERKED TO JESUS.

Four Senegambian Butchers Were Wafted to Heaven on Yesterday from Scaffolds.

Two of Them, in Louisiana, Died with the Sweet Confidence of Pious People.

While Yet Two Others, in Mississippi, Expired Exhorting the Public to Beware of Sisters-In-Law.

How the Capital Sentence Was Executed and How the Victims Stood It.

Diabolical Rape Case on Trial at Spring Lake---The Girl's Story.

An Indianian's Unsuccessful Attempt at Wife-Murder and Suicide.

Miscellaneous Criminal Record.

HELLUM AND HARRIS.
[Special Telegram.]
ONE OF THE WORST ON RECORD.

MONROE, La., Nov. 26.—The murder for which Alcee Harris and Tony Hellum suffered on to-day, was one of the worst cases on record, and if such a case can possess additional aggravation, it will be found in the fact that the woman Harris was the wife of the murdered man, and that she assisted in killing him, that she might enjoy without interference her guilty amours with Hellum.

THE WIFE SUSPECTED.

In April last, Harris began to suspect that his wife was not as circumspect in her conduct as loyal wives should be, and upon instituting an

A FAMOUS HEADLINE IN THE CHICAGO "TIMES"

but when he left the city, about 1876, it was all gone but five hundred. The clowns of Hairtrigger Block and Gamblers' Row were the Hankins brothers, Al and George, who cared nothing for fine clothing and were notoriously superstitious even for gamblers. They burned an old shoe each morning to bring good luck, and put a pinch of salt and pepper on every seat to hoodoo the players. While the game was in progress one or both of the brothers hovered over the playing tables with a shaker, ready to sprinkle salt and pepper upon any sucker who might have a run of luck. Sometimes a player resented these attentions and had to be thrown out, but in general it was held that a gambler had a right to cast any spells which he believed might be effective. Perhaps because of their magic, Al and George Hankins prospered in Chicago for more than three decades; for almost a year in the 1880's their Clark Street houses showed a clear gain of $1,400 a day. But in the end it profited them nothing. Al was sick and broke when he was smothered to death in a folding bed, and George was virtually a pauper when he died in 1912 at Gary, Indiana.

The biggest of the " big gamblers " in war-time Chicago was George Trussell, called by one old-time sharper " a shrewd, cunning Yankee from Vermont," but said by others to have been born in Cook County. In any event, Trussell first appeared in Chicago in the late 1850's as bookkeeper in a commission house. Later he worked in a bank, but was discharged for playing faro, and in 1860, when he was about twenty-seven years old, he became a roper and capper for a small faro bank. Early in 1861 he opened a house of his own, and within another year had become interested in half a dozen places in partnership with Old Bill Leonard, Otis Randall, and Jim Judd. Late in 1862, however, Trussell withdrew from the syndicate and confined his activities to a house in Randolph Street and another in Dearborn Street. During the next four years Trussell was in the heyday of his power; he "feed the accommodating police most munificently," and while he was unable to prevent the opening of new gambling-houses, any sharper who incurred his enmity soon found himself the object of destructive raids.

Trussell was the idol of the young sports of Chicago, and contemporary accounts agree that he was an unusually handsome man; he was "tall, straight as an arrow, and might have stood as model for one of Remington's Indian-fighting cavalry officers." Sober, Trussell was pleasant enough, but quiet to the point of taciturnity; drunk, he was talkative and quarrelsome, ready to fight upon the slightest provocation. His pet aversion was Cap Hyman, "an insufferable egotist, an excitable, emotional jack-in-the-box" with an irascible temper, who was variously believed to be an English Jew, the scion of a rich Southern family, and the son of an Eastern merchant. In liquor, Hyman was given to shooting up the town, a practice which led the *Tribune* to remark that "the practice of shooting people upon the most trifling provocation is becoming altogether too prevalent in this city."

When Hyman and Trussell happened to be drunk at the same time, they invariably went gunning for each other, while the sports of Hairtrigger Block laid bets as to which would be killed first. More than once the heroes exchanged shots, but they were notoriously poor marksmen and never hit anything but bar mirrors and street signs. The police let them alone as long as their target practice was confined to Hairtrigger Block, but Hyman frequently created such a disturbance elsewhere that he had to be arrested and fined a few dollars, sums which he meticulously deducted from his regular protection payments. One such occasion was in 1862, when Hyman staggered into the lobby of the Tremont House, fired a few shots, and refused to permit anyone to enter or leave the hotel for an hour. But when

74

Police Captain Jack Nelson appeared Hyman immediately pocketed his revolver and surrendered. "Jack can shoot too quick for me," he said afterward.

It was customary for the big gambler of this period to have as his mistress the madame of a brothel, known in sporting circles as an "establishment," and to parade his personal strumpet, decked in jewels and fine raiment, as visible evidence of his prosperity and success. George Trussell's inamorata was Mary Cossgriff, also called Irish Mollie and Mollie Trussell; she always insisted she had been married to the handsome sharper, but was never able to produce a wedding certificate. She had come to Chicago in 1854 from Columbus, Ohio, and was chambermaid at the American House for several years, until she was seduced. Almost immediately she entered a bordello, in those days the natural and accepted sequel to a single false step. Early in 1864 Trussell installed her as madame of an "establishment" in Fourth Avenue, later Custom House Place.

For more than two years Trussell and his Mollie were an obviously happy and devoted couple; he took her for a daily ride in his carriage, appeared with her at the theaters and race-tracks, lavished money upon her, and otherwise demeaned himself as a considerate and resourceful lover. But in the summer of 1866 the gambler became half owner of the famous trotting horse Dexter, and from that moment his interest in Mollie began to decline; he spent more time with his horse and less and less time with his mistress. Like most women of her class, Mollie's nature was compounded of almost equal parts of childlike devotion and insane jealousy. She dearly loved her gambler, but she was murderously enraged by his neglect, particularly when her friends began to taunt her with playing second fiddle to a horse. They quarreled bitterly and frequently. The climax in their relations came on September 4, 1866. Trussell had promised to take her to the opening of the fall season at the Chicago Driving Park and then preside over a select dinner party at the "establishment," but he did neither, and about ten o'clock in the evening Mollie went down to Hairtrigger Block in search of him. He was drinking at the bar of Seneca Wright's saloon in Randolph Street when she came in, attired, as the *Tribune* put it, "in a gorgeous white moire dress, with a light shawl thrown over it, and seemed as if she had just come from some dancing party." But under the shawl Mollie's trembling hand clutched a revolver, and when Trussell angrily told her to go home she shoved the weapon against his side and pulled the trigger. She shot him again as he ran out a side entrance, and once more as he dodged into Prince's livery stable. At the third shot Trussell fell dead, and Mollie flung herself upon his body, screaming:

"Oh, my George! My George! He is dead!"

In December 1866 Mollie was tried before a jury and found guilty of manslaughter. She was sentenced to one year at Joliet, but was pardoned by Governor Richard J. Oglesby before she entered the prison. She returned to her brothel and was well known in the red-light district for another fifteen years. So far as available records show, she made no claim to Trussell's estate, which amounted to approximately $75,000, and it was generally believed that this renunciation of whatever rights she may have had bore some relation to her pardon. Trussell left $31,563.58 in cash, and almost as much more in gambling I.O.U.'s, which were never collected. Besides his two gaming-houses, he owned several pieces of real estate, two of them on State Street near Monroe. His share of Dexter was sold by his executor for $10,000. His personal property, which brought $8,000 at auction, included five gold watches appraised at $1,445, two diamond pins valued at $1,700, one revolver, one single-barrel pistol, five hats, and twelve pairs of "cassimere pantaloons."

Cap Hyman's mistress was none other than Gentle Annie Stafford, once the terror of the Sands, who had come up in the world and was now, thanks to her lover's generosity, madame of a fine establishment at No. 155 North Wells Street. She had also taken on flesh, and was pointed out to strangers as the fattest brothel-keeper in town. Having seen the tragic end of her friend Mollie Trussell's illicit romance, Gentle Annie began to yearn for the security and sanctity of marriage, but Cap Hyman only laughed and chucked her under her several chins, reminding her that he was by no means the marrying type. He changed his mind on the afternoon of September 23, 1866, when Gentle Annie, armed with a long rawhide whip, stormed into his gambling-house at No. 81 Randolph Street, dragged him from the sofa upon which he had been dozing, knocked him downstairs, and then chased him up the street, her whip curling around his shanks at every jump. A few weeks later Cap Hyman and Gentle Annie were legally made one at a swell wedding attended not only by the cream of the Chicago underworld, but by delegations from St. Louis, Cincinnati, New Orleans, and Louisville.

During the feast that followed this brilliant social event, Cap Hyman announced that he and his bride had leased Sunnyside, a tavern at what is now North Clark Street and Montrose Avenue, but which was then well outside of the city limits, and would operate the place as " a high-toned roadhouse." The grand opening, for invited guests only, must have been a bizarre and colorful affair. Captain Jack Nelson was the guest of honor, and other gentlemen included various city and county officials, the blue bloods of the gambling world and the race-track, young business men with sporting proclivities, and reporters from each of the newspapers. The ladies were brothel-keepers who were friendly with Gentle Annie, and some thirty sirens from the staff of Gentle Annie's own establishment. For weeks before the opening Madame Stafford had painstakingly drilled her charges in the etiquette proper to the occasion, and they had listened eagerly to her instructions — all but one young red-headed strumpet who pish-toshed the whole business. She said that not only had she come from a good family, but she had read books, and knew perfectly well how to be a lady. She proved it at the party; whenever a gentleman was presented to her, she looked him straight in the eye and demanded:

"Who's your favorite poet? Mine's Byron."

The newspaper reporters were driven to Sunnyside in a huge four-horse sleigh, and when they arrived Cap Hyman took them into his office, gave them a drink, and made a little speech. "I would like you gentlemen of the press to understand," he said, "that this affair will be straight to the wink of an eyelash. All the ladies are here on their honor, and Mrs. Hyman will see to it that nothing unseemly takes place." Frederick Francis Cook, who was there as a reporter for the *Times,* said that the festivities began with dancing, decorous in the extreme. "You were ceremoniously introduced, engagement cards were consulted, and all the rest of the little formalities that distinguish like functions in the *haut monde* were strictly observed. Yes, the make-believe was quite tremendous." But decorum was thrown out the window after the reporters had been sent back to Chicago, and thereafter the guests were free to express their personalities in their own peculiar fashions. Before the party ended in a free-for-all fight at dawn, case after case of champagne had been guzzled, Cap Hyman had shot out the lights, Gentle Annie had chastised several madames for distributing their business cards, and half a dozen ambitious harlots had opened the sleeping-quarters upstairs for purposes of trade. But the little redhead was still plaintively inquiring: "Who's your favorite poet?"

The grand opening of Sunnyside was an enormous social success, but as " a high-toned roadhouse " the place was a dismal financial failure. Before six months had passed, Cap Hyman and Gentle Annie had abandoned the enterprise and returned to Chicago, the gambler to his tricks, and the madame to her strumpets. Hyman suffered a mental and physical breakdown a year or so later, and about 1876 died insane in a West Side boarding-house, with Gentle Annie by his side. After Hyman's death she ran a brothel in Custom House Place for several years, but dropped out of sight about 1880.

6

FOR several years after the close of the Civil War a respectable but not very prosperous laborer named Patrick O'Leary lived in the three rear rooms of a frame cottage at No. 137 DeKoven Street, on Chicago's West Side, with his wife Catherina and their five children, one of whom, James, later made his mark in the world — as Big Jim O'Leary he was a rich and powerful gambler. The two front rooms of the cottage were occupied by the family of Patrick McLaughlin, and in the rear was the two-story shanty used by the O'Learys as a barn, in which was kept a store of loose hay, a horse and a wagon, occasionally a calf, and five cows which Mrs. O'Leary milked twice daily, peddling the milk about the neighborhood. High wooden fences connected the barn with sheds and other out-buildings on adjacent property, and the alley north of the O'Leary cottage was strewn with old boxes, discarded lumber, and other rubbish of a highly combustible nature.

On the evening of Sunday, October 8, 1871, Dennis Sullivan, a drayman, called on his friends the O'Learys and found them in bed; they had retired early, Mrs. O'Leary said, because she " had a sore foot." Sullivan and O'Leary

79

talked for a few minutes about the unprecedented drought
— only an inch of rain had fallen since July 1 and the whole
Northwest was parched and dry, forest fires were raging
in Michigan and Wisconsin, and the grass of the prairies
was burning in a hundred localities. About half past eight
o'clock Sullivan started home, walking slowly along De-
Koven Street toward Jefferson. Half-way down the block
he stopped, filled his pipe, and sat on the curbing to enjoy
a quiet smoke. But as he raised his head to light the tobacco, shielding his match against the strong wind, the
drayman saw a bright, pulsating glow in the O'Learys' barn.
Crying the alarm, Sullivan rushed into the shanty and managed to drag out a calf, whose hair had caught fire. But
when he went back to save the horse or a cow, his wooden
leg caught in a crack between two boards and he barely escaped with his own life.

That was the beginning of the great Chicago fire;
within two hours it was raging over a hundred acres, de-
vouring pine houses, sheds, and barns as if they had been
so many match-sticks, and was beyond all possibility of control. Several things had enabled the flames to make such
rapid progress in such a short time. Foremost was the fact
that Chicago, as the *Tribune* had said, was " a city of ever-
lasting pine, shingles, shams, veneers, stucco and putty ";
of sixty thousand buildings, two-thirds were constructed entirely of wood, with roofs of shingles, tar, and felt, all bone-
dry from the drought and almost as inflammable as a bunch
of firecrackers. The Fire Department was undermanned
and possessed insufficient equipment; fewer than two hundred men depending upon seventeen fire-engines, eighteen
pieces of other apparatus, and forty-eight thousand feet
of hose. But at least a third of the hose, and several of the
engines and hose-carts, had been lost or damaged at previous fires and had not been replaced or repaired. Moreover,
the firemen were exhausted; they had answered thirty alarms

in a week, and only the day before had fought for fifteen hours against a $750,000 blaze on the West Side. And when the DeKoven Street fire was reported to the watchman in the Court House tower, he made a mistake in the location, and sent an engine company stationed a mile and a half away instead of one of the four which were comparatively

From an old print

THE GREAT CHICAGO FIRE

near by. Finally, throughout the conflagration a wind which at times reached the proportions of a gale blew without ceasing from the southwest.

Half an hour before midnight the fire crossed the Chicago River into the South Side, ignited the roof of a shanty at Adams and Franklin Streets, and leaped almost at once to the new eighty-thousand-dollar stables of Frank Parmalee's bus company. Conley's Patch and Shinbone Alley vanished in a flash of fire and smoke, and the blazing rookeries disgorged their prostitutes, pimps, and hoodlums to join the throng swarming back over the West Side bridges and through the tunnels. Gamblers' Row disappeared and so did Hairtrigger Block, and swinging slightly eastward the flames roared through the business district, destroying many important factories and all of the principal stores, wholesale houses, hotels, theaters, newspaper offices, and public buildings. Only two structures were left standing in the 460 acres bounded on the west, north, and east by the Chicago River and Lake Michigan, and on the south by a line running diagonally from Congress Street and Michigan Avenue to Polk and Wells Streets. In the early hours of Monday morning, October 9, the flames jumped the main stream of the Chicago River to the North Side and " went through that section of seventy-five thousand people as fast as a man could run "; 1,450 acres were burned over, and of 13,800 buildings fewer than five hundred were spared. Among the first to go were the waterworks and pumping station in Chicago Avenue, and the new structure of the Chicago Historical Society at Dearborn and Ontario Streets. With the latter went priceless and irreparable records, among them the original draft of Lincoln's Emancipation Proclamation.[1]

7

AHEAD of the reaching flames surged great masses of homeless and bewildered people, blistered and scorched by the terrific heat, carrying bundles and babies and invalids, dragging trunks and carts, stumbling, falling, trampling women and children, fighting, cursing, and screaming in such a frenzy of terror that sometimes their cries could be heard above the thunderous tumult of the fire. " The people were mad," said the Chicago *Post*. " Despite the police — indeed, the police were powerless — they crowded upon frail coigns of vantage, as fences and high sidewalks propped

---

[1] Andreas said that the only objects recovered from the ruins of the Society's building were the charred fragments of a few books, and a small vial containing a section of tapeworm.

82

on wooden piles, which fell beneath their weight, and hurled them, bruised and bleeding, in the dust. They stumbled over broken furniture and fell, and were trampled under foot. Seized with wild and causeless panics, they surged together, backwards and forwards, in the narrow streets, cursing, threatening, imploring, fighting to get free. Liquor flowed like water; for the saloons were broken open and despoiled, and men on all sides were to be seen frenzied with drink. . . . Everywhere dust, smoke, flame, heat, thunder of falling walls, crackle of fire, hissing of water, panting of engines, shouts, braying of trumpets, wind, tumult, and uproar.

"The brute creation was crazed. The horses, maddened by heat and noise, and irritated by falling sparks, neighed and screamed with affright and anger, and roared and kicked, and bit each other, or stood with drooping tails and rigid legs, ears laid back and eyes wild with amazement, shivering as if with cold. Dogs ran hither and thither, howling dismally. Great brown rats, with beadlike eyes, were ferreted out from under the sidewalks, by the flames, and scurried along the streets, kicked at, trampled upon, hunted down. Flocks of beautiful pigeons, so plentiful in the city, wheeled up aimlessly, circled blindly, and fell into the raging fire beneath."

From the blazing dens of the underworld came swarms of hoodlums, thieves, and prostitutes, hurrying to reap the richest harvest of loot that had ever fallen to the lot of American criminals. They hunted singly and in packs, snatching what they wanted from the drays and carriages and carts; breaking into saloons, stores, and homes, filling their bellies with liquor and their pockets with money and jewelry, covering their backs with fine clothing and their fingers and arms with rings and bracelets, dragging costly furniture into the streets and viciously ripping it to pieces because it must be abandoned to the flames. " They smashed windows with their naked hands," said the Chicago *Post,* "regardless of the wounds inflicted, and with bloody fingers rifled till and shelf and cellar, fighting viciously for the spoils of their forage. Women, hollow-eyed and brazen-faced, with filthy drapery tied over them, their clothes in tatters and their feet in trodden-over slippers, moved here and there — scolding, stealing, fighting; laughing at the beautiful and splendid crash of walls and falling roofs." Soon after midnight, with the Court House on fire, three hundred and fifty prisoners were released from the jail in the basement. They immediately broke into a jewelry store and looted it.

William S. Walker, a Chicago journalist, said that long before daybreak on Monday the looting had culminated in scenes of daring robbery unparalleled in the annals of disaster:

"As the night wore on, and the terrors aggregated into an intensity of misery, the thieves, amateur and professional, dropped all pretense at concealment and plied their knavish calling undaunted by any fears of immediate retribution. They would storm into stores, smash away at the safes, and if, as happily was almost always the case, they failed to effect an opening, they would turn their attention to securing all of value from the stock that could conveniently be made away with, and then slouch off in search of further booty. The promise of a share in the spoils gave them the assistance of rascally express-drivers, who stood with their wagons before doors of stores, and waited as composedly for a load of stolen property to be piled in as if they were receiving the honestly-acquired goods of the best man in town. . . . The scenes of robbery were not confined to the sacking of stores. Burglars would raid into the private dwellings that lay in the track of the coming destruction, and snatch . . . anything which their practical senses told them would be of value. Interference was useless. The scoundrels . . . were inflamed with drink, and were alarmingly demonstrative in the flourishing of deadly weapons. Sometimes women and children, and not infrequently men, would be stopped as they were bearing from their homes objects of especial worth, and the articles would be torn from their grasp by gangs of these wretches."

Alexander Frear, a New York politician who had been Boss Tweed's spokesman in the New York Legislature, saw the looting in part of the business district. He thus described it in an article for the New York *World:*

". . . I could see up Dearborn Street as far as the Portland Block, and it was full of people all the distance, swaying and surging under the reign of fire. Around on Lake Street the tumult was worse. Here, for the first time, I beheld scenes of violence that made my blood boil. In front of Shay's magnificent dry goods store a man loaded a store-truck with silk, in defiance of the employes of the store. . . . I saw a ragamuffin on the Clark Street bridge, who had been killed by a marble slab thrown from a window, with white kid gloves on his hands, and whose pockets were stuffed with gold-plated sleeve-buttons. On that same bridge I saw an Irish woman leading a goat that was big with young, while under the other arm she carried a piece of silk. Lake Street was rich with treasures; and hordes of thieves forced their way into the stores and flung out the merchandise to their fellows in the street, who received it without disguise, and fought over it openly. I went through the street to Wabash Avenue, and here the thoroughfare was choked with all manner of goods and people. . . . Valuable oil-paintings, books, pet animals, musical instruments, toys, mirrors, and bedding, were trampled under foot. Added to this, the goods from the stores had been hauled out and had taken fire; and the crowd, breaking into a liquor establishment, were yelling with the fury of demons, as they brandished champagne and brandy bottles. The brutality and horror of the scene made it sickening. A fellow, standing on a piano, declared that the fire was the friend of the poor man. He wanted everybody to help himself to the best liquor he could get; and continued to yell from the piano until someone, as drunk as himself, flung a bottle at him and knocked him off it. In this chaos were hundreds of children, wailing and crying for their parents. One little girl, in particular, I saw, whose golden hair, worn loose on her back, had caught fire. She ran screaming past me, and someone threw a glass of liquor upon her, which flared up and covered her with a blue flame."

The authorities were powerless to stop the looting, but they did succeed in checking the outbreak of incendiarism which seems inevitably to follow and accompany every great conflagration. Firebugs were active from Monday night, when the fire burned itself out against the open spaces of Lincoln Park, until Wednesday evening, by which time the city was being patrolled by two thousand special policemen, four hundred men of the regular force, six companies of the Illinois militia, and four companies of regular troops of the United States Army, all under the command of General Phil Sheridan, who ruled Chicago under martial law until October 22. Seven men caught setting fires were shot, and an eighth was stoned to death by a mob of infuriated citizens at Fourteenth Street and Fourth Avenue, where his body lay in the street for twenty-four hours as a warning to his kind. " It is not recorded," wrote Andreas, " that a woman was shot or hanged by the military, police or citizens, but several were taken in the act of incendiarism."

8

T H E Chicago fire was by far the most disastrous conflagration of the nineteenth century; in twenty-four hours it took two hundred and fifty lives,[1] devastated an area of three

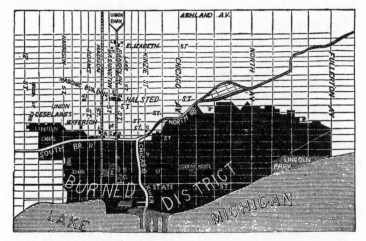

BURNED DISTRICT OF THE GREAT FIRE

and one-half square miles, burned 98,500 persons out of their homes, and destroyed 17,450 buildings, with a property loss of approximately $200,000,000. Hundreds of books, newspaper and magazine articles, poems, speeches, and plays were written about the catastrophe; no stereoptican collection was complete without views of Chicago before and after the fire, and as late as the early 1900's lec-

---

[1] That many bodies were found. At least as many more were believed to have been consumed in the fire, which in places reached temperatures as high as three thousand degrees Fahrenheit.

turers with magic-lantern slides were still drawing curious crowds. The disaster was the text of innumerable sermons, and scores of ministers declared that God had destroyed the city in punishment for its sins; the Reverend Granville Moody of Cincinnati was convinced that the calamity had been visited upon Chicago because it had voted down a proposition to close the saloons on Sunday. "It is retributive judgment," he declared, "on a city that has shown such devotion in its worship of the Golden Calf."

But nothing that was said or written about the fire solved the mystery of its origin. Legend has it that Mrs. O'Leary went into the barn to milk one of her cows, and that the animal kicked over a kerosene lamp, a tale which was given some color by the discovery of a broken lamp in the ruins. But both O'Leary and his wife declared, in affidavits, that no member of their family had entered the barn after nightfall, and that there had been no lighted lamp on their premises at any time during the evening. Another story was that Patrick McLaughlin or his wife had gone to the barn to get fresh milk for an oyster stew; the McLaughlins were having a party to celebrate the arrival of Mrs. McLaughlin's cousin from Ireland. But they swore that no one had left their rooms except one young man, who went to the corner for a bucket of beer. "Before God," Mrs. McLaughlin testified, "nobody went out to get milk." A third story of the fire's origin was that it was started by some boys smoking pipes and cigars in the hayloft. In later years Big Jim O'Leary said that was what had happened. But he always insisted that he knew none of the boys and was not himself a member of the group.

9

ON the morning of October 10, 1871, W. D. Kerfoot, a well-known real-estate agent and operator, went to the ruins of his office in Washington Street between Clark and Dearborn. With the assistance of his clerk and the latter's father, he cleared away the hot ashes and built a board shanty sixteen feet long and twelve feet wide. Atop the structure he placed a board on which had been lettered: "Kerfoot's Block," and on the front nailed a large sign:

W. D. KERFOOT

EVERYTHING GONE BUT WIFE, CHILDREN AND ENERGY.

This was the first building erected in Chicago after the great fire. But by the 18th of October, ten days after the start of the conflagration, business was being carried on in 5,497 temporary structures, and within a year a hundred thousand men were constructing ten thousand permanent buildings at a cost of almost $46,000,000. By the end of another decade Chicago was a bigger and grander city than even its most optimistic booster had ever imagined it would be; it had a population of almost 600,000 and was forging ahead toward the million mark, which it reached in 1890.

10

No part of Chicago was rebuilt more quickly than the saloons, brothels, gambling-houses, and other resorts and habitations of the underworld. In less than a year after the fire, conditions were even worse than in 1857 or in the early years of the Civil War — 2,218 saloon licenses, or approximately one to every hundred and fifty inhabitants, had been granted by the city during the first eight months of 1872, and, as John J. Flinn wrote, "concert halls, dives, brothels and gambling hells flourished" in unrecorded numbers. "Every train load of strangers," said Flinn, "contained a large percentage of disreputable characters. Gamblers, bunko-steerers, confidence men, sharpers, and criminals of every description arrived in shoals " [1] — to prey upon the disorganized and almost defenseless city; and the Police Department,

THE LEGENDARY START OF THE GREAT
CHICAGO FIRE

hurriedly and inefficiently reorganized and scarcely large enough to patrol the burned district and protect new and unfinished buildings from vandals and looters, could do nothing to stop them. Again no man's life and property were safe, and citizens who ventured out at night were almost certain to be robbed, while the newspapers were filled with accounts of crimes and editorials demanding the arrest and punishment of criminals. The *Times* printed a list of Chicago's homicides in seven years, and cried: "Nearly

---

[1] *History of the Chicago Police*, page 136.

a hundred murders since 1865 and not a single neck stretched!" Many of these killers were known by the police to have found refuge in a district known as Little Hell, at Crosby and Larrabee Streets on the West Side. The heart of Little Hell, and, as an old Chicago guide-book put it, "the center of all the glorious doings that made Little Hell historical," was a long, low building called the Barracks, which was erected by relief organizations in 1871 to house families whose homes had been destroyed. But the respectable residents soon left, and the Barracks was filled with ruffians who spent all their time drinking and fighting. "Every night," said the guide-book, "a patrolman would come in for help to subdue a riot. Little Hell was a terror district for several years, and many a bloody murder was committed within its precincts."

11

EARLY in 1872 an organization called the Committee of Seventy was formed by "leading citizens and a large number of clergymen," with the avowed purpose of preventing crime and promoting legal reforms. But the committee was soon captured by the temperance movement, and it confined its activities to issuing statements declaring that the prevalence of crime and lawlessness was due entirely to the unrestricted sale of liquor, and advocating as a remedy that the saloons be closed on Sunday. On September 10, 1872 the newspapers published a call for a mass meeting to devise ways and means of helping the police combat crime. The call was signed by sixty-two business men, headed by Henry C. Greenebaum, president of the German Savings Bank, and said in part:

"Never was there a time in the history of Chicago when there was less security for person and property than now. . . . One jostles the elbow of a murderer at every angle of the street, and yet the law seems powerless to bring the evil-doers to justice. The police are weak and their leaders inefficient; juries are uncertain and not always incorruptible. . . . There is hardly a day but that the body of some victim is lifted dripping from the river, his gaping wounds like those of poor murdered Duncan, having each a tongue that calls out loudly for revenge. . . . The sad recurrence of cold-blooded murders in our midst cannot longer be allowed to pass unnoticed by our citizens generally, with due regard to the safety of society. The people of Chicago must demand that murderers shall be hanged."

The mass meeting, held at the Board of Trade Hall on September 12, was attended by several hundred prominent citizens who cheered Henry Greenebaum's assertion that there should be no prison sentences for murderers. "The only way to protect society against such criminals," he said, "is to hang them." A Committee of Twenty-five was appointed to aid the police "in the prompt arrest, speedy trial, and sure punishment of criminals," and two weeks later the committee perfected its organization, with Greenebaum as permanent chairman, and adopted resolutions which said: "unfortunately the city is infested by a very large number of professional thieves, burglars, gamblers, prostitutes, and roughs. Chicago, great in everything, has seemed to offer an alluring field for those gentry to come to ply their vocations and revel in their coarse appetites."

The Committee of Twenty-five, with the moral and financial support of Chicago's leading business men, could probably have been of great assistance to the police had it carried out the purposes for which it was organized. But it likewise succumbed to the blandishments of the temperance reformers, and the banker Greenebaum, a liberal and a leader of the German element, immediately resigned in disgust. Within a few months the whole matter of law-enforcement had degenerated into a bitter and senseless squabble over the question of closing the saloons on Sunday. Mayor Joseph Medill, one of the owners of the Chicago *Tribune,* yielded to the pressure early in 1873 and ordered the Sunday closing law put into effect, but the attempt to enforce it met with dismal failure; there were three thousand saloons in Chicago by that time, and few policemen could be spared from other duties to watch them. The temperance forces were overwhelmingly defeated in the fall elections of 1873; and in the spring of 1874, despite a dramatic march upon City Hall by six hundred clergymen and " praying women " — crusaders who had created a furor in the East by invading saloons, kneeling on the floors, and asking God to reform the bartenders — the City Council passed an ordinance legalizing the sale of liquor on Sunday.

12

FOR more than two decades after the great fire there was little or no change in this dismal picture of confusion and disorganization; those were boom times for every phase of underworld activity. The *Times'* crusade was abandoned when Editor Storey retired from the active management of the paper in 1879, and after the abject failure of the Committees of Seventy and Twenty-five no reform group made any serious attempt to combat political corruption or to challenge the constantly increasing power of the underworld until the Civic Federation was organized in 1894. Throughout this period, in which the physical expansion of Chicago by far exceeded that of any previous era in its history, the Police Department continued to be probably the most inefficient organization of its kind in the United States. It was poorly

93

paid and riddled with graft, kicked about by politicians and boodling city officials, intimidated by thugs and hoodlums, dominated by gambling kings and saloon-keepers, helpless to protect the city from criminals, and unable to handle with any degree of intelligence the riots and disturbances which accompanied the railroad and street-car strikes of 1877 and 1885, the Haymarket bomb explosion of 1886, and the other labor troubles and radical outbreaks that kept Chicago in an almost constant turmoil. In 1872 the police force numbered 450 men of all grades. Twenty years later, when Chicago had a population of 1,208,676 and covered an area of 182 square miles, the department comprised a total of 1,870 men, of whom only 1,168 were available for patrol. Not more than one-half of these were on duty at one time, or approximately one patrolman to every twenty thousand inhabitants.

CHAPTER IV

"THE WITHERED ROSE LEAVES OF SOCIETY"

IT WAS during the decade of the Civil War, and the three or four years immediately following the disaster of 1871, that prostitution became the biggest and most profitable business of the Chicago underworld and one of the city's major political and sociological problems. There were two principal reasons why commercialized vice managed to gain so firm a foothold in such a comparatively brief period of time. In the first place, the police made no attempt to halt the overwhelming flood of "the withered rose leaves of society," as the Chicago *Journal* called them, which began to pour into Chicago at the outbreak of the Civil War; and failed to prevent the harlots, ninety per cent of whom had been burned out of their brothels and assignation houses, from re-establishing themselves after the great fire. In the second place, public opinion in those times regarded prostitution as inevitable, and in general favored toleration of the evil as long as it remained unobtrusive. It is doubtful if even the Sands would have been destroyed if its wickedness hadn't been so blatant — and if William B. Ogden hadn't been interested in the land. By the time Chicago awoke to the extent and seriousness of the menace, the open brothel had become closely allied with the saloon business and the politicians and was able to exist almost without interference, or even regulation, for nearly half a century.

2

THE number of brothels in Chicago during the 1860's was never officially determined, but, estimating from newspaper accounts and from available police and court records, there must have been between two hundred and two hundred and fifty, not counting the assignation houses and those directly attached to saloons. They harbored approximately two thousand prostitutes, as indicated by the fact that in 1867 the police made 1,670 arrests of inmates of disorderly houses, and 542 arrests of keepers of such resorts. Neither madames nor strumpets were thus annoyed more than once or twice a year, and those who knew politicians or influential saloon-keepers were seldom annoyed at all. And it is extremely improbable that in any one year the police arrested more than one-half of the women who made a living from vice.

Besides the low dens of Conley's Patch, Shinbone Alley, and the Chicago Patch, the bordellos of war-time Chicago were principally on Franklin, Jackson, Wells, Clark, State, Monroe, Dearborn, Sherman, Quincy, Van Buren, Adams, Griswold, Congress, Polk, Madison, Green, and South Water Streets; and on Fourth, Blue Island, and Chicago Avenues. Streetwalkers were everywhere; in the middle of 1860 it was estimated by the *Tribune* that two thousand "chippies" plied their unholy trade in the retail business district alone. They maintained living and business quarters on the top floors of stores and office buildings, and walked the streets both day and night, boldly accosting every man who passed and screaming insults at all who ignored their solicitations. If a citizen wished to complain to the police of the insolence and persistence of these harpies, or report the depredations of the confidence men, sneak thieves, pickpockets, purse-snatchers, and shoplifters, who likewise

96

swarmed in the business section, he usually had to go to Court House Square, where, according to Frederick Francis Cook, "several policemen could generally be found hanging about to prevent rival hackmen from murdering each other, or a combination of the pestiferous crew from doing a stranger to death, both being not infrequent happenings. Anywhere else a policeman was seldom seen — outside of saloons." [1]

Lou Harper's elegantly furnished establishment at No. 219 Monroe Street was the finest brothel in war-time Chicago, and was the city's first parlor-house, a type of bagnio which charged high prices and provided any sort of erotic amusement a customer might desire. Madame Harper's house, which she called the Mansion, was not for the ordinary seeker after illicit pleasures; she catered to the business and professional man and the rich young man-about-town and attempted to surround her shabby business with an atmosphere of gentility. Her girls wore evening gowns instead of wrappers or chemises, and were introduced to visitors by name instead of being herded into the parlor and lined up for selection. She frowned upon drunkenness and unnecessary vulgarity and was the first to discard the red lights and huge house-numerals by which bordellos were usually identified. On the front door of the Mansion was a small brass plaque with "Miss Lou Harper" neatly engraved upon it, and the business card of the house said simply:

THE MANSION

219 Monroe Street
Twenty Beautiful Young Ladies

None of the other brothels of Lou Harper's time equaled the Mansion in swank and magnificence, but there

---

[1] *Bygone Days in Chicago*, page 171.

were several which were frequented by the same class of men and were almost as popular. Among them were Kate Anderson's Senate; the houses run by Annie Stafford and Mollie Trussell; Rose Lovejoy's place on Fourth Avenue, where lived a strapping big strumpet known as Mountain Nell, who sang sentimental songs and also acted as Madame Lovejoy's bouncer; and Annie Stewart's establishment at No. 441 South Clark Street, a famous address in the annals of the red lights. Madame Stewart opened her house in 1862 and enjoyed half a dozen prosperous years. Her Chicago career ended on July 11, 1868. On the afternoon of that day Constable Marcus Donahoe and G. O. Dresser, a justice of the peace, visited the house, and while the justice talked to one of the girls, Donahoe and Madame Stewart played euchre for the drinks. After several games and as many bottles of wine she accused him of cheating, and when he tried to choke her, she snatched a revolver from beneath her pillow and shot him dead. She was arrested, but on July 15 was brought into Circuit Court on a writ of habeas corpus and set free after policemen had testified that the marks of Donahoe's fingers had been visible on her throat. Judge Erastus Smith Williams ruled that she "had not forfeited her rights to self-protection by resorting to the disreputable life of a cyprian."

The largest bordello in Chicago before the great fire, and also one of the toughest, was the notorious Ramrod Hall, a rambling, one-story wooden structure on Quincy Street near Wells. It was kept by Kate Hawkins, who ruled her flock with a horsewhip frequently applied. Madame Hawkins seldom had fewer than thirty girls, and sometimes as many as fifty were quartered in the house. Men were frequently slugged and robbed in Ramrod Hall, the inmates were nearly always drunk and most of the time fighting, and a night seldom passed when the police were not summoned to quiet the battling bawds or eject obstreperous customers. The biggest fight in the history of Ramrod Hall occurred on the night of March 3, 1871. It began when Mary Woods, whom the *Times* described as " a very lucrative piece of furniture," announced that she was leaving the Hall to be married. Madame Hawkins threatened to whip the girl and tried to lock her in a room, but Mary's friends came to her aid and within a few minutes all of the harlots, with their pimps and a few customers, were involved in a furious melee in which fists, teeth, feet, beer bottles, and articles of furniture were used as weapons. When the police arrived, the interior of Ramrod Hall had been wrecked and half the fighters lay unconscious on the floor.

Even lower in the red-light scale than Ramrod Hall were Madame Jennie Standish's place in Wells Street; and Belle Jones's den in Clark Street, which in 1871 could boast of harboring " the oldest dones [1] in the world " — Nellie Welch and Mollie Moore, past sixty and still going strong. One of the inmates of Madame Standish's house was Mollie Holbrook, who was described by Inspector Thomas Byrnes of the New York police as " the most notorious and successful female thief in America." She first appeared in Chicago about 1865 as the wife of Buck Holbrook, a gambler and safe-robber, who owned a gaming place on Clark Street and an assignation house on Randolph, over which Mollie presided. Holbrook was sent to prison at Joliet early in 1871 for robbing a bank, and Mollie entered the brothel of Madame Standish. She left Chicago in a hurry a few weeks before the great fire of 1871, when the police discovered that she had organized her fellow harlots into a band of pickpockets and shoplifters and was using the bagnio as a warehouse for stolen goods. Meanwhile Buck Holbrook had been shot by a prison guard while trying to escape from Joliet, and Mollie married Jimmy Hoey, a sneak thief and pickpocket; Inspector Byrnes said that this precious

---

[1] Current slang for prostitutes.

crook was "an unprincipled scamp who lived entirely upon the proceeds of his wife's stealings."

Mollie Holbrook returned to Chicago in 1873 and opened an assignation house, where she fleeced a rich Western cattle man out of $25,000 with the badger game. For this she served a short prison term, and during the next ten years was jailed several times in Boston, New York, and other cities. In New York she was sent to prison for a year, but was pardoned by Governor Grover Cleveland when she gave the police information that helped convict Marm Mandelbaum, a noted fence.

3

SHINBONE ALLEY, the Chicago Patch, the rookeries of Wells Street, and Mother Conley's Patch were obliterated by the great fire, but within half a decade after the rebuilding of Chicago had begun, a dozen vice districts of even greater extent and viciousness had been established, all swarming with harlots, footpads, pimps, and pickpockets and crowded with brothels, saloons, and dives of every description. To their inhabitants and the police they were known by such picturesque names as the Black Hole, Little Cheyenne, the Bad Lands, Satan's Mile, Hell's Half-Acre, the Levee, Coon Hollow, Biler Avenue, and Dead Man's Alley. All of these localities except the Black Hole, which was on the West Side, were on the South Side in the area bounded by Wabash Avenue, the Chicago River, and Van Buren and Twenty-second Streets. Two or three underworld settlements developed on the North Side, but they never were of much importance compared with those in the other divisions of the city. During the 1870's there were also two famous colonies of prostitutes in the downtown business section — one in the Bryant Block at Randolph and Dearborn Streets, and the other in the "marble fronts" at Nos. 143–149 East Monroe Street. The *Times* described the Bryant Block as "a nest of harlots" and on August 5, 1877 said that "the police regard the assemblage of women in this structure as one of the worst crowds in the city, and now and then reports reach them of orgies held there that would seem to indicate that ancient Sodom and Gomorrah have phœnixed themselves somewhere in the neighborhood."

The two upper floors of the "marble fronts" on Monroe Street were, as the *Times* said, in 1877, "the abode of such notorious old jades as Waterford Jack and her peculiar crew." Waterford Jack, also known as the "millionaire streetwalker," was one of the most remarkable, not to say industrious, women of her class that Chicago ever produced; she once boasted that she had walked the streets every night, rain or shine, for ten years, entertaining from five to twenty men a night at prices ranging from one to ten dollars. In the middle 1870's Waterford Jack organized a band of streetwalkers, stabled them in the marble fronts, and acted as their manager and business agent. She saw to it that they kept themselves clean and as attractive as possible, and each day assigned the territory to be patrolled, sending the youngest and prettiest girls to the hotels and railroad stations. Their earnings were turned over to Waterford Jack, who paid the police for protection, hired lawyers and bondsmen when necessary, and gave each strumpet a small allowance for food and clothing. The remainder she banked, first deducting a small percentage for herself. Several of the band saved enough in a few years to open bordellos of their own. Waterford Jack always said that she would retire when she had accumulated thirty thousand dollars, and since she dropped out of sight about 1880, it may be assumed that she had made her pile. A red-light newspaper called the *Chicago Street Gazette* said of her in 1877:

"Waterford Jack has $22,000 in the bank, every cent of which she had picked up (so to speak) on the streets of Chicago. Jack (her right name is Frances Warren) has made money. It is said to her credit that she never stole a cent and was never drunk in her life. She is a pug-nosed, ugly-looking little critter, but for all that she has prospered in her wretched business, and now stands before the world the richest street-walker in existence."

4

THE Black Hole was a group of Negro saloons, cribs, and bawdy houses at Washington and Halsted Streets, in the heart of a vice area bounded by Sangamon, Halsted, Lake, and Monroe Streets. It was in this section that the first concert saloon established in Chicago after the fire was opened at Madison and Peoria Streets in 1873 by Johnny Harmon, described by the *Tribune* as "a fierce-looking fellow." Harmon employed from six to eight girls and gave them twenty per cent of their sales of liquor; their income from this source averaged from twelve to fifteen dollars a week. The place made money for several years, until Harmon put this sign over the bar:

GENTLEMEN WILL PLEASE KEEP THEIR HANDS OFF THE WAITER-GIRLS, AS IT INTERFERES WITH THE DISCHARGE OF THEIR DUTIES.

Business fell off immediately, for snatching at the waiter-girls was considered rare sport, and in most concert saloons of the period not only was it encouraged, but private rooms were provided in which the practice could be carried to its logical conclusion. On Peoria Street next door to Harmon's establishment was the New Era Cigar Store, run by the notorious Welch sisters, Mamie and Eva, who gave a half-hour in the back room with every two-dollar purchase of tobacco.

The pride of the Black Hole in the 1870's and 1880's was Noah's Ark on West Washington Street near Halsted, a queer old rookery of three stories, once a pretentious mansion, which the *Times* in 1877 said was owned by Alderman Jacob Beidler, rich lumber-dealer and head of a pious and prominent family. "Noah's Ark is now to the West Side," said the *Times*, "what Under the Willow used to be to the South Side, and all it needs is a Roger Plant at its head to make it equally notorious and infamous." Like Roger Plant's resort, Noah's Ark was a seething hive of corruption, housing two saloons and half a dozen brothels, while what had been the drawing-room was partitioned by curtains into cubicles just large enough to accommodate a cot. These holes were rented to streetwalkers, who charged from twenty-five to thirty-five cents, depending upon whether the customer removed his shoes. Two of the denizens of Noah's Ark evolved a unique system of robbery. One, seizing the exact moment when the attention of her client was completely distracted, would clasp him tightly in her arms, while the other cracked him on the head with a club and hurriedly went through his pockets. Then, dazed by the extraordinary experience, he was kicked into the street.

The largest bagnio in Noah's Ark was Ham's Place on the second floor, where a score of dusky sirens received company clad in white tights and green blouses cut with a startling economy of material. The police never really knew who owned this dive, but it was believed to be one of the properties of Diddie Biggs, who ran another brothel in Halsted Street, in which the most popular girl was a midget named Julie Johnson; she gave erotic exhibitions with a Negro nearly three times her height and more than twice her weight. One of the members of Diddie Biggs's staff was a piano-player, three-hundred-pound Del Mason, who alternated between Ham's Place and the house on Halsted Street. Del Mason's husband, a Negro thief and desperado variously known as Joe Dehlmar and Bill Allen, was the central figure in what John J. Flinn conservatively called " one of the most remarkable incidents in the history of the police department."

In a fight on the afternoon of November 30, 1882, Bill Allen killed one Negro and seriously wounded another, and that night murdered Patrolman Clarence E. Wright when Wright attempted to arrest him in a shanty at Washington and Clinton Streets. Allen fled to the basement of Diddie Biggs's house in Halsted Street, but the police didn't know he was there until December 3, when the Negro gave Julie Johnson a nickel and sent her out to buy a newspaper. Instead she told the police where Allen was hiding, and for two dollars sold his nickel to Mike McDonald, the famous gambler, who thereafter carried the coin as a lucky piece. Patrolman Patrick Mulvihill started into Diddie Biggs's basement to capture the Negro, but Allen shot him through a window and then ran down an alley. Help was summoned, and within half an hour two hundred policemen were searching for Allen throughout the Black Hole. Meanwhile word spread that the game had been flushed, and a mob quickly began to form. By mid-afternoon, according to John J. Flinn, " upwards of ten thousand people armed with all sorts of weapons from pocket pistols and pitchforks to rifles, were assisting the police in the hunt." [1]

About half past three o'clock in the afternoon Allen was killed in an exchange of shots with Signal Sergeant John Wheeler, who found the Negro crouched in a feedbox in the back yard of a house on West Kinzie Street. Allen's body was dumped into a patrol wagon and taken to the Desplaines Street police station. Reports were circu-

[1] *History of the Chicago Police,* page 409.

lated that the Negro had been captured but not killed, and when the wagon reached the station-house it was met by a mob which cried: "Lynch him!" and "Get a rope!" While Captain John Bonfield and half a dozen policemen threatened the crowd with their revolvers, the patrol wagon was driven into an alley and the corpse quickly shunted into the station through a window. "Thus balked of its prey," wrote Flinn, "the crowd became frenzied and threatened to tear down the station. Threats and promises were all in vain, and a serious riot seemed inevitable. Chief Doyle mounted the wagon and assured the crowd that the Negro was really dead. They hooted and yelled, shouting that the police were concealing the man and encouraging each other to break in the windows of the station." [1]

Chief Doyle finally hit upon a novel way to quiet the crowd and convince the rioters that Allen was dead. The Negro's body was stripped, laid on a mattress, and placed in front of a barred window where it could be seen from the alley. Then a line was formed, and "the crowd passed in eager procession, and were satisfied by a simple glance at the dull, cold face. All the afternoon that line moved steadily along, and the officers were busily occupied in keeping it in order. The crowd increased rather than diminished, and until darkness settled down they were still gazing at the dead murderer. After dark a flaring gas jet at the head of the body brought it out in strong relief, and all night long the line of curious people filed by for a glimpse of the dead." [2]

Allen's body remained on exhibition for forty-eight hours, and then, after an inquest had been held, it was offered to his wife, Del Mason, for burial. But she refused it. She said:

"I wouldn't give a dollar to help bury the stiff!"

---

[1] Ibid., page 413.   [2] Ibid., page 415.

5

T H E R E was scarcely any distinction between the Bad Lands and Little Cheyenne, both of which were on Clark Street between Van Buren and Twelfth, but the police regarded the section south of Taylor Street as having a slight edge in depravity, and for that reason it was known as the Bad Lands. The whole stretch of Clark Street was described by a Chicago detective as "about as tough and vicious a place as there was on the face of the earth," with almost every house a saloon, a dance hall, or a brothel. "Around the doors of these places," said the detective, "could be seen gaudily-bedecked females, half-clad in flashy finery, with loose wrappers, and others wearing short scarlet dresses which never came below their knees, with many-colored stockings and fancy shoes. Many of them wore bodices cut so low that they did not amount to much more than a belt." [1]

The boss of the Bad Lands for many years was Big Maud, another of the gigantic Negresses who seem to have been so plentiful in Chicago; if legend is correct, she was bigger and a more ferocious fighter than even the Bengal Tigress. Big Maud ran a dive called the Dark Secret, near Twelfth Street, where for twenty-five cents a man could get a drink, a woman, a bed for the night, and, nine times out of ten, a broken head. Another famous character of the Bad Lands was Black Susan Winslow, who ran "one of the vilest houses of prostitution" in a dilapidated two-story wooden frame shack in Clark Street under the approach to the Twelfth Street viaduct. The roof of this dive was level with the sidewalk, and entrance was by means of a rickety stairway. Several gaping holes in the roof and walls had been stuffed with old newspapers, and the ceilings were less

---

[1] *Hands Up! In the World of Crime*, by Clifton R. Wooldridge.

than six feet high, so that a man of ordinary stature was compelled to stoop, and consequently was at a great disadvantage if he had to defend himself against robbery. For the privilege of living in this den, Black Susan paid forty dollars a month, except during the World's Fair of 1893, when the rent was raised to a hundred and twenty-five. From two to five girls lived with Madame Winslow, and they employed unusual methods of attracting the attention of men passing along the sidewalk. For a long time they rang a sheep-bell, set off an old alarm clock at regular intervals, and tapped on the windows, at the same time hissing like snakes. But all of this meant work, so finally they "rigged up an electric battery and attached it to the figure of a woman with a metallic arm and hand, which would strike the window and rebound, making a motion to 'come in.' "

Many complaints of robbery in Black Susan's house were made to the police, and in the course of half a dozen years a score of warrants were issued for her arrest. But every policeman who attempted to serve one of the documents returned to the station-house completely baffled, unable to figure out a way to get his prisoner out of the place. For Black Susan weighed 449 pounds and was wider in every direction than any door or window in her dive; the police never did know how she got in there in the first place. The problem was finally solved by Clifton R. Wooldridge, a famous detective of the 1890's. When Wooldridge set out to arrest Black Susan, he went in the patrol wagon and drove through an alley to the back door. Having read his warrant to the accompaniment of gleeful cackles by Black Susan, who was certain of his ultimate discomfiture, Wooldridge removed the back door from its hinges and sawed out the frame and about two feet of wall. Then he placed two oak planks, each sixteen feet long and a foot wide, on the door-sill and the rear end of the patrol wagon. One of the horses was unhitched, a heavy rope was tied around Black Susan's waist and attached to the animal's collar, and Detective Wooldridge shouted: "Giddap!" The horse lunged forward, and Black Susan was dragged out of her chair and skittered up the plank for about three feet before she began shrieking; Wooldridge hadn't bothered to get dressed lumber, and Madame Winslow's tug-like beam was full of splinters. When the rope was removed, she waddled painfully up the planks, and during the ride to the police station she lay prone in the bed of the wagon, while one of her girls sat beside her, pulling out the splinters. "After this," said Wooldridge, "the police had no more trouble with Susan Winslow."

Little Cheyenne was named in honor of Cheyenne, Wyoming, which was the toughest of the so-called "railroad end towns" that sprang up during the building of the Union Pacific.[1] The first of the Little Cheyenne dives north of the Bad Lands, Larry Gavin's gin-mill at Taylor Street, and the Alhambra next door, were typical of the entire disstrict. The Alhambra was a den of the type which the slang of the times called a "goosing slum" — a small, low-ceilinged room with smelly sawdust on the floor, bad liquor behind the bar, and a few tables at which streetwalkers of the lowest class waited gloomily for someone to buy a drink or make an indecent proposal. In the 1870's the Alhambra was run by three old women, one of whom boasted that she once had been the belle of Mother Herrick's Prairie Queen on State Street. Of Larry Gavin's place, the *Times* in 1872 said that "taking all things into consideration, it is about as tough a hole as one would like to visit. Rickety old chairs are occupied by females even more dilapidated. The saw dust floor reeked with tobacco juice and the upsetting of bar-slops. It was one of the vilest of places." A *Times* reporter took samples of liquor from Gavin's and the Al-

---

[1] In retaliation, Cheyenne called its vice district "Little Chicago."

hambra and had them analyzed, and reported that Gavin's whisky was full of "pepper and acids," but that the Alhambra's brandy "contained nothing worse than rat poison."

Disreputable as the Alhambra and Larry Gavin's groggery must have been, they were scarcely worse than a dozen other resorts in Little Cheyenne, notably the Pacific Garden Saloon, Concert Hall and Oyster Parlor at Van Buren Street, which was founded by a noted dive-keeper named Jerry Monroe, later owned by Jim Fitzsimmons, and eventually became a mission;[1] and the fifty-cent brothels run by Nellie St. Clair and Candy Molly Jones. The latter was so called because every man who entered her house received a stick of candy as a souvenir. Another ornament of Little Cheyenne was Lesser Friedberg, a fence and pawnbroker who operated a place on Clark Street and another on State Street in partnership with Original Andrews and Sheeney George. Friedberg was sent to prison for five years in 1878 for complicity in the murder of Patrolman Albert Race, who was killed when he interfered with the unloading of goods stolen from a department store. When Friedberg was released, he found that his wife had divorced him and sold all of his property. He began drinking heavily, and for several years afterward was arrested every few months for vagrancy. As an old guide-book says, "There is a moral here, but you may not see it."

Probably the toughest denizen of Little Cheyenne was a Negro woman named Hattie Briggs, who was more than six feet tall, weighed two hundred and twenty pounds, and "was as black as a stick of licorice and as ugly as anyone could imagine" — an arresting spectacle in the long scarlet coat which she habitually wore. She ran a brothel and thieving den on Clark Street near Polk, and another, with

---

[1] It was in this mission that Billy Sunday was converted and decided to quit professional baseball and become an evangelist.

the able assistance of Ginger Heel Paine, on Custom House Place. The price of a girl in one of Hattie Briggs's dives was supposed to be twenty-five cents, but it was seldom that a customer escaped without being robbed. Hattie scorned the slow and sometimes complicated methods of robbery used in other resorts; she simply grabbed her victim, slammed him against a wall two or three times, took his money, and threw him out. She was raided several times a week, but cared nothing for the small fines imposed by the courts, and she operated for almost a decade before the police finally succeeded in driving her out of Chicago.

Hattie Briggs's downfall began early in 1892, when she became infatuated with a young Negro thief and gambler named William Smith. She gave Smith a pocketful of money and set him up in the saloon business, and immediately, as the saying went, he became "too big for his britches." He promenaded little Cheyenne clad in a silk hat, light lavender pants, white vest, yellow shirt, bright blue coat, and patent-leather shoes with white spats or gaiters. His shirt-front gleamed with diamond studs and his fingers with rings; he carried a gold toothpick behind his ear, and four different-colored pencils in his vest pocket, and was attended by a uniformed messenger boy who carried his messages and orders. Sometimes, to impress his cronies, Smith dashed off a message to the Mayor or the Chief of Police, and a few of them actually reached City Hall, where they caused considerable wonderment. Hattie Briggs encouraged her lover's delusions of grandeur; she said she was making so much money she didn't know what to do with it, and intended to buy all the saloons and brothels in Chicago, elect Smith as Mayor, and abolish the police force.

The antics of this precious pair, especially Smith's grandiloquent claims of political influence which he didn't possess, sorely irked the police, but no action was taken against him until a night in April 1892, when he interfered with a detective who was trying to arrest Ginger Heel Paine. A warrant was obtained, and Smith's saloon was raided by twenty annoyed policemen, who arrested the great man and twenty-two of his henchmen after a fight in which considerable damage was done both to Smith and to his bar fixtures. Smith was fined a hundred dollars, and his saloon license revoked. Then the police went after Hattie Briggs. Blanket warrants were issued, and squads of detectives began to arrest her at all hours of the day or night, dragging her to the police station from ten to twenty times every twenty-four hours. After ten days of this, Hattie had enough — she hired a moving-van and trundled herself and her girls over to Lemont, where she opened a dive on Smoky Row.

6

BILER was the popular pronunciation of Boiler, a nickname which was applied to Pacific Avenue because of the large number of locomotives which rumbled and clanked day and night along its western edge. From early in the 1870's to the late 1890's Biler Avenue was "one of the most disreputable streets of the city, built up with hastily constructed tenements which were occupied by the most depraved of men and women, black, white and mixed." Most of the Biler Avenue bordellos were of the lowest class; about the only parlor-house on the thoroughfare was the Golden Gate, kept by Jennie Williams, who thus recalled her novitiate on San Francisco's Barbary Coast. Madame Williams's establishment received some unfavorable publicity in early January of 1874, when one of her girls committed suicide and left a note saying: "Please bury me in my silk dress and bracelets"; but the newspapers quoted her at some length a month or so later when she testified before the Board of Health and the Police Board, which were going through the motions of trying to find some way of regulating brothels. Madame Williams expressed the opinion that such resorts should be licensed.

More typical of Biler Avenue than the Golden Gate was Dan Webster's big groggery and bagnio at Nos. 130–132, which the *Times* in 1876 described as " an epitome of hell," and as an " infernal hell hole. There it is," the *Times* continued, "that the rottenest, vilest, filthiest strumpets, black and white, reeking with corruption, are bundled together, catering indiscriminately to the lust of all." Webster, a Negro, professed great indignation at the *Times'* exposé; he complained that he paid high for protection and deserved more consideration. The *Times* said that the building occupied by Webster was owned by Michael C. Hickey, Superintendent of Police, and Hickey was tried before the Police Board as a result of the uproar. But he was acquitted, the Board holding that he could not possibly have known of the character of his tenants. Another owner of property in the Biler Avenue district was Carter Harrison, five times Mayor of Chicago. " Our Carter," said the *Times* of August 5, 1877, " owns the entire block [on Harrison Street] between Clark Street and Pacific Avenue. On the corner of Clark, and running west to the middle of the block, stands a hotel. The other half of the block is occupied by four or five ordinary frame houses. One is used for a lager-beer saloon, another for a restaurant, still another for a tobacco store, a fourth as a hotel on a small scale, and right among these, as snug as a bug in a rug, Our Carter has allowed a number of gay damsels to nestle down, and they are rather homely ones at that."

7

Hell's Half-Acre, in which every building was occupied by a groggery, a bordello, a concert saloon, a low gambling den, an assignation house, or streetwalkers' cribs, and which the police never entered save in pairs, and seldom even then, was the block bounded by Polk, State, and Taylor Streets and Plymouth Place, now Plymouth Court. The center of the Half-Acre's social activity for many years was the Apollo Theater and Dance Hall on Plymouth Place, which was notorious during the 1870's and 1880's for its masquerade balls sponsored by the brothel musicians, or "professors," at which the dancers removed not only their masks at midnight but most of their clothing as well. The Apollo was still in existence as late as 1910, but after the middle 1890's it was merely a tough drinking and dancing place frequented by low-class prostitutes and their pimps.

In the middle of Hell's Half-Acre was Dead Man's Alley, a thirty-foot passage which ran from Polk to Taylor Street between State Street and Plymouth Place. The alley was always cluttered with trash, and lined up on one side, in the 1890's, were half a dozen abandoned old hacks which were used by Negro prostitutes. "This alley is frequently selected by footpads, highwaymen, strong-arm women and robbers," wrote Detective Wooldridge, " as a place in which to divide stolen property. Daily complaints were made to the Harrison Street station of robberies, cutting and shooting affrays which occurred in Dead Man's Alley, and as sure as a peddler or a stranger passed this alley, he was held up." [1] For more than a decade Dead Man's Alley was dominated by a gang of Negro footpads captained by Henry Foster, better known as the Black Bear, whose method of robbery was to wrap his powerful arms around a victim, rush him down the alley, and fling him to the ground, where his pockets were quickly rifled. The strong-arm work was done by the Black Bear and the other male members of the gang, but the brains of the band was a skinny little Negress named Minnie Shouse, who lured

---

[1] *Hands Up! In the World of Crime*, page 316.

113

men to the mouth of the alley, divided the loot, and negotiated the sale of watches, rings, and other stolen articles. Minnie Shouse was arrested three hundred times in half a dozen years, and was held for trial in the Criminal Court as often as thirty-six times in a single year; at one time her bail in various cases pending against her totaled $20,000. But she was " a good thief," and professional bondsmen were always ready to go her bail in any amount necessary. She escaped punishment, by legal chicanery, by returning a portion of the stolen money or by paying a policeman to threaten her victim with arrest for consorting with a prostitute, until early in 1895, when she was sent to prison for a year for robbing a farmer. The Black Bear got into serious trouble soon after Minnie Shouse had been locked up, and on July 1, 1895 he was hanged for the murder of a saloon-keeper.

Adjacent to Hell's Half-Acre, and really a part of it, was Custom House Place, originally Fourth Avenue and now Federal Street. It was two blocks west of Plymouth Place and ran southward from Jackson Street between and parallel to Clark and Dearborn. During the Civil War there were perhaps eight or ten brothels in the northern part of Custom House Place, among them Mollie Trussell's house, but after the great fire this portion of the thoroughfare was largely taken over by business, and the madames and their bawds moved south of Harrison Street. Until a few years after the turn of the twentieth century Custom House Place from Harrison to Twelfth Streets was probably the most renowned red-light district in the United States; it was at once the site of many of Chicago's vilest dens and some of its most elegant parlor-houses. Detective Clifton Wooldridge thus described Custom House Place as it appeared in 1893, when it was at the height of its fame, during Chicago's first World's Fair:

NIGHT SCENES IN CUSTOM-HOUSE PLACE

"Here at all hours of the day and night women could be seen at the doors and windows, frequently half-clad, making an exhibition of themselves and using vulgar and obscene language. At almost all of these places there were sliding windows, or windows that were hung on hinges and swung inside. These swinging or sliding windows were used by the women to invite pedestrians on the street to enter these places and also for the purpose of exhibiting themselves. Extension fronts were built to many of these houses from which a better view could be had of the police and pedestrians.

"All of the houses were equipped with electric bells, and a sentinel whose duty it was to watch for the police and give a signal to the inmates, was stationed at each end of the street between Polk and Harrison. . . . It was no unusual thing in those days to see from fifty to one hundred women lounging in the doors and windows in this one block at one time. The habitues of this place embraced every nationality, both black and white, their ages ranging from eighteen to fifty years. The costumes worn by these people embraced every kind known to the human race, from that of the Hottentot to the belle of the ball. Some were in tights, some having nothing on but a loose Mother Hubbard, made of some flashy material which resembled a mosquito bar, through which the entire form of the woman could be seen. Others were dressed as jockeys, while others had no sleeves in their dresses. The waist was cut so low that their bosoms were entirely exposed, and some were dressed almost exclusively in the garb which nature gave them when they were born. . . . In these houses could be found every low and demoralizing phase of life that the human mind could think of. Many of these women were even lower than brutes.

116

"Exorbitant rents were charged for these buildings, some of them bringing as high as $250 to $275 per month. Several enterprising landladies rented and furnished from one to four houses each and sublet them for from $15 to $25 per day in advance. Among the worst characters on this street was Mary Hastings, who rented and furnished four of these places and received as high as $25 per day for each of them. . . . In order to pay these exorbitant prices these women were compelled to commit crimes, and nearly every man who entered one of them was robbed before he got out."[1]

The activities of the prostitutes in Custom House Place at length became so obnoxious that in 1896 a committee from the Civic Federation called upon Mayor George B. Swift and demanded that he enforce the law against the maintenance of disorderly houses. The committee declared that the harlots were a menace to society, that their orgies could be seen by the passer-by through the windows of the dives, and that they were leading astray many young boys who were drawn to the district by curiosity. Accompanied by Chief of Police J. J. Badenoch, Mayor Swift made a tour of Custom House Place and said that he was profoundly shocked and disturbed by what he had seen. He immediately ordered the brothel-keepers to paint their windows and keep them closed.

8

T H E Mary Hastings briefly mentioned by Detective Wooldridge was not only one of the worst characters in Custom House Place; she was one of the worst in the entire city. She was only in her middle twenties when she came to Chicago in 1888, but she was already a veteran of the brothels,

---

[1] Ibid., pages 482–4.

having operated or been an inmate of houses in Brussels, where she was born, and Paris, Toronto, British Columbia, Denver, Portland, and San Francisco, where she had served six months in prison for practices which appalled even the Barbary Coast. In Chicago she established a bordello at No. 144 Custom House Place, about half-way between Polk and Harrison Streets, and a year or so later opened a saloon at No. 136, the license being issued without question or investigation. This latter property was operated for her by Tom Gaynor, her principal lover, or "solid man," who eventually defrauded her out of all her money and property. In 1892 she furnished and sublet the four dives referred to by Detective Wooldridge, and that same year built another house on South Dearborn Street near Twenty-second. For several years she avoided trouble with the police by paying the patrolman on the beat two dollars and a half a week, together with free drinks, meals, and girls whenever he wanted them. She also made regular payments to ward politicians and to the inspectors and captains of the Harrison Street police station. Once, when she complained that she was being assessed too heavily, a police captain replied: "Why, damn you, what are you made for but to be plundered?"

Madame Hastings supervised the operation of all her properties until they were taken from her by her solid man, but she lived at No. 144 and gave the establishment her close personal attention. This was a comparatively small house, with never more than twelve girls, and usually eight or ten. But what it lacked in size it made up in viciousness; Madame Hastings often boasted that all of her harlots had been thrown out of "decent houses" for stealing and fighting, and declared that if a girl was good enough to get into one of the first-class parlor-houses, she was too good for No. 144 Custom House. She boasted also that no man could imagine an act of perversion or degeneracy which she and her strumpets would not perform — and proved it at the "circus nights" which were held two or three times a month. Except for these exhibitions and an occasional brawl, the daily routine of the brothel seldom varied. William T. Stead thus described it:

"In the morning just before twelve, the colored girl served cocktails to each of the women before they got up. After they dressed, they took another refresher, usually absinthe. At breakfast, they had wine. Then the day's work began. The girls sat in couples at the windows, each keeping watch in the opposite direction. If a man passed, they would rap at the window and beckon him to come in. If a policeman appeared, the curtains would be drawn and all trace of hustling would disappear. But before the officer was out of sight, the girls would be there again. They went on duty fifteen minutes at a time. Every quarter of an hour they were relieved, until dinner time. At five they dined, and then the evening's business began. . . . About four or five in the morning, when they were all more or less loaded with drink, they would close the doors and go to sleep. Next day it would begin again, the same dull round of drinking and hustling, debauch and drink." [1]

From the beginning of her career in Chicago, Madame Hastings occasionally bought girls from the procurers, and sometimes financed the activities of these human vultures. Early in 1893 she entered the business herself on a fairly large scale, making frequent trips to other cities and returning with young girls, usually from thirteen to seventeen years old, whom she had induced to accompany her to Chi-

---

[1] *If Christ Came to Chicago,* by William T. Stead; Chicago and London, 1894; page 44.

Mary Hastings after the
arrest in 1897

128

Mary Hastings arrives
in Chicago in 1888

W. LAYMAN

MARY HASTINGS AND ONE OF HER
BROTHELS

cago by promising them jobs. Most of these children were taken to the house at No. 128 Custom House Place, where they were locked in a room and their clothing taken away. Then they were broken in to what in red-light circles was known as " the life," a process which involved rape and almost unbelievable brutalization; once in Madame Hastings's house three young girls were locked in a room overnight with six Negro men. Girls thus procured were used to fill vacancies in the Hastings resorts or were disposed of to other madames; they sold readily at from fifty to three hundred dollars each, according to age and beauty. The police, who placed procuring in an even lower category than hustling, knew of Madame Hastings's activities, but were unable to obtain conclusive evidence against her until the fall of 1895, when she brought nine girls into Chicago from Cleveland. Four of the victims managed to escape by climbing down a rope made of bed sheets tied together. Three made their way to the Harrison Street police station, but the fourth disappeared and was never seen again. The other five girls were rescued by a raiding party of detectives.

Two indictments were returned against Mary Hastings, and she was released on bail provided by Tom Gaynor. She immediately went to Canada, and when her case was called for trial, the bail was forfeited. Then she returned to Chicago, the bail money was refunded to Gaynor, and the case again set down for trial. The same procedure was gone through, and in one way or another Madame Hastings managed to evade trial until the summer of 1897, by which time the witnesses had scattered and the state was compelled to abandon the prosecution. Meanwhile Madame Hastings had assigned all of her property to Tom Gaynor, and when she attempted to take charge of her brothel, he threw her out. He finally gave her two hundred dollars and she went to Toledo. As far as the records show, she was never again in Chicago.

9

I N later years Chicago's entire red-light district was known as the Levee, but originally the name was applied only to a row of brothels, cribs, and dives on South State Street between Harrison and Taylor and was so used to indicate the toughness of the area, the levee districts of the river towns being perhaps the most disorderly localities in the country. The Levee was a part of Satan's Mile — State Street from Van Buren to Twenty-second — which also included Coon Hollow, south of Taylor Street. Most of the denizens of Coon Hollow were Negroes, but there was a scattering of whites, and several bawdy houses where white women were kept for the pleasure of Negro men. " The tough saloons in this district," said Detective Wooldridge, " were the resort of the most desperate burglars, thieves and sure-thing gamblers. Even the children here were taught to steal. Barefooted boys would rush out and jump on the footbars of the street cars as if to steal rides, and then snatch pocketbooks from women."

Many of Chicago's most dangerous criminals oper- ated or made their headquarters in Satan's Mile, but it is doubtful if any of them acquired a greater degree of un- savory renown than did Kitty Adams, a white strong-arm woman who for almost a dozen years was known as the Terror of State Street. She first appeared in Chicago about 1880 as the wife of George Shine, a pickpocket, but she left him within a few months and became an inmate of a Negro brothel in Coon Hollow, where she learned the power of a properly handled razor. Thereafter she always carried a razor concealed in the bosom of her dress, and never hesitated to use it; she once sliced off the ears of one of her black lovers, and on another occasion, during a quarrel with the driver of a scavenger wagon, she cut a six-inch gash in the side of one of his horses. About 1886 Kitty Adams established herself in a streetwalker's crib in the Levee and began a new career as a footpad. For several years she worked with a handsome young woman named Jennie Clark, who picked up men on the streets and maneuvered them into alleys. There Kitty Adams would pounce upon the victim, throw an arm around his neck and hold his head back, and threaten him with her razor while Jennie robbed him.

The Chicago police estimated that Kitty Adams committed at least a hundred robberies a year from 1886 to 1893, when a man was at last found who was willing to testify against her and she was sent to prison. But the gates of Joliet had scarcely clanged behind her when Jennie Clark began circulating a petition asking Governor John P. Altgeld for a pardon on the ground that Kitty Adams was dying of tuberculosis. The Governor ordered an investigation, and when Kitty was taken before the Board of Pardons, she punctured her gums with a toothpick and coughed and spat blood at such a rate that the sympathetic members of the Board were convinced she wouldn't live a week. They so reported to the Governor, and the pardon was granted. Kitty at once returned to the Levee and her old trade, and was arrested time after time, but the only charge the police could successfully bring against her was disorderly conduct, and she was always discharged after paying a small fine. In August 1896 she and Jennie Clark were arrested for robbing an old man of five dollars. Kitty Adams skipped her bail, but Jennie Clark appeared for trial when the case was called in Superior Court before Judge James Goggin, who was famous for his eccentric decisions. It was in this case that Judge Goggin made his celebrated ruling that any man who went into the Levee district deserved to be robbed, and that the robbers should not be punished. Jennie Clark was released, and the fugitive warrant which had been issued against Kitty Adams was withdrawn. It was another two years before the police could rid Chicago of the Terror of State Street. In 1898 they sent her to Joliet on an indeterminate sentence, and she died in prison, ironically enough, of tuberculosis.

10

O f all the brothels in Chicago's old red-light districts, the ones that gave the police the most trouble were the panel-houses, actually more robbing dens than bordellos, and so called because of sliding panels in doors and interior walls, through which a thief could enter or reach into a room and plunder a man's clothing while he was being entertained by a prostitute. A room in one of these resorts never contained any other furniture than a bed and a single chair or sofa placed near the panel. An unsuspecting man would naturally deposit his clothing on the chair, where it could easily be reached; if he didn't, it was dragged carefully across the floor with a long pole that had a hook at one end. It was always difficult to obtain a conviction in a panel-house case, for the victim never saw who robbed him, and the harlot who had enticed him into the house could obviously have had no actual hand in the theft.

This particular system of robbery was said by a New York detective to have been devised by a notorious New York thief and brothel-keeper known as Moll Hodges, who operated several panel-houses in Philadelphia as well as in the metropolis. The first such resort in Chicago was opened at Clark and Adams Streets about 1865 by Lizzie Clifford, who had been one of Moll Hodges's robbing women in New York. Lizzie Clifford's house was destroyed in the great fire, and Chicago seems to have been relatively free of these dives until the middle 1880's, when they began to appear in large numbers. By 1890 there were no fewer than two hundred, most of them on Custom House Place, Clark and State Streets, and Plymouth Place. In 1896 the police estimated that an average of $1,500,000 was stolen every year in the panel-houses. As much as ten thousand dollars was often reported as having been taken in a single night, and in virtually every twenty-four-hour period for years from fifty to one hundred complaints of panel-house thieving were received at the Harrison Street station. The police succeeded in closing fifty-two panel-houses in the latter part of 1896, and forty-five more in 1898. During the next year the keepers of twenty-eight such dens were arrested, and at the same time indictments were found against several property-owners who had rented houses to the thieves. There is no record that any of the property-owners went to jail, but by centering the attack upon them the police soon put an end to the business.

The man principally responsible for the successful campaign against the panel-houses was Detective Clifton Wooldridge, known to the underworld as " that damned little fly-cop," and an unusual character. Sometimes Wooldridge was a comic figure, especially when he arrested a girl for smoking a cigarette on the street, when he mounted the shoulders of a thief whom he had captured and rode pickaback to the lockup, and when he was arrayed in one of the seventy-five disguises which he kept in the squad room of the Harrison Street station. He was much given to bombast and boasting — he called himself " The World's Greatest Detective, the Incorruptible Sherlock Holmes of America," and wrote in one of his books that " no braver, more honest or efficient police officer ever wore a star or carried a club." [1] Nevertheless he was a really great policeman; he probably caused the red-light district more headaches than any other Chicago officer. He ornamented the police force from 1888 to 1910, and in that time made 19,500

----

[1] *The Devil and the Grafter;* Chicago, n.d.; page 11.

INTERIOR OF A PANEL-HOUSE

arrests, sent two hundred crooks to the penitentiary and three thousand to the House of Correction, rescued a hundred girls from brothels and white-slavery, recovered a hundred thousand dollars' worth of stolen property, closed a hundred panel-houses, broke up a hundred fake matrimonial bureaus, refused five hundred bribes of from five hundred to five thousand dollars each, was shot at forty-four times, and was wounded half that often. Wooldridge was a small man, not more than five feet six inches tall and weighing about 155 pounds, but he was a veritable wildcat in a fight, as many a husky hoodlum learned to his sorrow. He carried two guns, and although he never killed a man, he put many bullets into arms, legs, and fleeing posteriors.

During the early 1890's, with some slight assistance from the remainder of the Police Department, Detective Wooldridge broke up one of the most extraordinary gangs of criminals that ever operated in Chicago, or, for that matter, anywhere else — a group of Negro women footpads who prowled the vice areas of the South Side and committed hundreds of holdups before they were finally sent, one by one, to prison. They usually worked in pairs and were armed with revolvers, razors, brass knuckles, knives, and sawed-off baseball bats; one of their favorite tricks, if a victim didn't raise his hands quick enough to suit them, was to slash him across the knuckles with a razor. Among these female ruffians were Emma Ford and her sister Pearl Smith, Flossie Moore, Hattie Washington, Laura Johnson; Mary White, better known as the Strangler, who was said by the police to have stolen $50,000 in less than three years; and Ella Sherwood, an opium addict who was noted for her violent temper. Once, in 1893, Ella Sherwood gave a saloon-keeper $375, the proceeds of a robbery, to keep for her until the hue and cry had subsided. When he refused to return the money, she broke all of his windows with a baseball bat and then stood in the doorway and emptied two revolvers into the mirrors and bottles behind his bar. For several years these women made their headquarters at No. 202 Custom House Place, one of the several panel-houses kept by Lizzie Davenport, perhaps the most successful thief of this class in Chicago; the police said that in a period of eight or ten years $500,000 was stolen in Lizzie's resorts. It was not unusual for from ten to fifteen robberies to occur in her Custom House Place in one night. To protect her thieving women from the police, Lizzie Davenport built a closet of three-inch oak planks, with a massive door, in which they hid when a raid threatened. Wooldridge drove them out, however, by boring holes in the door and blowing pepper into the closet.

Wooldridge said, and the records bear him out, that the most dangerous of the strong-arm women were Flossie Moore and Emma Ford, both of whom were expert pickpockets as well as gifted stick-up artists and panel-workers. Emma Ford must have been a remarkable-looking woman — slightly over six feet tall, weighing two hundred pounds, arms so long that she could scratch her knee-caps without stooping, an almost masculine physique, and tremendous strength combined with catlike agility. " She would never submit to arrest," said Wooldridge, " except at the point of a revolver. No two men on the police force were strong enough to handle her, and she was dreaded by all of them." She was equally dreaded by the wardens and guards of the various prisons in which she served short sentences. Once in the Cook County Jail she nearly drowned a guard by holding him submerged in a water-trough; in the House of Correction she went on a rampage in the laundry and terribly disfigured half a dozen other female convicts with a hot flatiron; and in Denver, where she and Pearl Smith killed a man before coming to Chicago, she held a prison guard off the floor by his hair while she plucked out his whiskers and threw them in his face. After each term in prison Emma Ford resumed her interrupted career of crime, and as late as 1903 she was still the terror of the Levee.

Flossie Moore was described by Wooldridge as "the most notorious female bandit and footpad that ever operated in Chicago." She was certainly the most successful; she was active in the Levee and other vice districts from late in 1889 until the late spring of 1893, and in that time stole more than $125,000. She once said that a holdup woman who couldn't make $20,000 a year in Chicago should be ashamed of herself. She always carried a big roll of bills in the bosom of her dress and another in her stocking. She kept a shyster lawyer on her payroll at a hundred and twenty-five dollars a month, appeared at balls given by Negro prostitutes and brothel-keepers in gowns that had cost five hundred dollars each, and gave her lover, a white man known as Handsome Harry Gray, an allowance of twenty-five dollars a day. She was arrested and released on bail as often as ten times in a single day, and in one year was held for trial in the Criminal Court thirty-six times, her bail bonds aggregating thirty thousand dollars. She paid ten thousand dollars in fines into the Harrison Street police court, and once when she was fined a hundred dollars, she sneered at the judge and said: "Make it two hundred. I got money to burn!" Despite the frequency with which she was arrested, Flossie Moore managed to escape punishment until March 1893, when she was sent to Joliet for five years for robbing an elderly farmer of forty-two dollars. The prison authorities said she was one of the most unruly women ever confined at Joliet; she twice tried to kill the matron, and spent six months in solitary confinement. She returned to Chicago at the expiration of her sentence, but soon went east, and was last heard of in New York about 1900.

IN later years the so-called parlor-houses, well-furnished brothels which harbored the handsomest girls and charged the highest prices, and in which customers were comparatively safe from robbery, were more or less concentrated in

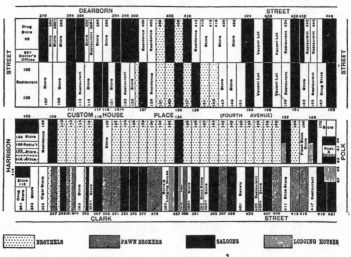

MAP OF ONE OF CHICAGO'S RED LIGHT

DISTRICTS, 1893

particular localities; but during the thirty years that followed the great fire they were scattered throughout the various red-light districts and were often interspersed among dives of the lowest character. The finest bordello in Chicago, Carrie Watson's famous house at No. 441 South Clark Street, was in the heart of Little Cheyenne, with Charley Kunnican's saloon and assignation house on one side and on the other a " circus house " run by Kitty Plant, of Roger's tribe, which was notorious for exhibitions in which women and animals participated. Mollie Fitch was

130

on Washington Street, on the outskirts of the Black Hole; and near by on Randolph Street was Frankie Wright, called by a red-light newspaper "that good old girl." Madame Wright's house was known as the Library, because of a bookcase containing half a dozen never read books. Half a block from the Library was Rose Manson's "Looking-Glass House," in which all of the ceilings and walls were covered with mirrors. Madame Manson was the wife of a Clark Street gambler, and the mistress of Eddie Jackson, a famous pickpocket.

Lizzie Allen's place was on Congress Street, and Ida Morrison was on State in the midst of panel-houses and cribs. Both were near the Park Theater, where dancing by naked women was one of the least objectionable features of the performance. William T. Stead said that the Park was "an outrage . . . an exhibition which would be more in place in Sodom and Gomorrah than in Chicago." On Plymouth Place, in Hell's Half-Acre, was Dora Claflin's bordello, with a panel-house on either side, one of them run by the appropriately named Madame Skinner. Maggie Edwards was on Custom House Place, and so were Jennie Goodrich, Jennie Costello, Vina Fields, next door to the terrible Mary Hastings, and Emma Ritchie, better known as French Em, whose brothel in the late 1870's, with fifty "boarders," was the largest in Chicago. French Em also employed the most famous of brothel musicians, a violinist known as Lame Jimmy, until he was lured away by Carrie Watson in the early 1880's. Lame Jimmy's annual benefit ball, held in the Apollo Theater and Dance Hall, was the high point of the year's social activity. The last one was in 1893, when a policeman was killed in a brawl.

During the late 1870's and the early 1880's the doings of the parlor-house madames and their girls, with animadversions upon the lower orders of strumpethood, were chronicled in several weekly newspapers, or rather

131

one newspaper under various names, which were published by a sporting character named Shang Andrews. He also produced a score of fictionized accounts of the lives of Chicago courtesans, which had a large sale among the prostitutes. Here are a few extracts from Andrews's papers:[1]

Chicago Sporting Gazette, August 4, 1877:
There is a lot of snide young tid-bits at 376 State Street.
Whatinell has become of little drunken May Willard?
Lulu De Vere, the child courtesan, has removed from Goodrich's to the Hotel de Costello.
French Mary, 678 State Street, take a tumble, and don't send to respectable houses for girls, for you know that no ladies board in your low rum shop.

Chicago Street Gazette, September 8, 1877:
Lulu Lee, the little streetwalker, has gone into a house to endeavor and reform herself, but we think it will prove a failure.
Lizzie Allen has put on her fall coat of veneer and varnish, and she is now the finest looking woman in Chicago.
Eva Hawkins is on one of her drunks again.

Chicago Street Gazette, September 22, 1877:
No. 70 Wells Street is now the cosiest little place on the North Side.
There is a dive on North LaSalle Street, called a wine hall, kept by an old procuress, and most any night you can find a congregation of boys, prostitutes, old cats, thieves and vags.
Little May Willard, an old time bummer at Costello's, is on a drunk.

---

[1] The originals from which these excerpts were taken are in the possession of L. E. Dicke of Evanston, Illinois, whose collection of Chicagoana is probably the largest in existence.

Chicago Sporting Gazette, August 11, 1877:

Miss Kit Thompson of 483 South Clark had better let up on taking other girls' men in her room and buying booze for them.

Laura and Carrie are keeping house at 109 Franklin.

The Sutherlands (Jet and Ida) who keep a "goosing-slum" on North Clark Street, have not paid the $20 borrowed from a lady friend.

The giveaway of West Washington Street is Stella Foster, the most charitable done in Chicago — so all the boys say that know her.

Chicago Life, March 23, 1878:

Mollie Fitch is instructing Nettie in the etiquette pertaining to the parlor.

Little French Carrie is at 310 State Street.

Blanche, at Allen's, had better keep her feet in soak for awhile, and not put them out of the window.

There are two new arrivals at the house of Miss Jennie Williams. They are said to be stunners.

Chicago Life, April 27, 1878:

TO RENT — The elegant, spacious house at No. 84 Fourth Avenue — first class in every respect, and very desirable for a party capable of running a No. 1 place.

The circus house, 70 Wells Street, is drawing crowded houses, and performances take place any hour of the day or night.

Sporting Life, August 3, 1878:

Big Lotta, having succeeded in bilking French Em out of $60 or more, is now stabled at Liz Allen's. The critter is spavined, ring-boned, and has the heaves, and is no earthly account wherever she may be.

The friends of Gracie Harmon say she is not near as

bad as she is painted. The girl is doing the best she can, and that's all anybody can do.

Chicago Street Gazette, September 29, 1877:
That lady at 492 State Street has got some new stock at last.

They have two new strawberry blondes at Hotel de Goodrich.

Lizzie Moss has got sober.

What has become of Bad Mollie?

The Fitch mansion has two new ladies, both brunettes.

Chicago Street Gazette, September 15, 1877:
Ada Huntley is now happy — she has a new lover — Miss Fresh, from Pittsburg.

Miss Jessie Curtis, the star boarder at 519 State Street, is looking nice, and shows up fine of late. She has let up on booze, we hear. That's right, Jessie; don't drink, and you will always prosper.

The pretty little Josie Miller has refurnished and fitted up in elegant style No. 70 Wells Street, and her lady-like manner is sure to win her many friends.

Chicago Street Gazette, October 13, 1877:
We are happy to inform the public that the old-timer, Frankie Warner, has left the city.

There are two new arrivals at 514 State Street — Lottie Maynard and Sadie Mason.

Little drunken May Willard, the pocket-book snatcher and lager-beer guzzler, went through a granger on the West Side lately.

Chicago Street Gazette, October 20, 1877:
Lottie Maynard should not be so fresh with other girls' lovers, or she will hear something to her disadvantage.

134

May Willard, why don't you take a tumble to yourself and not be trying to put on so much style around the St. Marks Hotel, for very near all of the boys are on to you; and when you register, please leave the word " New York " out, for we know it's from the Bridewell you are.[1]

The landlady at 414 State Street should hire somebody to drive her cattle home nights, after they have got through grazing at the garden.

French Em has fitted up the most elegant room in Chicago for her friend Mollie Weston. Miss Em is a lady of excellent taste, as well as rare personal beauty, and we have no doubt that the apartment is the neatest and most luxurious of any in the country. *Vive la Ritchie!*

The famous Eugenia de Groot arrived in Chicago a few days ago, and is making herself comfortable at the mansion of Caroline Watson. Eugenia is as dashing as of old — a gay, giddy girl of the period.

Miss Libbie is now boarding at 551 State Street.

Jessie Curtis, star boarder, is still at 519 State Street.

Mary McCarthy has gone to the insane asylum.

Little Kittie, of Stiles, says she has been on a big drunk. You had better look out, Kit, or bug juice will get the best of you.

12

CARRIE WATSON — she was christened Caroline Victoria — was the daughter of a fairly well-to-do middle-class family in Buffalo, New York, where she was born in 1850. The legendary tale of her beginnings in Chicago is more than a little fantastic. It recites that, seeing her sisters and their friends working in stores or as servants for a few dollars a week, she took stock of her capabilities and coldly decided

---

[1] May Willard was not a running gag, but a notorious streetwalker who was always in trouble. She " reformed " eventually, and in 1893 ran a brothel of her own in Custom House Place.

that her greatest opportunity lay in the field of prostitution. So in 1866, eighteen years old and a virgin, she came to Chicago, had a talk with Lou Harper, and became an inmate of the Mansion in order to learn the business and fit herself for a career as a madame. Her apprenticeship continued for two years, in which time, it must be assumed, she learned a great deal. When Madame Annie Stewart left Chicago in 1868 after the killing of a constable, Carrie Watson took over the lease of the brothel at No. 441 South Clark Street, between Polk and Taylor, and immediately installed new furniture and new girls. Later, with the aid of her solid man, Al Smith, who ran a saloon and gambling-house at No. 91 South Clark Street, she bought the property. Madame Stewart had admitted anyone who rang the bell, but from the beginning, Carrie Watson catered exclusively to the carriage trade and was just beginning to build up a nice list of clients when the great fire disrupted business of every description. The Watson legend says her house was destroyed in the conflagration, but as a matter of fact it was almost two blocks south of the burned district and was not damaged.

Al Smith passed out of Carrie Watson's life about the time of the fire, and in 1872 she acquired a new solid man in the person of Sig Cohen, who ran a big gambling joint at 194 South Clark Street, over the door of which he had installed a large sign saying: " Diamond Broker — Open Day and Evening." The business relationship between Carrie Watson and Cohen is not clear; Shang Andrews's papers frequently referred to him as the "landlord" of No. 441, but Carrie Watson paid the taxes, and in William T. Stead's list of brothels her name appears as the owner of the property. Whatever the arrangement may have been, it was apparently satisfactory; in 1878 the *Chicago Street Gazette* noted that Cohen was teaching Madame Watson how to play

FRONT PAGE OF *THE CHICAGO STREET GAZETTE*

casino, and declared that he was "the happiest sheeney in seventeen states."

Early in 1873 Carrie Watson and her solid man made extensive alterations in No. 441, and when they were completed the brothel was the finest resort of its kind that America had ever seen — a three-story, brownstone mansion with five parlors, more than twenty bedrooms, a billiard-room and — if legend be correct — a bowling alley in the basement. The furniture was upholstered in the finest of damask, voluptuous rugs covered the floors, the walls were hung with costly paintings and tapestries, a three-piece orchestra played the music of the day, wine was brought into the parlors in solid-silver buckets and served — at ten dollars a bottle — in golden goblets. The girls — twenty to thirty ordinarily, but twice that many during the World's Fair — received company in gowns of diaphanous silk, and performed their ancient rites upon sheets of purest linen. In every particular the house was conducted with great circumspection — there were no red lights over the doorway and no red curtains at the windows, and there was no hustling. The only advertising of the resort, so the story goes, was done by a parrot, trained to say: "Carrie Watson. Come in, gentlemen." This ornithological pimp spent its waking hours in a cage outside the door.

It may be that with the passage of time some slight exaggeration has crept into the Carrie Watson saga, but it is a fact that for at least twenty-five years the brothel at No. 441 South Clark enjoyed world-wide fame for its high prices, the loveliness and amiability of its inmates, and the luxurious surroundings in which the wages of sin were collected. And Carrie Watson herself — a rich woman who delighted in visible displays of her wealth — was scarcely less renowned for her silks and diamonds, her two snow-white carriages with bright yellow wheels, her four coal-

black horses, her Negro coachman in scarlet livery, her char-
ities, and the fact that she paid a larger personal-property
tax than many Chicago millionaires.[1] " Carrie Watson is a
smart woman," wrote William T. Stead, " said to be liberal in her gifts to the only churches in her neighborhood,
one a Catholic just across the way and the other a Jewish
synagogue which local rumor asserts is run rent free owing
to Carrie's pious munificence. This is probably a slander,
but its circulation is significant as proving that Carrie Watson can be all things to all men." [2] It is little wonder that
Shang Andrews's *Sporting Life* cried enthusiastically: " In
all the world there is not another Carrie Watson!"

During the many years in which Carrie Watson was
the undisputed queen of the brothels, her principal competi-
tors were Lizzie Allen, a Milwaukee girl whose real name
was Ellen Williams; and Vina Fields, a Negress. Lizzie
Allen came to Chicago in 1858, when she was eighteen years
old, and for a year or two was an inmate of Mother Herrick's Prairie Queen. Later she moved to the Senate, and
about 1865 she invested her savings in a small three-girl
establishment on Wells Street. This house was burned in
the great fire, but Lizzie Allen had prospered, and in 1872
she built a large two-story place on Congress Street, which
she operated for almost twenty years. Her house was never
such a show-place as Carrie Watson's, but it was handsomely
furnished, and its twenty-five to thirty boarders were care-

---

[1] In 1893 Carrie Watson's personal property was assessed at $4,000.
Carter Harrison, Sr., was assessed at $300, and Mayor John P. Hopkins at
$150. The sixty-eight aldermen were assessed a total of $1,700; sixty were
not assessed at all. Joseph Medill, John R. Walsh, and Victor F. Lawson, rich
newspaper-owners, were assessed respectively at $2,600, $1,000, and $300.
Other curious personal-property assessments included C. T. Yerkes, the traction
king, at $4,000; Lyman J. Gage, banker, at $1,000; William A. Pinkerton,
the wealthy detective, at $400; L. Z. Leiter, merchant, at $1,000; DeWitt C.
Creiger, former Mayor, nothing.
[2] *If Christ Came to Chicago*, page 250.

fully chosen for their youth and beauty; at one time in
the 1880's more than half of them were said to be under
eighteen.

There is no record of a solid man in Lizzie Allen's life
until 1878, when she met Christopher Columbus Crabb,

APPENDIX F.   BLACK LIST.
OCCUPIERS, OWNERS AND TAX-PAYERS OF PROPERTY USED FOR IMMORAL PURPOSES.

NO.	STREET.	DESCRIPTION.	KEEPER.	OWNER.	TAXES PAID BY
423*	Clark St....	Saloon	....	Annie M. Howard ...	Jacob Franks, 163 Clark-st.
429	"	Saloon and assig- nation house.	Joe Moll	Sidney A. Kent	A. E. Kent.
435	"	Saloon and assig- nation house.	C. F. Kinnucan.	Albert E. Kent.....	
441	"	House of ill-fame	Carrie Watson .	Caroline V. Watson ..	Caroline Watson.
443	"	" "	Kitty Plant ...	No record	S. Hofman, 744 W. Monroe-st.
445	"	" "	Daisy Plant	No record	
447	"	" "	Miss Lulu ...	Jenney Lehr.........	Mrs. M. Myer.
449				Andrew Iuerotte	Mrs. R. Iuerotte, 457 S. Clark-st.
451	"	" "	May Blank	Samuel Hofman ...	S. Hofman, 744 W. Monroe-st.
459	"	Saloon		Andrew Iuerotte	Mrs. R. Iuerotte, 457 S. Clark-st.
463	"	House of ill-fame	Miss Lillie	Philo C. Hildreth..	Philo C. Hildreth; 523 N. Weber-st., Colorado Springs, Col..
467	"	" "	Cora Clark ..		
469	"	Saloon		Blg., Le Grand O'- Dell. Deed in trust to Thos. H. Bliss.	Bliss & Hanscomb.
471	"	House of ill-fame ...	Jennie Moore..		W.W. Strong, 436 Washing'n-bl.
471½	"	" "	Thos. May	Rosa Foster.........	Rosa Foster, 685 W. Indiana-st.
473	"	" "	Jessie Wilson.	Est., Hannah Meyer Lease, W. T. Adams.	W. T. Adams, 125 La Salle-st.
477	"	Saloon and house of ill-fame.		Livi Winsberg.....	T. H. Schintz, 81 Clark-st.
477½	"	" " "	F. Whittaker .	C. E. Robinson est..	
479	"	" " "	Wm. Reidy..		
481	"	" " "	J. Finley....	William Short	Knight & Marshall.
481½	"	House of ill-fame	Ada Dick		
483	"	Saloon and house of ill-fame.		Sarah B.& Hariet Port.	Wm. Port, 5046 State-st.
495	"	" " "	Adolph Miller	Bldg.; W. M. Jenks.	J. Lafe. Curtis, 69 Dearborn-st.
497	"	" " "	Joe Moll	Lease, L, Friedberg.	

A PAGE FROM WILLIAM T. STEAD'S

BLACK LIST

described by Mayor Carter Harrison, Jr., as " an imposing
looking rooster," who was then a clerk in Marshall Field's
store, making fourteen dollars a week. Later he worked in
Mandel's store. In 1887 Crabb left the mercantile field and
entered the real-estate business for the sole purpose of handling Lizzie Allen's property, which by that time included
half a dozen houses and several parcels of real estate. He
also became financial adviser to Mollie Fitch, from whom he
inherited about $150,000 when she died a few years later.
About 1888 Crabb and Lizzie Allen built a twenty-four-room
house on Lake View Avenue, but were prevented by the
police from using it for immoral purposes. In 1890, at a

139

cost of $125,000, they erected an imposing double house at No. 2131 South Dearborn Street, which under the management of the Everleigh sisters eclipsed Carrie Watson's brothel in grandeur and became the most celebrated bawdy house in the world. Lizzie Allen called the resort the House of Mirrors, and occupied it as a bordello until early in 1896, when she leased it to Effie Hankins, and retired after thirty-eight years in the business of prostitution. In March of that year she transferred all of her real estate to Crabb and made a will leaving him everything she possessed. When the will was probated, it was shown that the value of her estate was in excess of $300,000, and some of the newspapers estimated it as high as a million. On September 2, 1896 Lizzie Allen died. She was buried in Rosehill Cemetery, and on her tombstone was inscribed: " Perpetual Ease." [1]

Vina Fields kept the largest brothel of her time; there were never fewer than forty boarders in her place, and during the World's Fair her staff of harlots numbered between seventy and eighty. All of her girls were Negroes, but only white men were allowed in the establishment. She operated her resort in Custom House Place for almost fifteen years, beginning in the middle 1880's, and in that time no complaint against her was ever made to the police; she was never raided, and, so she said, she never paid a cent for protection. She gave her girls a larger percentage of their earnings than any other madame in Chicago, and enforced rigid discipline. " The rules and regulations of the Fields house," wrote Stead, " which are printed and posted in every room, enforce decorum and decency with pains and penalties which could be hardly more strict if they were drawn up for the regulations of a Sunday School." [2] Among other things, they

---

[1] Crabb died on January 5, 1935, in his eighty-third year. He left an estate of $416,589.81, of which $315,681 was bequeathed to the Illinois Masonic Orphans' Home.

[2] *If Christ Came to Chicago*, page 247.

forbade hustling at the windows, drunkenness, and indecent exposure in the parlors and hallways. Twice a week Madame Fields held court, and the girls who had transgressed were fined, set to menial tasks, refused the privileges of the parlors, and in extreme cases expelled. One unruly strumpet whom she got rid of in a hurry in 1889 was Flossie Moore, the notorious strong-arm woman. Stead wrote further of this paragon of madames:

"Strange though it may appear, [she] has acquired the respect of nearly all who know her. An old experienced police matron emphatically declared that 'Vina is a good woman,' and I think it will be admitted by all who know her, that she is probably as good as any woman can be who conducts so bad a business. . . . She is bringing up her daughter who knows nothing of the life of her mother in the virginal seclusion of a convent school, and she contributes of her bounty to maintain her unfortunate sisters whose husbands down south are among the hosts of unemployed. Nor is her bounty confined to her own family. Every day this whole winter [1893–4] she had fed a hungry, ragged regiment of the out-of-works. The day before I called, 201 men had had free dinners of her providing." [1]

---

[1] Ibid., pages 247–8.

CHAPTER V

"THERE'S A SUCKER BORN EVERY MINUTE"

THE HISTORY of gambling and the allied arts of the confidence man in Chicago from the great fire until the middle 1890's is largely the history of Michael Cassius McDonald, bounty-broker, saloon and gambling-house keeper, eminent politician, and dispenser of cheating privileges; any gambler or swindler who wished to operate outside of the red-light districts had to "see Mike" and arrange to pay over a large proportion of his stealings for division among the police, various city officials, and the members of McDonald's syndicate. As the close friend and chief adviser of Harvey D. Colvin and later of Carter Harrison, Sr., and as a leader of the Cook County Democracy for a dozen years, Mike McDonald was the boss of Chicago, and by far the most powerful gambler in the history of the city. "He never held office," wrote Richard Henry Little, a well-known Chicago journalist, "but he ruled the city with an iron hand. He named the men who were to be candidates for election, he elected them, and after they were in office they were merely his puppets. He ran saloons and gambling houses, protected bunko steerers and confidence men and brace games of all kinds without let or hindrance." [1] He could have controlled prostitution also, but

---

[1] Chicago *Record-Herald*, August 18, 1907.

he never had any use for the more repulsive forms of criminality. As one of his friends expressed it, " A crook has to be decent to work with Mike."

This finicky gambling prince began his career in 1864, when he was about fifteen years old, as a swindling news butcher on a railroad train from Niagara Falls to Detroit, roping for gamblers and selling fake prize packages and phony jewelry. Later he worked on trains running between New Orleans and Chicago. He was a professional gambler long before he had attained his majority and in 1861 was important enough to be one of the signers of a call which urged " all Irishmen " to fight for the Union. But as far as Mike McDonald was concerned, " all Irishmen " meant all other Irishmen; instead of risking his own precious neck in the war, the young sharper organized a gang of bounty-jumpers, and thickened his bank-roll with commissions on the bounties which the various regiments paid his hoodlums for enlisting. During the Civil War McDonald occasionally helped bank a faro game, and late in 1867 he and a trickster named Dan Oaks opened a gaming place at No. 89 Dearborn Street, which they operated until the building was destroyed in 1871.

Oaks and McDonald ran brace games exclusively, and prospered, although one of their coups in 1869 very nearly cost McDonald a prison term — he took thirty thousand dollars from the defaulting assistant cashier of the Chicago Dock Company, and spent three months in jail, unable to furnish bail of sixty thousand dollars. He was finally tried, and was acquitted because he had hired a score of witnesses to swear that his games were honest and that the defaulter had begged with tears in his eyes to be allowed to play. But the expenses of the trial were very great, and when McDonald reopened his Dearborn Street house he was unable to pay the protection demanded by the police. In consequence, the place was raided two or three times a week for almost

143

a year, and McDonald was frequently arrested and fined. He felt that he was being persecuted, and developed a hatred of the police that lasted all his life; when he became politically powerful nothing gave him more pleasure than to break or humiliate a policeman. Out of this violent antipathy came a famous joke, for many years a favorite of minstrel-show end men, and still heard occasionally, in one form or another, on radio programs and in what's left of vaudeville. It was originated by Mike McDonald when a man came into his resort with a subscription list.

"We're raising a little money, Mike," he said. "We'd like to put you down for two dollars."

"What's it for?" asked McDonald.

"Well, we're burying a policeman."

"Fine!" said Mike. "Here's ten dollars. Bury five of 'em!"

2

McDONALD's fortunes began to improve immediately after the fire of 1871. Early in 1872 he opened a house in State Street in partnership with Nick Geary, a noted thief who was afterward killed by the police in Philadelphia; and a few months later he acquired an interest in Johnny Dowling's saloon and gambling-house on the West Side, from which he took a hundred thousand dollars as his share of the profits in less than a year. With his pockets bulging with money and more coming in every day, McDonald then turned his attention to politics. He soon became a leader of the saloon-keepers and other " liberals " who were fighting the Sunday closing law, and helped organize the People's Party, contributing a large sum to its campaign fund. In the fall of 1873 he won the Mayoralty for his friend Harvey D. Colvin, who was known in sporting circles as something of a high roller. In private life Colvin was general agent of the United States Express Company.

Colvin's predecessor, Joseph Medill, had attempted to suppress gambling and had actually closed several houses and driven a few sharpers from the city. But with Colvin in City Hall and Mike McDonald sitting atop the political heap, the gamblers returned, and Chicago was once more a swindler's paradise. " Of all the free and easy cities in the Union," wrote an old-time gambler, " Chicago at this time was the worst. The Mayor manifested utter indifference to the enforcement of the laws, and it was said that his personal example was not of a kind to instill into the mind of the average citizen a respect for authority. The games opened their doors upon the city's principal streets, their proprietors carrying on their nefarious business with as little concealment as though they had been engaged in legitimate commercial pursuits." [1]

Throughout the 1870's, except for the three years when Monroe Heath was Mayor, there were at least thirty first-class gambling-houses running wide open on Clark, Dearborn, State, and Randolph Streets in the business district, and on Halstead and Madison Streets on the West Side. Among the big resorts were those operated by the Hankins brothers, Johnny Dowling, George Holt, Theodore Cameron, and Old Man Dunne, all of whom had been in business before the fire. In the early 1880's the number of houses of this description was augmented by the famous resorts of Harry Romaine, Johnny Walpole, Ed Wagner, Curt Gunn; Pat Sheedy, considered the best poker-player of his time; Billy Fagan, in whose House of David one room, according to a sign on the door, was " reserved for prayer meetings and gospel services "; and Harry Varnell, who kept his place open twenty-four hours a day and employed fifteen croupiers, twenty-five faro dealers, and from forty to fifty ropers and cappers. In addition to operating their houses, Harry Var-

---

[1] *Fools of Fortune*, by John Philip Quinn; Chicago, 1892; page 402.

nell and the Hankins brothers were associated with Mike McDonald about 1885 in a bookmaking syndicate which controlled the gambling at the Chicago and Indiana racetracks, and in one season made eight hundred thousand dollars.

3

As soon as Harvey Colvin had been elected, Mike McDonald formed a partnership with Harry Lawrence and Morris Martin, who had been running a brace game on State Street, and the trio established a resort, which they called "the Store," in a large four-story brick building, later the home of the Hamilton Club, on the northwest corner of Clark and Monroe Streets. Except for a small shoe-store on the corner, McDonald and his associates occupied the entire structure, with a saloon on the first floor, the largest gaming place in Chicago on the second, and a boarding-house on the third and fourth. "Every form of gambling known," said Richard Henry Little, "flourished on that wonderful second floor. The most expert manipulators of cards that ever dealt a second or shifted a cold deck sat behind the tables."[1] While the house was being equipped Harry Lawrence was considerably worried by the magnitude of McDonald's plans, and frequently expressed concern over the large number of roulette wheels and faro tables which were being installed.

"There's too many, Mike," he protested. "We'll never get enough players to fill up the games."

It was then that McDonald coined one of the truest of aphorisms.

"Don't worry about that," he said. "There's a sucker born every minute."

The Store was opened for business late in 1873, with the three partners owning equal shares, but Lawrence and

---

[1] Chicago *Record-Herald*, August 18, 1907.

Martin dropped out of the firm after a few years, and thereafter McDonald ran the place alone. For two decades the Store was the sporting center of Chicago, and the principal rendezvous of city officials, politicians, and the big shots of the underworld. And for most of that period, especially during Colvin's administration and the four consecutive terms of Carter Harrison, Sr., it was to all intents and purposes the City Hall. From his office on the second floor Mike McDonald ran the city. There he held conferences with officials, and collected and dispersed the tribute paid by other gamblers and the gangs of confidence and bunko men.[1] About twice a year, for the benefit of the newspapers and the reformers, McDonald submitted to raids — accompanied by reporters, the police swarmed into the Store, smashed a few old wheels and tables which had been set up for the purpose, and arrested half a dozen dealers and croupiers, upon whom small fines were imposed.

The occasional police officer who succumbed to a sense of duty and ordered a raid on the Store without first notifying McDonald and obtaining his permission was quickly disciplined and was lucky if he wasn't kicked off the force. One who felt the weight of McDonald's displeasure was Simon O'Donnell, an honest and capable officer and perhaps the best-known policeman in Chicago, who was appointed Superintendent when Carter Harrison was first elected Mayor in 1879. O'Donnell received many complaints of robbery and brace games in the Store and in the fall of 1880 ordered a real raid on the resort. He was too popular to be discharged outright, but he was immediately reduced

---

[1] There was a difference between a confidence man and a bunko man. The former operated all kinds of swindles, while the bunko man specialized in playing banco, sometimes called bunko, which was an adaptation of the old English game of eight-dice cloth. In time the word "bunko" was applied to all swindling games. A history and description of banco, too long for inclusion here, may be found in my *Sucker's Progress, An Informal History of Gambling in America* (New York, 1938).

to a captaincy and for years was given the toughest assignments in the department. To succeed him as Superintendent, Mayor Harrison named William J. McGarigle, who was McDonald's man from head to toe. McDonald tried to elect him sheriff of Cook County in 1882, but failed, although McGarigle easily carried the city, and then had him appointed Warden of the Cook County Hospital. In 1886 McGarigle handled a slush fund of fourteen thousand dollars with which McDonald made a deal with the Board of Aldermen and the Board of County Commissioners. He bribed them to award to the American Stone and Brick Preserving Company, which was McDonald, a contract to paint the Court House with a secret preserving fluid invented by Harry S. Holland, one of McDonald's pals. The job was completed in December 1886, and Mike presented a bill for $128,250. Having no money in its treasury, the County Board gave McDonald warrants, of which he cashed some sixty-seven thousand dollars. But the Board which succeeded the grafters refused to pay any more when a newspaper reporter exposed the bribery and revealed that the preserving fluid was nothing but chalk and water. Several of the boodlers were sent to prison and McGarigle was convicted, but escaped to Canada. He was not seen in Chicago again for twenty-two years. McDonald was not even prosecuted.

McDonald's attempt to capture the shrievalty of Cook County brought about the only quarrel he ever had with Carter Harrison, who had warned Mike that McGarigle was not strong enough to carry the county outside of Chicago. To show that he could be the boss when necessary, Mayor Harrison in December 1882, a month after the election, ordered the police to raid every gambling-house in the city. Squads of policemen simultaneously invaded more than twenty resorts, among them the Store and those operated by Harry Romaine, Pat Heffrous, Johnny Walpole, and Jim Belknap, who was notorious in the sporting world as the only square gambler in Chicago. Several wheels and tables were destroyed by the raiding parties, and two wagon-loads of equipment hauled away. The sacred person of Mike McDonald was not taken to the lockup, but the police arrested a hundred and twenty-five other keepers and dealers, including McDonald's brother-in-law and his one-armed dice expert, Nick Hogan, of whom a policeman said: " If he had two arms he'd have all the money in the world." Mike McDonald acted as attorney for the sharpers when they were arraigned in police court, and such was his mastery of the law that they were all discharged. Meanwhile he had made his peace with Harrison, and the Store was reopened within a few hours after the raid. The other houses, however, remained closed for several days.

4

T H E boarding-house on the upper floors of the Store was the exclusive business of McDonald's wife, Mrs. Mary Noonan McDonald, whose hatred of the police, at least during the early years of her marriage, was almost as intense as that of her husband. The policemen who carried out the fake raids on the Store had strict orders not to go above the second floor, but occasionally during Mayor Monroe Heath's administration, at which time Mike McDonald was less influential than when Colvin or Harrison was in City Hall, she had trouble with officers who insisted upon searching the rooms of her boarders. On November 23, 1878, when several policemen blundered into her kitchen and began peering into the cupboards, she became so enraged that she fired at them with a revolver, putting a bullet into Patrolman Florence Donohue's arm. She was arrested, but thanks to McDonald's influence and the legal acumen of A. S. Trude, a famous criminal lawyer who often represented Mike's henchmen, she was discharged on the ground that she had merely defended her home against invasion. McDonald's saloon license was revoked by Mayor Heath, but was restored within a week.

Most of Mrs. McDonald's boarders were dealers and croupiers who worked in the Store, and the confidence and bunko men who operated either under McDonald's direct supervision or in independent gangs under his protection. However they worked, the division of spoil was the same — forty per cent to the swindler, twenty to the police, and the remaining forty to McDonald and his syndicate. Out of the latter share McDonald provided bail bonds, hired witnesses and lawyers and fixed juries when necessary, made "loans" to city officials and politicians, and took care of the ropers and tipsters who put the finger on ripe prospects. Any crook could run his games in Chicago on that basis, but the occasional smarty who attempted to operate without making arrangements with McDonald was promptly kicked out of town by the police, or locked up and allowed to cool his heels in jail for a few weeks. As a result of the protection furnished by McDonald, Chicago was infested by hundreds of the slickest swindlers in America, among them such celebrated confidence men and bunko-players as Tom and John Wallace, George W. Post, Lou Ludlum, Red Adams, Snitzer the Kid, Johnny Martin, Snapper Johnny Malloy, Kid Miller, Dutchy Lehman, Boss Ruse, Dutch Bill, Black-Eyed Johnny, Appetite Bill, Jew Myers; Charley Gondorf, called King of the Wire-Tappers, and his brother Frederick; Jim McNally; Charley Drucker; Johnny Norton and Red Jimmy Fitzgerald, who took seven thousand dollars in 1882 from Charles Francis Adams, famous diplomat; Hungry Joe Lewis, who swindled Oscar Wilde out of several thousand dollars that same year; Jim Arlington, who was killed by White Pine Martin in front of the Store in 1875 after a bitter quarrel over a few dollars taken from a sucker;

and Tom O'Brien, perhaps the most expert of all American swindlers, who was King of the Bunko Men until he went to Paris in 1895 and murdered Reed Waddell, inventor of the gold-brick fraud. During the World's Fair in 1893, with the aid of George Post, Lou Ludlum, Red Adams, Frank Smith, and Pete Conlish, O'Brien made five hundred thousand dollars in five months.

The most active of McDonald's crooks during the early years of the master's reign was John Turner, better known as Hank Davis, a faro dealer, forger, thief, top-rank confidence man, and captain of a gang which included Billy Brush, Ross Saulsbury, and Jim Fay. If a woman was needed to carry out a scheme, Davis used Saulsbury's wife, who was a lady of education, the daughter of an upstate New York clergyman and a graduate of a Mid-Western college. But she had also been a prostitute and was an inmate of a brothel in Niagara Falls when Saulsbury married her. On a lone-wolf expedition to Pennsylvania in 1874, Saulsbury was captured and sent to prison, and his wife immediately went to live with Davis. She accompanied him on a tour of the South in the fall of 1875, and when they returned to Chicago, Davis went on a spree. On November 25, very drunk, he called upon his old friend Charles D. Whyland, owner of the St. Elmo Saloon and Restaurant on South Dearborn Street, and invited Whyland and his wife to dinner. The saloon-keeper replied that he and Mrs. Whyland could not receive Mrs. Saulsbury socially, whereupon Davis drew a revolver and fired three bullets into Whyland's body. Whyland died within an hour. When told later that he might hang, Davis said: "It was an unfortunate scrape, and I can't blame anything but drink." Instead of being hanged, however, Davis was sent to Joliet for twenty-one years.

5

W H E N Carter Harrison, Sr., completed his fourth term as Mayor of Chicago in 1887, and John A. Roche was elected on a law-and-order platform to succeed him, Mike McDonald's domination of the more genteel divisions of the underworld came to a temporary end. Mayor Roche told the gamblers and confidence men that they would have to shut up shop, and soon proved by repeated raids and many arrests that he meant what he said. The swindlers left the city in droves and many sharpers closed their resorts, while those who remained, including the omnipresent Hankins brothers, ran their games very carefully under cover, resigning themselves to at least two years of lean pickings. McDonald, always the opportunist, immediately severed his connection with the confidence and bunko gangs, abolished the gamblers' slush fund, sublet his wife's boarding-house to a Mrs. Ross, who had been in business at the same location before the fire as " the only scientific astrologer in the west," and turned the Store over to Parson Davies, a well-known sporting man. Then Mike took his fortune of more than two million dollars, which he had accumulated since 1873, into the field of honest business, thus enhancing rather than diminishing his importance as a Democratic politician. He bought the Chicago *Globe* and ran it for two years, though not very successfully; became treasurer of the company which built Chicago's first elevated railroad, the Lake Street line; and acquired a quarry near Lemont from which he sold stone and gravel to the city and county at a big profit.

McDonald also built a magnificent home on Ashland Avenue, near the residence of his friend Carter Harrison, in which he installed his wife and their two children. But

Pearl Smith   (sisters)   Emma Ford

Mary White   Flossie Moore

FOUR FAMOUS STRONG-ARM WOMEN

Mrs. McDonald had been mistress of the mansion for only a few months when she suddenly disappeared, and McDonald told the newspapers that she had eloped with Billy Arlington, a minstrel singer who had come to Chicago as a member of the Emerson Troupe. The gambler set out in pursuit and finally brought his wife back from San Francisco, where, he said, he had found her living with Arlington at the Palace Hotel. Apparently McDonald and his wife were reconciled, but in 1889 she was gone again, this time, according to McDonald, with the Reverend Joseph Moysant, Assistant Rector of the Catholic Church of Notre Dame, with whom she had worshipped at a private altar in the McDonald home. After living half a dozen years in Paris, the priest entered a monastery and Mrs. McDonald returned to Chicago, where she opened a boarding-house.

Meanwhile McDonald had renounced the Catholic faith and obtained a divorce. In 1898, when he was about sixty-six years old, he married Dora Feldman, a twenty-three-year-old Jewess and the ex-wife of Sam Barclay, a professional baseball-player. As a little girl she had been one of the playmates of the McDonald children. McDonald built a mansion for his bride on Drexel Boulevard, and they lived together until February 21, 1907, when she shot and killed Webster Guerin, a young commercial artist. She told the police that Guerin had been her lover for several years, and talked freely of her affection for the artist and her dislike of Mike McDonald. The one-time gambling king never recovered from the shock of the killing and his wife's disclosures, and after several months in a hospital died on August 9, 1907. On his deathbed he was again received into the Catholic Church, and proclaimed Mary Noonan McDonald to be his only wife in the sight of God. But he left her none of his fortune. After his funeral the first Mrs. McDonald talked to newspaper reporters for the first time; she told them she had never eloped, either with the minstrel man or with Father Moysant, but had left home both times because of McDonald's unbearable cruelty, and that he had hounded her until his death. Dora McDonald, to whom McDonald left one-third of his estate and a special defense fund of forty thousand dollars, was tried early in 1908 and acquitted.

6

As far as gambling and confidence games were concerned, the lid was on in Chicago all the time that John A. Roche was Mayor. But it was tilted a little when DeWitt C. Cregier succeeded Roche, and a little more when Hempstead Washburne became Mayor in 1891, and it blew off with a bang when Carter Harrison, Sr., was elected for the fifth time in the spring of 1893, with the aid of a large campaign fund collected from the gamblers by Mike McDonald. After the election Carter Harrison, as William T. Stead put it, "took steps to recoup those patriots who had supplied him with the sinews of war." A syndicate was formed, managed by McDonald, to collect from every gambler and confidence man a fixed percentage of his profits, ranging from forty to sixty-five per cent, in return for which the crooks were guaranteed against interference by the police. "This sum," said Stead, "which amounted during the World's Fair, in some districts, to a colossal fortune, was divided. Many people had a finger in the pie before the residue reached Mr. Harrison. But however many there were who fingered the profit en route, there was enough left to make it well worth the Mayor's while to allow the houses to run. Everyone in Chicago knew perfectly well that they were running. . . . They were all in existence and prospered under the protection of the administration. One of the most famous hells was running immediately over the saloon of Alderman John Powers." [1]

Harrison had promised during his campaign that he would give the World's Fair crowds a wide-open town, and he more than kept his word. Until he was assassinated on October 9, 1893, by a disgruntled office-seeker, Chicago was the most wide-open town that America had ever seen, or probably ever will see. And it was also, with the possible exception of New York in the days of Boss Tweed, the most corrupt, and, for that matter, had been for a decade. Everyone in Chicago capable of reasoning knew that virtually all departments of the city government reeked of graft and bribery, but nobody felt called upon to do anything about it. Chicago stewed comfortably in the juices of its own corruption until the arrival of the Englishman William T. Stead, who came to see the World's Fair and remained to start a reform movement.

In the autumn of 1893 Stead made several speeches, and early in 1894 he published a book called *If Christ Came to Chicago*. Both his platform appearances and his writings caused sensations; huge crowds heard him speak, while seventy thousand copies of his book were sold before publication and twice that many afterward. He told and wrote of whole blocks given over to prostitution, and of prominent citizens pocketing the rent from infamous resorts; of politicians and saloon-keepers buying elections with whisky; of tax-dodging so nearly universal that the assessed valuation of Chicago was lower than in 1873, although there had been an increase of a million in population; of policemen collecting from fifteen to a hundred dollars a week from brothels and dive-keepers, and levying tribute upon criminals of every description. He published a Black List of occupiers, owners, and taxpayers of property used for immoral purposes. He recounted Mayor Harrison's deal with the gam-

---

[1] *If Christ Came to Chicago*, pages 223-4.

blers and described the operations of other gambling and swindling syndicates protected by city officials. He declared that fifty thousand homeless men were tramping the streets of Chicago, out of work, with no place to sleep but the police stations and the corridors of City Hall and no food except what they could grab from the free-lunch counters of the saloons; he quoted the *Herald's* calculation that sixty thousand persons were fed free every day by the saloon-keepers. He explained in detail the grafting methods of the City Council, and cited the statement of a corporation lawyer who said: " There are sixty-eight aldermen in the City Council, and sixty-six of them can be bought; this I know because I have bought them myself." [1] He quoted the Chicago *Record* for February 19, 1894:

" How much does it cost to pass a franchise through the City Council? There is no set price, because one franchise may be worth more than another. The highest price ever paid for aldermanic votes was a few years ago when a measure giving valuable privileges to a railway corporation was passed in the face of public condemnation. There were four members of the Council who received 25,000 dollars each, and the others who voted for the ordinance received 8,000 dollars each. An official who was instrumental in securing the passage of the measure received the largest amount ever given in Chicago for a service of this kind. He received 100,000 dollars in cash and two pieces of property. The property was afterward sold for 111,-000 dollars. In one of the latest ' boodle ' attempts the aldermen voting for a certain franchise were supposed to receive 5,000 dollars each. One of them, however, had been deceived and was to get only 3,500 dollars. When he learned that he had been ' frisked '

---

[1] Ibid., page 169.

156

of 1,500 dollars he wept in anger and went over to the opposition, assisting in the final overthrow of the steal.

"The ' 5,000 dollars per vote ' is the high-water mark in the Council for the last four years. During 1891 and 1892 there were a dozen ordinances which brought their ' bits,' yet in one case the price went down to 300 dollars. In spite of what has been said of the good old times these two years were among the most profitable ever known in criminal circles.

"When it becomes necessary to pass an ordinance over the Mayor's veto the cost is 25 per cent. more than usual."[1]

The immediate and principal result of Stead's disclosures was the formation of the Civic Federation of Chicago, the first reform organization to command the respect and support of any considerable number of citizens. The English journalist suggested such a body at a mass meeting in November 1893, and by the middle of the following February the Federation had been incorporated by the state, and had completed its organization with the election of Lyman J. Gage, eminent banker and later Secretary of the Treasury, as president. The Federation set to work immediately, organizing a system of relief for the hordes of men who had been thrown out of work by the depression and panic of 1893. Within the next few years it had waged successful campaigns against dirty streets and graft in the collection of garbage, pushed through Chicago's first Civil Service Law, and retired a score of boodling aldermen to private life. In the summer of 1894 the Federation declared war against the gamblers.

For a brief period after the shooting of Carter Harri-

---

[1] The *Record* also said: " In a fruitful year the average crooked alderman has made 15,000 to 20,000 dollars."

son, the syndicate headed by Mike McDonald continued to collect from the gambling-houses and the confidence men, but it was never known who got the former Mayor's share of the fund. In all likelihood McDonald got it. If so, it was his last ride on the gravy train, for with the election of John P. Hopkins as Harrison's successor, Mike McDonald dropped completely out of the picture; never afterward did he possess any political influence or have anything to do with gambling. A few weeks after Mayor Hopkins had moved into the City Hall, the Reverend O. P. Gifford of the Civic Federation called upon him and demanded that the gambling-houses be closed. The Mayor replied that it was impossible to suppress gambling in a city as large as Chicago, but that a means of regulating it might be found. Next day every gambling resort in Chicago was closed by the police, although the Mayor professed to know nothing about it. The newspapers duly chronicled the closing, but the general opinion was expressed in the *Inter-Ocean's* headlines:

"Not on the square! Gambling houses are ordered to suspend operations! It is only a blind! Done for the purpose of concentrating the privilege to rob! Houses will be open again as soon as those under the ban are driven out!"

The gamblers expected to reopen their resorts within a few days, and when two weeks passed and permission was still not forthcoming, they circulated a petition, alleging irregularities at the special election, which compelled Mayor Hopkins to defend his right to the office. The Mayor thereupon said to the newspaper reporters: "No gambler who spends his money in fighting me in this contest will open his place while I am Mayor. I may not be able to stop gambling entirely, but I will be able to stop these men from run-

ning open houses."[1] On February 14, 1894 Chief of Police
Michael Brennan announced that he had closed two gambling-houses which had attempted to operate. "I guess if
any houses open up," said Chief Brennan, "the police will
know their duty." Apparently they at least knew what was
expected of them, for on the afternoon of the same day on
which Chief Brennan made this statement, every gambling-
house in Chicago started its games and began running without any attempt whatever at secrecy.

During the spring and summer of 1894 the Civic Federation, through a special subcommittee headed by the Reverend W. G. Clarke, repeatedly gave the Mayor lists of
gambling-houses and asked him to take action. But Mayor
Hopkins either gave evasive answers or denied flatly that
there was any gambling going on in Chicago. Finally he said
that he had permitted a few houses to open at the request
of business men. "It is surprising," he said, "how many
reputable business men want gambling to continue. I have
had representatives of prominent wholesale houses tell me
that they have great difficulty in entertaining their country
customers because they cannot take them around to gambling-houses."[2] To the Civic Federation this was not sufficient reason for permitting the gamblers to violate the law,
and the Reverend Mr. Clarke's committee decided to try
direct action.

Forty operatives of Matt Pinkerton's detective agency
were employed and sworn in as special constables, and with
Pinkerton in command assaults were made in September
1894 upon Billy Fagan's House of David and upon the resorts operated by John Condon and Harry Varnell. They
seized all of Condon's gambling equipment, but a writ of
replevin compelled them to return it. At Varnell's the constables broke down the doors and scrambled over a barri-

---

[1] *If Christ Came to Chicago*, page 228.
[2] Ibid., page 230.

cade of chairs and tables, but at the moment of victory were arrested on warrants issued by a justice of the peace. At the House of David they were successful. Billy Fagan's wheels and tables were carted away and were burned in the furnace at City Hall when Judge Theodore Brentano refused to honor a writ of replevin issued by the Coroner. This outbreak of civic ·anger so frightened the gamblers that for several months, as far as agents of the Federation could ascertain, not a wheel was turned nor a card dealt, professionally, anywhere in Chicago. A few of the larger houses began to reopen early in 1895, but for the most part they operated under cover, and were frequently harassed by the police; with no Mike McDonald to guide them they were unable to get together on a plan for protection. The business remained unorganized until the rise of Big Jim O'Leary and Mont Tennes around the turn of the twentieth century. And by that time the character of gambling had changed; the big money was no longer in roulette and faro, but in poolrooms and handbooks.

7

BIG JIM O'LEARY, who died a millionaire in 1926, was the son of the Mrs. O'Leary who owned the famous cow. He first appeared in Chicago gambling circles as a handy man for the bookmaking syndicate in which Mike McDonald was associated with Harry Varnell and the Hankins brothers. Later he worked for Silver Bill Riley, probably the first man in Chicago to run a place exclusively for betting on the races. For a gambler, Riley was curiously straightlaced. He regarded drinking and card-playing as immoral, permitted no swearing or cigarette-smoking in his poolroom, and excluded minors. In the late 1890's Jim O'Leary had an interest in John Condon's gambling-house, and in 1900

160

DETECTIVE CLIFTON R. WOOLDRIDGE
AND A FEW OF HIS DISGUISES

Upper right, as a bum; upper left, as a cattle man;
lower right, as a society man; lower left, in private life

he and Blind John[1] ran a casino at Hot Springs, Arkansas, where they made $250,000 profit in a single season. A year later both Condon and O'Leary were members of a syndicate which established at Long Beach, Indiana, twenty-three miles from the Chicago City Hall, a gaming resort which was intended to eclipse the famous houses of Richard Canfield in New York and Saratoga. But most of the projected features of the place — stockades, barbed-wire fences, lookout posts for armed sentries, alarm-boxes, cages for ferocious dogs, and a network of tunnels — never passed beyond the stage of blueprints. The resort had two grand openings in 1901, but the expected crowds failed to materialize, and it was abandoned.

With the collapse of the Indiana enterprise, Big Jim O'Leary opened a gambling-house on South Halsted Street, near the Stockyards, and began to organize a string of poolrooms and handbooks. He also formed a syndicate, composed of John Condon, Bud White, Harry Perry, and Social Smith, besides himself, which controlled gambling on the South Side for more than a decade, operating from four hundred to six hundred poolrooms and handbooks. For three years, from 1904 to 1907, the syndicate operated a floating poolroom on the steamboat *City of Traverse*, the first gambling ship in American history. Every afternoon, with a thousand horse players aboard, the *City of Traverse* put out from the Illinois Central docks in South Chicago and sailed back and forth on Lake Michigan until the day's races had been run. The police finally put the boat out of business by arresting the passengers as they disembarked, and by scrambling the wireless messages which gave the odds and results of the races. The last trip was made in May 1907, when the *City of Traverse* carried forty-two

---

[1] Condon lost his eyesight from disease in 1899, but the disaster failed to affect his career as a gambler. Thereafter he was led about by a servant.

sports, eighteen detectives, and seven newspaper reporters.

O'Leary's house on South Halsted Street was one of the most lavishly equipped gaming resorts ever opened in Chicago. Not only did it provide facilities for all sorts of gambling, but for the further convenience and comfort of the players there were bowling alleys, a billiard-room, a Turkish bath, and a restaurant. The principal attraction, however, and the biggest money-maker, was the huge pool-room, with its luxurious chairs and couches, servants to bring drinks, and the charts giving odds and results of every race in the United States and Canada. In this room, and in his outside handbooks as well, Big Jim O'Leary made book not only on the races but on almost everything else — football and baseball games, prize-fights, wrestling-matches, elections, even crops and the weather; he once made, and won, a bet of ten thousand dollars that there would be eighteen days of rain in a certain May. In 1911, when he talked of retiring and tried to sell his Halsted Street house to Cook County for an emergency hospital, O'Leary told a newspaper reporter that he had never paid a dollar for protection. " I could have had all kinds of it," he said, " but let me tell you something. Protection that you purchase ain't worth nothing to you. A man who will sell himself ain't worth an honest man's dime. The police is for sale, but I don't want none of them." [1]

Big Jim always boasted that his resort, with its massive iron-bound oaken doors, steel plates in the outer walls, and inner walls of heavy oak covered with zinc, was " fire-proof, bomb-proof and police-proof." It did resist several attempts to burn it, and bombs planted near it during the gamblers' war of 1907 caused no damage, but the police frequently managed to gain an entrance by battering down the outer doors with axes and sledge-hammers. Occasionally they ar-rested some of O'Leary's customers and bookmakers, but

---

[1] Chicago *Record-Herald*, December 3, 1911.

usually Big Jim was ready for them. Once when a detachment of policemen swarmed into the house they found the poolroom bare of all furniture except a plain kitchen table, at which sat an old man devoutly reading a prayer-book. On another occasion O'Leary loaded his inner walls with red pepper, and when the police struck their axes into the zinc they were so blinded that for most of them hospital treatment was necessary. The eyes of three were so inflamed that they were off duty for a week.

While O'Leary and his syndicate were establishing themselves on the South Side, other combinations were gaining control of gambling in the remaining divisions of the city. On the West Side the rulers were Alderman Johnny Rogers, Patsy King, and Johnny Gazzola. In the Loop district the chieftains were Tom McGinnis, Pat and John O'Malley, and, according to the Illinois Crime Survey,[1] Aldermen Hinky Dink Mike Kenna and Bath House John Coughlin. On the North Side the king was Mont Tennes, owner of saloons and racehorses and ostensibly a dealer in real estate. For several years Tennes's principal lieutenant was Hot Stove Jimmy Quinn, so called because his favorite expression was: "He'd steal a hot stove!" By 1910, however, Hot Stove Jimmy had more or less abandoned gambling and, according to evidence gathered by the Chicago Civil Service Commission, was associated with Mike Kenna and Barney Grogan, a West Side politician, in a vice trust which sold protection at prices ranging from twenty-five dollars a month for a poker game to a hundred dollars for a brothel selling liquor.

---

[1] Page 868. Part III of this report, by John Landesco, contains an extremely detailed account of gambling and other phases of organized crime in Chicago.

8

T H E report of the Illinois Crime Survey, published in 1929, said that if the complete life history of Mont Tennes were known in every detail, " it would disclose practically all there is to know about syndicated gambling as a phase of organized crime in Chicago in the last quarter century. He was avowedly a real estate man, for a period the owner of a cash register company, and for more than a score of years the proprietor of the General News Bureau, controlling the wires for the gathering and dispensing of race track news in Chicago and principal parts of the United States. Repeated exposés have always found him in control of strings of handbooks and gambling houses in Chicago and other urban centers." [1]

Tennes dominated gambling on the North Side as early as 1901, but he first came into city-wide prominence about 1904, when he suddenly appeared as the backer of several hundred handbooks and formed an alliance with the West Side ring headed by Johnny Rogers. Within another year Tennes had made himself the biggest man in Chicago race-track gambling by obtaining a monopoly of the racing news — he bought the Payne Telegraph Service of Cincinnati for three hundred dollars a day and relayed it to poolroom-keepers and bookmakers, who each paid him from fifty to one hundred dollars. In addition, they turned over to him one-half of their total receipts, out of which Tennes paid one-half of the losses. Tennes thus became the virtual dictator of every gambling joint in Chicago, for none could operate without the telegraph service which only he could furnish. Threatened with extinction, the Loop and South Side syndicates declared war, which began in June

[1] Page 867.

1907 with the slugging of Tennes while he was out walking with his wife. Between that time and the first of October, eight bombs were exploded, three on property belonging to Tennes, one at O'Leary's house on South Halsted Street, one in John Condon's home, and one in the basement of a saloon owned by John O'Malley. After the sixth bomb Chief of Police George M. Shippy said: " It looks as if there was a big gamblers' war on in Chicago. I still maintain, however, that there is no gambling worthy of the name in existence here at the present time."

The war continued, with an occasional slugging and bombing, until the summer of 1908, when Tennes made peace with O'Leary and the principal members of the Loop syndicate. A new combine was formed, in which Tennes was by far the most important figure, and by the spring of 1909 he was absolute master of race-track gambling. Two years later, by virtue of his influence with the police, which was greater than that of any other gambler since Mike McDonald, he was able to extend his rule to other branches of the business, and to dominate the roulette, dice, and card men who had begun to open houses in Chicago as soon as Carter Harrison, Jr., was elected Mayor for the fifth time, in April 1911. By June of that year twenty-five resorts were operating in the Loop alone, and by August this number had increased to fifty, while craps and poker games were going full blast in many of the downtown hotels. They paid these fees to the Tennes syndicate for protection:

Poolrooms — forty to fifty per cent of the win.
Roulette — forty per cent of the win.
Faro — fifty per cent of the win.
Craps — sixty per cent of the win.
Poker and other games — fifty per cent of the house take.

Meanwhile, in 1910, Tennes had organized the General News Bureau to compete with the Payne Service, and succeeded in driving Payne out of business after a bitter struggle which provoked investigations, long drawn out but futile, by the Interstate Commerce Commission and the Attorney-Generals of three states. About the time that Tennes took the Loop gamblers under his wing, he had also become the boss of race-track gambling all over the United States and Canada. He had corrupted the police of a score of cities, was enforcing his decrees with guns and dynamite, and was making profits of several million dollars a year. In Chicago alone ninety poolrooms paid $3,600 a week for the service of his News Bureau.

During the next ten or twelve years Tennes figured prominently in a score of investigations and anti-gambling crusades, and once was even indicted. But the indictment was withdrawn for lack of evidence, and the investigations and crusades accomplished nothing. There was no indication that Tennes would ever be toppled from his throne until William E. Dever was elected Mayor of Chicago in 1923. As Chief of Police, Mayor Dever appointed Captain Morgan Collins, and in less than a year Collins had driven gamblers out of the Loop and had closed two hundred handbooks which had been earning Tennes an annual profit of $364,000. By the first of January 1924, gambling was probably as dead in Chicago as it ever had been, and about the middle of that year Tennes announced his retirement.[1]

---

[1] Tennes gave up actual ownership of poolrooms and handbooks, but retained control of the General News Bureau until 1927, when he sold a half-interest to Moe Annenberg, newspaper and magazine publisher of New York and Philadelphia, one of whose properties is *Racing Form*. In 1929 Tennes sold forty per cent of his share to Jack Lynch, who ran the Sportsman's Club and was an important figure in gambling for several years, and the remaining ten per cent to his nephews. A series of articles on Annenberg's career, by John T. Flynn, appeared in *Collier's Weekly* in January and February 1940.

THROUGHOUT the 1890's and the first half-dozen years of the twentieth century the Negro gambler Mushmouth Johnson, who possessed considerable political influence because he could deliver large blocks of black votes, dominated the policy business in Chicago, as well as many games of poker, craps, and faro in the Bad Lands and Little Cheyenne — all small stuff, too trivial to interest the big syndicates. During most of this period Johnson was also the boss of gambling in the Chinese quarter, assessing the resorts there three dollars a table a week for protection. His only rival was Bob Mott, who ran a saloon at No. 2700 South State Street. Mott ascended to the policy throne when Johnson died in 1907.

Mushmouth Johnson — his real name was John V. — came to Chicago from St. Louis in the middle 1870's, and for half a dozen years worked as a waiter in the restaurant of the Palmer House. In 1882 he was employed as floor man in Andy Scott's gambling-house at No. 205 South Clark Street, and after a few years Scott gave him an interest in the place. Later, in partnership with George Whiting and Al Bryant, Mushmouth Johnson opened a house at No. 311 South Clark which for almost a decade was the best-known cheap resort in Chicago — it catered to players of all races, offered all games, and bets as low as a nickel could be made at its wheels and tables. Johnson sold his interest in this place in 1890 and opened a saloon and gambling-house at No. 464 State Street, which was never closed for seventeen years. The only other large establishment in which he was interested was the Frontenac Club on Twenty-second Street, which was opened on May 1, 1906, by Johnson, Tom McGinnis, and Bill Lewis. Only white men were admitted, and to get inside, a prospective player had to show at least ten dollars in cash at the door. The profits of the Frontenac Club in the first year of its operation averaged two hundred dollars a day and were split three ways at six o'clock every morning.

In common with many other gambling-house keepers, Mushmouth Johnson never played cards or dice for money and never made a bet on the races. He was supposed to have accumulated a fortune of $250,000, but a year or so before his death he told a friend that he possessed not more than fifteen thousand, all of which had been made in the saloon business. In the long run, he declared, he had lost money on his gambling enterprises. " I have spent more than $100,000 for fines," he said, " and a huge sum for police protection. I have had to pay out four dollars for every one I took in at the game."

10

MUSHMOUTH JOHNSON's resort on State Street was in the heart of Whisky Row, the west side of State from Van Buren to Harrison, where for more than thirty years every building was occupied by a saloon, a wine-room with girls, a gambling-house, or all three combined. Most of these places were simply thieving dens, the rendezvous of sneaks, safe-blowers, pickpockets, burglars, and the lower orders of confidence men; and the gambling, with every man on both sides of the tables an expert cheat, must have been something to see. Besides Mushmouth Johnson, the most important of the Whisky Row dive-keepers, in the order of their appearance, were:

Tom McGinnis, who arrived in Chicago about 1883 from St. Louis, and for a few years peddled potatoes from a cart. In 1888 he appeared in State Street and opened a saloon and gambling place called the Berlin Café. The police finally closed it in 1899, but McGinnis reopened the dive within a week as the Elk. He sold the property in 1903 and said that he had saved three hundred thousand dollars and was going to Arizona to raise cattle. Instead he moved into the Loop and became a member of the syndicate which controlled gambling in that part of the city. He was also associated with Jim O'Leary in several gaming ventures on the South Side.

Al Connolly, who was Democratic Committeeman from the First Ward for many years. He started his place on Whisky Row in 1891, and during the World's Fair was notorious as a fixer and bondsman for sneak thieves and pickpockets.

Johnny Rafferty, who established himself on Whisky Row in 1893. After Mike McDonald's retirement he became head man of the confidence gangs. Rafferty received considerable newspaper notoriety around 1900 because of his frequent use of the expression: " I love a good thief." In 1903, when the Chicago *Journal* called him a crook, Rafferty indignantly offered to prove that he had " never gouged out an eye, cut off a goat's tail, beaten a policeman, held up a train, or bitten off a bulldog's nose."

Sime Tuckhorn, who ran one of the toughest places on Whisky Row, the hangout of thieves and hoodlums of the lowest type. He sold the dive in 1901 and opened the Olympis Café, at Wabash Avenue and Hubbard Court, which was a favorite meeting-place of white-slavers. It was torn down in 1910 to make way for the Blackstone Hotel and the Blackstone Theater, and Tuckhorn started the Skiddoo Café on Quincy Street. The owner of this property tried to eject Tuckhorn when he learned the character of the Skiddoo, but the dive-keeper refused to leave until a wrecking crew began to demolish the building.

Andy Craig, who was a bondsman, a politician, a dive-keeper, a fence, a pickpocket, a pander, a burglar, and the brother of Toronto Jim, a notorious hoodlum and crook of the 1880's. In 1891 Andy Craig served a prison sentence for burglary, and in 1897, after a four-year career as a pickpocket, he opened a saloon in Custom House Place and branched out as a fence and a banker for thieves. Late in 1898 he moved to Whisky Row and established the Tivoli Saloon, which he boasted was equipped with eight thousand dollars' worth of mirrors, and became a bondsman and a ward heeler for Aldermen Kenna and Coughlin. For several years he handled all of the bail bonds for Jim O'Leary's handbook men. As a politician he was powerful enough to compel the police to remove his picture and record from the Rogue's Gallery. In 1903, however, an aldermanic commission which investigated graft in the Police Department ordered Craig's saloon license revoked for flagrant violation of the law, and in 1904 Craig sold the Tivoli to Howard McPherson, a cigar-dealer. "There is no use trying to do business," said Craig, "when a lot of reformers are after you. They'll get you sooner or later." But they were a long time getting Andy Craig. Twenty-five years after the sale of the Tivoli he was still active in the underworld as one of Al Capone's agents in the management of brothels and assignation houses.

Bob Duncan, who was better known as King of the Pickpockets. He had two places on Whisky Row, one a concert saloon with girls and an assignation house upstairs; and the other a saloon with craps and faro in the back room. The saloon was the best-known hangout of pickpockets and professional tramps in the United States. One of the famous hoboes who made Duncan's place their Chicago headquarters was Wyoming Slivers, who left the road about 1896 and married a widow in Minnesota. She died after a few years and left him ten thousand dollars, and Slivers and a score of his cronies went on a six months' spree in which ten of them died of delirium tremens and Slivers himself lost an ear and three fingers in fights. The members of no fewer than twenty mobs of pickpockets spent their leisure time leaning against Duncan's bar or sitting at his tables, especially around 1900, when he possessed considerable influence as a fixer and a bondsman. Among them were such renowned knights of the nimble finger as Eddie Jackson, Dan Kelly, Paddy Gorman, Buck Troy, Bill Ryan, Paddy Masterson, Jim Barry, and Pat Kennedy. The most expert of them all was Eddie Jackson, who lifted his first poke in 1887 at the age of fourteen. Jackson always worked with a mob of three or four men, and sometimes hired a policeman to help confuse his victims. In the 1890's and the early 1900's Jackson operated exclusively in the Loop district, and often stole as much as fifteen hundred dollars in a single week. He paid a large retaining fee to Black Horton, a famous Negro lawyer and politician, and when working with his mob he reported to Horton every hour. If he failed to report, the lawyer hurried to the police station with a bail bond and a writ of habeas corpus. During the forty years in which he was active as a pickpocket, Eddie Jackson was arrested at least two thousand times. He paid a few fines, but usually escaped prosecution by returning a part of the stolen money. He went to jail but twice — for ten days in 1893, and for a year in 1897. He died in 1932, a pauper, in the Cook County Hospital.

Nothing remains of the careers of Andy Craig, Bob Duncan, Mushmouth Johnson, and the other princes of Whisky Row except meager police records and newspaper accounts and the faltering recollections of a few old-timers. But the bullet-headed proprietor of the Lone Star Saloon and Palm Garden, who was the lowliest and by far the toughest of all the denizens of the Row, has become a legendary character — he is immortalized in the American lauguage and is probably mentioned somewhere in the United States every hour of the day. For this terrible little man — he was only five feet and five inches tall and weighed about a hundred and forty pounds — was the veritable Mickey Finn whose name is used everywhere as a synonym for a knockout drink.

The Chicago police never knew very much about the early history of Mickey Finn. Sometimes he said he had been born in Ireland, but on other occasions claimed Peoria as his birthplace. He first appeared in Chicago during the World's Fair of 1893 as a lush worker, robbing drunken men in the Bad Lands and Little Cheyenne districts of South Clark Street. For a few months in 1894 Mickey Finn tended bar in Toronto Jim's dive on Custom House Place, but he was too tough and belligerent even for that notorious hangout of hoodlums and desperadoes. He was always fighting, and was at length fired after he had knocked out a man's eyeball with a bung-starter, a feat which he duplicated at the Lone Star a few years later when a customer failed to produce sixty cents to pay for a round of drinks.

For a year or two after leaving Toronto Jim's resort Mickey Finn was a pickpocket in the red-light district and a fence for small-time thieves and burglars. About 1896 he opened the Lone Star Saloon and Palm Garden, at the southern end of Whisky Row near Harrison Street, which Police Inspector Lavin once described as " a low dive, a hangout for colored and white people of the lowest type." Finn ran the Lone Star for seven or eight years, and during most of that time continued to operate as a fence. He also maintained a school of instruction for young pickpockets, and taught that branch of thievery to the streetwalkers who frequented his resort, encouraging them to rob the men whom they picked up and brought into the Lone Star for drinks. The faculty of this school, besides Mickey Finn himself, included his handsome wife, Kate Roses; and his bartender, whom he called " the Patsy." Kate Roses also had charge

172

of the " house girls," who were supposed to exert all their wiles to induce visitors to drink, and to entertain them in any other manner for which they were willing to pay. The last of these ladies, and the ones who finally brought trouble to Mickey Finn, were Isabelle Ffyffe, known as the Dummy because she had scarcely any of her buttons; and Gold Tooth Mary Thornton, whose single tooth was crowned with the precious metal. Both the Dummy and Gold Tooth Mary testified in 1903 before the aldermanic graft commission.

The Lone Star Saloon and Palm Garden — the Garden was a back room decorated with a scrawny little palm tree in a pot — was a robbing den from the beginning, although for a year or so Finn and his staff confined their activities to picking pockets and rolling an occasional drunk. But about 1898 Mickey Finn met a Negro voodoo doctor named Hall, who sold love potions and charms to the inmates of the bawdy houses, and cocaine and morphine to dope addicts. From the voodoo man Finn procured a large brown bottle filled with " a sort of white stuff " which the police never identified, but which was probably hydrate of chloral. Gold Tooth Mary said that when Mickey Finn returned to the Lone Star from his interview with Doctor Hall he said to her in great glee:

" See the nice bottle, Mary? We'll get the money with this. I give the doc an extra dollar to make it strong."

With the " sort of white stuff " as a starting-point, Mickey Finn invented two knockout drinks of which he was inordinately proud. One, which he called the " Mickey Finn Special," was compounded of raw alcohol, water in which snuff had been soaked, and a liberal portion of Doctor Hall's mixture. The other, called " Number Two," was beer dosed with the " white stuff " and further fortified by a dash of snuffwater. Finn put up a sign behind his bar which read: " Try a Mickey Finn Special," and the house girls and the streetwalkers who worked with him on a percentage basis were instructed to urge the concoction upon every man with whom they drank. It tickled Mickey Finn's fancy to have a customer order by name the drink which would knock him out. If the sucker insisted upon drinking beer, he was given " Number Two," which was capable of dealing him almost as hard a jolt as the " Special."

" When the victims drink this dopey stuff," said Gold Tooth Mary, " they get talkative, walk around in a restless manner, and then fall into a deep sleep, and you can't arouse them until the effect of the drug wears off."

If strangers happened to be in the Lone Star when a man succumbed to one of Mickey Finn's paralyzing potions, the victim slumbered undisturbed in his chair until they had gone or had themselves been doped. Then the Patsy and the house girls dragged him into one of two small rooms at the rear of the Palm Garden, which Finn called his " operating rooms." The actual robbing was done by Mickey Finn and Kate Roses, but first, curiously enough, Finn always put on a derby hat and a clean white apron. The drugged man was stripped to the skin and carefully searched for a money belt, and everything of any value at all was taken from his pockets. If his clothing was of good quality, Finn kept that also, and substituted ragged cast-offs. Usually Finn threw his victims into an alley behind the Lone Star, but sometimes he left them lying on the floor of the " operating room " all night and kicked them out next morning. They were seldom hard to handle when they awakened; most of them were befuddled for several days, and few could remember when or where they had been robbed. Dummy Ffyffe said that Finn was " terribly brutal " to men whom he had doped; he always carried a bung-starter into the " operating room " and tapped a victim on the head at the first sign of returning consciousness. Gold Tooth Mary hinted at even darker doings:

" I saw Finn take a gold watch and thirty-five dollars

from Billy Miller, a trainman," she said. " Finn gave him dope and he lay in a stupor in the saloon for twelve hours. When he recovered he demanded his money, but Finn had gone. . . . Miller was afterward found along the railroad tracks with his head cut off."

Gold Tooth Mary told the aldermanic graft commission that she had seen many men besides Miller drugged and robbed in the Lone Star, and that she had quit her job in the early fall of 1903 because of Finn's increasing brutality.

" I was afraid I would be murdered for the two hundred dollars I had saved up," she said, " and I did not want to be a witness to any more of the horrible things I saw done there. I was afraid I would be arrested some time when some victims who had been fed on knockout drops would die. When I saw his wife put the drugged liquor to the lips of men I could not stand it, as bad as I am. Oh, it was just awful to see the way men were drugged and stripped of their clothing by Finn or his wife. Finn had an idea that most men wore belts about their waists to hide their money. He had robbed a man once who hid his money that way, and he never neglected searching the ' dead ones ' to the skin."

Gold Tooth Mary testified that Mickey Finn had often told her that he would never be arrested because he paid the police for protection and possessed great influence with Aldermen Hinky Dink Mike Kenna and Bath House John Coughlin, but nobody was ever asked by the graft commission to explain or deny Finn's boastings. The police made a raid upon the Lone Star after Gold Tooth Mary and Dummy Ffyffe had appeared before the commission, but found nothing except a few bottles of liniment and cough medicine. They reported that in the absence of specific complaints it would be impossible for them even to arrest Finn. The only action the graft commission could take was to order Mickey Finn's saloon license revoked, which was done, and on December 16, 1903 the doors of the Lone Star were closed. Mickey Finn left Chicago for a few months, but returned in the summer of 1904, and for several years tended bar in a resort on South Dearborn Street. Meanwhile he had sold the formula for his " Special " to half a dozen ambitious dive-keepers, and the potion was known throughout the underworld simply as a " mickey finn." The name was soon applied to knockout drinks of every description.

CHAPTER VI

THE MONSTER OF SIXTY-THIRD
STREET

IN THE middle 1890's Chicago temporarily forgot the
disturbing revelations of William T. Stead and the Civic
Federation to marvel at the extraordinary career of a young
doctor named Herman W. Mudgett, but better known as
Henry H. Holmes. Gentle and almost effeminate in appearance and manner, with mild blue eyes and a soft and musical voice, and possessing an almost irresistible attraction
for women, Mudgett was nevertheless a forger, a bigamist,
a swindler, a horse-thief, and a murderer who maintained
a fantastic " castle " equipped with trapdoors, secret stairways, sound-proof rooms, torture chambers lined with sheet
iron and asbestos, a crematory, vats of corrosive acids and
quicklime, and apparatus with which he articulated the skeletons of several of his victims and prepared them for sale
to medical schools. This thrifty butcher was finally hanged
for the murder of one of his accomplices in a bizarre insurance fraud, and enough evidence was available to have
hanged him for a dozen other killings. But the actual number of persons who met death at his hands was never known,
although police and newspaper estimates ranged from thirty
to several hundred. He once described himself as " an honest
dealer in human remains," but the New York *World* called
him " the first criminal of the century," and the Chicago
Journal said of him:

"The nerve, the calculation and the audacity of the man were unparalleled. Murder was his natural bent. Sometimes he killed from sheer greed of gain; oftener, as he has himself confessed, to gratify an inhuman thirst for blood. Not one of his crimes was the outcome of a sudden burst of fury — 'hot blood' — as the codes say. All were deliberate; planned and concluded with consummate skill. To him murder was indeed a fine art; and he reveled in the lurid glamour cast upon him by his abnormal genius. Even with the shadow of the noose dangling over his head, he evolved a so-called confession, detailing with horrible calmness how he had exterminated twenty-seven fellow creatures, and coldly setting forth the varied and bloody tortures he employed. One could almost see the fiendish grin on his thin and bloodless lips as, in the gloom of his cell, he set down the terrible tale. But the man was an atrocious liar, and several of those with whose murder he charged himself have since denied his story with their own lips. The statement was prompted by a perverted ambition to be regarded as the 'greatest' monster who ever walked in the form of man, and an incongruous desire to win for the education of his little son the $5,000 offered for the 'confession' by a newspaper."

Mudgett, or Holmes, was born in 1860 at Gilmanton, New Hampshire, where his father, a respected and prosperous citizen, had been postmaster for almost a quarter of a century. He was notoriously a bad boy, frequently in trouble, and in later years was principally remembered for his cruelty to animals and smaller children. His only redeeming trait appears to have been a fondness for study; he was the brightest pupil in the local schools. In 1878, when he was eighteen years old, young Mudgett eloped with the seventeen-year-old daughter of a well-to-do farmer of Loudon, New Hampshire, and that same year he began to study medicine at a small college in Burlington, Vermont, paying his tuition with a small legacy which had been inherited by his

HERMAN W. MUDGETT, ALIAS
H. H. HOLMES

wife. In 1879 he transferred to the medical school of the University of Michigan, at Ann Arbor, and while studying there committed his first serious crime with the aid of another student who is said to have become, in later years, a prominent physician in New York. The accomplice insured his life for $12,500 and soon thereafter disappeared, while Mudgett stole a corpse from the dissecting-room of the medical school, identified it as that of the missing student, and

179

collected the insurance. A few months after this coup Mudgett completed his medical studies and left Ann Arbor, abandoning his wife and infant son. Mrs. Mudgett returned to Gilmanton and is said never to have seen her husband again.

Not even Pinkerton detectives, who procured most of the evidence which sent Mudgett to the gallows, were able to learn very much about his activities during the half-dozen years that followed his departure from Michigan, although they came across his trail in several cities and states. For a year or so he was engaged in legitimate business in St. Paul, and so gained the respect and goodwill of his neighbors that he was appointed receiver for a bankrupt store. He immediately stocked the place with goods bought on credit, sold them quickly at low prices, and vanished with the proceeds. From St. Paul he went into New York State as agent for a New England nursery, and for a while taught a district school in Clinton County, boarding at the home of a farmer near the village of Moore's Forks. He seduced the farmer's wife, and disappeared one night leaving an unpaid board bill and a pregnant landlady. In 1885 he opened an office in the village of Wilmette, a North Shore suburb of Chicago, posing as an inventor and using the name of Holmes. Without troubling to divorce his wife in New Hampshire, he married Myrtle Z. Belknap, daughter of a wealthy resident of Wilmette, but she left him after he had twice tried to poison her father and had attempted to obtain possession of his property by means of forged deeds. When Belknap threatened to have him arrested, Holmes hastily left Wilmette and went to St. Louis, where he served three months in jail as the result of an attempted land swindle. It was in St. Louis that Holmes met the two men who were destined to bring about his destruction — Marion Hedgspeth, a famous train-robber who was awaiting sentence to the penitentiary; and Benjamin F. Pietzel, a small-time swindler who was finding it extremely difficult to earn a dishonest living for his wife and five children.

Early in 1889 Holmes appeared in downtown Chicago with the A.B.C. Copier, a machine for copying documents, and about the only honest device with which he was ever connected. He operated from an office in the Monon Block on South Dearborn Street, but the copier was a failure, and Holmes again vanished, leaving his creditors with worthless notes aggregating nine thousand dollars. A few months later he turned up in the Englewood section on the South Side, as a clerk in a drug store owned by a widow named Holden, at Wallace and Sixty-third Streets, a neighborhood which served as a base for his operations during the next several years. About the first of 1890 Mrs. Holden disappeared, and Holmes told the neighbors that she had sold him the business and " moved away." Apparently no one was sufficiently interested to find out what actually had happened to her, and she could not be found when the police finally began to investigate Holmes's activities.

2

IN 1892 Holmes built on the southwest corner of Wallace and Sixty-third Streets, directly opposite the drug store which he had " bought " from Mrs. Holden, the building which was popularly known as Holmes's Castle — an imposing structure of three stories and a basement, with false battlements and wooden bay windows covered by sheet iron. It occupied an area of fifty by one hundred and sixty-two feet, and contained between eighty and ninety rooms. Holmes himself drew the plans and closely supervised every detail of construction, and, as far as the police could learn, never paid anyone a cent for the materials which went into the building. He also changed workmen frequently, often discharging them in a great fury and refusing to pay their wages, so that no one else knew the terrible secrets of the Castle until he was arrested in the summer of 1895.

The detectives who devoted several weeks to searching and making a floor plan of the Castle found nothing out of the ordinary on the first and third floors; the latter was cut up into small apartments which were apparently never occupied, and the former into larger rooms which were rented for business purposes. Three or four were used by Holmes himself for a drug store, restaurant, and jewelry store. But the second floor of the building proved to be a veritable labyrinth, with narrow, winding passages leading to hidden stairways, cleverly concealed doors and rooms, blind hallways and trapdoors, all so arranged as to facilitate escape and confuse pursuit. Holmes's private apartment, consisting of bedroom and bath and two small chambers which he used as offices, was on the second floor front, facing Sixty-third Street. In the floor of his bathroom, concealed under a heavy rug and carefully fitted, the police found a trapdoor, from which a stairway descended to a small room about eight feet square. There were two doors to this chamber, one opening on a stairway which led downward to the street, and the other giving access to a chute which extended to the basement.

Besides Holmes's quarters, the second floor contained thirty-five rooms. Half a dozen were fitted up as ordinary sleeping-chambers, and there were indications that they had been occupied by the various women who had worked for the monster, or to whom he had made love while awaiting an opportunity to kill them. Several of the other rooms were without windows, and could be made air-tight by closing the doors. One was completely filled by a huge safe, almost large enough for a bank vault, into which a gas-pipe had been introduced. Another was lined with sheet iron covered by asbestos, and showed traces of fire. Some had been sound-proofed, while others had extremely low ceilings, and trapdoors in the floors from which ladders led to smaller rooms beneath. In all of the rooms on the second floor, as well as in the great safe, were gas pipes with cut-off valves in plain sight. But these valves were fakes; the flow of gas was actually controlled by a series of cut-offs concealed in the closet of Holmes's bedroom. Apparently one of his favorite methods of murder was to lock a victim in one of the rooms and then turn on the gas; and the police believed that in the asbestos-lined chamber he had devised a means of introducing fire, so that the gas-pipe became a terrible blow-torch from which there was no escape. Also in Holmes's closet was an electric bell which rang whenever a door was opened anywhere on the second floor.

The basement of the Castle, which was seven feet deep under the entire building and extended under the sidewalk on Sixty-third Street, was Holmes's disposal plant, where he burned or otherwise destroyed the bodies of his victims, or removed the flesh from their bones and prepared the skeletons for articulation. In a corner of the huge underground room, beneath the chute which ran from the second floor, was a dissecting-table and a case of gleaming surgical knives, with sufficient evidence to indicate that they had frequently been used. Under the table was a box containing several skeletons, all of females. Built into one of the walls was a crematory, with a heavy iron grate to hold the fire, and another grate, fitted with rollers, by means of which a body could be slid into the flames. "A curious thing about this retort," said the New York *World,* " was that there was an iron flue leading from it into a tank. There was no other entrance to this tank. . . . A white fluid was discovered in the bottom of the tank which gave forth an overpowering odor." Buried in the floor of the basement the police found a huge vat of corrosive acid and two of quicklime, in any of which a body would have been devoured within a few hours. A pile of loose quicklime was also found in a small

183

room built into a corner, and in it was the naked footprint of a woman. Scattered about the basement were several mysterious machines, the purpose of which was never learned, although it was believed that one, in shape somewhat similar to the rack of the medieval torturer, was the " elasticity determinator " with which Holmes once said he had been conducting experiments. He had a theory that the human body, by proper manipulation, could be stretched to twice its normal length, and held that universal application of the process would produce a race of giants. Another unexplained mystery was encountered by workmen who were digging a tunnel through the cellar wall toward Sixty-third Street. Said the New York *World:*

". . . they encountered a wall that gave forth a hollow sound. As soon as this wall was broken through a horrible smell was encountered and fumes like those of a charnel house rushed forth. A plumber was sent for, and the workmen gathered about while he proceeded to investigate. The first thing the plumber did was to light a match. Then there was a terrific explosion that shook the building, while flames poured forth into the cellar. The plumber was the only man who escaped uninjured, and an ambulance took the other workmen to the hospital. Then a thorough search of this mysterious chamber was made by the police. They found that the brick wall had concealed a tank curiously constructed. This tank had contained an oil whose fumes, the chemists say, would destroy human life within less than a minute. There were evidences about the cellar of this mysterious and deadly oil having been used. . . . A small box was found in the center of the tank. When this was opened by Fire Marshal James Kenyon an evil-smelling vapor rushed out. All ran except Kenyon, who was overpowered by the stench.

He was dragged out and carried upstairs, and for two hours acted like one demented."

Half a dozen human bones, and several pieces of jewelry which were identified as having belonged to one of Holmes's mistresses, were found by detectives in a large wood-burning stove in the center of the basement, and scraps of blood-stained linen were discovered in a near-by ash-heap. " In a hole in the middle of the floor," said the *World,* "more bones were found. These have been examined by physicians, who declare that they include, among others, the bones of a child between six and eight years of age. There were seventeen ribs in all, part of a spinal column, a collar-bone, and a hip-bone. In spite of the retort, the deadly oil tank, and two vaults of quicklime, all working at the same time, is it possible, it was asked, that Holmes was murdering people so fast that he had to bury some of them? "

When Holmes built the Castle he told his neighbors that he intended to operate the second and third floors as a boarding-house during the World's Fair, which opened in the spring of 1893, a few months after the completion of the building. The New York *World* declared that there were many reasons to believe that the monster contemplated gathering in victims among the visitors to Chicago. " There are hundreds of people," said the *World,* " who went to Chicago to see the Fair and were never heard of again. The list of the ' missing ' when the Fair closed was a long one, and in the greater number foul play was suspected. Did these visitors to the Fair, strangers to Chicago, find their way to Holmes' Castle in answer to delusive advertisements sent out by him, never to return again? Did he erect his Castle close to the Fair grounds so as to gather in these victims by the wholesale, and, after robbing them, did he dispose of their bodies in his quicklime vats, in his mysterious oil tank with its death-dealing liquids, or did he burn them in the elaborate retort with which the basement was provided? "

These questions were never satisfactorily answered, although detectives did learn that Holmes had advertised the Castle as a boarding-house. No fewer than fifty persons, reported to the police as missing, were traced to the place, but there the trail ended, and the detectives were unable to find sufficient evidence to justify the popular belief that Holmes had killed any or all of them.

3

T H E police believed that the first persons murdered in the Castle were Mrs. Julia Conner, the wife of I. L. Conner, of Davenport, Iowa, and her eight-year-old daughter, Pearl. The Conner family came to Chicago in 1890, soon after the disappearance of Mrs. Holden, and Holmes employed both Conner and his wife in the drug store, the former as a clerk and the latter, a strikingly handsome woman, as bookkeeper. Mrs. Conner soon became the monster's mistress, and Conner quit his job and left Chicago when Holmes told him that his wife had been unfaithful. Mrs. Conner and the little girl remained with Holmes for almost two years, the longest period that any woman except his first wife ever lived with him. During some six months of that time she ran the drug store alone while Holmes went to Texas, where he was a member, and probably the leader, of a gang of swindlers, murderers, and horse-thieves which operated in that state and in Arizona. The gang was finally dispersed by Texas Rangers, but Holmes escaped and returned to Chicago before a warrant which had been issued for his arrest could be served.

While he was in Texas Holmes became acquainted with a young girl named Minnie Williams, who with her sister Nannie owned property in Fort Worth valued at about fifty thousand dollars. In the late summer of 1892 Minnie

Williams came to Chicago and moved into the Castle, and Holmes introduced her about the neighborhood as his private secretary. Actually she was his mistress, and her mad infatuation with the monster was obvious to everyone who saw them together. Within two hours after her arrival she

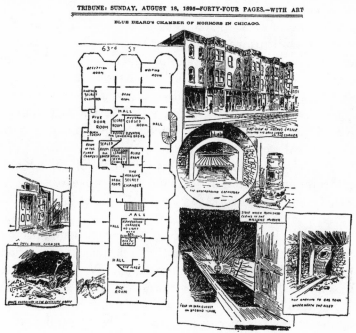

BLUE BEARD'S CHAMBER OF HORRORS IN CHICAGO.

From the Chicago *Tribune*

HOLMES'S CASTLE

had quarreled with Mrs. Conner over Holmes, and within ten days Mrs. Conner and her daughter had disappeared. After his arrest Holmes told detectives that Mrs. Conner had died while he was performing a criminal operation and that the little girl had " wandered away." Eventually, however, he admitted that he had murdered both the woman and her child because of Minnie Williams's jealousy. " But I would have got rid of her anyway," he said. " I was tired of her."

Minnie Williams lived at the Castle for more than a year and probably knew more about Holmes's affairs than any other person. The police said that it would have been impossible for her not to have had guilty knowledge of many murders. Besides being responsible for the killing of Mrs. Conner and her daughter, Minnie Williams was believed to have instigated the murder of Emily Van Tassel, a Chicago girl who worked for Holmes early in 1893 and vanished within a month; and of Emeline Cigrand, a nineteen-year-old blonde who is said to have been the prettiest of the monster's victims. Miss Cigrand, a girl of good family and excellent character, was a stenographer in the Keeley Institute at Dwight, Illinois, when Holmes's friend Ben Pietzel went there in the fall of 1892 to take the gold cure for drunkenness. Upon his return to Chicago Pietzel told Holmes of the girl's beauty, and Holmes offered her a large salary to work for him in Chicago. She accepted the job, came to the Castle, and never left it. Holmes said afterward that he had locked her in his sound-proofed room and forced her to have illicit relations with him, and that he had killed her because Minnie Williams objected to sharing him with another woman. Miss Cigrand was engaged to Robert E. Phelps, a wealthy man many years her senior, who was never seen again after he had called at the Castle. Holmes told the police that Phelps had died during the course of an " experiment."

In the early summer of 1893 Nannie Williams came to the Castle from Texas to visit her sister. Holmes made violent love to her and apparently had no trouble in persuading her to sign over to him her share of the Fort Worth property. Nannie Williams disappeared in July 1893, and it was understood by those who had met her in Chicago that she had gone back to Texas. In the fall of 1893 Ben Pietzel took charge of the Castle, and Holmes and Minnie Williams went to Denver, where the monster, under the name of Howard, married Miss Georgianna Yoke of Richmond, Indiana, whom he had met in Indianapolis several years before. After living in Denver for several weeks with the two women, neither of whom knew of the existence of the other, Holmes sent Miss Yoke back to her home in Indiana, telling her that he would soon join her, and returned to Chicago with Minnie Williams. He made several trips with Miss Yoke during the next two years, but was never with her more than a few weeks at a time. Apparently, however, he really loved her. At any rate, as she testified at his trial, he was always kind to her and made no attempt to take her life.

About the first of December 1893 Minnie Williams transferred her Texas property to Holmes, and soon afterward she disappeared; she was last seen alive on December 15. When he was questioned by detectives after his arrest Holmes at first insisted that Minnie Williams had killed her sister in a fit of jealous fury and had fled to Europe with a young man; but he finally admitted that he had killed both the Williams sisters, and that their skeletons, as well as those of Emily Van Tassel and Emeline Cigrand, were in the box found in the basement of the Castle.

4

THE facilities of the Castle were also utilized by Holmes in innumerable swindling operations, in some of which he was assisted by Mrs. Conner and Minnie Williams. He served good food in his restaurant, but virtually every article offered for sale in the jewelry and drug stores was a fake; the gold jewelry was brass, the diamonds were glass, and no matter what sort of pills were ordered, the customer received powdered chalk, occasionally colored and perfumed. For more than a year Holmes sold water from Lake Michigan over the counter of his drug store at five cents a small glass, assuring the people of Englewood that it was the finest mineral water in the world and had come from an artesian well in his basement. Perhaps the most elaborate of his swindles was the celebrated gas-generator, which deceived many people and was hailed as an important invention by which gas could be manufactured from water. In the basement of the Castle Holmes built a queer-looking contraption of pipes and tanks, with a furnace underneath, and when everything was ready he notified the gas company, which sent an expert to make an examination. "What the expert saw," said the Chicago *Tribune*, " was a contrivance such as he had never seen before, with a stream of water running in at one end and a strong flow of gas at the other. Holmes assured him that the cost of manufacture was next to nothing, and the result was that the gas company gave the invention such a strong recommendation that Holmes was enabled to sell it to a Canadian for $2,000. When the machine was taken out it was discovered that Holmes had tapped the gas company's mains and thus generated his great illuminator."

5

W H I L E in jail in St. Louis, Holmes told Marion Hedgspeth, the train-robber, that he had evolved a fool-proof scheme to defraud an insurance company, but that he required a shrewd lawyer to help work out the details. Hedgspeth referred Holmes to his own attorney, Jeptha D. Howe of St. Louis, and Holmes promised to send the bandit five hundred dollars if the plan was successful. Apparently Holmes did nothing about this particular idea for several years, though in the meantime he attempted an insurance swindle without assistance. He took a cadaver to a seaside resort in Rhode Island, registered as H. H. Holmes, and then burned and otherwise disfigured the head of the body and left it on the beach. Shaving his beard and making other alterations in his appearance, he returned to the hotel, registered under another name, and inquired for his friend Holmes. When the body was found on the beach he identified it as that of Holmes, and presented an insurance policy for twenty thousand dollars. But the insurance company suspected fraud and refused to pay, and Holmes returned to Chicago without attempting to press his claim.

In the early summer of 1894 Holmes held a conference with Ben Pietzel and Jeptha D. Howe, and the three compounded a plot whereby Pietzel was to take out life insurance and then disappear, while Holmes was to procure a body, identify it as that of Pietzel, and collect the insurance. As soon as the plan had been completed, Pietzel insured his life for ten thousand dollars at the Chicago office of the Fidelity Mutual Life Association, and in August went to Philadelphia, where he opened an office at No. 1316 Callowhill Street under the name of B. F. Perry, posing as a patent attorney. On September 3, 1894 Pietzel's body, with the face blackened and blistered as if from burns, was found on the floor of his office. Near by was a broken bottle which had contained benzine, and the first theory evolved by the police was that Pietzel, who of course they thought was Perry, had been killed in an accidental explosion. But an autopsy showed that his death had been caused by chloroform. Meanwhile the police had learned that "Perry" had come to Philadelphia from St. Louis, and the police of that city were asked to find his relatives. About three weeks after the finding of the body Jeptha D. Howe appeared in Philadelphia and said that the dead man was in reality Ben Pietzel, and that he was empowered by Mrs. Pietzel to collect the insurance. Later Holmes arrived in Philadelphia with Pietzel's daughter, Alice, and he also identified the body as that of Pietzel. The insurance was paid without question. Of the ten thousand dollars, Howe took twenty-five hundred and Holmes the remainder. Holmes afterward gave Mrs. Pietzel five hundred dollars, but took the money back within a few days on the pretense that he would invest it.

The ironic feature of the business was that actually no fraud had been perpetrated on the insurance company. Pietzel's life had been insured, and Pietzel was certainly dead; Holmes had murdered him three days before his body was found. But neither Howe nor Mrs. Pietzel knew this; they thought that Pietzel was alive and that Holmes had substituted a body in order to collect the insurance, and that Pietzel would return to his family in a few months. Howe regarded the whole matter as a closed incident, and when he returned to St. Louis he told Marion Hedgspeth about the scheme and how well it had worked. But when Hedgspeth failed to receive the five hundred dollars which had been promised him by Holmes, he told the Warden of the prison about the conversation he had held with Holmes while the latter was in jail. The Warden notified the insurance company, and the Pinkerton Detective Agency was employed to investigate. Detective Frank P. Geyer of Pinkerton's Philadelphia office was assigned to the case, and he was soon convinced that the body found in Callowhill Street was really that of Pietzel, and that Pietzel had been murdered. Geyer suspected Holmes, partly because of Holmes's unsavory record as a swindler, and partly because he had identified the body and was known to have called upon Pietzel several times while the latter was masquerading as B. F. Perry. Police departments throughout the United States were asked to arrest Holmes, and the Texas authorities were requested to revive their warrant charging him with horse-stealing, so that he could be held if caught.

But Holmes proved to be very elusive. After he had collected and divided the insurance with Jeptha Howe, he returned to St. Louis, where he found Mrs. Pietzel ill and frightened. He persuaded her to take her eldest and youngest children and go to her parents' home in Galva, Illinois, and promised to meet her in Detroit in two weeks with Alice, Nellie, and Howard. Her husband also, he said, would be in Detroit. Holmes arrived in Detroit several days before the appointed time and put the three children in a boarding-house. Then he went to Richmond, Indiana, returned to Detroit with Georgianna Yoke, and installed her in a second boarding-house. When Mrs. Pietzel arrived she was lodged in still another house. Then he began to move about the country, apparently having learned that Pinkerton's were on his trail. " During these travels," said the Chicago *Journal,* " Holmes carried with him three separate detachments — Mrs. Pietzel, Miss Yoke, and the children — all within four blocks of each other in all the different cities, almost travelling together, under Holmes's leading strings, and yet each detachment ignorant of the presence of the other two." This fantastic journeying continued for nearly two months, but on November 17, 1894, Holmes appeared in Boston, alone, and was arrested and sent to Philadelphia.

A week after Holmes's arrest Miss Yoke was located at her parents' home in Indiana, and Mrs. Pietzel was found in Burlington, Vermont, where Holmes had established her in a rented house to await the arrival of her family. Holmes had lived at the house for several days, but left in great annoyance when she found him digging a hole in the back yard. The police believed that he was digging her grave, but for some unknown reason decided not to kill her. Mrs. Pietzel was arrested and taken to Philadelphia, but was soon released, and no charge was ever made against her.

Holmes flatly refused to tell what had become of the three Pietzel children, Nellie, Howard, and Alice, and Detective Geyer set out to find them and so complete his case against the monster. In Chicago he learned that Holmes's mail had been forwarded every day to Gilmanton, New

Hampshire; from Gilmanton it had been sent to Detroit, from Detroit to Toronto, from Toronto to Cincinnati, from Cincinnati to Indianapolis, and so on. For more than eight months Geyer followed Holmes's trail throughout the Middle West and Canada, stopping at every city to investigate every house that had been for rent at the time Holmes was supposed to have been there — literally hundreds of them. In Detroit the house that Holmes had occupied with the children was still vacant, and there was a big hole in the cellar floor. But nothing was found in the hole. In Toronto Geyer searched for eight days before he found a house at No. 16 Vincent Street which had been rented to a man with two little girls. Holmes had borrowed a spade from a neighbor with which to dig a hole for storing potatoes, and Geyer borrowed the same spade and dug in the same place. Several feet under ground he found the bodies of Nellie and Alice Pietzel. In an upstairs bedroom was a large trunk, with a piece of rubber tubing leading into it from a gas pipe. It was clear that Holmes had induced the girls to enter the trunk, probably during a game of hide and seek, and had asphyxiated them.

During the few days in which they lived in Toronto the Pietzel girls had told neighbors that they had a little brother in Indianapolis, and with this clue in mind Geyer went to the Indiana city and painstakingly searched nine hundred houses. Finally, in the suburb of Irvington, he found the place that Holmes had rented and in which he had lived for nearly a week. Fortunately for Geyer's investigation, the house had been vacant since the departure of the monster, and the stove used by Holmes was still in the kitchen. And in the stove the detective discovered the charred body of Howard Pietzel. Holmes told a great many different stories when confronted with the evidence which had been unearthed by Detective Geyer; he insisted that Pietzel had committed suicide, and declared that the three children had been murdered by a mythical young man who had made the mythical trip to Europe with Minnie Williams. But in his famous " confession," which he wrote while awaiting execution, Holmes said that he suffered greatly when he was informed that Geyer had found the bodies of Alice and Nellie Pietzel in Toronto. " I saw again," he said, " the two little faces as they had looked when I had hurriedly left them — felt the innocent child's kiss so timidly given — heard again their earnest words of farewell."

6

THE indictment returned by the Grand Jury charged Holmes with the murder of Ben Pietzel. His trial, which began on October 28, 1895, was one of the most sensational of the century, and the newspapers reported it in a manner which would have done credit to the modern tabloid. And they had first-rate material with which to work. Besides the mysteries of the Castle, which were recounted at length in the testimony of various witnesses, Holmes created several exciting scenes in the courtroom, broke down and wept when Georgianna Yoke appeared as a witness for the state, and at length discharged his lawyers and attempted to conduct his own defense. But the skill and shrewdness he displayed in questioning witnesses and arguing points of law were of no avail; the trial ended in six days with a verdict of guilty of murder in the first degree. Afterward the jurors said that they had agreed in one minute, but had remained out for two hours and a half " for the sake of appearances."

Holmes's case was appealed to the Pennsylvania Supreme Court, which affirmed the verdict, and on April 30, 1896 the Governor refused to intervene. On May 7, 1896, nine days before his thirty-sixth birthday, Holmes was hanged in Moyamensing Prison.

" It is safe to assume," said the Chicago *Journal* on the

afternoon of the execution, " that a sigh of relief will go up from the whole country with the knowledge that Herman Mudgett or Henry H. Holmes, man or monster, has been exterminated — much the same as a plague to humanity would be stamped out."

7

C H I C A G O never produced another killer of Holmes's caliber, but the murderous activities of Herman Billik, who flourished some ten years after Holmes had been hanged, aroused almost as much interest as had the evil exploits of the monster of the Castle. Billik, a handsome, stoutish Bohemian with piercing black eyes and, like Holmes, a way with women, was a fortune-teller; he read the future for twenty-five cents and carried on a lively trade in charms and potions. He was also something of a hypnotist and claimed to possess mysterious occult powers which he had inherited from his mother. That accomplished lady, he said, was a witch. However, when Billik murdered six persons, all members of the same family — father, mother, and four daughters ranging in age from twenty-two to twelve years — he relied, not upon spells or supernatural forces, but upon arsenic.

Billik, whose real name was Vajicek, came to Chicago in the autumn of 1904 from Cleveland, where his mother had been in business as a fortune-teller for several years. He established himself and his family, consisting of his wife, two sons, and a daughter, in a small house in West Nineteenth Street, where he hung out a sign announcing that he was " The Great Billik, Card-Reader and Seer." Three doors away was the modest residence of Martin Vzral, his wife, Rose, and their seven children. Vzral was a milkdealer and one of the most prosperous citizens of the Bohemian quarter; he had more than two thousand dollars in the bank, owned his own home, and his business regularly earned a net profit of from seventy-five to one hundred dollars a week.

Although it was afterward established that Billik had chosen the Vzrals for his victims even before he moved into the neighborhood, he made no attempt to approach the family for several days, during which time his arrival, and the air of mystery with which he managed to surround his movements, were the principal topics of conversation for blocks around. Finally he strode into the milk depot and ordered a can of milk, and as Vzral handed over the filled container Billik stared fixedly at him, muttered a few words of unintelligible gibberish, and at length said impressively:

" You have an enemy. I see him. He is trying to destroy you."

Billik let the milk-dealer worry for a few days, and then he called upon the Vzrals and told Martin Vzral that his enemy was another milkman across the street. The fortune-teller offered to use his supernatural gifts in Vzral's behalf, and at midnight, while the nine Vzrals looked on in awe, Billik brewed an evil-smelling potion on the kitchen stove and then ceremoniously threw the mixture upon the stoop of the rival's home. " Now," said Billik, " you will prosper. He cannot harm you." Since Vzral was a man of industry, he did prosper; his business continued to increase as it had been doing for months. But to Billik and his charms went the credit; he was hailed as the savior of the Vzral family. He refused pay for the great service, but was at length prevailed upon to accept a loan of twenty dollars.

The Vzrals were a good Catholic family, but were very superstitious, and they saw no reason to doubt that Billik was everything he claimed to be; moreover, with their own eyes they had seen him cast a spell which had warded off a great danger. They listened, fascinated, to his recital of the supernatural wonders he had performed, and to his tales

197

of his mother, the witch. Within a few weeks Billik's domination of the family was complete; the Vzrals seemed to exist for no other purpose than to serve the fortune-teller. He spent as much time at the Vzral home as he did at his own, and made love to Mrs. Vzral and her daughters under the beaming eyes of their husband and father. Mrs. Vzral's preoccupation with Billik was so intense that for days at a time she refused to leave the house, for fear he might come while she was away.

At every visit Billik borrowed money; by the first of January 1905 he had stripped Martin Vzral of his bank account and was absorbing most of the profits of the milk business. To provide more money, three of the Vzral girls went to work as domestic servants and turned their wages over to the greedy charlatan. He bought new clothing, set up a stylish horse and carriage, and made trips to New York, Saratoga, and California, for all of which the Vzrals paid. At his suggestion Mrs. Vzral insured the lives of her husband and four of her daughters in amounts ranging from two thousand to one hundred and five dollars. The only members of the family not insured were the oldest daughter, Emma, the son, Jerry, and the baby girl. And they were the only ones who survived Billik's machinations.

Early in March 1905 Martin Vzral began to show signs of awakening; he occasionally grumbled about money and deplored the state of business, and once went so far as to hesitate when Billik asked for a loan. To cure this attack of bad disposition, Billik gave Mrs. Vzral a white powder, which he said was a charm, and told her to introduce it into her husband's food. A few days later Vzral complained of pains in his stomach, as most people will when they are given doses of arsenic. Billik diagnosed the ailment as " stomach trouble," and treated Vzral with more white powder and a liquid which he poured into the sick man's mouth from a whisky bottle. Vzral died on March 27, 1905. Mrs. Vzral collected two thousand dollars in life insurance and turned it all over to Billik except a hundred dollars which he permitted her to keep for funeral expenses.

A few weeks after Martin Vzral's death, Emma and Mary Vzral went to visit Billik at Riverside, where he was telling fortunes in a tent. He showed Emma a queerly marked playing card and said: " This is the card of death. Mary will die soon." He was correct. Mary Vzral died of " stomach trouble " on July 22, 1905. Her life had been insured for eight hundred dollars, of which Billik took seven hundred. Soon after Mary Vzral's death her brother Jerry objected to the constant presence of Billik, and his mother promised to fix it so he would not see the fortune-teller any more. A day or two later Jerry Vzral became ill, but his sister Emma insisted upon calling a physician, and he recovered. The police believed that Billik had not intended to kill the boy, but had administered a small dose of poison to frighten him.

The next death in the Vzral family was that of Tillie, eighteen years old and insured for six hundred and twenty dollars, who succumbed to " stomach trouble " on December 22, 1905. For several months thereafter Billik rested from his labors, and it was not until August 1906 that Rose, fourteen years old and insured for three hundred dollars, died of the same ailment. Three months later Ella died. She was twelve years old and was insured for one hundred and five dollars. After the usual deductions for funeral expenses, the proceeds of all these policies were given to Billik by Mrs. Vzral. With no more insurance in sight, and with the milk business taken over by creditors, Billik persuaded Mrs. Vzral to sell her home. She received for it two thousand nine hundred dollars, and Billik took the money and made a leisurely trip to Buffalo and Niagara Falls. He told Mrs. Vzral that while away he would visit Cleveland and " fix " his mother, and that he would then inherit her fortune.

When Billik returned to Chicago he found the bewildered remnant of the Vzral family, with no money and scarcely any food, waiting to be put out of the home that was no longer theirs. On the night of his arrival Billik called to see Mrs. Vzral. He left her at four o'clock in the morning, and within an hour she was dead of poison.

8

DURING the two years in which Billik preyed upon the Vzral family the people of the neighborhood felt that the Vzrals were experiencing more than their share of misfortune, but no one suspected murder until a girl employed as maid in a North Side home was overheard by her mistress to remark to another servant that " somebody ought to investigate the deaths in that family." The mistress questioned the girl and learned that she had known Mary Vzral, and that Mary had said she was afraid of Billik but was unable to resist him. That night the woman repeated the conversation to her husband, and the husband was so impressed that he told the policeman on the beat. The policeman included it in his daily report, and eventually the report reached Inspector George M. Shippy of the Hyde Park police station, who assigned detectives to make an inquiry.

After a few days' investigation the body of Mary Vzral was exhumed, and chemists who examined the contents of her stomach found five grains of arsenic. Billik was immediately arrested, and in the early summer of 1907 was tried and found guilty of murder in the first degree. In July of that year he was sentenced to death, but reprieved by the Governor, and appeals to various courts, including the Supreme Court of the United States, prevented a final disposition of the case for nearly two years. Meanwhile Billik was held in Cook County Jail, where he was said to be the most popular man, with guards and other prisoners alike, who had ever been confined in the institution.

9

ONE of the unusual features of Billik's case was the extraordinary fight which was waged to save the charlatan's life. The battle was led by a Catholic priest, the Reverend P. J. O'Callaghan of the Paulist Fathers, and a nun, Sister Rose of the Order of the Sacred Heart; by means of mass meetings and private solicitation they raised most of the considerable sums of money required for Billik's legal expenses. The climax of the struggle came in June 1908, just before the appeal to the Supreme Court. A prayer service in Billik's behalf was held by Father O'Callaghan at the County Jail on June 7, at which was witnessed the strange spectacle of four hundred prisoners on their knees beseeching God to save the fortune-teller from the gallows. Another service was held at the jail two days later, at which prayers were offered by Father O'Callaghan, Jerry Vzral, Billik, and Billik's wife and ten-year-old daughter, while many of the prisoners wept and moaned. Billik's cellmate, a notorious burglar named Milwauski, clung to Billik, kissed him repeatedly, and wept openly throughout the long prayers. After the services the prisoners presented flowers to Father O'Callaghan, the jailer, and Sister Rose.

On the 10th of June a petition signed by twenty thousand persons was presented to the State Board of Pardons, and five mass meetings were held in Billik's behalf on the West Side, at which hundreds of women wept and screamed that Billik should not be hanged. At all of the meetings Father O'Callaghan was the principal speaker. Jerry Vzral also spoke, and tearfully declared that he had committed perjury at Billik's trial. Commenting upon the meetings, Inspector Shippy, whose approach to the case was perhaps less emotional than that of some, said: " Billik is a cold-blooded murderer of the worst type, and is simply deceiving the people who are working in his behalf."

Nevertheless, Billik was not hanged. In January 1909, upon recommendation of the Board of Pardons, Governor Charles S. Deneen commuted his sentence to life imprisonment. On February 1 he was transferred to the State Penitentiary at Joliet. He was pardoned by Governor Edward F. Dunne and released from prison on January 4, 1917.

CHAPTER VII

"A REIGN OF TERROR IS UPON THE CITY"

T HE TWENTY years that elapsed between 1890 and 1910 formed one of the most spectacular periods of growth in the history of Chicago; it increased in area to almost two hundred square miles and in number of inhabitants to 2,185,283, a gain of more than a million in the two decades; and it passed Philadelphia to become second only to New York in both population and commercial importance, with daily bank clearings of nearly forty million dollars and taxable property of an estimated value of two billions, five hundred million. " Chicago," said a magazine article in 1910, " is noted for the greatness of its financial institutions, for the excellence of its parks and public playgrounds, for its universities, its efficient public-school system, and for other educational, artistic, and morally uplifting institutions that give to Chicago an enlightened, a cultured, and a progressive citizenship."

But Chicago was also noted for other things — for the magnitude of its crime and sociological problems, for political corruption, for the inefficiency of its Police Department; for the laxity of its building laws, which had terrible consequences on December 30, 1903, when six hundred and two persons died in the Iroquois Theater fire; and for the polyglot character of its population. Unchecked and virtually unregulated, the stream of immigration that was little more than a trickle in the 1890's reached flood proportions during the first ten years of the twentieth century. The good and the bad of Europe poured into Chicago by the thousands, bringing with them their historic customs and hatreds, their feuds and vendettas, their characteristic methods of revenge and reprisal, settling in national groups and in the main resisting the slight efforts which were made to Americanize them. By 1890, of all American cities Chicago had the largest number of Poles, Swedes, Norwegians, Danes, Bohemians, Dutch, Croatians, Slovakians, Lithuanians, and Greeks; it had become the second largest Bohemian city in the world, the third largest Swedish, the third Norwegian, the fourth Polish, and the fifth German.

2

As in previous boom eras, the underworld more than kept pace with other phases of municipal expansion. The two decades into which Chicago crowded such extraordinary population growth and such cultural and commercial progress also saw the partitioning of the city among the powerful gambling syndicates, the perfecting of the unholy alliance between the open brothel and the politicians, a tremendous increase in the power of the saloon-keeper, widespread corruption in the Police Department, the appearance of the Black Hand extortionists and killers in the Italian and Sicilian quarters, and the development of criminal gangs of boys and young men, precursors of the great outlaw organizations of the prohibition epoch. It was these latter elements that were principally responsible for the great outbreak of crime and lawlessness which began in 1902 and continued, with brief periods of subsidence, for half a dozen years, during which conditions in Chicago were almost exactly as they had been in 1857 and immediately following the great fire of 1871, but on an infinitely larger scale. Crime reached unbelievable proportions; literally thousands of burglaries and holdups and hundreds of murders were reported to the police. In one period of six months in 1906 there was a burglary every three hours, a holdup every six hours, and a murder every day.

The newspapers began calling the attention of Chicago's " progressive and enlightened citizenship " to the situation in the early summer of 1903. In the fall of that year several civic organizations announced that they would join the fight against domination by the underworld, and in December a mass meeting of citizens appointed a Committee of Twenty-five and somewhat grandiosely instructed it " to eradicate crime in Chicago." The Citizens' Association procured a hundred and fifty indictments against Mushmouth Johnson and others for operating policy games, but none went to jail. The cartoonist Clare Briggs designed an elaborate suit of armor to be worn by citizens when necessity called them from the shelter of their homes at night, and Mayor Carter Harrison, Jr., seriously suggested that such hardy adventurers " might carry revolvers strapped outside their clothing." The Mayor promised a general cleanup, and the *American* sarcastically advised him to begin by making less flagrant use of the pardoning power vested in his office by the city charter; the newspaper pointed out that in six weeks, from October 1 to November 15, 1903, the Mayor had pardoned a hundred and ten men who had been sentenced to the Bridewell for robbery and other crimes. " Thieves and criminals," said the *American,* " thus are out on the streets plying their trade with revolver and slungshot almost before they have begun serving their sentences." A list was published, showing that many of the men freed had criminal records, and that in most instances the pardons had been requested by aldermen.

On December 7, 1903 the State Board of Pardons did its part toward adding to Chicago's criminal population by pardoning Jimmy Dunlap, for almost forty years one of

America's most celebrated burglars and bank-robbers, who had been sent to the State Penitentiary at Joliet in 1900 to serve a sentence of twenty years. About the same time the newspapers said that Mike Burke, a Chicago product who had stolen half a million dollars during a long and prosperous career as a pickpocket and sneak thief, was returning to Chicago to share in the great harvest of loot. The *American* suggested that a day be set aside to honor these famous citizens and that they be given the freedom of the city, on the ground that they would take it anyway unless it was nailed down. The following entertainment was proposed:

Banquet by the State Board of Pardons.

Luncheon at the Crooks' Club by William A. Pinkerton.

Open Air Reception, by Amalgamated Association of Prominent " Cits."

After the reception, a pageant, with these features in line:

Bank Robbers' Concert Band.

State Board of Pardons and James Dunlap on float, representing the onward march of progress.

Bandits' Fife and Drum Corps.

Mike Burke in a carriage, upon which are pinned watches, money, rings, diamonds, and purses he has stolen.

Confidence Men's Brass Band.

Local Order No. 326 of Citizens Who Have Been Robbed.

Prominent Burglars and Confidence Men in Buses.

Thugs on Horseback.

Authors of Dime Novels on Foot.

The Board of Aldermen suspended its own extensive grafting operations long enough in the late fall of 1903 to appoint a commission to investigate allegations of graft in the Police Department and to expose rumored collusion with the saloon interests and the underworld. The commission sat for weeks and heard millions of words of testimony. Eventually it revoked a few saloon licenses and made examples of a few policemen. In general, the police were exonerated, and shining with a fresh coat of whitewash the high officials of the department boasted that they would soon drive every known criminal out of Chicago; in statements to the newspapers they claimed that the city had the finest police organization in the United States. But their boasting dwindled to pained squeaks on March 19, 1904, when the papers published the preliminary report of Captain Alexander Piper, a former United States Army officer and later Deputy Police Commissioner of New York, who slipped into Chicago with a squad of New York detectives and made an exhaustive study of the police force at the behest of the City Club. Captain Piper's report declared that Chicago had many honest, capable, and intelligent policemen, but that as a whole the force was both inefficient and insufficient, with ten per cent of its personnel either decrepit or too fat for active service, and another hundred unfit by reason of viciousness and bad habits. There was practically no discipline, no protection was given pedestrians, and no pretense was made of handling traffic. The report said that many policemen were afraid of thieves, that many lacked sufficient intelligence to cope with crooks, that many shirked their duty, that the entire force was slouchy in appearance, that many loafed and drank in saloons while on duty, and that many were in collusion with saloon-keepers. Captain Piper's investigation found but one policeman whose uniform looked neat and clean, and of all of those found drinking, only one paid for his drink. The report recommended that a thousand men between the ages of twenty-one and twenty-five be added to the police force immediately, and that another thousand be added within two years.

DURING the last two months of 1905 and the first two of 1906 the crime wave reached its crest; the average citizen, and especially the average woman, was probably in greater danger of being robbed and murdered than at any other time in the history of Chicago. This was particularly true on the North Side, where for reasons never explained the number of policemen on duty had been reduced by one-half within less than ten years, although the growth of the district had been phenomenal. With nothing to stop them, bands of thugs and hoodlums prowled the streets from dusk to dawn. They robbed every pedestrian they encountered, and many of these holdups were remarkable for brutality; sometimes the footpads stripped their victims, tied them to lamp posts, and cut shallow slits in their flesh with razors and knives. They broke into stores and residences, held sex orgies and drinking parties on the lawns and porches of private homes, and pursued every woman they saw. If they caught her, she was dragged into an alley and raped. If she attempted to defend herself, she was beaten, in many instances fatally.

In the twenty-four hours which ended at ten p.m. on January 6, 1906, Chicago's crime record included four murders, seven suicides, and ten deaths from bomb explosions and other forms of violence. From July 26, 1905 to January 13, 1906, fifty-four homicides were reported. Twenty of the victims were women, all of whom had been criminally attacked either before or after death. The last of this series of murders was the brutal killing of Mrs. Frank C. Hollister, the wife of a printing-plant owner and a woman of considerable social prominence on the North Side, who left her home on the late afternoon of January 12 to sing at a funeral. She was found next day in a trash pile behind a fence on Belden Avenue. She had been raped, strangled with a coil of copper wire, and her body pounded almost to a pulp.

The murder of Mrs. Hollister threw the North Side into the most widespread panic that the district had experienced since the terrible days of the great fire. Many families abandoned their homes and sought refuge in downtown hotels; hundreds of others talked of leaving the city altogether. Women were afraid to leave their homes even in the broad light of day; after dark they cowered behind the protection of locked and barricaded doors and windows. In many residences lights burned throughout the night, and men remained on guard until dawn. Every stranger who rang a doorbell or passed through an alley was suspected, and the utilities companies canceled the regular tours of their inspectors and meter-readers after several had been shot at by frightened householders. The Chicago *Tribune* declared that " A reign of terror is upon the city . . . no city in time of peace ever held so high a place in the category of crime-ridden, terrorized, murder-breeding cities as is now held by Chicago." A report of the Cook County Grand Jury said that " it is our deliberate judgment that such a brazen exhibition of lawlessness cannot continue without official connivance." Mrs. W. C. H. Keough, a member of the Board of Education, said in the *Tribune*:

> " Hunting women and hitting them on the head with a piece of gas pipe seems to be the favorite sport of the Chicago man. The man lies in wait for his prey as an East Indian hunter awaits the approach of a tigress. It is considered rare evidence of sportsmanship to capture the prey near her home, just as it is regarded as proof of supreme skill when the hunter slays the tigress near her lair."

Throughout the city ministers prayed for divine protection for Chicago's women and children, and their congregations adopted resolutions demanding that the police curb the activities of the criminals. Committees were appointed to bring the resolutions to the notice of city officials. Mass meetings were held on both the North and West Sides, at one of which a speaker declared that " it has come to a point where no one is safe, especially our wives and children." In Garfield Park, on the West Side, a Law and Order League was organized at a meeting of a hundred and fifty representatives of fifty churches and half a dozen civic bodies, and committees were appointed to study all phases of the situation. The Police Committee of the City Council voted to add five hundred men to the force, but did nothing about weeding out incompetent officers or increasing efficiency. A mass meeting of citizens organized the Law Enforcement League, and in a stirring speech the Reverend W. H. Burns declared: " Chicago is worse than it has been since 1879. In those days I saw two men hanged to lamp posts, and it did some good, too." Another mass meeting, held at the Auditorium Hotel, appointed a committee to confer with Mayor Edward F. Dunne and Chief of Police John M. Collins. The North Shore Club also appointed a committee. The city fairly swarmed with committees, all furiously adopting resolutions and issuing statements.

But in two sections of the North Side there was action which, in connection with increased police activity, drove the worst of the criminals out of that district and brought about a gradual subsidence of the crime wave. In both Sheridan Park and Buena Park mass meetings appointed Vigilance Committees, which set briskly to work with a minimum of hullabaloo. In both sections protective patrol systems were organized, and the streets were patrolled night and day by private detectives heavily armed and clad in distinctive uniforms. Women who found it necessary to leave their homes were asked to notify the headquarters of the patrol services, which provided armed and uniformed escorts. No woman was attacked and no pedestrian was robbed in Sheridan Park or in Buena Park after these measures went into effect; a man with a gun was something the underworld could understand.

4

T H E most vicious of the thugs and hoodlums who terrorized Chicago around the turn of the twentieth century came from two districts — the thirty-eighth police precinct on the North Side, and the twenty-second precinct on the West Side. The thirty-eighth was south of Division Street and north and east of the Chicago River. It had a population of about thirty-two thousand, and four hundred saloons, or approximately one to every eighty inhabitants, and probably half that many blind pigs. The worst of these dives were in a section called Little Hell, a network of brothels, low hotels, concert saloons, and grog-shops between La Salle Street and the river. One of the hotels in Little Hell catered exclusively to male degenerates. Another was patronized only by dope addicts, and cocaine and morphine were sold openly over the desk. In virtually every resort knives and revolvers could be rented by the hour, and men could be found who were willing to commit any sort of crime for a few cents. In the first fifty-one days of 1906 the police of the thirty-eighth precinct made nearly nine hundred arrests, of which more than a hundred were for such serious offenses as murder, rape, burglary, and shooting and stabbing affrays. Ten times that many arrests would have been made if the area had been properly patrolled.

But the thirty-eighth precinct, despite the manifold villainies of Little Hell, was a paradise compared to the twenty-second, which was sometimes called the Maxwell Street district but was more commonly known as Bloody Maxwell. About two miles long and one mile wide, Bloody

Maxwell was bounded on the north by Harrison Street, on the west by Wood Street, on the south by Sixteenth Street, and on the east by the south branch of the Chicago River. It included the " dark river wards," the Ghetto, the Italian and Bohemian quarters, and large colonies of Russians, Lithuanians, Greeks, Poles, Irish, and Germans, with a total population of more than two hundred thousand and proportionately more saloons than any other district in the city. The precinct police station was on Maxwell Street three blocks west of Halsted, and " on all sides of the station," said the Chicago *Tribune*, " are corners, saloons and houses that have seen the rise, the operations, and often the death of some of the worst criminals the land has ever known." Two blocks from the station was the corner of Sangamon Street and Fourteenth Place, for more than twenty-five years notorious as the original Dead Man's Corner. More policemen were killed there by criminals, and more criminals by policemen, than at any other locality in Chicago.

At the southern end of Bloody Maxwell, on Johnson Street, was the Walsh School, a public institution and the scene of one of the most remarkable feuds in American annals — a war between rival gangs of schoolboys that started in 1881 and continued for almost thirty years, during which time several were killed and at least a score were shot or stabbed, or seriously injured by brickbats and clubs. The gangs called themselves the Irishers and the Bohemians, and allegiance was determined, not by nationality, but by place of residence; the boys who lived east of Johnson Street were Irishers, and those who lived west of Johnson were Bohemians. For years the boys carried knives and revolvers to school, and occasionally slashed and took pot shots at each other in the class-rooms, and fought desperate and often bloody battles in the streets and playgrounds. The last of the gun-fights occurred in December 1905, when some twenty-five Irishers led by Mike and George McGinnis, who were also co-captains of a smaller gang called the Twins, marched against an equal number of Bohemians commanded by Joe Fischer. Between forty and fifty shots were fired before the police arrived, but no one was hit. The age of the young gangsters ranged from ten to fifteen years, and many were so small that both hands were required to lift a revolver to firing position. For several years after the 1905 battle every boy who attended Walsh School was searched before being permitted to enter the building.

The Chicago *Tribune,* on February 11, 1906, described Bloody Maxwell as " the wickedest police district in the world." It continued:

" It is more than this. It is the most cosmopolitan police district in the world. Within its borders are to be found a greater variety of people and more different kinds of living than in any other similar district in the world. It is a division of the city composed of sections of dozens of European and even Asiatic cities . . . [it] is the crime center of the country. . . . Murderers, robbers and thieves of the worst kind are here born, reared and grow to maturity in numbers that far exceed the record of any similar district anywhere on the face of the globe. Reveling in the freedom which comes from inadequate police control, inspired by the traditions of criminals that have gone before in the district, living in many instances more like beasts than like human beings, hundreds and thousands of boys and men follow day after day and year after year in the bloody ways of crime. . . .

" Murders by the score, shooting and stabbing affrays by the hundreds, assaults, burglaries and robberies by the thousands — such is the crime record each year for this festering place of evil which lies a scant mile from the heart of great Chicago. . . . Murderers,

213

robbers, burglars, thieves, pickpockets, and criminals of all sorts are bred here with a facility that is appalling. . . . From Maxwell come some of the worst murderers, if not actually the worst, that Chicago has ever seen. From Maxwell come the 'smoothest' robbers, burglars and thieves of all kinds; from Maxwell come the worst tough 'gangs.' In general, it may be safely said that no police district in the world turns out such skilled and successful criminals, and certainly none turns out criminals of any kind in such numbers as are produced here. . . ."

The area which later became known as Bloody Maxwell was a " terror district," swarming with hoodlums, cop-fighters, footpads, burglars, and other criminals, as early as the middle 1850's. It continued to be Chicago's foremost crime nursery for almost three-quarters of a century, although there was a brief period in the 1880's when the police under Captain Simon O'Donnell, working out of the old Twelfth Street station, reduced the district, as John J. Flinn put it in his history of the Chicago police, " to a condition bordering upon respectability " by literally clubbing the underworld into submission. But Captain O'Donnell was soon transferred, and Bloody Maxwell immediately relapsed into its former state of riotous upheaval. Until half a dozen years after the great fire of 1871 the population was predominantly Irish, and the hoodlums possessed all the legendary combativeness of that race; life in Bloody Maxwell was one continuous fight. The general tendency was to go it alone; Irish ruffians of the old days scorned to call for help unless they were fighting the police or were attacked by far superior numbers. They began to form into gangs to combat what they considered to be the menace of the German and Jewish invasion of the district in the 1870's and the 1880's, and the German and Jewish rowdies and criminals organized in self-defense, as did those of other nationalities. For several years racial and national lines were strictly drawn, but in time origins came to make little difference; there were many gangs with members from half a dozen countries. Until the late 1890's, however, leadership was generally held by Irishmen.

The most dangerous of the gangs that flourished in Bloody Maxwell during the last fifteen years of the nineteenth century were the Johnson Street gang, captained by Buff Higgins, with Red Gary and Johnny Mortell as lieutenants; the Henry Street gang, which, under the leadership of the redoubtable Chris Merry, who was hanged for kicking his invalid wife to death, once fought a two-hour pistol battle with a posse of policemen; the Mortell-McGraw combination, commanded by Bill Mortell, who eventually went to prison for a long term, and Jack McGraw, who reformed and thereafter led a peaceful and prosperous life as a bricklayer; and the McGanns, composed of Jimmy McGann, who had only one leg but was remarkably agile, and his five sons. McGann and his rowdy progeny were successful thieves and cop-fighters for many years, but in 1903, when the Chicago *Journal* took stock of the family, one of the sons was in the Reformatory, one in the House of Correction, one in the State Penitentiary, one in the Cook County Jail, and one was dead, killed by his father in a drunken brawl.

Of equal importance, though in a different category, was an extraordinary thieving outfit variously known as the Weiss gang and the White gang, which came into existence in 1866 when the six sons and two daughters of Widow Margaret Weiss of Maxwell Street all married into the Renich family of ten daughters and two sons. The children of these unions likewise intermarried, and by the late 1890's, with various cousins and other relatives, they formed a tribe of more than a hundred persons, all of whom were said by the police to be criminals, and about twenty of whom were in prison. For many years the general head-quarters of the gang was an isolated house on Cooper Street in Lake View, from which the police frequently removed wagonloads of stolen property. The titular leaders in the 1890's were George and Mary Miller, but the brains of the tribe was Mrs. Renich's sister, Eva Gussler, better known as Eva the Cow, who was one of the most expert pickpockets and shoplifters that ever operated in Chicago. Eva the Cow planned and directed the thieving enterprises in which the gang engaged, and also had charge of the young, who were taught to steal as soon as they were able to walk. One of the unusual methods by which children of the tribe were used in shoplifting was discovered in 1903, when the police arrested Mary Boston and her five-year-old niece in a department store. Mrs. Boston wore a very ample dress with large pockets sewed into the lining, and as she moved slowly about the store the little girl walked along under her skirts. When the woman saw something she wished to steal, she unostentatiously knocked it off a counter to the floor, and the child picked it up and put it in one of the pockets.

A criminologist who examined Chris Merry after he had finally been locked up described him as " the choicest flower ever garnered from this field of crime." But " this," said the Chicago *Tribune,* " was sarcasm. Merry was one of the worst criminals that ever lived in Chicago." Actually, Merry's criminal record was surpassed by many, but it is doubtful if Bloody Maxwell or any other section of the city ever produced a more ferocious rough-and-tumble fighter. He was admirably fitted, both by temperament and by physique, for this popular sport; few men possessed sufficient courage to withstand the rush of his heavy, bull-necked figure, with its enormously long arms, huge hands and feet, and dish face, in which were set a button nose and pig-like eyes. Habitually Merry was sullen and morose, but he was subject to terrible fits of anger on little or no provoca-

216

tion. At such times, as the *Tribune* said, " he became a demon unleashed, and acted more like a mad animal than like a human being." In action, Merry continually snarled and grunted; he fought with teeth, fists, feet, and any other weapon that came to hand, and permanently disfigured many men who had dared stand up against him. The police generally let him alone, but when it did become necessary to bring him in, a squad of six or eight men was sent to accomplish the task.

Ostensibly Merry was a peddler, but the wagon which he drove about Bloody Maxwell was little more than a receptacle for stolen goods and a means of flight. Emboldened by his prowess and the widespread fear with which he was regarded, the Henry Street gang became the most successful thieving outfit in the district; Merry and his men frequently drove along Maxwell and Halsted Streets in broad daylight, boldly taking what they wanted from stores and outside stands and throwing the articles into the peddler's wagon. To a large extent, however, the gang specialized in stealing " silk," which in the gangland of those days meant anything that might be found in a tailor's shop — buttons, thread, bolts of cloth, trimming, clothing, even sewing-machines and pressing-irons. Merry is also said to have introduced, at least into Bloody Maxwell, a form of robbery known as the " kick-in," the essentials of which were used with great success in later years by John Dillinger and other noted outlaws. With half a dozen gangsters in his wagon, Merry would drive up to a previously selected shop or store. One man remained on the wagon with the reins in his hands and two stood guard with revolvers on the sidewalk, threatening pedestrians and watching for the police, while Merry kicked in the door of the store with his big feet and carried out the loot. Then the thieves escaped in the wagon, exactly as Dillinger made his getaway in an automobile.

Buff Higgins was a typical product of Bloody Maxwell. He never did a day's work in his life, but lived on the proceeds of burglaries, gang stealings and holdups, and when he was not occupied in crime he loafed in saloons and brothels. He preceded Merry by several years, and his reputation as a fighter never equaled that of the troglodytic Chris, but in his time he was regarded by the police as one of the most dangerous criminals of the district. Stories of his doings are still to be heard among the old-timers of Maxwell Street, but several men who had known him well told a reporter for the *Tribune* in 1906 that he was " an arrant coward at heart, and only succeeded in being a bad man because of his readiness to use the revolver when things threatened to go against him." He always carried two guns, and was an excellent shot.

Higgins was born in Ireland in 1871 and was brought to the United States by his parents when he was two years old. In 1874 the family moved to Chicago and settled on Johnson Street, in the Maxwell district. Buff attended the Walsh School for several years, and in the early 1880's was one of the captains of the Irishers; he led those juvenile desperadoes in several forays against the Bohemians. He quit school when he was about thirteen years old, and organized a boys' gang which broke windows, robbed fruit stands, stoned peddlers, and tormented merchants. By the time he was fifteen, Buff Higgins was an accomplished thief and a familiar figure in the saloons and bawdy houses, and at eighteen he was the acknowledged leader of the Johnson Street gang. Higgins was active as a gangster king for some five years; he committed innumerable burglaries and holdups, killed at least two men, and wounded half a dozen others, including two or three policemen. He was frequently arrested, but merchants and others whom he had robbed and the men he had shot refused to testify against him for fear of reprisals by his fellow gangsters. He was never in really serious trouble until the early morning of September 3, 1893, when he broke into the home of Peter McCooey at No. 153 Johnson Street. With him were Red Gary and Johnny Mortell, the latter " a notorious character " who was sentenced to life imprisonment in 1880 for killing a policeman, but was paroled within two years by the sympathetic State Board of Pardons.

The three men entered McCooey's bedroom after filling a bag with plunder from other parts of the house, and Higgins was rifling a pair of trousers when McCooey suddenly awoke and jumped out of bed. Higgins promptly shot him. McCooey, who had known Higgins, lived long enough to name his murderer, and the burglars were arrested after a desperate fight with a squad of police. Gary and Mortell were sent to prison, but Higgins was convicted of murder in the first degree. On March 23, 1894, in his twenty-third year, he was hanged in the Cook County Jail.

As organized criminal combinations the Johnson Street, Henry Street, and Mortell-McGraw gangs vanished with the death or imprisonment of their leaders, but scores of other gangs continued to make Bloody Maxwell as much of a terror district as it had ever been while under the sway of Chris Merry and Buff Higgins. Chief among these outfits were the Daly gang, with headquarters in Maxwell Street, which was broken up in 1905 when the police arrested Tom and Jack Daly and sent them to Joliet for burglary; the Forty-Two's, of Taylor Street, originally a neighborhood play group which in time became a notorious gang of pickpockets, automobile-strippers, and window-smashing burglars; and the Valley gang of Fifteenth Street, which was organized in the middle 1890's in the area just south of the Ghetto and was in existence for some forty years.

The first important leaders of the Valley gang were Big Heinie Miller and Jimmy Farley, expert pickpockets and burglars, who flourished in the early 1900's. They went to the penitentiary in 1905, together with two other members of the gang, Tootsie Bill Hughes and Cooney the Fox, who were described by the police as the smoothest thieves that ever worked in the Maxwell Street district. After the arrest of Miller and Farley the gang was captained for sev-

THE HANGING OF BUFF HIGGINS

eral years by Red Bolton, who likewise ended his career in the state prison, serving a life sentence for murder. Bolton was succeeded by Paddy Ryan, better known as Paddy the Bear, a red-faced, waddling obscenity — he was only a little more than five feet tall and weighed more than two hundred pounds — who ran a dingy saloon in South Halsted Street and was one of the most feared men in the history of Bloody Maxwell. He was assassinated in 1920 by Walter Quinlan, called the Runt, who had usurped the wife of an imprisoned gangster and for this breach of etiquette had been terrifically beaten. The Runt served a few years in prison, and when he was released opened a saloon at Seventeenth and Loomis Streets which became a rendezvous for gangsters and trigger-men. In one raid on the Runt's saloon the police confiscated a dozen automatic pistols, ten bullet-proof vests, and two machine-guns. The Runt was finally killed by Paddy the Bear's son, Paddy the Fox.

The most successful chieftains of the Valley gang were Terry Druggan and Frankie Lake, renowned beer barons of the prohibition era. Under their leadership the gang concentrated its efforts on bootlegging and rum-running, and eventually controlled a string of breweries. The leaders made millions, and even their lowliest retainers, as they often boasted, "wore silk shirts and rode in Rolls-Royce automobiles." In 1924, for refusing to answer questions put to them by Judge James Wilkerson of the United States District Court, Druggan and Lake were sentenced to a year's imprisonment for contempt of court. Several months later a newspaper reporter called at the county jail to see Druggan, but when he asked for the gangster he was told:

" Mr. Druggan is not in today."

" Then I'll talk to Frankie Lake," said the reporter.

" Mr. Lake also had an appointment downtown," the jailer said. " They will be back after dinner."

The dazed newspaper man returned to his office, and an investigation disclosed that both Druggan and Lake, in return for twenty thousand dollars in bribes, as they testified later, had been given extraordinary privileges. Supposedly incarcerated and treated the same as other prisoners, they had actually spent much more time in Loop restaurants and in their own luxurious apartments than in jail; they had been permitted to come and go as they pleased, and the death cell of the jail had been turned into a private office where they received their gangsters and issued their orders. As a result of the exposures, Sheriff Peter Hoffman and Jailer Wesley Westbrook were each sentenced to three months in jail for contempt of court.

5

BLOODY MAXWELL and the thirty-eighth police precinct were the most prolific of Chicago's crime-breeding areas, but they were only two out of many. Criminal gangs developed in and dominated every slum district in the city — there were the Market Streeters at Market Street and Chicago Avenue, the Car Barn Bandits on Monticello Avenue near the Chicago River, the Briscoe gang on Fortieth Street, the Feinberg gang on Twenty-third Street, the Formby gang on Fullerton Street, the Brady gang on Milwaukee Avenue, the Trilby gang at Carroll Avenue and Elizabeth Street, the Kinzie, Morgan, Austin, and Green Street gangs, and a hundred others besides. The Chicago *Tribune* made a careful study of conditions early in 1906 and arrived at a conclusion strangely similar to that reached by the newspapers and law-enforcement agencies twenty years later, when Al Capone was at the height of his power. Said the *Tribune*:

> " Chicago is gang-ridden to such extremes that the safety of life, property and happiness are only proverbs, and, like many proverbs, absolutely untrue, and the real facts are that life, property and happiness are only safe when they are protected by locality, strength of arm, or firearms. Chicago is infested by gangs of hoodlums to whom the law is a thing to mock at and by whom the revolver and bullet and the strong arm of the officer are the only things that are feared, and who, after dark in every locality, and through the day time in many localities, menace the decent citizen's life and belongings

at every step. Chicago is terrorized by . . . criminals who have helped to make the name ' Chicago ' a byword for crime-breeding throughout the country."

The most appalling aspects of the situation as disclosed by the *Tribune* were the youth of the gangsters and the tender age at which boys of the slum areas became involved in activities which led straight to criminal careers. " It is not unusual," said the *Tribune,* " for a boy six years old to be arrested for a serious offense. Boys who should be at home learning their ABC's are often found armed with cheap revolvers and knives. At Maxwell Street station the arrests of boys under sixteen average nearly sixty a month. Most of these arrests are for larceny or burglary. Some are for holdups." Scarcely any of the thugs captured by the police during the lawless years of the early 1900's were as old as twenty-five years; most of them were between seventeen and twenty-two, and the average was about twenty. One of the most vicious groups of the period, the Formby gang, was led by three boys — David Kelly, Bill Dulfer, and Jimmy Formby — whose ages were respectively sixteen, seventeen, and eighteen. Formby and Dulfer were the gunmen of the gang. Formby killed a street-car conductor in the summer of 1904, and Dulfer killed two men while robbing a saloon. Afterward he boasted that he had shot both his victims at the same time. " I didn't even have to aim to hit 'em," he said. " Just held a gun in each hand and let go. They both came down. I saw 'em fall, that was all I wanted." When Formby was arrested he asked the police to charge him with murder instead of robbery. " I'm a killer," he said, " not a robber."

6

O F all the early twentieth-century gangsters in Chicago the most spectacular, and the ones who received the greatest measure of publicity, were Gustave Marx, Harvey Van Dine, and Peter Neidermeyer, who called themselves the Automatic Trio, but were better known to the police and to the newspaper-reading public as the Car Barn Bandits. From July 8 to November 27, 1903, these boys — Marx and Neidermeyer were each twenty-three years old and Van Dine was twenty-one — killed eight men, including two detectives, wounded five others, and committed eight robberies, the proceeds of which amounted to less than twenty-four hundred dollars. There was a fourth member of the gang, Emil Roeski, a loutish sort of fellow who wouldn't sleep in a bed or use a knife and fork. Roeski fetched and carried for the Automatic Trio; he killed no one, and touched very little of the stolen money. " I never got much," he said after he had been arrested. " They used to buy me something to eat and give me a few nickels once in a while."

The development of Marx, Van Dine, and Neidermeyer conformed to an all too familiar pattern. Together with Roeski, they were born and reared in the slum districts of the northwestern part of the city, near the yards of the Northwestern Railroad, where, as the *Tribune* said, " the streets are ill-kept, the houses congested, and the corner saloon, with its cheap whisky and cheaper beer, furnishes the great, the popular, and practically the only source of amusement and recreation to the male element of the population." Marx's father was a fairly prosperous truck farmer, and the parents of Van Dine and Neidermeyer were laborers, poor but respectable. The boys were kept in school until they had graduated from the grammar grades, and apparently were then permitted to go their own ways. Instead of trying to find work or complete their education, they took to the streets and joined the Monticello Pleasure and Athletic Club, a gang of youthful thieves and rowdies which maintained headquarters in the cellar of an abandoned building on Monticello Avenue near the north branch of the Chicago River. Roeski also joined the club, but quit after a year or so and went to work in a brewery.

By virtue of their superior education and a natural aptitude for leadership, Marx, Van Dine, and Neidermeyer soon dominated the Monticellos, and led the young ruffians on innumerable thieving expeditions, raiding fruit and vegetable stands, clothes-lines, and unattended wagons, and stealing practically everything they could carry away. They became heroes among the other boys when they broke into a new building in the neighborhood and stole a large quantity of lead pipe and brass fittings, which they sold for more than a hundred dollars. They were arrested for this, but the evidence against them was insufficient, and they were quickly released. As they grew older, their crimes became more serious; they began to hold up pedestrians, to commit burglaries and rob stores, and to pick pockets and snatch an occasional pocketbook. They continued to live at home, and explained their wealth of pocket money by saying that they were " working for a man." Apparently their parents suspected nothing, although after the boys had been captured both Mrs. Van Dine and Mrs. Neidermeyer said that they had often begged their sons to lead better lives. Mrs. Marx blamed everything on " dime novels, whisky, cigarets and evil associates."

In the summer of 1903 the Automatic Trio decided to become big-time bandits. They bought a dozen pistols and some three hundred rounds of ammunition, and prepared a hideaway, a dugout in the Indiana sand dunes about two miles from Miller's Station, on the Pennsylvania Railroad. They asked Roeski to join them, and, as he put it, " I wasn't getting much wages, so I quit my job and they fixed me out with guns."

The first of a series of crimes which were to make the four boys, for a few months, the most important criminals in Chicago was committed on July 8, 1903 — the robbery

225

of the Clybourne Junction station of the Northwestern Railroad. They stole seventy dollars, and Neidermeyer shot, but didn't kill, the station agent.

On July 9 they held up the saloon of Ernest Spires at No. 1820 North Ashland Avenue, and killed a boy named Otto Bauder, who became frightened and tried to run behind the bar. "We cleared $2.35 out of that place," said Van Dine. "Shooting came cheap."

On July 10 and 12 they robbed saloons in Addison Street and Sheffield Avenue. Total proceeds from the two jobs, twenty-five dollars.

On July 20 the bandits held up the saloon of Peter Gorski at No. 2611 Milwaukee Avenue. Van Dine shot Gorski, who fell to the floor and pretended to be dead until the boys had departed with twenty dollars taken from the till. A few days later Gorski identified as his assailant a man who had been arrested for prowling around the Northwestern railroad yards. When Van Dine was told of the identification he said to the detectives: "That only goes to show, gentlemen, how positively foolish some of you can be."

On August 2 the Automatic Trio held up the saloon of Benjamin C. LaGross, at No. 2120 West North Avenue. Van Dine killed LaGross and Adolph Johnson, a customer. "I had two guns in my hands," said Van Dine, "and covered LaGross and Johnson. I let 'em have both guns at once and Johnson fell, hit in the stomach. LaGross got to the door and I gave him another shot. He dropped in the doorway. Then I went home. I slept fine. We got eight dollars out of that haul. We killed two men — four dollars apiece."

On August 30 the bandits stole $2,250 from the car barns of the Chicago City Railway Company at State and Sixty-first Streets. They also killed James B. Johnson, a motorman, and Francis W. Stewart, a clerk. Van Dine said that after this robbery they ran out of the car barn through the washroom and across a vacant lot, and then walked to

Jackson Park, a few blocks away, where they sat and talked for several hours. At daybreak they crawled into a clump of bushes and divided the money. Roeski's share was five dollars and the promise of food until the next robbery.

As far as the Chicago police could learn, these were the only crimes in which Marx, Van Dine, Neidermeyer, and Roeski were implicated, although in his confession Neidermeyer asserted that they had held up a stagecoach and a gambling-house in Nevada, in which one man was killed; and an Illinois Central railroad train near Paducah, Kentucky. But the Nevada and Kentucky authorities had no record of such robberies. Neidermeyer also said that he had stolen a large quantity of dynamite in Nevada and had brought it back to Chicago to " blow up some places." But he couldn't remember where he had hidden the explosive, and the police doubted if he had ever possessed it.

7

D U R I N G most of the three months that followed the car barn holdup the young thugs devoted themselves to spending the stolen money, principally on women and liquor. Meanwhile detectives were searching all over Chicago, and in time heard of the three young men who seemed to have much larger bank-rolls than their positions in the economic scale would justify. Inquiry disclosed the fact that they bore bad reputations, that their families were poor, that they had never worked, and that they had no way of getting money except by stealing. About the middle of November Herman W. Schuettler, Assistant Chief of Police, ordered Marx, Van Dine, and Neidermeyer brought in for questioning, and on the night of November 21 Detectives John Quinn and William Blake found Marx drinking in a saloon at Addison and Roscoe Streets. When Quinn put his hand on Marx's shoulder and said: " The Chief wants to talk to you," the bandit immediately drew two revolvers and began shooting. Quinn was killed in the first blast, but Blake shot Marx in the right leg, whereupon Marx threw down his guns and surrendered. But he protested bitterly when he was locked up in the Sheffield Avenue police station.

"You can't do anything to me," he cried. "I only shot a cop! Anybody's got a right to shoot a cop!"

Neidermeyer and Van Dine hung about the neighborhood of the station for several days after the arrest of Marx, planning to dynamite the building and rescue their comrade. But their plans were changed when they read in the newspapers on November 25 that Marx had confessed; they rented a room across the street, overlooking the entrance of the Sheffield station, and throughout that day and the next Van Dine sat at the window with a rifle in his hands. He had read that the police intended to take Marx to police headquarters, and he was waiting for Marx to come through the doorway. He intended to shoot his erstwhile pal "because he was a dirty squealer."

In the late afternoon of November 25 Van Dine abandoned his vigil, and with Roeski and Neidermeyer sought refuge in the dugout in the Indiana sand dunes. When he was asked later how he managed to get out of Chicago, Van Dine said with a grin: "Why, we went right down through the center of the city and took an electric car to East Chicago. From there we walked." While the three bandits were en route to Indiana, Marx was telling the police of the hideaway, and on the early morning of November 27 ten detectives and uniformed men, armed with rifles and revolvers, went out to East Chicago, crossed the state line into Indiana, and deployed among the sand dunes, where they were joined by several posses of farmers who had read in the newspapers that the thugs were supposed to be hiding in the neighborhood of Miller's Station. By nine o'clock the dugout had been found and surrounded, and a pistol battle ensued in which all three of the bandits, as well as Detective Joseph D. Driscoll and Detective Sergeant Matthew Zimmer, were wounded. Driscoll was seriously hurt and died four days later.

After some fifty shots had been fired, Roeski, Van Dine, and Neidermeyer left the dugout and, with pistols blazing in each hand, raced across the dunes and into a patch of woods. Policemen and farmers pursued them, but, as Roeski put it, "they had a scare to come near." Roeski, who had been shot in the stomach and was in considerable pain, left his companions in the woods and made his way along the tracks to the railroad station at Aetna, Indiana, where he collapsed on a bench and waited for the police. Van Dine and Neidermeyer went on to the village of East Tolleston, where they found a gravel train, with steam up, waiting on a siding while the engineer finished a cup of coffee. The two boys boarded the engine and pointed revolvers at the fireman, and Neidermeyer shot and killed a brakeman, L. J. Sova, who clambered over the tender and grabbed his arm. "He tried to take my gun away from me," said Neidermeyer later, "and I'm a bad man when anyone tries to do that."

The bandits compelled the fireman to uncouple the locomotive and run it two miles down the siding to East Liverpool, where further progress was stopped by a locked switch. They tried to smash the mechanism of the switch, but failed, so they abandoned the engine and ran across a stretch of prairie into a cornfield, where they encountered a posse of farmers armed with shotguns and surrendered without firing a shot. They were disarmed and turned over to the police.

Roeski, Neidermeyer, and Van Dine were brought back to Chicago on a special train. Assistant Chief Schuettler had planned to take them to an isolated police station where detectives could question them in private, but was ordered by Mayor Carter Harrison, Jr., to bring the prisoners to the office of Chief of Police Francis O'Neill. At the Archer Avenue railroad station the bandits were met by two wagon-loads of uniformed policemen and were escorted in style to the City Hall, where several thousand curiosity-seekers awaited them. In Chief O'Neill's office, crowded with police-men, newspaper reporters, and city officials, the bandits were treated more like conquering heroes or visiting celebrities than like desperate criminals. They were formally presented to Mayor Harrison, the Chief of Police himself tenderly washed Van Dine's face so he could have his picture taken, and the bandits beamed with pride as they listened to the ex-cited gabble about their great courage and extraordinary marksmanship, especially that of Van Dine. " He's a great shot," said a detective. " Zimmer was behind a tree, and Van Dine got him twice."

" I could have killed a dozen men," said Van Dine, " if there had been any pleasure in it."

After the wave of admiration had subsided, the three boys talked of their crimes with much boasting and great bravado, an attitude which they maintained throughout the trials which began in January 1904. Van Dine in particular seemed to look upon the trial as a show in which he was the principal actor; he strutted at every opportunity, and on the witness stand bragged that he was a bad man and a crack pistol-shot. On the third day of the trial he drew, for the delectation of the reporters and court attendants, three graves with headstones, on which he lettered these inscrip-tions:

Here Lies the Notorias Gus Marx, Desperado. Died Mar. 1st, 1904.
Here Lies the Famous Dead Shot, Peter Neider-meyer, aged 23. Died Mar. 1st, 1904.
Here Lies the Red Crook, Harvey Van Dine, aged 21. Died With His Boots on Mar. 1st, 1904.

Van Dine's prediction was correct, except as to time. The trial jury returned a verdict of guilty on March 12, 1904, and on April 22 Van Dine, Marx, and Neidermeyer were hanged in the county jail. Roeski, tried separately, was likewise convicted, but was sentenced to imprisonment for life. He was transferred to Joliet on the day that his comrades died on the gallows.

8

T H E Black Hand first became prominently identified with Chicago crime in the middle 1890's. Its depredations were confined almost entirely to the Italian and Sicilian settlements of Oak and West Taylor Streets and Grand and Wentworth Avenue, where it was a source of great terror for more than thirty years. During that time some four hundred murders were ascribed to the Black Hand by the police and by various organizations which were formed to combat the outlaws. The focal point of this activity was the intersection of Milton and Oak Streets, in the heart of Little Italy, where so many murders were committed that the locality became popularly known as Death Corner. This was the favorite slaughtering-place of a professional assassin called the Shotgun Man, who was believed to have been responsible for at least one-third of the thirty-eight unsolved Italian and Sicilian killings which occurred between January 1, 1910 and March 26, 1911. Four of the Shotgun Man's victims were killed in a single seventy-two-hour period of March 1911.

There were probably between sixty and eighty Black Hand gangs at work in Chicago during the first two decades of the twentieth century, but all of them appear to have been independent units; no two were ever found to be connected. Despite the magnitude of Black Hand operations, none of the extensive investigations undertaken by the police of

Chicago and other American municipalities disclosed a Black Hand organization of international, national, or even city-wide proportions. As the noted criminologist John Landesco said in the Illinois Crime Survey, the Black Hand was " only a method, a *modus operandi.*" It was used by individuals, by small groups, and by large and well-organized gangs; in Italy and Sicily it had been employed for generations by bands of the Mafia and the Camorra. The method was called the Black Hand because as a general rule the extortion letters which formed its initial phase bore the imprint of a hand in black ink, as well as crude drawings of a skull and cross-bones, and sometimes crosses and daggers.

The procedure of the Black Hand was both simple and direct. First, a victim was chosen, usually a man who had displayed signs of prosperity; the purchase of property, if the fact became public knowledge, was almost always followed by Black Hand activity. Sometimes two gangs chose the same victim, in which case it was customary to recognize priority rights. A letter, bearing some such signature as Black Hand, Mysterious Hand, or Secret Hand — the word " hand " was always present — was sent to the victim demanding money. If he ignored the letter or refused to pay, his home, office, or store was bombed. If he still refused to pay, he was murdered. Most of the Black Hand letters were blunt instructions to put a certain sum of money, ranging usually from one thousand dollars to five thousand dollars, in a certain place at a certain time, but some were very politely worded, in the best tradition of Latin courtesy. The following are typical:

"Most gentle Mr. Silvani: Hoping that the present will not impress you much, you will be so good as to send me $2,000.00 if your life is dear to you. So I beg you warmly to put them on your door within four days.

232

But if not, I swear this week's time not even the dust of your family will exist. With regards, believe me to be your friends."

"You got some cash. I need $1,000.00. You place the $100.00 bills in an envelope and place it underneath a board at the northeast corner of Sixty-ninth Street and Euclid Avenue at eleven o'clock tonight. If you place the money there you will live. If you don't, you die. If you report this to the police, I'll kill you when I get out. They may save you the money, but they won't save you your life."

"We all of us thank you for the success that has happened, but for your security do that which we have written in the first, and take good care of doing the exact things, and woe unto you people if you do not deliver the said sum, more than the past $1,000.00 at the stated place. If you don't do this now within the term of a week, we will think of something else. If we will not succeed here in Chicago in the other parts even to hell. Even if you leave the city we will think to revenge ourselves with a severe vengeance and precaution."

The Silvani letter was written by Joseph Genite, in whose home on Racine Avenue the police found a large quantity of dynamite and a dozen revolvers and sawed-off shotguns. The detectives believed, but were never able to prove, that Genite sold explosives to Black Hand gangs and rented the weapons to professional killers.

9

THE extent of Black Hand terrorization in Chicago was shown in an article in the *Daily News* of May 25, 1915, which said that in the first ninety-three days of that year fifty-five bombs had been exploded in the Italian district, and that not one of them had been set off for any reason other than the extraction of blackmail. " A detective of experience in the Italian quarter," said the *Daily News,* " estimates that ten pay tribute to one who is sturdy enough to resist until he is warned by a bomb. . . . Well informed Italians have never put the year's tribute to the ' Black Hand ' at less than half a million dollars." On March 17, 1911 the Chicago *Tribune* listed twenty-five unsolved Black Hand killings which had occurred in 1910; and on June 2, 1915 the *Record-Herald* said that the Black Hand had murdered forty persons in Chicago in 1911, thirty-three in 1912, thirty-one in 1913, and forty-two in 1914. In the first five months of 1915 six persons were killed and twelve bombs were exploded.

In attempting to combat the Black Hand gangs the police faced almost insurmountable obstacles. Innumerable arrests were made; in one raid on five saloons in the vicinity of Oak and Milton Streets, in January 1910, detectives rounded up a hundred and ninety-four Sicilians, most of whom were known criminals. But all were released within twelve hours because no evidence connecting them with specific crimes could be obtained. Many cases of both murder and extortion were brought into trial courts, but few convictions were secured, and most of those who were sent to prison were soon paroled through the connivance of saloonkeepers and crooked politicians. As soon as a Black Hand suspect was arrested, witnesses and members of the victim's family were threatened with death if they divulged information to the police. Judges, jurors, members of the prosecutor's staff, and their families likewise received threats. In one case a witness was about to tell the details of a Black Hand extortion plot when a man entered the courtroom and waved a red handkerchief at him. After that the witness refused to testify, and the state was compelled to abandon the

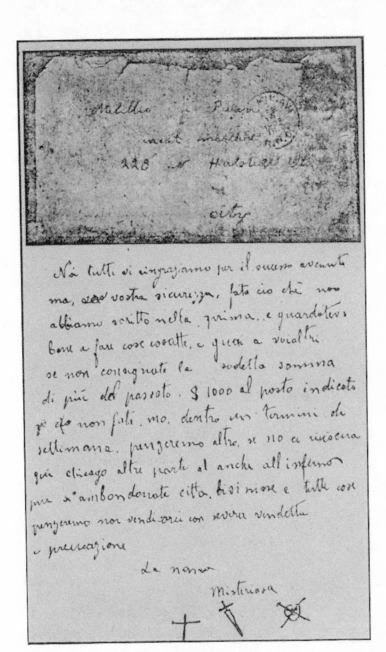

A BLACK HAND LETTER

prosecution. The *Record-Herald,* in an editorial on March 20, 1911, gave this concrete example of the difficulties encountered by the police in investigating Black Hand cases:

"A murder was committed here in Chicago, and the detectives, native and Italian, were set to work on the case. They succeeded in learning who the murderer was, but in spite of nets and traps, weeks passed in a vain hunt for him. Finally an Italian detective saw the 'wanted man' leave the home of the brother of the murdered man. When the police summoned the brother to explain the strange affair he declared that the murderer had been wounded and that he and his family had shielded and nursed the wretch back to life in order to kill him and thus duly and personally avenge the death of the beloved brother. This sort of story would astonish one in a melodrama; what are practical policemen in real life to make of it? How could it have occurred to them to look for the criminal in the home of the victim's own devoted brother?"

The White Hand Society, an organization of Italian business and professional men sponsored by the Italian Chamber of Commerce, the Italian newspapers, and several fraternal orders of Italians and Sicilians, was formed in 1907 to co-operate with the police in a campaign to exterminate the Black Hand. Although virtually every member of the Society was threatened with death, it was active for several years. Detectives were employed to help the police investigate Black Hand cases, and agents were sent to Italy and Sicily to inquire into the past histories of notorious gangsters, while as much protection as possible was given to witnesses and the families of victims. Several murderers and extortionists were sent to prison through the efforts of the White Hand, but they were soon paroled and resumed their

235

criminal activities. In 1912 the president of the White Hand Society, Dr. Joseph Damiani, told the *Record-Herald* that the members of the organization " were so discouraged by the lax administration of justice that they were refusing to advance further money to prosecute men arrested on their complaints." Little was heard of the Society after about 1912.

The Federal government began to prosecute extortionists for misuse of the United States mails late in 1910, and within a few years a dozen Black Hand gangsters had been heavily fined and sent to Federal prisons. Local politicians were unable to help them, and most of the convicted men served their full sentences. Owing almost entirely to government intervention, the method of extortion known as the Black Hand gradually disappeared. Bombings, murders, and extortion continued to be common, but in the majority of instances the demands for money and the threats of death were communicated by means other than the mails. All Black Hand activities decreased with the coming of prohibition, many of the extortionist gangs finding in bootlegging and rum-running a greater field for their talents. Some turned to banditry, notably the Sam Cardinelli gang, which for several years was regarded as one of the most vicious criminal mobs in Chicago, so tough that even the beer barons and their torpedoes were afraid of them. Cardinelli's principal trigger-man was Nicholas Viana, better known as " the choir-boy," who was only eighteen years old. This gang committed a score of murders and was involved in more than a hundred holdups before Cardinelli, Viana, and Frank Campione were hanged and another sentenced to life imprisonment.

10

T H E bomb as an instrument of terror and destruction appears to have been introduced into Chicago by the Black

236

Hand, but of the eight hundred or more such infernal machines set off during the first thirty years of the twentieth century not more than one-third, and probably even less, were detonated by the extortionists of the so-called Dirty Mitt. The remainder were exploded by gamblers, to destroy rival houses or call the attention of the police to them; by racketeers, to compel payment of tribute by business firms; by politicians, to intimidate voters and discourage opposition; and by labor-union terrorists, as a form of direct action. The bomb was also extensively used in racial conflicts; thirty of the one hundred and twenty-two bombs set off in Chicago from January 21, 1918, were directed against Negroes and were apparently intended to check the spread of black families into white residential districts. The race rioting of July 1919, in which thirty-eight lives were lost in " five days of terrible hate and passion let loose," as the Coroner's Jury described it, was essentially a part of the bombing war against the Negroes, and the logical consequence of the bitter feeling which the bombings had engendered.

Most of the bombing in Chicago during the World War period and in the 1920's was done by gangs of professional bombers and sluggers. The methods of one of these gangs were disclosed in 1921 when the police, after investigating the bombing of four laundries in which the engineers had been on strike, arrested Andrew Kerr, a member of the International Union of Steam and Operating Engineers. Kerr made a confession in which he said that the boss of the Chicago bombers was Jim Sweeney, whose gang hung out at Harrison and Halsted Streets and would accept any job of bombing, shooting, or slugging. Kerr named as Sweeney's principal lieutenants Soup Bartlett, an expert with explosives, and Con Shea, a notorious labor agitator, who Kerr said had been a bomber since he was sixteen years old. Kerr himself was attached to the bombing gang as a representative of the engineers' union; he accompanied the bombers and sluggers on their expeditions to see that the union was not cheated. For this he received fifteen dollars a week strike benefit. He told of one occasion when union officials gave Sweeney a list of twenty-five persons who were to be slugged, and the addresses of several laundries which were to be bombed. The gang was finally broken up late in 1921 when Sweeney and Bartlett were sent to Joliet on indeterminate sentences.

Sweeney was succeeded as king-pin bomber by Joseph Sangerman, manufacturer of barbers' supplies and boss of the barbers' union. "He was the directing genius of the bombing trust," said the Illinois Crime Survey, "the contractor of bombing. As an officer in the barbers' union, his specialty at first was the hiring of bombers to discipline barber shop owners who did not work in agreement with barbers' rules, but finding that his gang could 'turn a trick' effectively and escape detection, he began to accept commissions in other fields." Sangerman was arrested in 1925, and told the police that he maintained, on regular salaries, a bombing crew of five men and one woman, and that his prices for bombings and sluggings ranged from fifty to seven hundred dollars. His star bomber was George Matrisciano, alias Martini, who was said by the police to have been one of the most expert that ever worked in Chicago. He manufactured the bombs, which were usually made of black powder, and carried in his pockets two sticks of dynamite for emergencies, as well as an automatic pistol. The report of the Crime Survey said that Matrisciano conceived his role in terms of operatic melodrama; he was proud of his ability, and greatly cherished a newspaper clipping in which he was called a "terrorist." Several indictments were found against Matrisciano, but before he could be arrested he was killed, according to the Crime Survey, by "the guns of the officers of the barbers' union."

11

T H E first political bombings of importance in Chicago occurred during the struggle for control of the Nineteenth Ward between Alderman John Powers and Anthony D'Andrea, which began in 1916 and ended in 1921 when D'Andrea was killed by an assassin armed with a sawed-off shotgun. Powers had been boss of the ward since 1888; he was a saloon-keeper, protector of gamblers and criminals, and one of the most notorious of the boodling aldermen of the 1890's. D'Andrea himself was no shining light of morality; he was a labor-union official and a prominent figure in the councils of several Italian fraternal societies, but he was also an ex-convict, and his record as a whole was distinctly unsavory. Commenting upon his career in 1916, the *Tribune* said: " Anthony Andrea is the same Antonio D'Andrea, unfrocked priest, linguist, and former power in the old ' red light ' district, who in 1903 was released from the penitentiary after serving thirteen months on a counterfeit charge. D'Andrea's name has also been connected with a gang of Italian forgers and bank thieves who operated at one time all over the country."

D'Andrea's first appearance in politics as a candidate for office was in 1914, when he ran for County Commissioner but was unsuccessful. Two years later he opposed James Bowler, junior alderman from the Nineteenth Ward and one of Powers's henchmen, in the primary election of February 1916. The killings began that same month, when Frank Lombardi, a ward heeler who had been active against D'Andrea, was shot in a Taylor Street saloon. D'Andrea was defeated, but tried again in October 1919, running for the Democratic nomination for representative in the Constitutional Convention. He was again defeated, the courts throwing out the vote of an entire ballot when the Citizens'

Association produced fifty-six voters whose names appeared on the poll but who swore they had not voted. Meanwhile D'Andrea had been elected president of the Unione Siciliana, one of the strongest foreign organizations in the United States, and had gained control of four more labor unions.

The first bomb exploded in the Powers-D'Andrea feud was set off on September 28, 1920, on the front porch of Alderman Powers's home in McAllister Place. Early in 1921 D'Andrea announced himself as a non-partisan candidate for alderman against Powers, and on February 7 a bomb was exploded in a hall on Blue Island Avenue where adherents of D'Andrea were holding a rally. Five persons were severely injured. During the next two weeks two more bombings were reported, one at D'Andrea's headquarters and the other at the home of one of D'Andrea's lieutenants. There were innumerable fights, and several shootings and stabbings. Alderman Bowler issued a statement declaring that the D'Andrea faction had imported gunmen to terrorize the Nineteenth Ward. He continued:

" Conditions in the Nineteenth Ward are terrible. Gunmen are patrolling the streets. I have received threats that I was to be 'bumped off' or kidnapped. Alderman Powers' house is guarded day and night. Our men have been met, threatened and slugged. Gunmen and cutthroats have been imported from New York and Buffalo for this campaign of intimidation. Owners of halls have been threatened with death or the destruction of their buildings if they rent their places to us. It is worse than the middle ages."

D'Andrea was defeated by four hundred and thirty-five votes at the election on February 22, 1921, but Powers's victory failed to end the bombings and killings. Early in March 1921 two of Powers's principal supporters were killed. D'Andrea denied knowledge of the murders, but several members of his organization were arrested as suspects. A week after the double killing, D'Andrea announced that he was through with Nineteenth Ward politics. Nevertheless the war continued, with several more bombings, until it reached a climax with the death of D'Andrea on May 11. Two of D'Andrea's intimate friends, Andrew Orlando and Joseph Sinacola, swore to avenge his death. They were likewise murdered, Orlando in July and Sinacola in August.

12

ANOTHER series of political bombings attracted international attention during the primary campaign of 1928, in which Senator Charles S. Deneen's faction of the Republican Party opposed the faction headed by Mayor Big Bill Thompson and State's Attorney Robert E. Crowe. The Crowe-Thompson machine was one of the most powerful Chicago has ever seen; in alliance with Governor Len Small it controlled practically all of the jobs and patronage in the city, county, and state. Several bombs were exploded during the early days of the campaign, most of them directed against supporters of Thompson and Crowe; and on March 21, 1928 assassins murdered Diamond Joe Esposito, café-owner and racketeer, said by police to have been the power behind the famous Genna gang of bootleggers. Diamond Joe was also a warm personal friend of Senator Deneen and one of the Senator's most influential lieutenants.

On the morning after Esposito's funeral, bombs were exploded at the homes of Senator Deneen and Judge John A. Swanson, the Deneen candidate for State's Attorney, and Crowe thereupon made one of the worst blunders in the history of Chicago politics. He issued a statement saying that he was " satisfied that the bombings were done by leaders in the Deneen forces . . . and were done mainly to discredit

Mayor Thompson and myself." A similar statement was soon thereafter made by the Mayor. The reaction against Crowe was tremendous; as the *Tribune* said, " the callous, cynical note in this led to public exasperation." Newspapers which had been supporting the State's Attorney turned against him, several mass meetings were held to denounce his candidacy, and the Chicago Crime Commission, which had been friendly to him, issued an open letter recommending his defeat. The Commission declared that Crowe was " inefficient and unworthy of his great responsibility," and that " his alliances are such as to destroy public confidence in his integrity."

In the election the Deneen faction was overwhelmingly victorious. " It was purely a revolt," said the Illinois Crime Survey, " an uprising of the people, expressing themselves through the ballot. The birth of ' Moral Chicago ' was hailed throughout the world."

CHAPTER VIII

THE SCARLET SISTERS AND
THEIR TIMES

O N NOVEMBER 25, 1895 the first trolley car clattered down South Clark Street, and in April 1897 Carter H. Harrison, Jr., was elected Mayor of Chicago for the first time. A few months after his inauguration Mayor Harrison ordered the police to clean up Clark Street and make it fit for occupancy by decent people, giving as his reason the fact that he had received many complaints from citizens who were compelled to use the new car line as transportation to and from business. Carrie Watson immediately sold her mansion and retired, with her parrot and her carriages, to a comfortable home in the suburbs, and a few of the lesser Clark Street madames transferred their girls and other belongings to the West Side. Some went southward and established vice districts in South Chicago, principally on Harbor Avenue and The Strand, and on Thirty-first Street from Cottage Grove Avenue to the Rock Island railroad tracks, where a dive called the Arsenic Club was a landmark for many years.

In the main, however, the brothel-keepers of Clark Street gradually moved into the region around South Dearborn and Twenty-second Streets, where a red-light district had been developing since the late 1880's when the police drove from South State Street a few harlots who had been edging toward the business section. But the evacuation of

Clark Street proved to be a slow process; six years after the Mayor's order had been issued the *Record-Herald* complained that the thoroughfare between Polk and Twelfth Streets was still largely given over to cheap brothels, dives, and low saloons in which a drink of whisky could be had for five cents. Many of these grog-shops flaunted huge signs claiming to have originated nickel whisky, and fights frequently occurred between rival claimants of the dubious honor.

Soon after his election in 1903 for the fourth consecutive time, Mayor Harrison made another attack upon Clark Street, and at the same time began to close the brothels of Custom House Place and Plymouth Place,[1] the madames of which likewise moved to the Twenty-second Street district. No action was taken against Little Hell on the North Side or the long-established vice area on the West Side, where the evil fame of the Black Hole had been overshadowed by that of the Jungle, which comprised a dozen connected shacks at Peoria and Monroe Streets. Six men, four of whom were saloon-keepers, owned these dens, and kept in them from sixty to one hundred women, who were known as " air-walkers " because of their peculiar bouncing gait, the result of the excessive use of encaine, a cheap substitute for cocaine. None of these harlots was ever permitted to leave the shacks unless accompanied by a pimp. They solicited naked from the doors and windows of the Jungle, charged twenty-five to fifty cents, catered to white men and Negroes alike, and robbed every man who failed to keep his wits about him.

Scarcely less vicious than the Jungle was a fifty-cent brothel at No. 75 South Peoria Street, which was managed by Bessie Lane. The dive was owned, however, by Leona Garrity, who lived in a fine house in the North Shore suburb of Glencoe. There she posed as Mrs. Lemuel Schlotter, the

---

[1] The names of these thoroughfares were changed to Federal Street and Plymouth Court.

wife of a traveling salesman, and for several years tried un-successfully to chisel her way into Glencoe society. On June 20, 1907 Madame Garrity was arrested for harboring a six-teen-year-old girl, known as Florince, in her brothel, and was tried before a jury and found guilty. She was sentenced to prison for from one to fifteen years. Bessie Lane was also convicted, but the jury recommended mercy on the grounds that Leona Garrity was most to blame. " There she was," said one juror after the trial, " posing as a society woman and living high on the money turned over to her by her agent." Part of the evidence introduced by the State's At-torney consisted of Madame Garrity's account-book, in which was set down the number of men who visited the house each day, the number entertained by each girl, and the earn-ings of the inmates. This book showed that on four consecu-tive days six of the regular girls received three hundred and ninety-four men and were paid a total of $98.50, a like sum going into the pockets of the madame. Two of the six girls received two hundred and six men in five consecutive days, and of this number one hundred and thirty were entertained by Florince, forty-five of them in a single day. Florince's total earnings for the five days was $32.50. The record of the two girls was thus recapitulated by the State's Attorney:

	Sun.	Mon.	Tues.	Wed.	Thurs.	Total	Ave.
Kitty							
No. of men	24	14	12	9	17	76	15
Florince							
No. of men	20	23	21	21	45	130	26

2

B Y the middle of 1904 open vice on Chicago's South Side, except for scattered call flats and assignation houses on Michigan Avenue, was confined to the Thirty-first Street and South Chicago areas, and to a much larger and more important district bounded by Clark Street, Wabash Avenue, and Eighteenth and Twenty-second Streets. This territory, which besides the four boundary streets included such thoroughfares as State and Dearborn Streets and Archer and Armour Avenues,[1] was the segregated district known throughout the world as the Levee. It was the largest, the most notorious, and the most vicious of all Chicago's concentrations of vice; it combined the worst features of the Bad Lands and Little Cheyenne, and the most disreputable superlative that could be imagined would fail to do it justice. It had saloons, wine-rooms, and dance halls of unbelievable depravity. Its streets and alleys and dives swarmed with harlots, footpads, sluggers, degenerates, dope fiends, sneak thieves, pickpockets, and bums; and with hundreds of pimps, organized as the Cadets' Protective Association. It had panel-joints and goosing-slums, deadfalls and parlor-houses, and shanties with muslin partitions for streetwalkers; one group of twenty-five-cent brothels, occupied by Negro girls and known as Bed Bug Row, was at least as bad as the cribs of New Orleans or the cow-yards of San Francisco. It had peep-shows which catered especially to boys, and provided entertainers for stag parties; in 1908 a famous peep-show performer, the Merry Widow Kiddo, aroused something of a scandal by dancing naked at a social function given in honor of a police lieutenant. It had gangs of panders and white-slavers, which maintained stockades and "breaking-in" dens, and classes in which young girls were taught various methods of perversion after they had been "broken-in" by professional rapists. It had drug stores where dope addicts congregated and openly gave one another injections of cocaine and morphine which had been purchased at the counters; one such store provided a hypodermic needle. It had a King and Queen of the Cokies, Eugene Hustion and his wife Lottie, who kept a supply of thirty pounds of cocaine

---

[1] Armour Avenue is now the southern extension of Federal Street.

and half as much morphine in a Dearborn Street flat and sent salesmen on nightly tours of the brothels. Lottie Hustion was a college graduate who spoke five languages, and in her spare time composed music, painted portraits, and did fancy needlework.

3

THE show-place of the Levee, and the shining symbol of open and protected vice, was the brothel at Nos. 2131–3 South Dearborn Street, the three-story, fifty-room, $125,000 double mansion which had been erected in 1890 by Lizzie Allen and Christopher Columbus Crabb. This was the world-famous Everleigh Club, run by those extraordinary sisters Ada and Minna Everleigh, who started in the business of prostitution with no previous experience and no under-world connections — neither had ever been an inmate of a bawdy house nor even so much as entered such a resort — and became the most successful madames of whom any record remains. When they retired, still in their early thirties, after twelve years in which the doors of the Everleigh Club were never closed except to allow the harlots to catch up on their sleep, the sisters had a million dollars in cash, some two hundred thousand dollars' worth of jewelry, uncollectable I.O.U.'s from customers totaling twenty-five thousand dollars; and books, paintings, rugs, statues, and other valuable articles for which they had paid a hundred and fifty thousand dollars. They had enough furniture to equip a small hotel, including between forty and fifty brass beds inlaid with marble and fitted with specially-built mattresses and springs, and twenty gold-plated spittoons which had cost six hundred and fifty dollars each. For them the wages of sin were economic security and a comfortable old age.

The Everleigh sisters were born in a small Kentucky village near Louisville, Ada in 1876 and Minna a little more than two years later. They were the daughters of a lawyer, said to have been wealthy, and received the finishing-school education which in those days was considered sufficient for Southern gentlewomen. Only a few of their most intimate friends in Chicago knew their origin and identity, but Minna, who was the leader in their joint enterprises and handled the money, always signed her bank statements and legal papers as Minna Lester, and the latter was probably their real family name. They told friends that they called themselves Everleigh in honor of their grandmother, who always signed her letters " Everly Yours." In 1897 the sisters married brothers in their home town, but left them within a year; both husbands, they said afterward, were brutes who often tried to strangle them. Neither ever married again. In fact, according to several old-time Chicagoans who knew them well in the palmy days of the Everleigh Club, neither even had a lover, in which respect they differed from at least ninety-nine per cent of their fellow madames.

After leaving their husbands the sisters joined a theatrical troupe, and for a year or so traveled about the Middle West playing bits in melodramas of the *East Lynne* variety. Between them they had about thirty-five thousand dollars, most of which represented an inheritance that had been paid upon marriage, and Minna Everleigh said in later years that they were " looking for a nice town in which to invest our money." They played in Omaha early in 1898, and found that city, then one of the really wide-open towns of the country, preparing to open the Trans-Mississippi Exposition and expecting large crowds. Everywhere they had gone the two girls — Ada was twenty-three years old and Minna not quite twenty-one — had heard of the enormous fortunes which were being made by well-conducted brothels, and they decided that prostitution offered maximum returns with minimum risk.

In the spring of 1898 the Everleighs leased a bordello in Omaha, redecorated the resort, put in new girls and raised

248

prices, and operated it throughout the period of the Exposition. They made money, but business declined as soon as the free-spending Exposition crowds had departed; the sports of Omaha refused as one man to pay ten dollars for a girl and twelve dollars for a bottle of wine. The sisters concluded that only a city with a large sporting population could support the sort of brothel they wished to conduct, and they spent several months looking over the field in Washington, New York, New Orleans, and San Francisco, but without finding a suitable opening. In the winter of 1899 they arrived in Chicago, having heard that Madame Effie Hankins, who had leased the Dearborn Street house shortly before the death of Lizzie Allen in 1896, was anxious to sell and try her luck in New York. The Everleighs bought the lease, fixtures, and girls for fifty-five thousand dollars, paying twenty thousand down and agreeing to pay the balance in six months, and immediately discarded the fixtures and discharged the girls. Carpenters and decorators were summoned, and the house was redecorated and refurnished from cellar to garret. A new staff of harlots, many of whom had never before worked in Chicago, was engaged, and on February 1, 1900 the brothel was reopened as the Everleigh Club.

4

UNDER the management of the gifted sisters the Everleigh Club was the most notorious, the most luxurious, and at the same time the most consistently profitable bordello that the United States, and probably the rest of the world as well, has ever seen. European visitors, marveling at its gaudy splendor, said that it eclipsed anything to be found in Paris; and by comparison the celebrated Mahogany Hall of Washington, the famous Clark Street house of Carrie Watson, and the finest brothels in New York, San Francisco, and New Orleans were squalid hovels fit only for the amorous frolics of chimpanzees. " No house of courtesans in the world," said the Chicago *Tribune,* " was so richly furnished, so well advertised, and so continuously patronized by men of wealth and slight morals." Even the report of the Vice Commission of Chicago, coldly judicial in its evaluations and dealing strictly with facts, said that the Everleigh Club was " probably the most famous and luxurious home of prostitution in the country."

During the twelve years of their active career the sisters Everleigh spent nearly two hundred thousand dollars on the furnishings of this glittering palace of sin, and even men who had been accustomed to luxury since childhood were astounded at its magnificence. Less fortunate visitors were completely bowled over by the curtains and hangings of golden silk, the great divans and easy chairs upholstered in silk damask, the thick and expensive rugs and carpets, the gold spittoons, the inlaid beds, the solid mahogany tables covered with slabs of imported marble, the paintings and tapestries, the statues, the cases of iridescent sea-shells, the cages of sweetly singing canaries, the solid silver dinner service, the gilded bathtub especially for the use of customers, the gold-rimmed china and crystal glassware, the golden trays and champagne buckets, the tablecloths of Irish linen and Spanish drawnwork, the half-dozen pianos, one of them heavily gilded and made to order at a cost of fifteen thousand dollars, the ornamental incense-burners, and the thousand and one *objets d'art* and elegant knickknacks.

There were two entrances to the Everleigh Club, each leading into a spacious hallway fragrant with perfume and decorated with potted palms and other greenery, through which peeped statues of Greek goddesses. From the hallways mahogany staircases wound gracefully upward to the love bowers of the courtesans, each of which was sumptuously furnished according to the taste of its occupant, with the exciting colors of red and gold dominating the decorative schemes. On the first floor were the music-room, the library, an art gallery which was said by connoisseurs of the period to contain a few really good paintings; the grand ballroom, lighted by chandeliers of cut glass, the hardwood floor inlaid with rare woods in mosaic patterns; the dining-room paneled in walnut and containing a mahogany table large enough for fifty diners; and the Pullman Buffet, a reproduction in mahogany of a section of a railroad dining-car. Also on this floor were some of the twelve parlors, each of which was virtually sound-proof and could be completely cut off from the remainder of the house by closing the heavy double doors. These parlors were called the Gold, Moorish, Silver, Copper, Red, Rose, Green, Blue, Oriental, Chinese, Egyptian, and Japanese Rooms, and were appropriately decorated and furnished — in the Gold Room the furniture was encrusted with gilt; in the Copper Room the walls were paneled with hammered brass; in the Blue Room everything was collegiate, with pennants and pillows of blue leather ornamented with pictures of Gibson girls; in the Moorish Room was the inevitable Turkish corner, with its voluptuous couches and draperies; in the Japanese Room was a heavily carved teakwood chair resting upon a dais, the whole covered by a canopy of yellow silk. The *Tribune* once said that the Japanese Room was " a harlot's dream of what a Japanese palace might look like inside." And in every room were the two objects that probably aroused more comment than any other feature of the brothel — the gold spittoon, and a fountain which at regular intervals squirted a jet of perfume into the incense-laden air.

The visitor to the Everleigh Club was met in the hallway by the gracious Madame Minna, clad in a trailing gown of silk and literally blazing with jewels — she customarily wore a diamond dog-collar, half a dozen diamond bracelets, a ring on each finger, and a great stomacher of diamonds, emeralds, and rubies. There was no lining up for selection as in the majority of bordellos; wearing evening gowns and whatever jewelry they possessed, the harlots drifted elegantly from parlor to parlor and were formally introduced to gentlemen who desired their services. They were, at any rate, carefully chosen. " I talk with each applicant myself," said Ada Everleigh in 1910. " She must have worked somewhere else before coming here. We do not like amateurs. Inexperienced girls and young widows are too prone to accept offers of marriage and leave. To get in a girl must have a good face and figure, must be in perfect health, must understand what it is to act like a lady. If she is addicted to drugs, or to drink, we do not want her." The sisters had no difficulty in keeping the " membership " of the Club filled with desirable girls; usually there was a long waiting list, and the prostitutes who were accepted were unquestionably the cream of the harlot crop. The work was lighter and the pay higher in the Everleigh Club than elsewhere — the courtesans there actually received half of their earnings without the deductions common in other houses — and to have worked in the celebrated resort was regarded in red-light circles as a mark of distinction and a badge of merit. Everleigh-trained girls were in demand in brothels throughout the country. Few, however, ever became known outside their profession. An exception was Belle Schreiber, notorious as one of the white sweethearts of Jack Johnson, the Negro pugilist. She was also the girl who caused Johnson to be indicted for white-slavery in 1912, the Federal government alleging that he had brought her from Pittsburgh to Chicago for immoral purposes in 1910, long after she had left the Everleigh Club.

5

THE operating expenses of the Everleigh Club were enormous — the annual overhead ranged from fifty thousand to seventy-five thousand dollars, and included such unavoidable

ADA AND MINNA EVERLEIGH

Courtesy of King Features Syndicate, Inc.

items as six thousand dollars for rent, from twenty thousand to thirty thousand for servants, music, and entertainment — the Club employed from fifteen to twenty-five cooks and maids, three orchestras, and a piano-playing "professor" for the interludes, and frequently imported special dancers for its circuses — and from ten thousand to fifteen thousand a year for protection, in return for which the sisters were never molested and the name of the resort never appeared on any of the police lists of bawdy houses. But the proceeds were likewise enormous. The gross receipts of the opening night were one thousand dollars, and there were not many nights when the take was so small; occasionally it was as high as five thousand. The average was between two thousand and twenty-five hundred dollars, of which from three to five hundred was net profit and went into the bulging bank account of the scarlet sisters.

The scale of prices established by the Everleigh sisters was ten, twenty-five, and fifty dollars, depending upon the character of the service required by the customer and how long he wished to retain sole rights to a selected harlot. But the ten dollars was little more than an entrance fee, and the man who failed to spend at least fifty dollars in the course of a visit to the Club was requested not to come again. Wine was sold in the parlors at twelve dollars a bottle and in the bedrooms at fifteen dollars, but beer and hard liquor were unobtainable at any price. Admittance to a circus cost twenty-five to fifty dollars, depending largely upon the lewdness of the show and the quality of the dancing, and these performances were never staged for fewer than five spectators. Supper parties, for which the house was famous — the Club was said to employ one of the finest chefs in the United States — cost from fifty dollars a plate up, which included wine but not girls. The host at such a function would indicate to one of the madames how much he wished to bestow upon the prostitutes invited to entertain his guests, and these amounts

253

would appear on his bill as incidentals. The most expensive party of this sort is said to have been given in 1910 by the young son of a railroad president, who paid two thousand dollars, besides harlot hire, for a supper for half a dozen friends. Every dish was an out-of-season delicacy.

From the beginning the Everleigh Club catered particularly to rich men, but for a year or so it was open to all comers. As a regular clientele was gradually established, the Club became more and more exclusive, and during the last four or five years of its existence no man was admitted unless he was known to the sisters or one of the girls, possessed a letter or card of introduction, or had been recommended by telephone. Visitors from out of town, strangers to Chicago, were required to prove their identity and financial standing. Slumming parties and sightseers in general were rigorously excluded, but exceptions to this rule were made for a few crusaders and mission workers with whom the Everleighs had become friendly, and to whom they frequently made sizable donations. These were permitted to visit the brothel in the afternoon, distribute their tracts, pray for the souls of the harlots, and endeavor to reform them. There is no record that any ever succeeded. Occasionally a prostitute left the Club to be married, but none ever quit for the sole purpose of leading a better life, which for girls of their class would have meant working in a factory or a department store for from six to ten dollars a week. In the Everleigh Club a popular girl could easily make a hundred.

Lucy Page Gaston, the famous anti-cigarette crusader, was one of the favored reformers. She appeared at the Club regularly several times a month with anti-tobacco literature which the girls solemnly accepted and promised faithfully to read. Once Miss Gaston dashed into the kitchen, where Minna Everleigh was in conference with the chef, and cried:

" Minna, your girls are going straight to hell! You must stop them!"

254

" What can I do ? " inquired the madame.

" Make them quit smoking cigarettes ! "

Another crusader popular with the Everleigh Club was a man, noted for his good works among the denizens of the Levee, who after much prayer and meditation decided to experience the sin against which he had so often thundered. One of the harlots agreed to make him a special price of twenty-five dollars, and they climbed the stairs to her boudoir, where he handed her a fifty-dollar bill.

" I'll get your change," she said, and left the room.

When she returned he was pacing back and forth in great agitation.

" I've changed my mind," he said. " Can't we just sit and talk for an hour or two ? "

" Yes," said the harlot, " but in that case you don't get any change."

6

T H E R E was great rivalry among the parlor-house madames of the Levee to secure the patronage of rich young men, and whenever a report spread that such a prize was in the district, on the loose with his pockets stuffed with money and blank checks, the keepers of the big houses hurriedly dispatched cadets to bring him in for plucking. The Everleighs, who permitted no pimps on their premises and forbade their girls to have any dealings with these human lice, took no part in such undignified scrambles, but the playboy usually visited the Club anyhow, because of its infinitely superior attractions. As a result, the Everleighs were cordially hated throughout the Levee, and rival madames and their cadets frequently tried to involve the sisters in serious trouble and so drive them from Chicago.

One of these attempts, which if it had succeeded would have closed the Club and sent the Everleighs to prison and possibly to the gallows, was in connection with the death of Nathaniel Ford Moore, the twenty-six-year-old son of James Hobart Moore, president of the Rock Island Railroad and one of the country's most important capitalists. Young Moore, whose career as a playboy began when he found a check for a hundred thousand dollars under his breakfast plate on his twenty-first birthday, visited the Everleigh Club on the night of January 8, 1910. But his condition was such that Minna Everleigh refused to sell him any more wine, and in consequence of this decision quarreled with one of her harlots, who stormed out of the Club screaming that she would be avenged. At one o'clock in the morning of January 9 Moore left the Club in a taxicab. Shortly after dawn on January 10 Minna Everleigh was called to the telephone, and the strumpet who had flounced out of the house in such a rage told her that Moore had died in a brothel kept by Vic Shaw at No. 2104 South Dearborn Street, and that Madame Shaw and her cadets were planning to put the body into the Everleigh Club furnace. Accompanied by a friend, Minna Everleigh hurried down the street and forced her way into Vic Shaw's place, and after considerable uproar Madame Shaw finally admitted that young Moore had been found dead in bed about half an hour before dawn. Upon Minna Everleigh's insistence the police were notified, and the body of the young man was removed to his home on Lake Shore Drive. In later years Minna Everleigh told the State's Attorney that Moore had died of an overdose of morphine placed in his champagne, but the verdict of the Coroner's Jury was that death had been caused by heart disease. An autopsy disclosed no trace of drugs.

Another and even more fantastic scheme was attempted late in 1905, when a young man, a member of one of Chicago's foremost families, accidentally shot himself in his home. Between the shooting and the death of the young man five days later, a report was circulated in the Levee that he had been shot during a quarrel in the Everleigh Club; and that the newspapers had suppressed the story because his father was an important advertiser. There was no foundation whatever for the rumor. Investigations by the police, by newspaper reporters, and by private detectives proved beyond question that the shooting had been accidental and that it had actually occurred in the young man's home. Moreover, it was shown conclusively that not only had he never visited the Everleigh Club, but that he had never even been seen inside the segregated district, and that his reputation was of the highest. Nevertheless the rumor persisted — it spread throughout the country and is still heard occasionally in Chicago — and the enemies of the sisters seized upon it as a golden opportunity. They enlisted the aid of Pony Moore, a Negro gambler and thief who operated the Turf Exchange in Twenty-first Street. Moore offered one of the Everleigh harlots twenty thousand dollars if she would make an affidavit that she had seen Minna Everleigh shoot the young man. The courtesan agreed, but Minna Everleigh overheard her talking to Moore on the telephone, and with the aid of a friendly police lieutenant succeeded in thwarting the plot.

The Levee regarded it as significant that Pony Moore's saloon license was revoked a few days after the collapse of the scheme to discredit the Everleighs, an action which came as a great surprise to the gambler because he called himself "Mayor of the Tenderloin" and boasted that he controlled the district. As a matter of fact, even as a dive-keeper Pony Moore was relatively unimportant, but his personal peculiarities occasionally thrust him into public notice, and he looked upon any mention of his name in the newspapers as an indication of power. He framed and hung behind his bar, among other clippings, one that described the huge diamond stud which he wore secured to his shirt-front with a silver bolt and a small padlock. Pony Moore's greatest ambition was to pass as a white man, and to that end he applied strong bleaches to his skin, at length achieving a pasty gray with brown splotches. He also tried various preparations for straightening his hair, and it finally became a violent green, but remained kinky, so he shaved it off altogether. In the middle 1890's Moore visited Newport, Saratoga, and other Eastern watering-places and attracted considerable attention by changing his costume every hour, and by the number, brilliance, and odd arrangements of his diamonds.

7

THE destruction of the Everleigh Club was finally accomplished, not by its enemies, but by the sisters themselves; they had set out to make their resort the best-known bawdy house in the United States, and they succeeded only too well. Their downfall was the direct result of their arrogance, their methods of advertising, and their persistent flouting of a growing public opinion against segregated vice. Minna announced that she intended to write her memoirs, and called in a Chicago literary man for advice. At every opportunity the Everleighs broke into print, especially during the final years of their reign as queens of the Levee. And since they had always made pets of the reporters — anything a working journalist wanted, from wine to women, was on the house — their names often appeared in the newspapers. Every afternoon the sisters went for a ride, at first in a handsome carriage drawn by a team of black horses and driven by a liveried coachman; and later in an automobile, a huge open machine painted a bright yellow, with an enormous bunch of artificial flowers attached to the hood. Accompanying them was one of the most beautiful of their harlots, a different girl each day, gaudily bedecked in silks and satins and loaded with jewelry; and when the sisters swept into a bank to make their daily deposit, the strumpet remained in the car, so that all men might see and marvel at the loveliness which was for sale at the Everleigh Club.

After about 1906 ninety per cent of the sermons preached in Chicago on the subject of the open brothel were directed against the Everleighs, but instead of seeing in these attacks a premonition of disaster, the sisters regarded them as good publicity. In the summer of 1911, further to attract attention to the resort, Minna Everleigh wrote and published an elaborate brochure, illustrated with photographs of the Club and setting forth its varied luxuries and enchantments, and declaring that the two things in Chicago which the visitors must not miss were the stockyards and the Everleigh Club. "With double front entrances," said the brochure, "the twin buildings of the Club are so constructed as to seem as one. Steam heat throughout, with electric fans in summer, one never feels the winter's chill or summer's heat in this luxurious resort. Fortunate indeed, with all the comforts of life surrounding them, are the members of the Everleigh Club." There was nothing really offensive about the booklet, and fewer than five hundred copies were actually distributed. But unfortunately for the sisters, one of them fell into the hands of Mayor Carter Harrison. Enraged, the Mayor, at noon on October 24, 1911, ordered the police to close the resort "because of its infamy, the audacious advertising of it, and as a solemn warning that the district had to be at least half-way decent."

The Mayor's order was transmitted immediately to John McWeeny, the General Superintendent of Police, but McWeeny ignored it for more than twelve hours. Meanwhile the afternoon newspapers had published the news that the Everleigh Club was doomed, and the brothel had the busiest night of many years; crowds of men hurried to the Club to say good-by and break a last bottle of wine with favorite strumpets. At the height of the revelry Minna told reporters that the police had notified her that the Club would probably

259

have to close within a few hours, but she declared that she was not in the least worried by the Mayor's action. She said to the Chicago *American:*

"You get everything in a life time. Of course, if the Mayor says we must close, that settles it. What the Mayor says goes, as far as I am concerned. I'm not going to be sore about it, either. I never was a knocker, and nothing the police of this town can do will change my disposition. I'll close up the shop and walk out with a smile on my face. Nobody else around here is worrying, either," she went on with a smile, waving a hand literally coruscated with diamonds toward the parlors, from which came sounds of music and bursts of laughter. "If the ship sinks we're going down with a cheer and a good drink under our belts, anyway."

At 2.45 o'clock on the morning of October 25, when it had become apparent that the politicians and the saloon-keepers could not induce Mayor Harrison to rescind the closing order, the doors of the Everleigh Club were locked and a policeman posted in front of the building with orders to allow no one to enter. Within twenty-four hours all of the harlots had departed to accept some of the hundreds of offers which had poured in by telephone and telegraph from all over the country; and in less than a week the sisters had put their furniture in storage and left the district. After a six months' vacation in Europe they returned to Chicago and bought a house on Washington Boulevard, with no intention, they said afterward, of attempting to operate a bagnio. But they were soon recognized, and sold the property to a man who, curiously enough, had made a fortune producing melodramas which exposed life in a brothel. Then the sisters went to New York, and as this is written they are still living there in strict retirement, rich, contented old ladies with nothing to remind them of the past but their fortune, a few photographs, and the gold piano.

8

THE house in South Dearborn Street was never opened again as a bordello. Ed Weiss, a well-known Levee figure, leased the building in January 1913, intending to pay the police twenty-five thousand dollars a year for protection and operate the property as a disorderly hotel, but the plan fell through and he gave up his lease. For several years the place was a Negro boarding-house, but during most of the two decades that followed the closing of the Everleigh Club it remained vacant. It was demolished in the spring of 1933.

9

NEXT to the Everleigh Club, the finest parlor-houses in the Levee were those operated by Vic Shaw, Zoe Millard, and Georgie Spencer, all of whom were active in the management of a society of madames called the Friendly Friends, which the Everleighs were not asked to join. Madame Shaw was a prominent red-light figure in Chicago for some forty years; after the Levee had been abolished she opened a luxurious call flat in South Michigan Avenue, and as late as 1938, though nearly seventy years old, she was busily running an under-cover joint on the North Side, near the Loop. Madame Millard was inclined to blame the Everleighs for everything that happened in the district; she frequently declared that they were " too damned exclusive," and once inflicted a terrible beating upon one of her own harlots for defending the sisters. Madame Spencer, whose brothel was on South Dearborn Street in the same block as the Everleigh Club, was the firebrand of the district; she was always in a furious rage about something, and her indignation when the police began to close the brothels was almost unbearable. One day, " redolent of riches and ablaze with diamonds," she dashed into the office of Police Captain Max Nootbaar, pounded his desk with her jeweled fist, and cried: " Listen to me, policeman! I'm rich. I own a hotel that's worth forty-five thousand dollars. I own a flat worth forty thousand, and these stones I'm wearing are worth another fifteen thousand. I'd like to see you interfere with my business." Captain Nootbaar listened politely, but continued to interfere with her business, and so successfully that she was driven from the Levee and retired with her fortune to California.

Despite the almost frantic efforts of Madames Shaw, Spencer, and Millard and their corps of pimps, the Everleigh sisters always said that the only real opposition they encountered was provided by Ed Weiss, who with his wife ran the brothel at No. 2135 South Dearborn, next door to the Club. Weiss first appeared in the Levee as part owner of Fred Buxbaum's dive at State and Twenty-second Streets, one of the toughest resorts in the city, which was on the ground floor of a famous assignation house, the Marlborough Hotel. Late in 1904 Weiss married Aimee Leslie, a " member " of the Everleigh Club, and the pair bought the brothel of Madame Julia Hartrauft; they got a bargain because the resort had just been held up by bandits who tied the madame to a chair and the girls to beds and escaped with ninety dollars in cash and three thousand dollars' worth of jewelry. The loot included an opal ring which Madame Hartrauft had bought the day before, and the madame said that the opal was responsible for her bad luck. Weiss remodeled and refitted the brothel and reopened it with his wife as madame and himself as general manager and head pimp. Their success was due in some measure to the luxury of the bordello's appointments and the beauty of its harlots, but it was also due, in part at least, to Weiss's shrewdness in putting most of the Levee's cab-drivers on his payroll. When a drunken spender poured himself into a cab and asked to be driven to the Everleigh Club, or to some other resort, as often as not he landed in Ed Weiss's place. And seldom knew the difference.

The brothel on the other side of the Everleigh Club, called the Sappho, was owned and operated by Weiss's brother, Louis. It was a first-class resort, but was never as popular as Ed's. Next to Georgie Spencer's house was a cheap brothel run by Mike Monahan, who in the 1890's was one of a brace of famous footpads known as " the long man and the short man." Between Monahan's place and the corner of Twenty-first Street were the Casino, run by Vic Shaw's husband, Roy Jones; and the bordellos of Emma Duval, who had usurped the title of French Em held so long by Emma Ritchie of Custom House Place; Harry Cusick, in later years manager of some of Al Capone's bawdy houses and payoff man for Johnny Torrio; Maurice Van Bever, an elegant pimp and pander who took the air daily in a fine carriage driven by a coachman clad in a high silk hat and a reddish-brown livery trimmed with solid-gold buttons.

On the west side of Dearborn Street, between Twenty-first and Cullerton, were Vic Shaw and Zoe Millard, besides the Frenchman's, Old Ninety-two, and French Charlie's. Across the street from the Everleigh Club were Madame Leo, Madame Frances; and the California, run by Blubber Bob Gray and his wife, Therese McCafey, which was the toughest parlor-house in the district. There were from thirty to forty girls in the California, wearing shoes, short, flimsy chemises, and nothing else. They stood naked in the windows and doorways whenever a policeman was not in sight, and two pimps were stationed on the sidewalk in front of the entrance, inviting every man who passed to come in. When customers appeared, the girls were paraded in a large room, bare of furniture except for a few benches placed against the walls, while Madame McCafey or her Negro housekeeper shouted: " Pick a baby, boys! Don't get stuck to your seats!" A dollar was the price, but fifty cents would

263

do if a man could prove by turning out his pockets that he didn't have the dollar. The California remained one of the vilest resorts on the Levee until the night of August 29, 1909, when it was raided by Federal immigration agents searching for alien women who had been brought to the United States for immoral purposes. They found six in the California. Blubber Bob Gray, who weighed three hundred pounds, tried to escape when the raiders entered, but stuck in a window, and three men were required to pull him out. He got out of trouble with much less difficulty, and within a year had reopened his brothel and was again a power in the Levee.

Several celebrated madames, both male and female, were located on Armour Avenue during the reign of the Everleighs. Frankie Wright, " that good old girl " of the 1870's, was between Eighteenth and Nineteenth Streets, still calling her bagnio the Library and still cherishing her bookcase and her uncut books. Big Jim Colosimo owned two large brothels, the Victoria at Armour and Archer Avenues, run for him by Sam Hare, and the Saratoga on Twenty-second Street, managed by a young New York gangster named Johnny Torrio, imported by Colosimo in 1908 as a bodyguard. The Victoria was so called in honor of Colosimo's wife, Victoria Moresco, who had opened it in the late 1890's. Colosimo himself spent most of his time at his famous café in Wabash Avenue near Twenty-second Street.

A notorious saloon called the Bucket of Blood was on Armour Avenue near Nineteenth Street, opposite Bed Bug Row; and between Cullerton and Twenty-first Streets were Dago Frank's, Eva Lowry's, another Van Bever dive; and Black May's, which provided light-skinned Negro girls for white men and was supposed to present the most bestial circuses ever seen in the United States. The Silver Dollar saloon and dance hall, owned by Jakie Adler and Harry Hopkins, was also in this block on Armour Avenue, and so

264

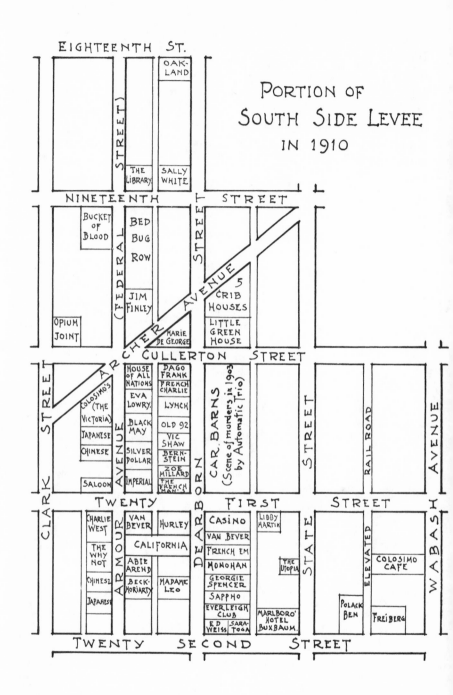

PORTION OF
SOUTH SIDE LEVEE
IN 1910

were George Little's combination saloon and brothel, the Imperial, and the celebrated House of All Nations, which had a two-dollar entrance and a five-dollar entrance. The same girls, however, worked both sides of the house. Also on Armour Avenue were two Japanese and two Chinese brothels, to which only white men were admitted. It was popularly supposed that the Oriental prostitutes, unable to withstand the rigorous Chicago climate, practiced their profession during the winter months clad in long woolen underwear. Near Twenty-first Street was a vicious resort called the Why Not? — perhaps in memory of Roger Plant of Under the Willow fame. The owner of this dive, John Pitt, was arrested and fined four hundred dollars in 1907 on complaint of a young girl who said he had kept her prisoner in the brothel for a year, forcing her to lead an immoral life. "They let me out of the house only a few times," she told the police, "and even then I was not allowed to go alone. My every act was watched. I was only seventeen when I was lured into this place by a man who seemed to me to be honorable. Pitt kept all the money I made, saying he was putting it into the bank for me."

As far as methods of operation were concerned, the brothels of the Levee differed in no important particular from the earlier bagnios of Clark Street and Custom House Place. In a few of the first-class resorts, and certainly in the Everleigh Club, a man was safe as long as he spent a reasonable amount of money, but in most of the bordellos a visitor was robbed whenever an opportunity occurred. To prepare him for "rolling," the victim was usually given morphine in wine or beer, a method which was recklessly used because of the widespread belief that the drug when thus administered could not be detected by an autopsy. Hard liquors were forbidden in the brothels and could be obtained in only a few places, but every resort sold wine, and all but the Everleigh Club handled beer. Enormous quantities of the latter beverage were disposed of; in 1910 it was estimated that the annual consumption of beer in the bordellos was more than seven million bottles. This liquor was bought for about four cents a pint and was sold by the madames at from twenty-five cents to a dollar. The so-called champagne used in the brothels cost from twelve to sixteen dollars a dozen, but the man who bought it paid from three to five dollars a bottle.

A few of the proprietors of the larger parlor-houses, notably Ed Weiss, Vic Shaw, and Georgie Spencer, provided small orchestras of from three to five musicians to play for the entertainment of their visitors, though only the Everleigh Club employed more than one. But a " professor," performing upon a banjo or a piano, was a standard feature throughout the district.

10

T H E investigation undertaken by the Chicago Vice Commission in 1910 disclosed that the average age of the parlor-house prostitute was twenty-three and one-half years, and that the professional life of a girl in the " big-time " resorts was seldom more than five years. After that she drifted downward into the lower-priced houses, then to the streets and the back rooms of saloons, and finally into such houses as those of the Jungle and Bed Bug Row. In consequence of this rapid turnover of what the vice lords callously called " stock," constant recruiting was necessary, and to supply the large demand and keep the brothels filled with fresh and attractive girls was the profitable business of the numerous gangs of procurers and white-slavers which operated, not only in Chicago, but in other large American cities as well. It was never established that a national organization of white-slavers existed, but it was often demonstrated that the gangs of the various cities used the same methods and worked together, and that girls were frequently shipped under guard all over the United States. Except in the cases of a few higher-ups, the protection paid by the brothel-keepers was seldom extended to white-slavers; even the politicians appeared to be horrified by such activities. But despite the efforts of police departments throughout the country the traffic was never brought under even a semblance of control until the Federal government entered the fight, operating at first under the immigration laws and later under the Mann Act of 1910.

One of the first Levee gangs of white-slavers with inter-city connections was organized about 1903 by Big Jim Colosimo and Maurice Van Bever. This gang was associated with similar outfits in New York, St. Louis, and Milwaukee, and was in successful operation for more than half a dozen years, in which time it was believed to have imported some two hundred girls into Chicago and sold them to brothel-keepers for prices ranging from ten to a hundred and fifty dollars. Most of these chattels were professional prostitutes, but many were young girls: one of whom there is official record was only a few weeks past her fifteenth birthday when she was brought to Chicago from Milwaukee and sold, for ten dollars and a proportion of her earnings for six months, to Bill Conroy, who ran the two brothels in Armour Avenue and Dearborn Street which were later owned by Maurice Van Bever. This girl was a prisoner for nearly six months, but in the spring of 1907, with the aid of a passer-by who was struck by her youthful appearance and obvious fear, she managed to escape through a window of the Dearborn Street house and make her way to the police station. There she told this story:

" My home is in Milwaukee. Some time ago I met a nice-appearing young man from Chicago in Milwaukee. He seemed interested in me and I thought he was honorable. He promised to get me a nice position in Chicago at eight dollars a week if I would come down here, and I came. I knew noth-

267

ing about Chicago. He took me straight to the house at 2115 Armour Avenue, and as soon as I entered the place I knew something was wrong. But I saw there was no chance to get away. My street clothes were taken away from me, and there was nothing for me to do but to submit to orders. They kept me at 2115 Armour Avenue a while and then transferred me to 2117 Dearborn Street. I stayed there until I thought I should go mad if I could not escape. I waited my chance and then crawled through a window."

The slaver who had sold the girl could not be found, but Conroy was arrested and tried on a charge of pandering. The girl's mother swore that she was less than sixteen years of age, but Conroy's lawyers, hired by the white-slave gang, brought into court a large number of witnesses, many of them supposedly reputable tradesmen from whom he bought his supplies. These men testified unanimously that the character of the girl was very bad, " so bad, in fact," as the *Record-Herald* put it, " that the stainless jointkeeper had rendered her almost a service by allowing her to live in his establishments." The girl was sent back to Milwaukee with her mother, but Conroy was acquitted.

The operations of the Colosimo and Van Bever gang were halted, for a few years at least, in 1909, when Federal agents discovered that the slavers had brought twelve girls to Chicago from St. Louis and placed them in Levee bordellos. Van Bever and his wife, Julia, were found guilty of pandering and were each fined a thousand dollars and sentenced to one year in prison. Convictions were also obtained against other members of the gang, among them Mike and Molly Hart, Dick and Julia Tyler, and Joe Bovo, who had accompanied the girls from St. Louis. Several of the prostitutes had been found in Big Jim Colosimo's two bagnios, but as the report of the Vice Commission said, Colosimo " could not be reached." His managers, Johnny Torrio and Sam Hare, were arrested, but could not be convicted because Joe Bovo refused to testify against them. This case marked the first appearance, in the newspapers and in a Chicago courtroom, of Johnny Torrio, who organized the first of the bootleg gangs in prohibition times and for several years was the biggest criminal figure in the United States.

Some of the white-slave gangs handled only foreign women, who were shipped out to them by the bands which operated in New York and other cities of the Atlantic seaboard. One such gang, headed by French Em Duval and her husband, with headquarters in French Em's dive on Dearborn Street, ran its own brothel on Armour Avenue and maintained a stockade in the suburb of Blue Island, known as the Retreat, where the women were kept to await buyers. Some of the rooms in the stockade were equipped with iron bars, and none of the women was allowed to have any street clothing until the time came to transfer her to the brothel by which she had been purchased. French Em and her fellow slavers made profits aggregating two hundred thousand dollars before the gang was finally broken up by Federal immigration inspectors in 1908.

Another gang with Eastern and foreign connections, said by the police to have been the best-organized band that ever worked in Chicago, operated from the Dewey Hotel on Washington Boulevard, on the top floor of which were its stockades and breaking-in rooms. This gang was composed almost entirely of Russian Jews and specialized in the sale of Russian Jewesses, who have always brought high prices in American bagnios. Once a week the slavers held a meeting to discuss the stock on hand, the bordellos to which girls were to be sent, and the prices to be charged, and to make arrangements for incoming shipments from the East. Occasionally, when large stocks of women had been accumulated, auctions were held at which the prostitutes were stripped, inspected by the brothel-keepers, and sold to the highest bidders. In one week in the late fall of 1906 twenty-five women

269

were thus disposed of at from twenty-five to one hundred dollars each. But the purchase price did not represent the whole of the profit to be gained from the sale of a harlot, for the prostitute's share of her earnings was, in most instances, turned over to the gang.

The most vicious of the white-slave gangs were those which found their victims among the underpaid domestic servants, factory girls, waitresses and department-store salesgirls, thousands of whom were struggling to keep alive on wages of from four to seven dollars a week. Starving for pleasure and amusement, and frequently for food as well, many of these girls were easy prey for the attractive women of middle age and the glib-tongued, well-dressed young men who were employed by the white-slavers as ropers. The women offered the girls better jobs, and the young men offered them romance, and took them to the theaters, the dance halls, and the wine-rooms. The end in any case was the same — the girl was eventually enticed into an apartment or a house, and having been " broken-in " was sold to a brothel. The extent of these operations was shown by the fact that during a period of about nine months in 1907 and 1908 the police arrested a hundred and fifty-seven women for roping and rescued three hundred and twenty-nine young girls from the bagnios. One of them, found in the House of All Nations in July 1908, had been sold by her brother, a Levee " professor."

Several white-slave gangs of this type had stockades and breaking-in places on South Wabash Avenue near Twenty-second Street. One at No. 2226 was discovered in the spring of 1907 when a desperate seventeen-year-old girl fought off five men with a long hatpin; she had been brought to the house by Emma Mosel, notorious in the Levee district for several years as a procuress, and equally well known on West Nineteenth Street as the honest and hard-working mother of five young children. Another clearing-house for white slaves at No. 2252 South Wabash Avenue was raided by the police in 1907 as the result of revelations by an eighteen-year-old girl who had been employed in a department store. On March 3, 1907 this girl was induced by a young man named Harry Balding, twenty years old, to accompany him to the Prima Dance Hall on Thirty-fifth Street. There she was drugged, and was then taken to the place on Wabash Avenue and kept prisoner for three days, during which time she was attacked almost continuously by Balding and three other young men. After she had thus been brutalized she was sold for fifty dollars to Roy Jones and Barry Cusick and installed in their brothel in Dearborn Street.

In the latter part of May the girl wrote a letter to her mother and threw it from the window of the bagnio, and a passer-by picked it up and put it in a mail-box. The mother notified the police, and the raid followed. Roy Jones and Cusick were arrested in their bordello and the girl released, and at the Wabash Avenue stockade the police took into custody Balding and two other young men, one of whom was eighteen years old and the other twenty. Bill McNamara, the older of this pair, confessed that he had been hired by Jones to rape girls brought into the place, and said: " I know that a man who would do such a thing ought to be taken out and shot." Convictions were obtained in all of these cases, but the punishments inflicted were not very severe. Balding was fined three hundred dollars and sent to jail for one year, but the others were only fined, in amounts ranging from one hundred to two hundred dollars.

II

T H E R E were between seven thousand and eight thousand legal saloons in Chicago during the first dozen years of the twentieth century — the number rose and fell according to the cost of liquor licenses and protection — and perhaps half as many speakeasies, or blind pigs, as they were called in those days. At least two-thirds of them operated a wine-room in connection with the bar, and it was estimated that an average of thirty thousand women, the vast majority either professional or semi-professional prostitutes, gathered in these places every night for a decade. An extensive investigation made by the *Record-Herald* in 1907 disclosed that virtually every resort of this type in the city was openly violating the law, in most instances with the connivance of the police and the politicians. These three places, all in the West Side vice district, were typical:

"119 Halsted Street, Bob Miller, prop.: Saloon open after one o'clock; men and women drinking in rear room; disorderly conduct the rule; men in last stages of intoxication; many asleep on the floor.

"135 Halsted Street, Mike Fewer, prop.: Conditions revolting; men in drunken stupor; women openly soliciting; girls eighteen and nineteen years old intoxicated; women in so-called vaudeville act indulging in disgusting contortions.

"225 Halsted Street, Billy Murphy, prop.: Women summoned by bartender from rear room on entrance of customer; in rear room men and women sprawling in various stages of intoxication."

The number of dance halls in Chicago varied from a hundred and fifty to three hundred,[1] with at least a hundred going full blast every night. Many others were closed except when rented to so-called pleasure clubs or societies, which periodically conducted masked balls with little or no police or other supervision. Young boys and girls were admitted to these affairs, drinks were served to them, and many of the

---

[1] The Vice Commission found approximately two hundred and eighty-five in the fall of 1910.

places provided rooms upstairs where drunken girls could be taken for purposes of rape or seduction. Newspaper reporters who visited Hoerber's Dance Hall on Blue Island Avenue during a masked ball given by a "pleasure club" in January 1905 found boys in knee pants drinking at the bar, and girls as young as twelve and fourteen years drinking and dancing with all comers. And Hoerber's resort was no worse than scores of others. Investigators for the Chicago Vice Commission, who attended a large number of these balls in 1910, found prostitutes at nearly every one. "These girls and women," said the Commission's report, "openly made dates to go to nearby hotels or assignation rooms after the dance. In some instances they were accompanied by their cadets who were continually on the lookout for new victims. Young boys come to these dances for the express purpose of 'picking up' young girls with whom they can take liberties in hotels, rooms or hallways of their homes."

Perhaps the most disreputable of the dance halls were the Prima on Thirty-fifth Street, Schumacher's on Ashland Avenue, the Dana on West Chicago Avenue, the Alma Club House at Madison and Paulina Streets; the Wellington Dancing Academy on North Clark Street, which was closed for a few months in 1904 following the suicide of a seventeen-year-old girl; Freiberg's Dance Hall on Twenty-second Street between Wabash Avenue and State Street, operated by Ike Bloom and his brother-in-law, Solly Freidman; and the Capitol on Twenty-second Street and the Omaha on Armour Avenue, both owned by Ed Weiss. The worst of the lot was Freiberg's, which was a typical resort of its kind — a bar opening on the street, and in the rear a long room with small tables scattered about the dance floor, an orchestra in the balcony, and a platform on which singers and dancers entertained with vulgar songs and suggestive cavortings. With the exception of the Everleigh Club, Freiberg's was probably the best-known resort in Chicago. The *Rec-*

273

ord-Herald in 1905 called it "notorious even among the other dens of revelry and orgy which make up the South Side Levee," and five years later the report of the Chicago Vice Commission described it as "the most notorious place in Chicago." The report continued:

> "Every girl who frequents this place is a professional prostitute, groomed and trained to coax money out of the pockets of visitors for the benefit of the managers and then to persuade him to go to a hotel or to their own flats. One of the rules of this place is that a girl is supposed to make each man spend at least forty cents for every round of drinks. The price of admission to men is twenty-five cents, in addition to a tip of ten cents for checking a hat. The girls are very aggressive, and do not wait for an invitation, but sit down at the tables, and as pointed out above, order a round of drinks that costs no less than forty cents. The mixed drinks brought to the prostitutes are counterfeit. For instance the girl orders a ' B ' ginger ale highball. This is colored water made in imitation of this drink. The cost is probably less than a cent, but the victim pays twenty-five or fifty cents for it. The business is run in a systematic manner; the prostitutes must be in their places at 9 p.m. If they are tardy, the manager ' calls them down.' "

The girls who worked in Freiberg's charged five dollars for their services, and as a rule took their customers to the Marlborough Hotel over Fred Buxbaum's dive in Twenty-second Street, in which Ike Bloom owned an interest. The price of a room there was usually five dollars, of which the girl got half. The average weekly earnings of a member of Ike Bloom's corps of prostitutes was about forty dollars, but an investigator for the Vice Commission found one girl who said she seldom made less than a hundred. However, she was an exceptional strumpet who had no pimp, didn't drink, and refused to "grease" the police. "I used to pay a lot of protection money to policemen," she said, "but I got wise in time. If they threaten to pinch me, why I say, go ahead and pinch me, then they won't. No, I never knew any of their names, but I could point them out to you any time. Hell, they all graft. There is not a policeman around here that doesn't hold us girls up, and I know it from experience. But you see us girls who have been around a long time get wise, and they don't get a nickel out of me any more. I think I make more than any of the girls around here, and I don't spend it on booze like the rest of them. That's why they never have anything."

Repeated attempts were made by reform organizations to close Freiberg's, but except for a brief period in the fall of 1903, when Bloom's liquor license was revoked by the aldermen's graft commission, and in 1905 when the doors of the dive were shut for a month by order of Mayor Edward F. Dunne, it was in continuous operation for thirteen years. Bloom's license was again revoked and the dance hall closed on August 24, 1914, after Mayor Carter Harrison had received from the Women's City Club a petition signed by 18,816 voters. In the crowd on the final night were two girls who said that they had spent every evening there for ten years. The resort was reopened late in 1915 when Big Bill Thompson proclaimed a wide-open town, and was operated for several years as the Vienna and the Midnight Frolics. Bloom was of little importance during the prohibition period, although his name was occasionally connected with a brothel or cabaret. He died in 1930 after a long illness which necessitated the amputation of both his legs.

12

THE multitudinous tasks involved in regulating competition, arranging for protection, acting as liaison agents for the police and the politicians, and collecting tribute from the keepers of brothels and other resorts, were performed by the so-called vice kings. On the West Side the chief monarchs were Jim Cross, head of the ring which controlled the Jungle; Mike de Pike Heitler, who was sent to Leavenworth Penitentiary for white-slavery in 1916; and Mike Fewer, who owned two concert saloons, the Blue Ribbon and the Globe, besides his Halsted Street dive. On the South Side, in the Levee, the most important figures were Ike Bloom, Big Jim Colosimo, Roy Jones, Maurice Van Bever, Blubber Bob Gray, Ed Weiss, Harry Hopkins and Jakie Adler of the Silver Dollar, Harry Cusick, Dago Frank Lewis; George Little, who also owned the Here It Is saloon on the West Side; and John Jordan, better known as Pops and the Immune, who was the husband of Georgie Spencer and the owner of a saloon at Twentieth Street and Wabash Avenue. Singly and in various combinations, for there were frequent changes of alliance and partnership, all of these men were on top of the heap at various times. Probably the most powerful over the longest period of time was Ike Bloom, whose photograph, handsomely framed, hung for several years in a place of honor in the squad room of the Twenty-second Street police station. It was removed in 1914 by Captain Max Nootbaar, an honest policeman who became enraged when Bloom called upon him to "make arrangements." Minna Everleigh once said: "Positively the dive-keepers feared Ike Bloom more than the Twenty-second Street police captain or any inspector ever placed in charge of the district."

The real rulers of the Levee, however, were those renowned aldermen, Bathhouse John Coughlin and Hinky Dink Mike Kenna, whose bailiwick, the First Ward, included all of the segregated district. In letters made public by the State's Attorney in 1914, Minna Everleigh declared that all orders relative to protection payments and other Levee

BATHHOUSE JOHN AND THE COVER
OF HIS FAMOUS SONG

activities came from Coughlin and Kenna through Ike Bloom and Solly Freidman. She said that the brothel-keepers were compelled to place their insurance with a company controlled by Bathhouse John; that they were ordered to buy all of their liquor from Freiberg's, in which Coughlin was commonly reputed to own a half-interest; and that they were given a list of four grocery stores at which they could buy their food supplies. In the course of their forty-year domination of the Levee and of the First Ward, Coughlin and Kenna were accused of grafting and collecting tribute from the district by virtually every newspaper in Chicago, and by every reform organization that was active after 1894. But none of the charges ever reached the point of prosecution, perhaps because in the main they followed the advice given to Coughlin by William Mason, for many years Representative at Large for Illinois and afterward United States Senator. Mason told Bathhouse John to stick to the "small stuff" and let the "big stuff" alone. The small stuff paid well enough for Coughlin to buy a racing stable of sixty horses and a country estate, with a private zoo, in Colorado.

Bathhouse John was the big noise of the Coughlin-Kenna combination, but Hinky Dink furnished most of the brains. Coughlin was first elected Alderman in 1892, but possessed slight influence until Kenna also became a member of the City Council in 1897. It was Hinky Dink who established the standard rate of fifty cents a vote, and who conceived the idea of organizing the First Ward Democratic Club, of which every registered voter was automatically a member and entitled to carry an identification card. With this organization, from their headquarters in Hinky Dink's Workingman's Exchange in South Clark Street near Van Buren, the pair of political spoilsmen controlled the First Ward from 1897 to Coughlin's death in 1938.[1]

The annual ball of the First Ward Club, by which

---

[1] Kenna is still living and still an alderman.

Coughlin and Kenna added from twenty-five thousand to fifty thousand dollars to their campaign fund every year, was held in the Chicago Coliseum during the Christmas holidays. The report of the Illinois Crime Survey described the ball as the "annual underworld orgy given by Alderman Michael Kenna and Alderman John Coughlin, bosses of the First Ward, for the purposes of retaining control of prostitutes and criminals of the First Ward Levee for political purposes and for political funds." Every harlot, every pimp, every streetwalker and pickpocket, every burglar and footpad, was expected to buy at least one ticket, and the keepers of the brothels, saloons, and other resorts had to take large blocks. The most important madames bought boxes, where they sat in state amidst their strumpets, guzzling champagne by the case and rubbing elbows with city officials and prominent politicians. On the dance floor swarmed the riffraff of the city, all masked, most of them drunk, and many of the ladies wearing what the newspapers delicately called "abbreviated costumes." As the *Record-Herald* said in 1903, "Disreputables from every levee resort in the throng, blackmailers and thugs paraded arm-in-arm with the police sent to guard pleasure-seekers from loss of jewelry."

Reform elements attempted every year to prevent the ball, which Bathhouse John called "the derby," but it was an annual affair for a decade. In 1908 the rector, warden, and vestry of Grace Episcopal Church asked the Superior Court for an injunction, but the court held that the matter was not within its jurisdiction. On December 13, two days before the ball was to be held, a bomb was exploded in the Coliseum, wrecking a two-story building used as a warehouse and breaking windows within a radius of two blocks. The police said that the bomb had been planted by "fanatical reformers." The ball was given as scheduled, and Bathhouse John told newspaper reporters that "it was the nicest Derby we ever had." But the Reverend Melbourne P. Boynton of the Lexington Avenue Baptist Church, who was there, said it was "unspeakably low, vulgar and immoral." Most people believed the preacher. The 1908 ball was the last. When Coughlin announced plans for the affair in 1909, such a storm of opposition arose that Mayor Fred Busse refused to issue a liquor license. On December 13 of that year Coughlin and Kenna gave a concert by Tony Fischer's band in the Coliseum, but fewer than three thousand persons attended, and two hundred policemen were on hand to see that no liquor was served. In consequence, the affair was probably the dullest the Levee had ever seen. No attempt was made to hold the ball in 1910 nor any year thereafter.

13

ALDERMAN COUGHLIN was called Bathhouse John because he had once been a rubber in a Turkish bath; Kenna was known as Hinky Dink, and sometimes as the Little Fellow, because he was a small man. Kenna possessed no illusions about politics; he was a shrewd, forthright man who said what he meant and meant what he said, and never went back on his word. There was never any doubt as to where he stood or what he intended to do. In many respects Bathhouse John was a bombastic jackass who attempted to conceal his political shenanigans behind a plethora of meaningless words about democracy and the rights of the working man. He was pompous, willing to perform any antic that would get his name in the newspapers, and addicted to the use of big words without the slightest idea of their meaning. Once he told Carter Harrison that he was certain to be re-elected Mayor "because of the honesty that has caricatured your every act."

As far as appearance went, Bathhouse John was himself a caricature. He customarily wrapped his heavy frame in a long, green frock coat and a vest of thick plush, beneath which, in cold weather, were two suits of heavy underwear, one of wool and one of balbriggan. On formal occasions he sometimes wore ordinary dinner clothes, but more often he would appear wondrously arrayed in silk hat, pink gloves, yellow shoes, a swallow-tail coat of bottle green, lavender pants, and a cream-colored vest blazing with diamond studs and embroidered with roses and carnations. This was the costume in which he led the grand march at the First Ward Ball. In 1899 Bathhouse John wrote a poem called " Dear Midnight of Love," which had all the literary quality of a first-grade essay on " Oh, See the Cat." Nevertheless, it was set to a sort of music and was sung at the Chicago Opera House, with some difficulty, by May de Sousa, a popular songstress of the period. The chorus follows :

> *Dear Midnight of Love, why did we meet?*
> *Dear Midnight of Love, your face is so sweet.*
> *Pure as the angels above, surely again we will speak;*
> *Loving only as doves, Dear Midnight of Love.*

Frequently thereafter the newspapers published poetic effusions, such as " An Ode to a Bath Tub," and " Why Did They Build Lake Michigan So Wide? " which were supposedly composed by Bathhouse John. In reality they were written by John Kelley of the *Record-Herald,* later a police reporter for the *Tribune,* who kept the gag alive for years.

CHAPTER IX

THE FIGHT AGAINST THE LEVEE

THE MOST dramatic of the many attacks made upon
segregated vice in the first decade of the twentieth century was the invasion of the South Side Levee by the famous
English evangelist Gipsy Smith during a series of revival
meetings held in the autumn of 1909. On October 15 Smith
announced his intention of leading " an army of Christians "
into the red-light district, and went ahead with his preparations despite the vigorous opposition of many religious leaders who believed that undesirable publicity would result.
The General Superintendent of Police, Leroy T. Steward,
finally promised to provide an escort of mounted policemen,
but said that he would do so to prevent possible rioting; he
regarded Smith's plan as " inherently vicious," and declared
that it would only advertise the Levee. The evangelist re-
torted that he wanted to advertise it, that sin must be exposed before it could be destroyed. He notified the newspapers and invited them to send reporters.

On the night of October 18 Gipsy Smith concluded his
service, in the Seventh Regiment Armory at Wentworth Avenue and Thirty-fourth Street, with a stirring prayer for
divine aid against the cohorts of evil. Then, with no word
of exhortation or command, he stepped from his pulpit and
walked slowly down the aisle and into Wentworth Avenue.
Behind him streamed his congregation of men, women, and
children, many of them wearing long black gowns and carry-

ing unlighted torches. In front of the Armory a squad of mounted policemen closed in around the evangelist, and three brass bands swung into line. But at first there was no music, and no light except the flickering gleam of the street lamps. For block after block Smith and his followers went forward in a silence broken only by the boom of a drum, the heavy tramp of feet, and an occasional jeering laugh from the great throng of idlers and scoffers which flanked the procession. The crusaders made no effort to march in formation; at some points they filled the street from curb to curb, and at others they straggled along two and three abreast. Newspaper estimates of their number varied from three thousand to twelve thousand, but all of the reporters agreed that the crowd which had come along to see the show was several times as large. At least twenty thousand persons were following Gipsy Smith when at length he reached the Levee.

As the evangelist stepped into Twenty-second Street he raised both hands above his head and began to sing, while the torches flared into flame and the bands struck up " Where He Leads Me I Will Follow." Slowly, almost at half-step, to the accompaniment of hymns played in the tempo of a funeral march, the crusaders shuffled back and forth through the district, traversing every street, passing and repassing every brothel and every dive. As they marched they sang, shouted prayers, and praised God, while the harlots, wondering and vaguely disturbed, watched from the upper windows of the bagnios. In front of the Everleigh Club, the House of All Nations, and other notorious resorts, the evangelist and his congregation knelt in the street, intoning the Lord's Prayer, reciting the Twenty-third Psalm, and singing " Where is My Wandering Boy Tonight? " After an hour the crusaders raised their voices in " Nearer, My God, to Thee " and marched out of the district; they followed Gipsy Smith to the Alhambra Theatre at State Street and Archer

282

Avenue, where the evangelist led them in a prayer service for the fallen.

The Levee received this strange visitation in almost utter quiet. Brothels, saloons, and dives were closed and darkened, and the streets were deserted save for a few prostitutes and pimps who huddled in the doorways. Even the hoodlums who formed a large proportion of the crowd of sightseers were curiously quiet; they voiced no threats and few jeers. But within ten minutes after the departure of the crusaders the Levee had sprung to life. Red lights gleamed, doors swung open, corks popped, music blared from pianos and banjos, and from their hiding-places swarmed the pimps, streetwalkers, and thieves. While Gipsy Smith prayed in the Alhambra Theatre the Levee enjoyed the biggest night in its history; hundreds of boys and young men whose previous knowledge of vice had been gained by hearsay now learned of it through first-hand experience. "We were certainly glad to get all this business," said one smug madame, "but I was sorry to see so many nice young men down here for the first time."

This was the theme of the great storm of criticism and reproach which broke over Chicago on the morning of October 19. The newspapers published complete and accurate accounts of the extraordinary march, but for the most part their editorials dismissed it as the futile gesture of a crank. Politicians laughed and city officials refused to comment, while many ministers hastened to disavow any connection with the invasion. But Gipsy Smith said: " Time will show that great good has been done," and his vision was clearer than that of any of his critics. The immediate results of the foray into the Levee were unquestionably bad, but ultimately it was shown to have made the first breach in the fortifications of entrenched vice. Nothing that had ever happened in Chicago, not even the publication of William T. Stead's startling book, had so focused public attention upon segregated prostitution; the city suddenly found itself more conscious than ever before in its history of the evil within its borders. Inspired by Gipsy Smith's success, three thousand members of the Woman's Christian Temperance Union, led by Mrs. Emily C. Hill, president of the Cook County Chapter, paraded through the downtown streets on January 27, 1910. Crowding into City Hall, they demanded that Mayor Fred Busse enforce the Revised Municipal Code of 1905, which forbade the operation of a house of ill-fame or assignation, and imposed a fine of two hundred dollars upon any person convicted of being a keeper, inmate, or patron of an immoral resort. Mayor Busse promised an investigation, and Mrs. Hill urged him to pray for divine guidance. The Mayor tartly replied that he would do so at the proper time and place.

2

On January 31, 1910, a momentous meeting of the Federated Protestant Churches, representing six hundred congregations, was held in the Central Y.M.C.A. building for the purpose of discussing " the social evil problem in Chicago." The Very Reverend Walter T. Sumner, Dean of the Episcopal Cathedral of SS. Peter and Paul, read a paper on the subject, and then introduced this resolution, which was unanimously adopted:

" Resolved, that the Mayor of the City of Chicago be asked to appoint a Commission made up of men and women who command the respect and confidence of the public at large, this Commission to investigate thoroughly the conditions as they exist. With this knowledge obtained, let it map out such a course, as in its judgment, will bring about some relief from the frightful conditions which surround us. Taking this report as a basis, let us enlist the support of every civic, protective, philanthropic, social, commercial and religious body in the city to carry out the plans suggested. If the present administration feels that it cannot subscribe to such a plan, make the report the basis of a pledge from the political parties at the next election and make it the basis for an election issue. But first get the plan. The city press will be back of any sane movement to improve present conditions. The Church certainly is. Social settlements have been agitating and endeavoring to reach some decision. The general public is in a mood to listen to such conclusions as such a Commission would reach."

A special committee transmitted the resolution to Mayor Busse, and on March 5, 1910 the Mayor announced the appointment of a Vice Commission of thirty members, among them such leading citizens as Dean Sumner; the Reverend James F. Callaghan of St. Malachy's Roman Catholic Church; Bishop C. T. Shaffer of the African Methodist Episcopal Church; Dr. Anna Dwyer, president of the Mary Thompson Hospital; Dr. W. A. Evans, City Health Commissioner; Dr. Frank W. Gunsaulus, president of Armour Institute; Harry Olson, Chief Justice of the Municipal Court; Alexander Robertson, vice-president of the Continental National Bank; Julius Rosenwald, president of Sears, Roebuck & Company; Edwin W. Sims, United States District Attorney; Professor Herbert L. Willett of Chicago University; Judge Merritt W. Pinckney of the Juvenile Court; and Edward M. Skinner of the Association of Commerce. At the same time the Mayor issued a statement to the newspapers in which he said: " As a matter of fact, the conditions incident to the vice problem in Chicago are better than they have ever been within present day memory. But," he continued, " we all want still better conditions if they can be had."

The Vice Commission was organized on March 15, 1910, with the election of Dean Sumner as chairman and Edwin W. Sims as secretary. On June 27, 1910, the City Council passed an ordinance officially creating the Commission and appropriating five thousand dollars to carry on its work of investigation. An additional five thousand was provided by the Council's Finance Committee early in 1911. To the amazement of all observers, the ordinance of June 27 was passed without a dissenting voice, even such foes of reform as John Powers, Hinky Dink Kenna, and Bathhouse John Coughlin voting aye. This apparent desertion of the vice lords was never satisfactorily explained, but it was generally thought that Mayor Busse and the members of the City Council had been led to believe that a majority of the appointees were in favor of continued segregation, and that the committee would so report.

On July 15, 1910, the Commission opened offices in the downtown business district, and actual field work was immediately begun by a large corps of investigators under the direction of George W. Kneeland, a social worker of wide experience.

Meanwhile two important events relating to the red-light district had occurred. Pointing out a possible new line of attack upon commercialized vice, a judge had issued an injunction restraining six persons from operating brothels in South Chicago, holding that the presence of an immoral resort damaged adjacent property; and the Police Department had promulgated twelve new rules governing the regulation of vice. These rules, which the Superintendent of Police said would be rigidly enforced, were as follows:

1. Messenger and delivery boys, or any person over the age of three or under the age of eighteen years, shall not be permitted either in the district or to enter the premises.

286

2. Harboring of inmates under legal age. . . . If inmates under age are found, the house shall be suppressed, and it shall be definitely understood that this action will be taken in any and all cases where this law is violated.

3. Forcible detention. No person, regardless of age, shall be detained against his or her will, nor shall iron bars or other obstacles be permitted upon any exit.

4. No women without male escorts shall be permitted in a saloon. All soliciting of this nature to be vigorously suppressed.

5. Short skirts, transparent gowns or other improper attire shall not be permitted in the parlors, or public rooms.

6. Men will not be permitted to conduct or be domiciled in a house of prostitution or to loiter about the premises. Males evidently subsisting on the income of inmates shall be arrested as vagrants.

7. Soliciting in any form shall not be permitted, either on the street, from doorways, from windows or in saloons.

8. Signs, lights, colors or devices, significant or conspicuous, indicative of the character of any premises occupied by a house of ill-repute, shall not be permitted.

9. Obscene exhibitions or pictures shall not be permitted.

10. Restricted districts. No house of ill-fame shall be permitted outside of certain restricted districts, or to be established within two blocks of any school, church, hospital, or public institution, or upon any street car line.

11. Doors. No swinging doors that permit of easy access or a view of the interior from the street shall be permitted. All resorts shall be provided with double doors which shall be kept closed.

12. Liquor. On and after May 1, 1910, no liquor will be permitted to be sold, carried in stock or given away in connection with any immoral place.

The promulgation of these rules less than two months after the appointment of the Vice Commission was symptomatic of the fact that the pressure of public opinion was already being felt by the police and the politicians. It was obvious, however, that they had been issued not so much for the purpose of regulating prostitution as to clean up the red-light districts to a certain extent, and to emphasize the advantages of segregation, before the work of the Commission actually got under way. The vice kings, however, refused to co-operate; they looked upon the activities of the Commission as nothing more than silly gestures by fanatical reformers. The rule against selling liquor was enforced for a few months, but the others were ignored. As the Vice Commission said later, "There has been lax observance of police regulations so long that police orders are not taken seriously."

3

T H E report of the Vice Commission embodied the findings of the most careful and searching study of the social evil ever undertaken in the United States; it revealed for the first time the extraordinary extent of commercialized prostitution and its enormous profits. In a period of six weeks of intensive work the Commission held ninety-eight special conferences, at which there appeared representatives of more than thirty philanthropic, civic, social, reform, and business organizations of such diverse interests and aims as the Anti-Cigarette League, Hull House, and the Retail Liquor Dealers' Protective Association. Prominent citizens, clergymen, professional reformers, and social workers were heard, and so were city and police officials, patrolmen, detectives, saloon-keepers, brewers, distillers, and keepers and inmates of brothels. Agents employed by the Commission visited bordellos, assignation houses, wine-rooms, saloons, dance halls, amusement parks, excursion steamers, even ice-cream parlors and nickel movie shows, observing conditions and interviewing madames, inmates, streetwalkers, pimps, factory girls, white-slavers, and bartenders. Despite the lack of sufficient funds, every phase of the problem was investigated, from the danger to respectable immigrant women to the effect of vice upon the lives of children who lived in areas adjacent to the segregated districts. The Commission's final recommendation, based upon its studies and a great mass of statistical information, was as follows:

"Constant and persistent repression of prostitution the immediate method; absolute annihilation the ultimate ideal."

That its recommendation might be put in force "effectually and unremittingly," the Commission urged the establishment of a Morals Court and the appointment of a Morals Commission. Both of these suggestions were eventually carried out by Mayor Carter Harrison, Jr., the former in 1913 and the latter in 1915. In its summary of existing conditions the report of the Vice Commission said in part:

"The first truth that the Commission desires to impress upon the citizens of Chicago is the fact that prostitution in this city is a *Commercialized Business* of large proportions with tremendous profits of more than Fifteen Million Dollars per year, controlled largely by men, not women. Separate the male exploiter from the problem, and we minimize its extent and abate its flagrant outward expression. . . . In juxtaposition with this group of professional male exploiters stand ostensibly respectable citizens, both men and women, who are openly renting and leasing property for exorbitant sums, and thus sharing, through immorality of investments, the profits from this *Business*. . . . Evidence has been produced showing that a highly respected and honored company, in whose hands respectable citizens entrust their money, has apparently assumed the trusteeship of four of the vilest houses of ill-fame in the Twenty-second Street restricted district. Again, several wealthy and prominent business men, whose advice is sought in matters pertaining to the civic welfare and development of Chicago, are leasing their houses on —— Street and —— Avenue for this business. One of these men has six houses in a part of the district where the most disgusting and flagrant violations of the law and police rules occur. The court records show that practically no effort had been made during the past three years to prosecute agents and real estate owners who are leasing and renting property for immoral purposes. The law affecting these persons is a dead letter. . . . During the month of October an investigator visited sixty-five real estate agents and owners, most of whom were located in residential sections of the city, and in forty-four instances they offered to rent rooms and flats. In each instance the investigator stated she wanted to rent the premises for a ' sporting house.'

" These statements may seem exaggerated and highly colored, but a careful, ultra-conservative study of conditions in this municipality has put the Commission in possession of absolute facts upon which to base these conclusions.

" In the second place the Commission believes that something can be done by law honestly and efficiently administered. Practically no attempt has been made in Chicago to enforce the present laws. In place of enforcing the law the police have been allowed to adopt arbitrary rules and uncertain regulations of their own, whereby certain sections of the city have become restricted districts. Here they established their own regulations which were without adequate legal foundation.

"The Commission has found in its investigation that the most dangerous immoral influence, and the most important financial interest, outside of the business of prostitution as carried on in houses, is the disorderly saloons. The proprietors of these places are using prostitutes as an adjunct to the sale of beer and liquor, and are allowing them to openly solicit for immoral purposes in their rear rooms. During the period of its investigation the Commission has secured definite information regarding 445 saloons in different parts of the city. The investigators have counted 929 unescorted women in these saloons, who by their actions and conversation were believed to be prostitutes. In fact, they were solicited by more than 236 women in 236 different saloons, all of whom, with the exception of 98, solicited for rooms, ' hotels,' and houses of prostitution over the saloons."

The inquiries of the Vice Commission proved conclusively that the policy of segregation had been a complete failure, and that not more than one-half of Chicago's immoral resorts were confined within the limits of the red-light areas. Said the report:

"New houses, especially in the flat buildings, are being established in residental districts at an alarming rate. In fact, there are more houses of this character in these sections of the city than in the so-called restricted districts. When the order was issued prohibiting the sale of liquor in the houses, many of the keepers removed from the restricted districts into the residential sections and opened flats. Many inmates have left the houses and now live in flats, where they sell liquor under a government receipt, procured at a cost of twenty-five dollars. 'There are five hundred flats opened up on the South Side since May 1st,' an inspector states. 'There are three hundred and sixty flats with prostitution on Cottage Grove Avenue and all over; that is, from Twenty-second Street south and east of State Street.' It is undoubtedly true that the result of the order has been to scatter the prostitutes over a wider territory. . . .

"There is quite a number of massage parlors, manicure establishments and Turkish baths, especially in the downtown district, which are in reality nothing but houses of prostitution of the most revolting and insidious type. It is practically impossible to secure legal evidence against these places. . . .

"Assignation hotels are scattered all over the city, especially in the downtown district and on the West and North sides. Prostitutes in saloons and on the streets use these cheap places. . . . There are also a great many assignation rooms, especially on the North Side from the river to Chicago Avenue and on the side streets west of State. These rooms are used to the same extent as the hotels and conditions in them are about the same. . . ."

On October 26, 1910, the Police Department issued, for the use of the Commission, a list which contained the addresses of 192 houses of prostitution, with 189 madames and 1,012 inmates; 272 flats with 252 keepers and 419 inmates; and forty-two hotels catering to an immoral trade, eight of them operated by women. This was a total of 506 resorts and 1,880 madames and harlots. But the Commission's investigators found an additional 514 houses, flats, saloons, and hotels, all used for immoral purposes and of which the police professed to have no knowledge, and 2,314 keepers and inmates who likewise had not been mentioned in the police list. These discoveries increased the total of resorts to 1,020, and of women known to be engaged in the business of prostitution to 4,194. "We again emphasize the fact," said the report, " that the Commission was unable to cover the entire city in its investigations, and that many resorts, their keepers and inmates, are still unrecorded. The estimation of 5,000 is, therefore, considered conservative but fair." This estimate, however, did not take the streetwalkers into account; their number was not determined, but was certainly not less than two thousand. The Commission also made no attempt to inquire into the extent of part-time or semi-professional prostitution, although the investigators reported that they had found hundreds of girls, employed in factories and department stores at from four to six dollars a week, who " hustled" at night in the dance halls and saloons to eke out the miserable wage upon which they had found it impossible to live decently. Had harlots of every classification been included, the Commission's estimate of the number of women who made a living, and in some instances a fortune, from vice would probably have been nearer fifteen thousand than five thousand.

The Commission's investigators found that many harlots in the brothels regularly entertained from fifty to seventy men a day. One madame, who kept a one-girl house in the West Side and herself practiced as a prostitute, testified that for more than a year she and her boarder had received from three hundred and fifty to four hundred men each week. Records of a South Side brothel seized in a white-slave case showed that in the twenty-two months from August 1906 to June 1908 the girls in this establishment, whose numbers varied from twelve to twenty, had entertained 179,599 men. After thorough investigation and examination of records of this description, the Commission estimated that the average number of men received each day by a girl in a regularly established brothel was fifteen. "Taking the number of women on the police lists alone, or 1,012," said the report, "and multiplying that number by the average number of services daily, or fifteen instances, or 15,180 daily, this makes a grand total of 5,540,700 per annum." But if five thousand women maintained this average, which was not at all unlikely, the annual number of instances of prostitution reached the stupendous total of 27,375,000.

The yearly profits of commercialized vice in Chicago, including the gains of owners, keepers, and inmates of brothels for "rent of house and body," and the returns from the sale of liquor in the resorts and in the 236 disorderly saloons which were investigated, were estimated by the Commission at $15,699,499. This figure was described as "ultra conservative," and was probably ten million dollars less than actual profits, since it did not include the earnings of streetwalkers and part-time prostitutes, nor the proceeds from liquor sales in the hundreds of resorts which were not covered by the inquiry. The estimate of the Commission was broken down into detailed listings by district and type of resort, with this final recapitulation:

Rental of property, and profits of keepers
and inmates $8,476,689
Sale of liquor, disorderly saloons only ... 4,307,000
Sale of liquor in houses, flats, and profits
of inmates on commissions 2,915,760
Total $15,699,449

On April 5, 1911, the report of the Vice Commission was submitted to Mayor Busse and the City Council, which

adopted a resolution ordering that it be "placed on file."
The Commission was continued in existence until June 1, and
was authorized to print and distribute copies of the report,
provided this could be done without expense to the city. It
made a book of almost four hundred pages, so forthright in
tone that the Post Office Department barred it from the
mails.

4

CHICAGO'S reaction to the revelations of the Vice Commission astounded even the most optimistic foe of segregation; it soon became clear that the devastating report had
completed the shift in public opinion which had been begun by
earlier exposés and intensified by Gipsy Smith's dramatic
march through the South Side Levee. Vice was no longer
looked upon as a necessary evil, but as a serpent of sin to
be scotched. Throughout the summer of 1911 Chicago was
aflame with the fires of reform. The newspapers were filled
with news of the activities of the crusaders, and with editorials commending their aims; clergymen preached scores
of sermons demanding that the red-light areas be closed and
the recommendations of the Vice Commission be put into
effect; every night the segregated districts were "slummed"
by swarms of social and rescue workers from the missions;
in Springfield, the state capital, legislators considered a measure designed to abolish vice areas throughout Illinois; reform
and civic organizations ceaselessly bombarded city officials
with statements and resolutions containing facts and figures.
Particularly active were the Law and Order League, led by
the Reverend Arthur Burrage Farwell; and the Committee
of Fifteen, under the chairmanship of Clifford W. Barnes.
The committee, the membership of which included such leading citizens as Julius Rosenwald of Sears, Roebuck & Company and Harold H. Swift of the famous meat-packing family, was a volunteer organization. It provided its own funds,

made investigations, and collected evidence which it presented to grand juries and the police.

The first indication that the politicians would succumb to the enormous pressure came in the fall of 1911. On October 12 Mayor Carter Harrison, Jr., who had succeeded Fred A. Busse soon after the submission of the Vice Commission's report, ordered the police to move all disreputable women from South Michigan Avenue and to close up all disorderly flats on that thoroughfare from Twelfth to Thirty-first Streets. Among the places which thus passed out of existence was the Arena, ostensibly a three-story private residence, with shuttered windows and a never-opened front door, set back some fifty feet from the sidewalk at No. 1340. Actually, the Arena had been Chicago's most famous assignation house for more than twenty years, the resort of sinners from the upper classes, but forbidden to streetwalkers. Customers of the resort were admitted through a door opening into a courtyard in the rear, and it was the boast of the management that no attaché of the Arena had ever looked upon the face of a woman visitor.

The closing of the Everleigh Club followed the attack upon the flats and hotels of South Michigan Avenue, and for several months thereafter, except for an occasional arrest, the police rested from their labors. The agitation against the segregated districts, however, continued with unabated vigor. The Civil Service Commission and the Cook County Grand Jury started inquiries. An aldermanic committee appointed by Mayor Harrison, at a cost of twenty thousand dollars, went over the ground that the Vice Commission had covered for half that amount. Obviously prepared to make a report recommending segregation, the committee lost its collective nerve and voted to continue its "investigations." Little more was heard from it. The State Vice Commission, authorized by the Legislature and headed by the Lieutenant Governor, Barrett O'Hara, began an inquiry into the connection between vice and low wages, the ultimate result of which was a rise in the prevailing wage for women and the formation of unions of department-store employees. The Committee of Fifteen returned to the fray in the latter part of August 1912, notifying Mayor Harrison that six dives in the South Side Levee were harboring girls under age. The Mayor promptly revoked the saloon license of Harry Cusick and Dago Frank Lewis, at No. 2035 Armour Avenue, and ordered the police to close the brothels of Cusick and Helen Turio in Armour Avenue, Leo Bernstein and Louis Weiss in Dearborn Street, and Marie de George in West Twentieth Street. From Bernstein's resort a fifteen-year-old girl was rescued. In Weiss's dive a sixteen-year-old girl was found. Neither Bernstein nor Weiss was prosecuted.

In early September 1912 Virginia Brooks, an attractive young woman and a crusader of the militant type, came to Chicago from the suburban town of Hammond, Indiana, where she had frightened half a hundred keepers of disorderly saloons into semi-respectability by organizing a hatchet brigade of women and threatening to emulate Carry Nation unless the liquor-sellers obeyed the law. Miss Brooks believed in dramatizing reform; she recalled the success of Gipsy Smith's march into the Levee and considered that the time had come for another demonstration of popular feeling. She interested the Chicago Civic Welfare League and other organizations in her plan, and on the afternoon of September 28, in a rainstorm of torrential proportions, more than five thousand men, women, and children marched northward in Michigan Avenue from Sixteenth to Washington Street and thence through Washington and State Streets to Jackson Boulevard. The procession was led by a band and a detachment of mounted policemen, followed by a delegation of clergymen singing "Onward, Christian Soldiers." Behind the preachers came groups of Girl Scouts, Boy Scouts,

Epworth Leaguers, members of the Women's Temperance Union and of the Catholic Temperance Society, students of the Baptist Missionary Training School and the Garrett and Moody Bible Institutes.

Interspersed among the marchers were many elaborate floats, graphically condemning vice of every description. One, presided over by Lucy Page Gaston, denounced cigarettes and bore a huge sign declaring that the players of the National League baseball team, the Cubs, "must cut out cigarettes." Another, equipped by the Norwegian churches of Chicago, was occupied by twelve young men in armor, and a thirteenth in pink tights, representing the god Thor. About his neck hung a placard saying: "The Great God Thor with his hammer. The Norwegians will help smite the saloons." As the *Record-Herald* put it, "The aim of the crusaders seemed to be rather diffuse." But at a mass meeting in Orchestra Hall they made it abundantly clear that their principal concern was the abolition of the red-light districts. A dozen speakers violently assailed city officials who had failed or refused to enforce the laws against vice. Virginia Brooks specifically attacked John E. W. Wayman, State's Attorney of Cook County.

Wayman was in an extremely uncomfortable position. Elected on the Republican ticket in 1908 by reform elements as a "white hope," he had not lived up to his reputation as an energetic young lawyer, and his work had been disappointing. He now sought renomination, and apparently was unable to make up his mind whether to espouse the cause of the crusaders, attempt to steer a middle course, or align himself with the segregationists. He fought with the Grand Jury, ignoring its investigation of the social evil, denouncing it as a "runaway jury," and declaring that its indictments were illegal. One of these true bills named A. E. Harris, Democratic precinct committeeman from the First Ward, and one of Hinky Dink Kenna's political henchmen. Under constant attack by Virginia Brooks and the Reverend Mr. Farwell, harassed both by the Committee of Fifteen and by politicians allied with the vice kings, Wayman was at length compelled to withdraw from the contest to succeed himself, realizing that defeat was inevitable. On October 3, 1912, the State's Attorney conferred with Chief Justice Harry Olson of the Municipal Court, who had been a member of the Vice Commission, and emerged from the Justice's chambers in what reporters described as a " furious passion." He immediately announced that he intended to close every vice resort in Chicago, and next morning obtained warrants for the arrest of one hundred and thirty-five keepers, owners, and agents of property used for immoral purposes.

The raids started during the early evening of October 4, and within five minutes after the first patrol wagon rumbled into the South Side Levee the district was in wild disorder, for reports had spread that everybody was to be locked up. " Electric pianos stopped as if paralyzed," said the *Record-Herald*. " Bright lights went glimmering. Into the streets poured a crowd of half-dressed women, some with treasured belongings tied in tablecloths. Others were packing suitcases as they moved, and most of them were running, a majority not knowing where they were going, but anywhere to get out of the district. In front of a few of the more pretentious establishments automobiles suddenly appeared. Women soon loaded them down, and they raced away." In every brothel entered by the police were found evidences of hurried flight: cooking pots bubbling on the kitchen stoves, half-empty bottles of beer and whisky scattered about the parlors, and the floors of the bedrooms littered with the clothing of men and women. The streets of the Levee were jammed with scurrying prostitutes and pimps, and with thousands of curiosity-seekers who had hurried southward from the Loop to watch the raids. Bands of Salvation Army and mission workers, with booming drums and blaring trumpets, rushed about the district, snatching at the souls of the terrified strumpets. Gangs of hoodlums looted the bordellos as rapidly as they were emptied of their inmates, driving away groups of reformers who attempted to hold religious services in the abandoned palaces of sin. A terrific clamor filled the air.

Through the uproar moved squads of detectives and uniformed policemen, backing patrol wagons up to the brothels and filling them with prostitutes and customers. The first arrest was that of Black May Douglas, who was permitted to ride to the police station in her own car. Then the detectives took into custody Julia Van Bever and such eminent vice lords as Ed Weiss, Roy Jones, and Big Jim Colosimo, all of whom were immediately released on bail. From Vic Shaw's resort the police took twenty women and one man; from Madame Amy's, ten girls; from Annie de Muncey's, sixteen women and twenty-five men; from Madame Suzanne's, five women and ten men; from Mamie Wilson's, five women and twenty men; from Marie Blanchey's, twenty women and thirty men; from Phyllis Adams's, twenty-four women and twenty men. Because of the flight from the Levee only twenty-three of Wayman's warrants were served, but more than a hundred dives were closed.

On the day following the first raids on the Levee, the dive-keepers struck back. They organized their own Committee of Fifteen, headed by Roy Jones and Big Jim Colosimo and including such notorious red-light figures as Blubber Bob Gray, John Jordan, Ed Weiss, and Ike Bloom, and began to raise the fund of forty thousand dollars with which they hoped to secure the passage of favorable legislation at Springfield. After a conference at Colosimo's restaurant in Wabash Avenue, the committee issued these orders to the harlots:

300

1. Get on your loudest clothes and more paint than usual and parade.

2. Go to residence districts. Ring doorbells and apply for lodgings.

3. Get rooms only in respectable neighborhoods.

4. Don't accost men on the streets, but be out as much as possible.

5. Frequent respectable cafés and make a splash.

The invasion of the prostitutes began at four o'clock on the afternoon of October 5, when hundreds swarmed into Michigan Avenue from Randolph Street to Hyde Park. At the same time other hundreds entered the downtown business district. Many were clad in garish silks and satins, with big plumed hats and faces daubed with paint; others, from the lowest dives, who had not been outside in daylight for months, wore bedraggled skirts pulled on over nightgowns and kimonos, and carried bundles of belongings slung on sticks in the traditional manner of the tramp. Downtown, they paraded back and forth, but did nothing to cause interference by the police. On Michigan Avenue they rang doorbells, explained that they had been driven from their homes, and asked for shelter. None was accommodated with rooms, but none would have accepted lodgings had they been offered; their object was to attract attention, and this they succeeded in doing until October 7, when they vanished as suddenly as they had appeared. Before the attack upon the Levee began, Miss Kate Adams, a prominent social worker, told the newspapers that she would care for all prostitutes who applied at her girls' home on Calumet Avenue. Aid was also offered by the Beulah Home, the Life Boat Home, the Florence Crittenden Anchorage, and the American Vigilance Association. But only one harlot asked for assistance, and on October 9, after a careful investigation, Miss Adams reported that she had been unable to find any who were homeless or hungry. Some had left the city, and others were being cared for by the vice kings.

The police continued to raid the South Side Levee on the 5th, 6th, 7th, and 8th of October, arresting inmates and keepers, and posting uniformed patrolmen in front of the brothels, and at the same time they began to close the resorts of South Chicago and the North and West Sides. Meanwhile a terrific hullabaloo had arisen as to the wisdom of the raids. The Chicago Protective League for Women issued a sixteen-page report declaring that the campaign of extermination was a " monstrous mistake "; but the American Vigilance Association, through its attorney, Clifford G. Roe, who as special prosecutor a few years before had broken several white-slave gangs, announced that it would " fight to the death against segregation." The aldermanic committee investigating vice asked the State's Attorney to reopen the Levee pending the completion of its inquiry, but Wayman flatly refused to do so. Instead he procured additional warrants, and prepared to prosecute the dive-keepers already under arrest. But the city administration, although permitting the Police Department to operate under his orders, refused to co-operate with the State's Attorney until November 20, 1912, when Mayor Harrison ordered the Superintendent of Police, John McWeeny, to close all resorts found to be operating. Said the *Record-Herald* of November 21:

" Five minutes of real police activity, which gives a rough idea of how such matters can be handled when they want them handled, wiped out the South Side Levee district in Chicago. It ceased to exist as if by magic, not because of enforcement of the law, but because of the apprehension of it. A few minutes before six o'clock last evening policemen began nailing the doors of Tommy Owens' café at 2033–35 Armour

302

Avenue. They were acting on the orders of Mayor Harrison, delivered at last in an unmistakable manner. Echoes of the blows of their hammers had hardly died away before the entire district was deserted. By six o'clock not a woman was to be found in it."

The *Record-Herald* said that Freiberg's Dance Hall and a few cafés on the fringes of the segregated district were not molested, but that " the Levee itself was darkened for all time." As a matter of fact, however, it was almost two years before the red lights were finally extinguished.

Wayman's last important act as State's Attorney was the prosecution of Police Inspector Edward McCann, who in former years had waged successful warfare against the dives of the West Side, on a charge of accepting bribes from brothel madames and saloon-keepers. McCann was convicted and sentenced to the State Penitentiary at Joliet. About the same time Inspector John Wheeler and Lieutenant John R. Bonfield were suspended after a hearing before the Police Trial Board on similar charges, and less than a year later Mayor Harrison removed Chief McWeeny from office for failing to close notorious resorts. Wayman retired from office early in 1913, and on April 17 of that year, as a result of overwork and great nervous strain, committed suicide at his home on Constance Avenue.

5

A T the conclusion of his raids on the South Side Levee, State's Attorney Wayman said he had closed the Levee and that it was up to the police to keep it closed. To carry out this task Mayor Harrison established the Morals Division and placed it under the direction of Major M. C. L. Funkhauser, formerly an officer of the Illinois National Guard, for whom the Mayor created the office of Second Deputy

Police Commissioner. Major Funkhauser was authorized to investigate conditions independently of the Police Department and to prosecute as a civilian. A morals squad of fifteen men was organized, and W. C. Dannenberg was appointed inspector — and almost immediately was offered twenty-two hundred dollars a month to protect the resorts of the South Side. When he refused, his life was threatened. The fact that the dive-keepers were willing to pay so much, as the Illinois Crime Survey said, "gave evidence of the profitableness to the police of the old segregated district."

Dannenberg's answer to the would-be assassins and bribers was a remarkably energetic drive upon vice. In less than six months his force made three hundred and fifty arrests, closed many dives and disorderly saloons, procured evidence of grafting in the Police Department, started action against owners of property in the Levee, and in many instances prevented the spread of prostitution into residential districts. Despite this showing, however, many Levee resorts reopened and operated under the protection of the regular police. The resorts' owners also used an elaborate spying and lookout system, employing pimps and hoodlums, who kept them informed as to the movements of the morals-squad officers.

Early in 1914 a man named Isaac Henagow, supposed by the underworld to have been an under-cover agent of the Morals Division, was killed by Jim Franche, alias Duffy the Goat, in Roy Jones's saloon in Wabash Avenue, whither Jones had moved when Wayman closed his dive in Dearborn Street. Jones's saloon license was revoked by Mayor Harrison, and Jones immediately began drinking heavily and complaining that he had been double-crossed. He threatened to talk, and did talk enough when drunk to indicate that the vice kings had formed a plot to murder Major Funkhauser, Inspector Dannenberg, and several members of the morals squad. Big Jim Colosimo and Maurice Van Bever offered Jones fifteen thousand dollars to go to Buenos Aires for three years, and an attempt was made to frame him on a charge of white slavery. Alarmed, Jones fled to Detroit.

In April 1914, a member of the Dannenberg force was stabbed to death while investigating the murder of Henagow. On the night of July 16, a few days after the departure of Roy Jones, two detectives of the morals squad, Joseph E. Merrill and Fred Amort, raided a resort known as the Turf, at No. 28 West Twenty-second Street. When they left the place a crowd of hoodlums followed them, yelling and throwing stones and bricks, and at length became so threatening that in front of the Swan poolroom near Michigan Avenue the detectives stopped and drew their revolvers. A moment later Detective Sergeant Stanley J. Birns and Detective John C. Sloop of the regular police rushed up and, seeing two men in plain clothes with guns in their hands, began shooting. Amort and Merrill returned the fire, and several shots were also fired from the crowd. Sergeant Birns was killed, and Sloop, Merrill, and John J. Carroll, a railroad fireman said to have been a Morals Division stoolpigeon, were wounded. Merrill said afterward that he and Sergeant Birns had been shot by a man wearing a gray suit, a leader of the gang of hoodlums which had followed the morals squad men from the Turf. This man was partially identified as Roxie Vanille, a New York gunman, friend of the notorious Gyp the Blood and cousin of Johnny Torrio, who had apparently shot Sergeant Birns by mistake. According to the newspapers and the State's Attorney's office, Vanille had been brought to Chicago to kill Inspector Dannenberg.

A few hours after the killing of Birns several prominent Levee figures, among them Torrio, John Jordan, Jakie Adler, Harry Hopkins, and Saffo the Greek, hurriedly left Chicago and sought refuge at Port Lamp Burke's roadhouse near Cedar Lake, Indiana. Madame Georgie Spencer, Jordan's wife, followed them next morning with five thousand dollars in cash with which to facilitate the escape of any who might be suspected of complicity in the Birns killing. Adler and Van Bever returned to Chicago on July 23 and were at once taken into custody by detectives of the State's Attorney's office, who also arrested Vanille, Big Jim Colosimo, and Joseph Moresco. Colosimo was locked up for the first and only time in his entire career; he spent half a day behind the bars in a police station before the State's Attorney would permit his release on bail. But none of these men would testify before the Grand Jury, and there was not sufficient evidence to expose the plot against Dannenberg or to justify the indictment of Roxie Vanille. All were released. Duffy the Goat was eventually tried for the murder of Isaac Henagow and at first was convicted and sentenced to hang. A new trial was granted, however, and he was finally acquitted on a plea of self-defense, although witnesses testified that Henagow was unarmed and had his arms straight down at his sides when he was shot.

6

MACLAY HOYNE, succeeding John E. W. Wayman as State's Attorney, announced that he would not interfere in a situation which he considered to be the business of the police. The killing of Henagow, Sergeant Birns, and the morals-squad detective, together with the repeated attacks by dive-keepers and hoodlums upon Inspector Dannenberg's men, brought about a reversal of this policy. Immediately following the murder of Birns, the State's Attorney began a grand-jury examination of the complicated vice situation and of the relations between the vice kings and the police and politicians. About the same time a similar inquiry was begun by the Civil Service Commission at the request of the Superintendent of Police, James Gleason, who had been appointed by Mayor Harrison after the removal of McWeeny. The State's Attorney found that prostitution in the Levee district was controlled by three rings, " which have been collecting money from the little fellows and splitting it with the police and the politicians." The largest and most powerful of these combinations was composed of Colosimo, Torrio, and Van Bever. Another was headed by Julius and Charlie Maybaum and included Ed Weiss, Jakie Adler, and Harry Hopkins. The third was led by Eddie Woods and the Marshall brothers, none of whom had been very important before Wayman's assault began. The Illinois Crime Survey showed that " each of these syndicates operated a string of saloons in the proximity of, or connected by passages with, clandestine flats or houses of prostitution." There were also many independent vice operators, among them such familiar figures as Harry Cusick, Judy Williams, Jew Kid Grabiner, and John Jordan.

On July 17, 1914 State's Attorney Hoyne told the newspapers that he intended to clean up the Levee, which, he declared, was " worse than ever before, infested by the worst criminals in Chicago, a segregated district of pickpockets, gunmen, robbers and burglars." But before Hoyne could take any definite action Mayor Carter Harrison, who had been subjected to constant pressure by the Committee of Fifteen and other reform organizations, ordered the transfer of Captain Michael Ryan of the Twenty-second Street police station, who the *Tribune* declared had been " denounced as either corrupt or incompetent. Men in uniform in Ryan's district," the newspaper continued, " are told to keep their eyes straight ahead, ignoring what is going on behind doors and windows, and watching only for disturbances on the street. They are told to do police duty as though the social evil did not exist around them." To succeed Ryan, the Mayor appointed Captain Max Nootbaar, a capable and honest policeman. Captain Nootbaar's first act

307

after assuming the command was to kick Ike Bloom out of the police station for trying to " arrange a deal." His second was to remove Bloom's picture from the squad room. His third was to order the saloons and dance halls in the district to curtain their windows or paste paper over the glass. And on July 26 Captain Nootbaar notified the resort-owners to close or be raided.

This ultimatum was given wide publicity in the newspapers, and although the dive-keepers, confident of protection from the politicians, were ready to continue operations, their customers, afraid of being caught in raids, stayed away with remarkable unanimity. An *Examiner* reporter, on the night of July 27, found the Levee quieter than ever before in his memory. Similar conditions prevailed on the 28th, and at dusk on the following day John Jordan expressed the general feeling when he paid off his waiters and entertainers and closed the doors of the saloon and wine-room which he had conducted at No. 2008 Wabash Avenue for more than ten years. " It's no use," said Jordan, " the Levee won't go again. I've seen reform come and reform go, but this is honestly the first time since the closing of the old Custom House Place and Federal Street tenderloin that it looked as if reform might stick."

Within another month Mayor Carter Harrison had dealt the final blow by revoking the liquor licenses of more than twenty First Ward saloons, including those operated by Colosimo, Johnny Torrio, John Jordan, and Ike Bloom. " Chicago," said Mayor Harrison, " is through with the segregated-vice idea." But Chicago was not through with prostitution. As the report of the Vice Commission had said three years before, " The Social Evil in its worst phases may be repressed, but so long as there is lust in the hearts of men it will seek some method of expression. Until the hearts of men are changed we can hope for no absolute annihilation of the Social Evil."

7

D URING the last few months of Mayor Harrison's final term Chicago was probably as free from organized vice as at any time in its history. Captain Nootbaar rigidly enforced the law in the old Levee district, the State's Attorney made considerable progress with grand-jury investigations, and the Morals Division under Major Funkhauser waged energetic warfare against dives and call flats, while the Mayor promptly revoked the license of any saloon that came under suspicion. But the situation changed completely when William Hale Thompson, advocate of a wide-open town, became Mayor on May 15, 1915. Captain Nootbaar was transferred to another and unimportant station, and Mayor Thompson began throwing obstacles in the way of Major Funkhauser, despite the strenuous objections of the Committee of Fifteen, with the obvious intention of eventually getting rid of the Morals Division altogether. Francis D. Hanna, an Inspector of the Division, was summarily discharged in March 1916 when he submitted to the Mayor a report which said, among other things, that " high-class " brothels operated without police interference, that prostitutes who got high prices were not arrested, and that the manner in which cases were handled in the Morals Court indicated collusion among police, bondsmen, lawyers, and defendants. In June 1918, Major Funkhauser and his most important assistants were placed on trial before the Police Trial Board, and women of the old red-light district were called in to testify against them. While these trials were in progress, the finance committee of the City Council abolished the Morals Division, and eliminated Major Funkhauser, by stopping the Division's appropriation.

No attempt was made to re-establish the restricted districts, but harlots soon began to carry on their trade more or less openly in downtown hotels and in residential districts, with an immediate increase in the number of call flats. Dance halls and wine-rooms which had been closed by Mayor Harrison reopened as cabarets, which Samuel P. Thrasher, Superintendent of the Committee of Fifteen, declared were " used as recruiting stations for the promotion of vice." The *Record-Herald,* after a survey of the situation in February 1916, said: " The cabaret evil is the illegitimate heir to the old vice rule. People who prospered when practically licensed prostitution was permitted in Chicago now find remuneration and familiar employment in some of the cabarets." Mr. Thrasher likewise said: " All the old vice promoters who can get into the cabaret business are in it to-day." These statements were verified by Kate Adams, who investigated conditions in October 1916. She found that Ike Bloom was again running Freiberg's, under the name of Old Vienna, and that Colosimo had reopened his resort on Wabash Avenue. Johnny Torrio and Jew Kid Grabiner were operating the Speedway Inn in the suburban town of Burnham, and Ed and Louis Weiss owned the Fountain Inn Cabaret at Halsted and Sixty-third Streets as well as the Canary Cottage on Cottage Grove Avenue. Dago Frank Lewis had opened the Columbia Café and Cabaret at Ogden Avenue and Van Buren Street, and Jakie Adler had two places in Burnham, one of them the notorious State Line Bar and Cabaret. John Jordan was managing the Garden Café on South State Street, and Charlie West had a similar dive on the same thoroughfare. Despite this resurgence of vice, however, many of the gains made by the Wayman and Hoyne crusades had been retained; the Committee of Fifteen said early in 1916 that only forty per cent as many immoral resorts were running as were in operation in 1912, and that streetwalking had been reduced by eighty per cent.

To offset the publicity which the newspapers were giving to the State's Attorney's grand-jury investigation,

310

Mayor Thompson began a graft inquiry of his own through the Police Civil Service Commission. It produced little of importance, although it did bring charges against a police captain because of conditions in the Warren Avenue district. One of Hoyne's principal witnesses was Captain W. P. O'Brien, who had been suspended after a quarrel with Charles C. Healey, the new Superintendent of Police. Captain O'Brien described the "unspeakable conditions of immorality" in the Negro sections of the South Side, and said that he had been ordered by Superintendent Healey not to molest certain dives because of their political influence. The State's Attorney also made public, early in 1917, the contents of a notebook which had been taken by his investigators from a lieutenant of the Lake Street police station. This notebook contained a list of shady hotels and the weekly rates of graft, ranging from forty to one hundred and fifty dollars. Several pages were devoted to a list of brothels, houses of assignation, Greek places and gambling joints, all marked "the Chief's places." One page showed which saloons could remain open on Sundays and after one o'clock. A list of gambling resorts, bagnios, and disreputable hotels was headed: "can't be raided." Another was headed: "can be raided."

As a result of the disclosures before the Grand Jury the State's Attorney ordered the arrest of Superintendent Healey, who was immediately released on bail of twenty thousand dollars. Indictments were found against two vice collectors, two police sergeants, and a Negro and an alderman. About the same time Mayor Thompson promised a cleanup of disreputable cabarets and saloons. But none of the indicted men were punished, and the cleanup was never made.

8

T H E most important criminal in Chicago during the decade which followed Wayman's raids on the South Side was Big Jim Colosimo, who ruled the underworld for a longer period than any other one man in the history of the city. He was also one of the few vice moguls who made more money after the Levee was closed than before. His receipts from the innumerable immoral enterprises which he either owned or controlled were conservatively estimated at fifty thousand dollars a month for some eight years, an enormous take for those times, though small compared with the gleanings of the racketeers and bootleg princes of the prohibition epoch. Colosimo was also a prodigious spender. He built a fine house for his father, and an even grander one for himself, and filled both with a remarkable assortment of gaudy and expensive junk. He supported a horde of impecunious relatives, some of whom earned their keep by working in his brothels and other dives. He maintained a large staff of liveried servants, and his two uniformed chauffeurs drove the biggest and shiniest automobiles that money could buy. His massive figure, clad in snow-white linen and a suit of garish checks, blazed with diamonds. He wore a diamond ring on every finger, diamond studs gleamed in his shirt front, a huge diamond horseshoe was pinned to his vest, diamond links joined his cuffs, and his belt and suspender buckles were set with diamonds. He bought diamonds by the hundreds from thieves and needy gamblers, and cherished them as other men cherished books and paintings. He carried them in his pockets in buckskin bags, and spent most of his leisure time playing with them, pouring them from one hand to another or heaping them in little piles upon a black cloth. His morals were those of the gutter and he was without honor or decency, but the police and the politicians fawned upon him; to them went a sizable portion of his unholy gains.

Ten years old when his father brought him to the United States from their native Italy, Colosimo spent all but two or three of his remaining thirty-nine years in the red-light district of the South Side. He began his career in the Levee as a newsboy and bootblack, but his rise was rapid. At eighteen he was an accomplished pickpocket, and a pimp with half a dozen industrious girls on his staff. For a year or so in his middle twenties he was a successful Black Hand extortionist. But in the late 1890's, after several narrow escapes from arrest, Colosimo abandoned most of these activities and obtained a job as a street-cleaner, the only honest occupation in which he was ever engaged. By 1900 he had been promoted to foreman, and had organized his fellow sweepers into a social and athletic club, which eventually became a labor union under the control of the notorious Dago Mike Carrozzo. As a reward for delivering the votes of the club to the First Ward Democratic machine, Alderman Hinky Dink Kenna made Colosimo a precinct captain, a post which carried with it virtual immunity from arrest, as well as many other privileges and opportunities. In 1902 Colosimo married Victoria Moresco, who kept a house of prostitution in Armour Avenue, and at once took over the management of the brothel. Within three years this precious pair had established another bordello, and about 1910 they opened the famous café in Wabash Avenue, which for many years was a center of Chicago's night life and a favorite resort of slumming parties. Meanwhile Colosimo had organized a white-slave gang with Maurice Van Bever, had brought Johnny Torrio from New York to be his bodyguard and right-hand man, and had acquired interests in several saloons and immoral resorts. He had likewise gained in political stature and influence, in direct proportion to the increase in his wealth and in the number of votes he was able to control.

During the palmy days of the Levee, Colosimo played second fiddle to Ike Bloom, but Bloom's power declined with the abolition of the red-light district, and Colosimo's rise began. His only setback, and that of brief duration, came when the license of his Wabash Avenue resort was revoked by Mayor Carter Harrison in the late summer of 1914. It was restored as soon as Thompson became Mayor. Colosimo made little effort to operate his Armour Avenue dives after Wayman and Hoyne had finally closed the Levee; instead, seeing clearly that the segregated district as such would never be reopened, he concentrated his energies upon gaining control of call flats and assignation houses, most of which were operated in connection with disorderly saloons and cabarets. He also led the fight against the Morals Division, handled most of the protection money collected by his own and other vice syndicates, and financed the invasion of Burnham by Johnny Torrio, Jew Kid Grabiner, and Jakie Adler, which marked the first real attack by Chicago criminals upon the suburbs. By the middle of 1915 Colosimo was the acknowledged overlord of prostitution on the South Side, and because of his political power was almost as important in other sections of the city.

Ironically enough, Colosimo's downfall was indirectly due to a romantic interest in one of the few respectable women he had ever known. This was Dale Winter, a young musical-comedy actress, who, stranded in Chicago after an unsuccessful theatrical tour, had accepted an engagement to sing in the Wabash Avenue cabaret, intending to quit the job as soon as she could get something better. But Colosimo at once fell in love with her, and she with him; perhaps she glimpsed a spark of decency in the depths of his black soul. In March 1920, Colosimo divorced Victoria Moresco and gave her fifty thousand dollars in full settlement of her marital claims. Three weeks later he and Dale Winter were married at Crown Point, Indiana, and after a two weeks' honeymoon returned to Chicago.

On the afternoon of May 11, 1920, less than a week after he and his bride had established themselves in his Vernon Avenue mansion, the vice king summoned his automobile and drove to his café as usual. His wife said afterward that she was prepared to accompany him, but he told her to remain at home because he had a business appointment. She was to meet him for dinner. Colosimo's café at this time consisted of two long rooms, called the north and south rooms, separated by a wall through which a wide archway had been cut. The main entrance led into a small lobby, at one side of which was the cloak-room. When Colosimo arrived he went directly to his office in the rear of the south room, where he found his secretary, Frank Camilla, discussing the day's menu with the chef, Antonio Caesarino. Colosimo talked to them for ten or fifteen minutes, but about half past four, remarking that his expected visitor was late, he walked through the north room and went into the lobby, evidently intending to step outside. A moment later Camilla and Caesarino heard two shots, and Camilla investigated. He found Colosimo's dead body lying on the floor of the lobby with a bullet wound in the back of his head. The second bullet had lodged in the plaster wall. From the angle at which the shots had been fired, the police concluded that the killer had been hidden in the cloak-room.

The funeral of Big Jim Colosimo, held on May 15, 1920, was the first of the gaudy burial displays which were the fashion in Chicago's underworld throughout the 1920's, and which as much as anything else focused the attention of the outside world upon the alliance of criminals and politicians. Archbishop Mundelein refused to allow the famous pander's body to be taken into a Catholic church or buried in a Catholic cemetery because of his divorce and remarriage, and services were held at the Colosimo home under the direction of a Presbyterian clergyman, the Reverend Pasquale de Carol. At the conclusion of a prayer by him, Alderman Bathhouse John Coughlin knelt beside the coffin and recited the Hail Marys and also pronounced the Catholic prayer for the dead. Five thousand persons, including a thousand members of the First Ward Democratic Club led by Bathhouse John and Hinky Dink Kenna, followed the hearse to the Oakwood Cemetery. But the most striking and significant feature of the funeral was not the size of the cortege nor the flowers which filled several carriages; it was the presence among the active and honorary pallbearers of three judges, an Assistant State's Attorney, a member of Congress, a state Representative and nine aldermen, marching side by side with such notorious white-slavers, thugs, thieves, and gangsters as Johnny Torrio, Ike Bloom, Andy Craig, and Jakie Adler.[1] "Such tribute from men set up to make and enforce our laws to a man who in much of his life was a law unto himself, is more than the tribute of friendship," said the Chicago *Tribune*. "It is a tribute to power, regardless of the source or justice of that power. . . . It is a strange commentary upon our system of law and justice. In how far can power derived from the life of the underworld, influence institutions of law and order? It is a question worthy of the thoughtful consideration of those entrusted with the establishment of law and order and of those dependent on and responsible for such trust."

9

W H E N Colosimo was murdered he was supposed to possess five hundred thousand dollars in cash and diamonds, in ad-

---

[1] When Tony D'Andrea was buried in May 1921, his honorary pallbearers included twenty-one judges and nine lawyers of more or less prominence. Among the active pallbearers were a special prosecutor for the State of Illinois, the Chicago City Sealer, and two representatives of the Hod Carriers' Union.

dition to his home, the Wabash Avenue resort, and his interests in other enterprises. But after weeks of search the vice king's lawyer announced that he had been able to find only forty thousand dollars' worth of precious stones and no cash at all, and if the remainder was discovered later the newspapers and the general public never knew it. An unverified story was current that Colosimo had a hundred and fifty thousand dollars in cash in his pockets when he was killed. Neither Victoria Moresco nor Dale Winter claimed any part of Colosomo's estate, and most of it eventually went to his father. The *Daily News* declared that the dwindling of the fortune " was ascribed to his paying tribute to the Black Hand." Despite his power, Colosimo was preyed upon by extortionists throughout his career as a vice mogul; as late as September 1919, he received two threatening letters demanding ten thousand dollars. Colosimo himself killed three Black Handers, and as chief of his bodyguard Johnny Torrio arranged lethal surprises for several others. But on many occasions Colosimo had met their demands.

10

The murder of Big Jim Colosimo is still a mystery, at least as far as legal evidence is concerned. The Chicago police have always believed, however, that the killing was planned by Johnny Torrio, and that Torrio paid Frankie Uale, a notorious New York gunman and national head of the Unione Siciliana, ten thousand dollars to do the job. Uale was arrested in New York, but one of Colosimo's porters, who had seen the assassin enter the café a few minutes after the arrival of the vice king, was terror-stricken when confronted by the famous killer and refused to identify him.

Torrio's motive for having Colosimo removed was clear and, by underworld standards, ample. During the first half-dozen years which followed his arrival in Chicago in 1908,

Torrio was apparently content to serve as a subordinate to Big Jim. But with the closing of the restricted districts his gifts as an organizer and a fixer were needed, and he became increasingly important in Colosimo's vice and political machine. When Dale Winter began to absorb most of the vice king's time and thought, Torrio obligingly took over the active management of his underworld interests, and at the same time assumed many of his political powers and privileges. Within a few years Torrio was a more important criminal figure than Colosimo, though Big Jim still held the reins and gobbled up most of the profits. Torrio had also gained a much desired foothold in Cook County by the successful invasion of Burnham, a feat made possible only by wholesale corruption of village and county officials. The Burnham resorts were lucrative and well protected, and Torrio frequently urged Colosimo to join him in a scheme to establish similar dives in other suburban towns and to link them together with a string of roadhouses. But Colosimo was so wrapped up in his new-found love that he manifested little interest in Torrio's ambitious plans. He was definitely in Torrio's way, and so he died.

II

ONE of Torrio's first acts after stepping into Colosimo's shoes ultimately had dire consequences for Chicago — he took under his wing a young New York hoodlum named Alphonse Capone, who had fled the metropolis under the mistaken impression that he had killed a man in a fist-fight in a Brooklyn saloon. Capone was only twenty-three years old when he came to Chicago, but he had already been questioned by the New York police in two murder cases and had made a name for himself as a slugger and gunman along the Brooklyn waterfront. He had also worked for the famous Five Points gang, one of the most feared criminal organiza-

318

tions in the country, of which several of his cousins were members. Since he came well recommended, Torrio put him to work immediately as watcher and bouncer in one of the Burnham resorts. But Capone displayed such aptitude that he was soon promoted to the post of manager of one of Torrio's toughest dives, the Four Deuces at No. 2222 South Wabash Avenue — a four-story brick structure with a saloon on the first floor, Torrio's general offices on the second, a gambling joint on the third, and a brothel on the fourth. In later years Capone was succeeded as manager of the Four Deuces by one of his brothers, Ralph, also known as Ralph Brown. A similar dive in which Torrio owned an interest was the Rex at No. 2138 South State Street, managed by Dennis Cooney, who was described by the *Daily News* as the righthand man of Alderman Mike Kenna.

During Al Capone's tenure as manager of the Four Deuces he became Johnny Torrio's first lieutenant and chief of the Torrio gunmen, but as far as the general public was concerned he remained an obscure member of Torrio's organization for more than two years after he arrived in Chicago. As late as August 1922 he was so little known that when he became involved in an automobile accident the newspapers referred to him as Alfred Caponi, and relegated their accounts of the incident to the back pages. In those days Capone was a typical hoodlum, coarse and brutal, given to vulgar talk and flashy clothing, with little to indicate that he was destined to evolve into the polished criminal of later years. In the underworld he was generally known as Scarface Al Brown, the nickname being due to two parallel scars on his left cheek. He claimed to have received these wounds while fighting in France as a soldier of the Seventy-seventh Division. Actually he was slashed with a knife during a brawl in a Brooklyn dance hall. His number was certified in the draft, but he was never called up for service in the Army.

319

CHAPTER X

THE BIG SHOTS

ONLY FOUR of the gangster chieftains who ruled, or attempted to rule, the Chicago underworld during the saturnalia of crime and corruption which has been called " a noble experiment " were recognized by their fellows as genuine Big Shots — Johnny Torrio, who succeeded Colosimo; Al Capone, who succeeded Torrio; and Dion O'Banion and Hymie Weiss, peerless gunmen, and pretenders to the throne who revolted against Torrio and Capone and were eventually crushed. The biggest of the Big Shots, of course, were Torrio and Capone, and although Capone achieved an international reputation and accumulated a great deal more money than ever fell into the hands of Torrio, the latter was the more accomplished criminal. Torrio built the machine of outlawry; Capone only kept it running, replacing and adding parts. Torrio maintained peace in gangland for more than three years by strategy and compromise, with only an occasional disciplinary murder; Capone ruled by the gun and the bludgeon and held his position by incessant fighting and frequent massacre of his enemies. Torrio's authority was so nearly absolute that he seldom carried a revolver and frequently walked the streets alone; Capone burdened himself with two holstered pistols under his armpits, wore a bulletproof vest, and rode in a seven-ton armored car equipped with a machine-gun. He went nowhere without a bodyguard.

As an organizer and administrator of underworld affairs Johnny Torrio is unsurpassed in the annals of American crime; he was probably the nearest thing to a real master mind that this country has yet produced. He conducted his evil enterprises as if they had been legitimate business. In the morning he kissed his wife good-by and motored to his magnificently furnished offices on the second floor of the Four Deuces. There he bought and sold women, conferred with the managers of his brothels and gambling dens, issued instructions to his rum-runners and bootleggers, arranged for the corruption of police and city officials, and sent his gun squads out to slaughter rival gangsters who might be interfering with his schemes. But he never accompanied his killers on these forays, for Torrio himself was not a gunman; he once boasted proudly that he had never fired a pistol in his life.

When the day's work was done, Torrio returned to his Michigan Avenue apartment and, except on rare occasions when he attended the theater or a concert, spent the evening at home in slippers and smoking jacket, playing cards with his wife or listening to phonograph records. Unlike most of his fellow gangsters, Torrio disliked to talk shop; his favorite topic of conversation was music, and he frequently astonished musicians by his knowledge of the works of great composers and his critical comments upon them. Though his bank account and safe-deposit boxes bulged with the proceeds of debauchery, Torrio eschewed dissipation with the holy scorn of the anchorite. He neither smoked nor drank, he was never heard to utter a profane or obscene word, and as far as he was concerned, the women who filled his bordellos were just so many articles of merchandise. His wife, a Kentucky girl who knew next to nothing of his business, called him " the best and dearest of husbands " and said that her married life had been " like one long, unclouded honeymoon."

ONCE the love-lorn Colosimo was no longer either an annoyance or a potential menace, Torrio went ahead with the expansion of his system of suburban bordellos and roadhouses. Under the command of Capone, Mike de Pike Heitler, Harry Cusick, and Charley Carr, his agents went into Stickney, Forest View, Posen, Burr Oaks, Blue Island, Steger, Chicago Heights, and other Cook County towns west and southwest of Chicago, in many of which there were large foreign populations, and soon transformed them from peaceful suburbs into brothel-ridden Babylons. Footholds were gained in these towns partly by corrupting village and county officials and partly by bribing property-owners. Before a resort was opened, the neighborhood was thoroughly canvassed, and if a man who owned a home near the proposed dive would agree not to cause trouble, Torrio solved some of his most pressing financial problems. Was he carrying a heavy mortgage? Torrio paid it. Did he need a new car, a new furnace, or a new suite of furniture? Torrio bought them. Did his house need painting or a new roof? Torrio sent carpenters and painters, and took care of the bill.

Many of the resorts thus established were more vicious than any of the old Levee dives, because they were operated without police supervision of any description. Some were elaborate cabarets with assignation houses attached, designed to appeal to automobile parties from the city. Others were combination dives similar to the Four Deuces and the Rex. Still others, catering principally to the foreign workers in the steel mills and manufacturing plants, were built like barracks, with bedrooms upstairs, and on the ground floor a large drinking and gambling room where prostitutes mingled with and solicited the customers. In most of these places the benches and tables were fastened to the walls and floor to prevent them from being destroyed during the brawls which were of frequent occurrence.

Some of Torrio's suburban dives housed from forty to sixty girls, who worked in three eight-hour shifts. The largest were the Stockade, a sixty-girl house in Stickney, and the fifty-girl Maple Inn near Forest View, a community which was so completely under Capone's domination that in the underworld it was commonly called Caponeville. The Stockade was more than an immoral resort; it was also a hideaway and a munitions dump. It was raided by the Chicago police after the murder of Assistant State's Attorney William H. McSwiggin in Cicero in 1926, and was found to be a veritable labyrinth of secret passages, and hidden rooms constructed under the roof and between the floor and ceiling of the first and second stories. One of these chambers was lined with cork, furnished with soft rugs and comfortable couches and easy chairs, and fitted with a speaking-tube and a dumbwaiter. A criminal secreted there could keep his own lookout through the punctured eyes of female figures painted on the ceilings of the saloon and gambling room. In several steel-lined panels built into the walls the police discovered large quantities of dynamite, rifles, shotguns, grenades, automatic pistols, machine-guns, and ammunition.

The decent citizens of Forest View, unable to prevent the invasion of their town by Torrio and Capone, waited for several years for the Cook County authorities to heed their complaints and close the Maple Inn, but were finally compelled to take matters into their own hands. After the raid upon the Stockade Al Capone, who by that time had succeeded Torrio as head of the operating syndicate, closed the resort, intending to resume operations as soon as the wave of public indignation had subsided. But the dive was never reopened. About daybreak on May 30, 1926, three automobiles drove up to the Inn and a score of Vigilantes jumped out and quickly surrounded the building. Over-

323

powering the Negro watchman, they smashed in the doors and set fire to the structure in half a dozen places. Fire companies were summoned from Berwyn and other towns, but the firemen made no attempt to extinguish the flames, although they laid hose lines and protected near-by property. When representatives of Capone urged them to save the Inn, they replied that they couldn't spare the water.

3

ALREADY the foremost vicemonger in the United States, with an annual income from prostitution of at least a hundred thousand dollars a year, Johnny Torrio began to organize the beer and liquor traffic of Chicago and Cook County in the late summer of 1920. He held long conferences with the leaders of the principal criminal gangs and persuaded them to abandon bank robbery, burglary, and banditry, for the time being at least, in favor of bootlegging and rumrunning. He promised them riches beyond their wildest dreams, and more than made good his promises. He formed an alliance with Joseph Stenson, member of a well-known family and a wealthy brewer before prohibition, and took over the five breweries which, according to the Illinois Crime Survey, Stenson was operating in partnership with Terry Druggan and Frankie Lake, co-captains of the Valley gang and trusted henchmen of Morris Eller, trustee of the Chicago Sanitary District and political boss of the Twentieth Ward. Utilizing Stenson's business experience and connections, Torrio acquired more breweries. Some were bought outright. Others were leased. A few remained in the hands of their original owners, while Torrio and his gangsters "fronted" for them — that is, assumed ownership and accepted responsibility in the event of trouble.

Torrio exercised general supervision over every phase of the liquor traffic, but to facilitate operations the city and county were divided into spheres of influence, in each of which an allied gang chieftain was supreme, with sub-chiefs working under his direction. A few of these leaders themselves owned and operated breweries and distilleries, but in the main they received their supplies from Torrio and were principally concerned with selling, making deliveries, protecting shipments, terrorizing saloon-keepers who refused to buy from the syndicate, and furnishing gunmen for punitive expeditions against hi-jackers and independents who attempted to encroach upon Torrio territory. The North Side was allotted to Dion O'Banion, captain of a famous gang of bandits, burglars, and safe-crackers. A portion of the West Side was earmarked for Terry Druggan and Frankie Lake, and the remainder, including the suburbs into which Torrio had already penetrated with his prostitutes, was ruled by Torrio's own men under the direction of Harry Cusick, Al Capone, and Frankie Pope, sometimes called the Millionaire Newsboy. Part of the South Side remained in Torrio's hands, and the rest of this rich area was split up among Danny Stanton; Ralph Sheldon, one of the many criminals produced by a notorious political club called Ragen's Colts; Polack Joe Saltis, once a more or less honest saloon-keeper in Joliet; and Frank McErlane, whom the Illinois Crime Survey called " the most brutal gunman who ever pulled a trigger in Chicago," a savage, merciless killer with small, piglike eyes set in a fat red face. McErlane's favorite weapon was a sawed-off shotgun loaded with slugs, and he was without fear, pity, or remorse.

As long as these alliances remained unbroken, Johnny Torrio commanded the services of between seven hundred and eight hundred gunmen, the most vicious aggregation of criminals ever brought together in one city. According to the well-known Chicago journalist James O'Donnell Bennett, ninety-five per cent of them were of foreign birth, and of this ninety-five per cent, eighty-five per cent were Italians

or Sicilians. Ten per cent were Jews, and most of the remaining five per cent were of Irish extraction. About forty
per cent were paroled convicts, from the ranks of the nine
hundred and fifty criminals who had been released from
Illinois penal institutions by the State Board of Pardons and
Paroles in less than three years.

4

THE most important of the independent gangsters for
whom Johnny Torrio made no provision in the allocation of
territory were the four O'Donnell brothers, Edward, Steve,
Walter, and Tommy, generally called the South Side O'Donnells to distinguish them from Myles and Klondike O'Donnell, unrelated but also criminals, who flourished on the far
West Side and in the suburban city of Cicero. The probable
reason for the exclusion of the South Side O'Donnells was
the fact that the leader and eldest of the four brothers, Edward, better known as Spike, was in prison at Joliet when
the country went dry, having been convicted of complicity
in the daylight holdup of the Stockyards Trust and Savings
Bank. A criminal since boyhood, Spike O'Donnell had been
sneak thief, pickpocket, burglar, footpad, labor slugger, and
bank-robber; he had shot half a dozen men, had been twice
tried for murder, and had been accused of several other
killings. He was also deeply religious, and not even the
prospect of a good murder or a holdup could keep him
from attending Sunday Mass at St. Peter's Catholic
Church.

Without this devout and gifted outlaw to lead them,
the O'Donnells were nothing more than good journeymen
burglars and gunmen; for more than a year they hung about
the Four Deuces, grateful for whatever crumbs might be
thrown to them by Torrio and Capone. But the fortunes of

the clan began to improve when Governor Len Small paroled Spike O'Donnell at the earnest request of six state senators, five state representatives, and a judge of the Criminal Court of Cook County. Within a few months after Spike's return to Chicago the O'Donnells hi-jacked several truckloads of Torrio beer, imported a crack New York gunman, Henry Hasmiller, and enlisted a dozen thugs, most of them convicts on parole, as truck-drivers, bodyguards, and beer drummers. Then Spike O'Donnell made arrangements with a Joliet jury and began running beer into the South Side territory which had been assigned to Joe Saltis and Frank McErlane. Drummers preceded the shipments, and by slugging and otherwise terrorizing saloon-keepers, a method of salesmanship devised by O'Donnell and immediately copied by other gang leaders, they soon built up what Spike O'Donnell described as a " nice little business."

By Torrio's orders the gunmen of the Saltis and McErlane gangs struck at the interlopers with the speed and ferocity of a cornered rattlesnake. On the night of September 7, 1923, a band of triggermen headed by Danny McFall and Frank McErlane, prowling the South Side in quest of O'Donnell beer drummers, surprised Walter and Tommy O'Donnell, George Bucher, Jerry O'Connor, and George Meeghan in Joe Platka's saloon on Lincoln Street. All escaped through side and rear doors except O'Connor, who was captured by McFall and marched out of the saloon. As he stepped into the street, McErlane blew his head off with a shotgun. Ten days later Bucher and Meeghan were snatched from an O'Donnell truck in the wilds of Cook County and forced into an automobile by two men who " took 'em for a ride," a phrase, incidentally, which is said to have been coined by Hymie Weiss. The bodies of Bucher and Meeghan, hands tied behind their back and their bodies filled with shotgun slugs, were found next morning in a ditch.

The ride murder, first of its kind, was repeated on December 1, 1923, when Morrie Keane was killed and Shorty Egan was seriously wounded and left for dead. A few months later Philip Corrigan was blasted with a shotgun while driving an O'Donnell beer truck, and Walter O'Donnell and Henry Hasmiller were shot to death in a gun battle at Evergreen Park. Meanwhile ten separate attempts had been made to kill Spike O'Donnell, and several bullets had found temporary lodgment in his body. He fought back savagely, but he lacked the guns to cope with his enemies. With the score seven to two in favor of Torrio's killers, Spike O'Donnell finally abandoned his " nice little business " and left Chicago. He returned in a year or so, after Torrio himself had fled, resumed his bootlegging activities, though on a smaller scale than before, and became interested in several racketeering enterprises. Apparently he had reached an understanding with Al Capone, for he was not molested. He also went into the wholesale coal business, and despite his long criminal record and the fact that his name appeared on the list of public enemies issued by the Crime Commission, his political friends obtained for him a contract to supply the city with coal.

Most of the killing in the war against Spike O'Donnell was done by the ferocious Frank McErlane, who included at least five of O'Donnell's men in his lifetime bag of thirteen. The others probably fell before the flaming pistols of Walter Stevens, the dean of Chicago gunmen — he was fifty-six in 1923 — and one of gangland's most picturesque figures. Stevens was first heard of in Chicago as a henchman of Mossy Enright, who with his gang performed prodigies of bombing, slugging, and murder on behalf of labor unions in the industrial wars in the early part of the twentieth century. Enright was killed in February 1920 by Sunny Jim Cosmano, a Sicilian gunman and blackmailer who was afterward deported, at the behest of Big Tim Murphy, best-known of

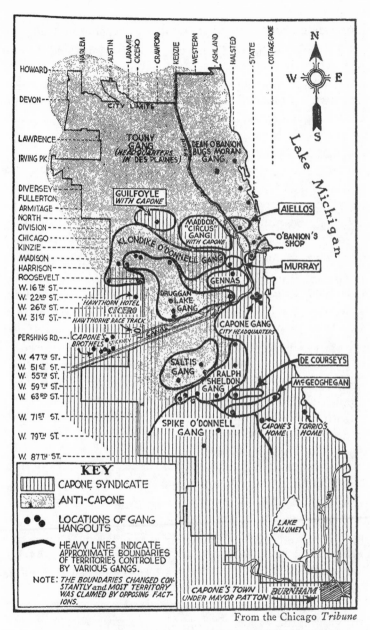

From the Chicago *Tribune*

ONE OF THE SEVERAL DIVISIONS OF
TERRITORY MADE BY THE GANGS

labor racketeers.[1] Stevens's name was connected with a dozen murders during his service with Enright, and he was definitely implicated in several, among them the killing of Peter Gentleman, a policeman's son turned bandit and gunman. The murder of a policeman in Aurora, Illinois, put Stevens in prison, but he was soon pardoned by Governor Len Small as a reward for services performed when the Governor was tried for malfeasance.

Like Johnny Torrio, Stevens kept his home life distinct from his business. He was well educated, a student of history, and an omnivorous reader, being especially fond of the works of Robert Louis Stevenson, Robert Burns, and Jack London. He never drank, and didn't learn to smoke until he was fifty years old. He adopted three children and gave them good educations, and cared for an invalid wife for more than twenty years, giving her the best medical attention obtainable. He was extremely puritanical in his views; he disapproved of the theater, expunged immoral passages from the classics before bringing them into his home, refused to permit his children to wear short skirts or to use rouge or lipstick, amused his fellow gunmen by inveighing bitterly against the so-called flaming youth of the period, and frequently made long speeches upholding old-fashioned ideals and morals. But he would kill a man for fifty dollars and crack a skull for twenty.

Neither Stevens nor McErlane was ever punished for thinning the ranks of Spike O'Donnell's gang. It was common knowledge that McErlane had murdered O'Connor, Meeghan, Keane, and Bucher, but Torrio was able to keep him out of jail for several months; the police finally arrested him because of the uproar raised by the newspapers. McErlane was indicted, and the Grand Jury ordered that he be

---

[1] Cosmano was one of the many Black-Handers who tried to blackmail Jim Colosimo, but was ambushed by Colosimo and badly wounded. He was in jail when Colosimo was murdered.

held without bail; but he was immediately set free under bonds, and in April 1924 the State's Attorney nolle-prossed the case. Similar dispositions were made of indictments found against Joe Saltis, Ralph Sheldon, and others accused of complicity in the killings. Danny McFall, an unimportant member of Torrio's gun squad — his value lay chiefly in the fact that he was a Deputy Sheriff — was tried for the murder of O'Connor, but was acquitted, and soon thereafter vanished from Chicago. Walter Stevens also retired, after an attempt had been made to kill him. In gangland it was said of Stevens, as of Torrio: "He could dish it out but he couldn't take it."

5

WHEN Johnny Torrio led his army of pimps and harlots into Chicago's suburbs he made no attempt to establish bordellos in Cicero, which not only was the largest community in Cook County outside of Chicago, but with a population of more than fifty thousand was the fifth largest city in Illinois and one of the state's most important manufacturing centers. It had long since outgrown the wildness of which the Chicago newspapers had complained in Civil War times, and in the main was a prosperous and law-abiding city. It was preyed upon, of course, by the usual assortment of crooked politicians, and harbored the normal quota of saloons, most of which remained open after prohibition went into effect and were supplied with beer by the West Side O'Donnells, Klondike and Myles. But there were no brothels in Cicero, and the only form of gambling permitted was slot machines, hundreds of which were in operation under the control of a politician named Eddie Vogel. In co-operation with the O'Donnells and Eddie Tancl, a Bohemian saloonkeeper who had a large following among foreign-born voters, Vogel dominated the city government headed by Mayor Joseph Z. Klenha.

It was probably fear of the West Side O'Donnells rather than the opposition of the politicians that had kept Torrio out of Cicero, for the O'Donnells disapproved of prostitution and would have nothing to do with it. But in the fall of 1923, having gained control of the remainder of Cook County, Johnny Torrio made a carefully planned and long expected assault upon Cicero. Characteristically, he employed strategy instead of force. Making no arrangements for protection, he sent a score of prostitutes into Cicero in October 1923 and opened a bordello on Roosevelt Road. The Cicero police immediately closed the dive and arrested the women. Torrio opened another resort at Ogden and Fifty-second Avenues. It was wrecked by the police, and the harlots locked up. Torrio then withdrew his forces, but two days later deputies from the office of Sheriff Peter Hoffman descended upon Cicero and confiscated every slot machine in the city.

Having thus served notice that if he couldn't bring prostitutes into Cicero no one else could operate slot machines, Torrio suggested a compromise and made a treaty of peace with Vogel and the O'Donnell brothers, which was scrupulously observed for nearly three years, to the great profit of all concerned. Under the terms of this pact Vogel's slot machines were returned to him, and the O'Donnells were granted exclusive rights to sell beer to the saloons on Roosevelt Road and in several other sections of the city. The treaty also confirmed their possession of that portion of Chicago's West Side in which they had been operating. Torrio agreed not to import harlots nor attempt to establish brothels, but was permitted to open gambling houses and cabarets, to sell beer anywhere in Cicero except in the territory allotted to the O'Donnells, and to use the city as a base for all of his operations except those connected with vice. Eddie Tancl, notorious for his bad temper and fighting ability, would take no part in the peace conference; he defied

Torrio from the start, and profanely declared that he would buy beer from whomever he pleased. He had long been friendly with the O'Donnells, but quarreled with them when they began delivering needled beer instead of real beer. Ordered by both the O'Donnells and Torrio to leave Cicero, he replied that he would leave only in his coffin, which he did. He was killed in November 1924 by Myles O'Donnell and Jim Doherty, ostensibly in a dispute over a meal check.

As soon as terms for the occupation of Cicero had been agreed upon, Johnny Torrio turned the city over to Al Capone, by now Torrio's right-hand man and a full partner in all Torrio enterprises, and departed on an extensive tour of Europe, accompanied by his wife and mother. He also took with him a million dollars in securities and letters of credit, which he deposited in European banks against the time, which a man of his intelligence must have recognized as bound to come, when he should be compelled to flee Chicago. He returned to America in the spring of 1924, leaving his mother to spend her declining years on a seaside estate in Italy, with half a dozen automobiles and a staff of thirty servants, the richest woman in the province. Meanwhile Al Capone had been organizing Cicero. Torrio had captured the city without firing a shot, but Capone consolidated the conquest in a blaze of gunfire and a wave of lawlessness.

The violence reached a climax on election day, April 1, 1924, which brought the most disorderly twenty-four hours in Cicero's history. Bands of heavily armed gangsters, commanded by Capone and campaigning for Mayor Klenha and the Democratic ticket, terrorized the city from dawn to dusk. A man was killed in Eddie Tancl's saloon. Two others were shot dead in Twenty-second Street. Another man's throat was slashed. A policeman was blackjacked. Citizens who attempted to vote Republican were slugged and driven from the polls. "Automobiles filled with gunmen paraded the streets," said the Illinois Crime Survey, "slugging and kid-

333

napping election workers. Polling places were raided by armed thugs and ballots taken at the point of the gun from the hands of voters waiting to drop them in the box. Voters and workers were kidnapped, taken to Chicago and held prisoners until the polls closed." Late in the afternoon honest citizens appealed to Chicago for help, and seventy policemen were sworn in as deputy sheriffs by County Judge Edmund K. Jarecki and rushed to Cicero by automobile. A police squad commanded by Detective Sergeant William Cusick came upon Al Capone, his brother Frank, Dave Hedlin, and Charley Fischetti, with pistols in their hands, standing in front of a polling place at Cicero Avenue and Twenty-second Street. Frank Capone shot at Patrolman McGlynn, but missed, and McGlynn killed him. Hedlin was wounded. Fischetti was chased into a field and captured after a gun battle in which no one was hurt. Al Capone fled down Cicero Avenue, encountered another group of policemen, and with a gun blazing in each hand fought them off until darkness came to his aid and he escaped. He was never arrested, though a long and fruitless investigation was made by the State's Attorney's office to learn where he and other gangsters had obtained their pistol permits. It developed that most of them had been issued by suburban justices of the peace. Frank Capone was given a funeral which eclipsed that of Big Jim Colosimo, with a silver-plated casket and twenty thousand dollars' worth of flowers. As a gesture of solidarity, every saloon and gambling-house in Cicero remained closed, with tightly drawn blinds, for two hours.

Mayor Klenha and his ticket were, not unexpectedly, elected by tremendous majorities, and Al Capone was master of Cicero. Almost overnight the city became one of the toughest in the United States. It was said that the way to determine when one crossed the Chicago line into Cicero was simply to sniff. " If you smell gunpowder, you're in Cicero." The one-time peaceful streets of downtown Cicero were filled with arrogant, roistering, swaggering gangsters, and crowded with saloons and gambling-houses. One hundred and sixty of these places ran full blast day and night, with sidewalk barkers urging passers-by to step in. Among them were the notorious Ship, owned by Capone and managed by Toots Mondi; the Hawthorne Smoke Shop, owned by Torrio and managed by Frankie Pope, where an average of fifty thousand dollars a day was bet on the races; and Lauterback's, which operated the largest gambling games in the country, with a hundred thousand dollars in chips frequently risked on a single turn of the roulette wheel. Whisky sold for seventy-five cents a drink, beer for thirty-five cents a stein, and wine for thirty cents a small glass. Torrio and Capone owned many of the gambling-houses and had shares in others. In every independent resort was posted an agent of the syndicate; his job was to protect the dive and see that Torrio and Capone received their split, which ranged from twenty-five to fifty per cent of the gross receipts. The house was also compelled to pay the salary of the agent.

Capone ruled Cicero from his headquarters in the Hawthorne Inn on Twenty-second Street; he occupied an entire floor, posted armed gangsters at every entrance, and installed bullet-proof steel shutters at the windows. His orders transcended all law; he was obeyed without question by the police, and by city officials and employees from the Mayor down to the lowliest street-cleaner. Once when Mayor Klenha failed to do as he had been told, Capone knocked His Honor (*sic*) down on the steps of the City Hall and kicked him as he struggled to his feet. A policeman who saw the assault twirled his night-stick and strolled away. On another occasion, when the town council seemed about to pass a measure which Capone had ordered them to defeat, gangsters broke up the meeting, dragged one of the trustees into the street, and slugged him with a blackjack. Arthur St. John, editor of the Berwyn *Tribune,* was kidnapped and shot because he protested against the invasion of Berwyn by Torrio's harlots and gunmen. His brother Robert, editor of the Cicero *Tribune,* was beaten because of his anti-Capone editorials and because he interfered with a disciplinary slugging which was being administered to a Cicero policeman.

6

THE fortunes of Johnny Torrio reached their peak immediately following the conquest of Cicero. In the late spring of 1924, in partnership with Al Capone, he was running twenty-five large brothels scattered throughout Cook County, probably twice as many gambling-houses and immoral cabarets in the suburbs and in Chicago, and was operating or handling the output of sixty-five breweries. He also controlled several distilleries, and was running enormous quantities of hard liquor into Chicago from Canada and the Atlantic seaboard, using trucks and automobiles with secret compartments built into the top and floors. Most of Torrio's breweries were in operation for nearly ten years; many continued to manufacture beer even after they had been officially padlocked by the Federal government. Trucks belonging to Torrio and allied gang leaders, loaded with beer and whisky and guarded by armed gunmen, rumbled day and night through the streets of Chicago and Cook County, supplying at least three-fourths of the twenty thousand drinking places which came into existence after the dry amendment had gone into effect on January 16, 1920.

Except for an occasional attempt at hi-jacking by Spike O'Donnell and a few other independent gangsters, Torrio's liquor convoys were seldom molested; on the contrary, whenever a particularly valuable shipment was made, the criminal guards were frequently supplemented by detachments of uniformed policemen. For as the money rolled in, Torrio expanded to appalling proportions the system of corruption by which he had kept his brothels immune from interference. He gave liberally to campaign funds, and bought policemen, prohibition and enforcement agents, judges, politicians, and city and county officials as he needed them; hundreds openly received their bribes each week at a payoff station conveniently established in a downtown office building. It was not without reason that Torrio boasted: " I own the police." Many officials, of course, refused to " go along " with the gangsters. Morgan Collins, Chief of Police from 1923 to 1927, was offered a thousand dollars a day, and on another occasion a hundred thousand dollars a month, if he would guarantee Torrio's operations against molestation. E. C. Yellowley, Federal Prohibition Administrator for Illinois, refused two hundred and fifty thousand dollars to drop padlock proceedings against a distillery. William F. Waugh, United States District Attorney, was offered fifty thousand dollars to abandon the prosecution of several important gangsters accused of violating the Volstead Act. But for all practical purposes Johnny Torrio dominated the political machines of Chicago and Cook County, and to a somewhat lesser degree the Federal enforcement agencies for those districts, throughout the first and second administrations of Mayor William Hale Thompson, just as Al Capone did during most of Thompson's third term. " In circles close to Capone," said the Illinois Crime Survey, " it was well known that he had contributed substantially to the Thompson campaign." [1] Chicago witnessed a typical demonstration of Torrio's power in 1923, when he compelled Governor Len Small of Illinois to pardon Harry and Alma Cusick, convicted of pandering while operating a Torrio brothel at Posen, before they had even begun to serve their sentences.

Torrio's payroll, exclusive of the huge sums disbursed

[1] Frank J. Loesch, president of the Chicago Crime Commission, was quoted as saying that the amount was $260,000. Judge John H. Lyle said it was $150,000.

for protection, was not less than thirty thousand dollars a week. The profits from his various criminal enterprises were never accurately computed, but evidence obtained by the authorities from time to time indicated that they totaled an enormous amount. The Chicago *Daily News* said in 1924 that Torrio's arrangement with the brewer Joseph Stenson put forty-eight million dollars into Stenson's pocket in four years. "Nobody," the *News* continued, "has ever risked a guess at the clearings of the many-sided Torrio." When the Stockade in Stickney was raided in 1926, the police confiscated records which showed that the average weekly net earnings of the dive since its establishment were five thousand dollars. The Maple Inn at Forest View earned almost as much, and it was estimated that Torrio and Capone pocketed a net income of three thousand dollars a week from each of the other suburban resorts. This was a grand total of approximately four million dollars a year, of which ten per cent, or about four hundred thousand dollars, was paid out for protection. Federal investigators declared that from vice and gambling combined Torrio and Capone divided net earnings of two hundred thousand dollars a week. Ledgers seized in a raid on the gangsters' headquarters, transferred in 1923 from the Four Deuces to an elaborate suite of offices on Michigan Avenue, listed profits of three million dollars a year from whisky, beer, and wine. But these ledgers formed only a small part of the syndicate's bookkeeping system; the police estimated that the total annual profits from the manufacture and sale of liquor were at least thirty million dollars. Edwin A. Olson, United States District Attorney, told the newspapers that Torrio and Capone operated on a gross basis of seventy million dollars a year.

7

WITH the police demoralized and helpless and the whole machinery of law-enforcement in a condition of collapse, criminals who for years had lurked in the dark corners of the underworld came brazenly into the open. They took service under the captains of the gangs and so shared generously in the golden flood of prohibition, but at the same time they didn't neglect their own specialties. Banks all over Chicago were robbed in broad daylight by bandits who scorned to wear masks. Desk sergeants at police stations grew weary of recording holdups — from one hundred to two hundred were reported every night. Burglars marked out sections of the city as their own and embarked upon a course of systematic plundering, going from house to house night after night without hindrance. Fences accompanied thieves into stores and appraised stocks of merchandise before they were stolen. Pickpockets and confidence men flourished as they had not done since the first World's Fair. Payroll robberies were a weekly occurrence and necessitated the introduction of armored cars and armed guards for the delivery of money from banks to business houses. Automobiles were stolen by the thousands. Motorists were forced to the curb on busy streets and boldly robbed. Women who displayed jewelry in night clubs or at the theater were followed and held up. Wealthy women seldom left their homes unless accompanied by armed escorts.

Chicago seemed to be filled with gangsters — gangsters slaughtering one another, two hundred and fifteen in four years; gangsters being killed by the police, one hundred and sixty in the same length of time; gangsters shooting up saloons for amusement; gangsters throwing bombs, called "pineapples"; gangsters improving their marksmanship on machine-gun ranges in sparsely settled districts; gangsters speeding in big automobiles, ignoring traffic laws; gangsters strutting in the Loop, holstered pistols scarcely concealed; gangsters giving orders to the police, to judges, to prosecutors, all sworn to uphold the law; gangsters calling on their friends and protectors at City Hall and the County Court House; gangsters dining in expensive restaurants and cafés; tuxedoed gangsters at the opera and the theater, their mink-coated, Paris-gowned wives or sweethearts on their arms; gangsters entertaining politicians and city officials at " Belshazzar feasts," some of which cost twenty-five thousand dollars; gangsters giving parties at which the guests playfully doused each other with champagne at twenty dollars a bottle, popping a thousand corks in a single evening; gangsters armed with shotguns, rifles, and machine-guns, convoying beer trucks; gangsters everywhere — except in jail. And all with huge bank-rolls; a gangster with less than five thousand dollars in his pocket was a rarity. They had so much money a new argot was invented to describe it. A thousand dollars was a grand, abbreviated to "gran'"; hundred-dollar bills were leaves, and twenty-five dollars was scornfully called two bits. Five-, ten-, and twenty-dollar bills were chicken-feed; they were given to newsboys for a paper, to hat-check girls in restaurants, to dazed panhandlers.

"It's all newspaper talk," said Big Bill Thompson, Mayor of Chicago.

8

JOHNNY TORRIO and Al Capone were riding high in the spring of 1924, but great trouble for them was looming on the horizon of the underworld, and most of it was to be caused by Dion O'Banion. As a boy, O'Banion sang in the choir of the Holy Name Cathedral and was remarkable for piety and obedience; as a man, he was a swashbuckling,

340

ambidextrous, flower-loving, cheerful murderer, who wore a carnation in his buttonhole and carried three pistols stowed away in special pockets built into his expensive clothing by expert tailors. Chief of Police Morgan Collins characterized O'Banion as " Chicago's arch-criminal " and declared that he had killed, or ordered killed, at least twenty-five men. But he was never brought to trial for any of these crimes, for politically he was only less important than Torrio or Capone. He was particularly powerful in the Forty-second and Forty-third wards on the North Side, and for years he and his gunmen had kept them safely in the Democratic column. So widely was his ability as a vote-getter recognized that a question-and-answer wheeze developed in Chicago: "Who'll carry the Forty-second and Forty-third?" "O'Banion, in his pistol pocket."

As the November 1924 election approached, Democratic politicians were disturbed by rumors that O'Banion intended to throw his strength to the Republicans. To avert such a calamity, a testimonial dinner was held in October at the Webster Hotel on Lincoln Park West, at which the gang leader was presented with a platinum watch richly encrusted with rubies and diamonds. Who sponsored the dinner and bought the watch was never divulged. Prominent among the guests were Frank Gusenberg, Schemer Drucci, George Bugs Moran, Maxie Eisen, Hymie Weiss; Louis Alterie, who besides being one of O'Banion's crack gunmen was president of the Theater and Building Janitors' Union; Jerry O'Connor, gambling-house owner and vice president of the union; and the union's secretary, Con Shea, notorious labor slugger and racketeer, who had served a term in Sing Sing for the attempted murder of a woman. But also present were Colonel Albert A. Sprague, Chicago's Commissioner of Public Works and Democratic candidate for United States Senator; County Clerk Robert M. Sweitzer; Chief of Detectives Michael Hughes, half a dozen police captains and lieutenants, and many lesser office-holders and politicians. When ordered by Mayor William E. Dever to explain why he had attended the dinner, Chief Hughes said he had understood that the party was to be in honor of Jerry O'Connor. "But when I arrived," he said, "and recognized a number of notorious characters I had thrown into the detective bureau basement a half-dozen times, I knew I had been framed, and withdrew almost at once."

The gang chieftain accepted the platinum watch with pleasure, but whoever put up the money for it did so in vain. For favors expected and received, by slugging, bribery, shooting, kidnapping, and the use of floaters and repeaters, O'Banion delivered both the Forty-second and Forty-third wards to the Republican ticket, headed by United States Senator Charles S. Deneen and Robert E. Crowe, the latter running for re-election as State's Attorney. Crowe defeated the Democratic nominee, Michael I. Igoe, nearly two to one.

9

O'BANION was a product of Little Hell, on the North Side near the Sicilian quarter and Death Corner, where tenements swarming with children were interspersed among brothels, disorderly saloons, and immoral cabarets. Throughout his formative years he was surrounded by criminal influences, and under the pressure of environment he soon forgot the moral lessons taught by the priests of the Cathedral. He became a thieving loafer and a member of the Market Street gang, and then a singing waiter in McGovern's Cabaret at Clark and Erie Streets, one of Little Hell's toughest dives. He sang sentimental ballads while picking the pockets of maudlin customers. At this time he was known as Gimpy O'Banion, because his left leg was a trifle shorter than the right, but no one ever called him Gimpy, and lived, after he had become a Big Shot. From robbing drunken revelers, O'Banion turned to highway robbery, burglary, and safe-cracking. He served three months in the Bridewell in 1909, when he was seventeen years old, for burglary, and three months in 1911 for assault. And that was all the time he ever spent in prison.

When prohibition came upon the land in 1920, O'Banion was well known to the police as a dangerous hoodlum and as chief of one of the most successful criminal gangs Chicago has ever harbored. His followers included such notorious gunmen and bandits as Handsome Dan McCarthy, Bugs Moran, Maxie Eisen, Frank Gusenberg; Vincent Drucci, better known as the Schemer; Two-Gun Louis Alterie, also called the Cowboy Gunman because he owned a ranch in Colorado; Hymie Weiss, who was O'Banion's alter ego and second in command of the gang; and Samuel J. Morton, called Nails, who had won the *Croix de guerre* in France and had returned from the World War a First Lieutenant in the United States Army. Morton died as the result of what his fellow gangsters regarded as despicable treachery; he was thrown and kicked to death while riding a horse in Lincoln Park. A committee of the O'Banion gang, determined to exact vengeance, kidnapped the horse a few days later, led it to the spot where Morton's body had been found, and solemnly "bumped it off," each gangster firing a shot into the animal's head.

Morton, known by the police to have committed several murders, was buried with elaborate religious, fraternal, and military honors, and his funeral was attended by the usual assortment of truckling city, state, county, and Federal officials. "Five thousand Jews," said the *Daily News,* "paid tribute to Morton as the man who had made the West Side safe for his race. As a young man he had organized a defense society to drive 'Jew-baiters' from the West Side." A year after Morton's death a memorial service was planned by his friends, and the printed announcement of the service

343

carried the names of Rabbi Felix A. Levi, the Reverend John L. O'Donnell, General Abel Davis, and Captain Ed Maher. It was also announced that Johnny Torrio, Hymie Weiss, Terry Druggan, and other criminals would participate. The principal address was to be delivered by a well-known lawyer, Frank Comerford. The plan was abandoned when General Davis withdrew from the committee; he said it would be a mistake to flaunt Morton's record " in the faces of decent citizens."

O'Banion's income from the liquor traffic, though not nearly so large as that of either Torrio or Capone, was sufficient to make him a very rich man; it was estimated by the police after his death that he had banked almost a million dollars a year from this source alone. He supplemented his booze earnings with the proceeds of frequent safe-robberies, payroll holdups, and hi-jackings. At least two of his exploits were noteworthy even for Chicago. He led his crew of gunmen into West Side railroad yards and stole a hundred thousand dollars' worth of Canadian liquor from a freight car; and in 1924 he carried out the famous robbery of the Sibley warehouse, trucking out one thousand seven hundred and fifty barrels of bonded whisky and leaving in their stead as many barrels of water. He was indicted for this, together with ten of his gangsters, four city detectives, and officials of the Sibley Warehouse Company, but no one was convicted. In 1922 O'Banion further augmented his income by buying a half-interest in William E. Schofield's flower shop on North State Street, directly opposite the Cathedral where he had once served as choir boy. As gangland's official florist O'Banion sold thousands of dollars' worth of flowers to the friends and foes of slain gunmen, for underworld etiquette demanded that a killer send expensive floral tributes to the funeral of his victim. Even without the business of the gangsters, ownership of the shop would have brought great prosperity to O'Banion, for he

344

had considerable business ability and possessed a consuming love of flowers. He had a knack of arranging blooms, and unless hampered too much by instructions his floral creations were, in many instances, works of art.

For three years after O'Banion joined Torrio's league of gunmen he appeared to be content with what he could get out of the North Side. But after the taking of Cicero he began to express dissatisfaction; several of his killers had supported Al Capone during the election-day rioting in the suburban city, and he had got nothing out of it but a brief word of thanks. To placate the disgruntled O'Banion, Torrio turned over to him a strip of Cicero territory in which the beer concession was worth about twenty thousand dollars a month. O'Banion soon quintupled this business; he canvassed the South and West Sides and persuaded fifty saloonkeepers who had been buying beer from the Sheldon, Saltis-McErlane, and Druggan-Lake gangs to move into Cicero, where they competed with saloons which were supplied by Torrio and Capone. Torrio demanded a share of the new revenue, and in return offered O'Banion an interest in the syndicate's earnings from brothels. But O'Banion refused. Like the O'Donnells, he was not interested in prostitution.

O'Banion also nursed a grievance against Torrio's allies the Genna brothers — Sam, Jim, Pete, Angelo, Tony, and Mike, known as the Terrible Gennas, who were the special pets of Diamond Joe Esposito and high in the councils of the Unione Siciliana. The North Side gang chieftain complained that the Gennas were "muscling in" on his territory and flooding the district with bad whisky which they sold for three dollars a gallon. O'Banion had been getting from six to nine dollars, but delivering a much better grade of liquor. He demanded that Torrio drive the Gennas back to the West Side, and when Torrio protested that he could not accomplish such a miracle of discipline, the fiery O'Banion angrily threatened to do it himself. This was a task which no one but the North Sider would even have considered, for of all Chicago gunmen the Gennas and their henchmen were the most feared.

Five of the six Genna brothers were typical Sicilian killers — haughty, overbearing, contemptuous, savage, treacherous, and at the same time devoutly religious; they went regularly to church, and carried rosaries and crucifixes in their pistol pockets. The exception was Tony, known in the Italian colony as Tony the Gentleman and Tony the Aristocrat, who studied architecture, built model tenements for his poor countrymen, was a patron of the opera, and lived elegantly in a downtown hotel. He never killed, but he attended all family councils at which murder was planned, and had a voice in all decisions. The qualities that Tony the Gentleman lacked were to be found in ample measure in the Gennas' principal followers — Sam Smoots Amatuma, the dandy of gangland, accomplished musician and double-crosser; Giuseppe Nerone, called the Cavalier, university graduate and teacher of mathematics; and those ferocious murderers John Scalisi and Albert Anselmi, beside whom Frank McErlane was the personification of loving-kindness. It was Scalisi and Anselmi who taught Chicago's gangsters to rub their bullets with garlic, to increase the chances of gangrene.

The Gennas put hundreds of Sicilians and Italians to work cooking corn sugar alcohol in West Side tenements in the vicinity of Taylor Street, using a process which is said to have been invented by their brother-in-law, Harry Spingola, a wealthy lawyer. In less than a year the Genna cookeries and stills were producing thousands of gallons of raw alcohol, which was cut, flavored, colored, and sold as brandy, whisky, or whatever the customer desired in the way of fine liquor. At the peak of their prosperity, early in 1925, the assets of the Gennas, including goodwill and a three-story warehouse on Taylor Street, were valued at five million

346

dollars; gross sales amounted to three hundred and fifty thousand dollars a month, of which at least a hundred and fifty thousand was profit. This lucrative business was protected by a police and political hookup arranged by Torrio and Esposito, by which the gangsters paid, monthly, sums which ranged from a small amount in the beginning to nearly seven thousand dollars in April 1925. Federal agents investigating the Gennas obtained a confession from their office manager, who said that five police captains were on the Genna payroll. He also said that four hundred uniformed policemen, mostly from the Maxwell Street station, besides many plain-clothes officers from Headquarters and the State's Attorney's office, called at the Genna warehouse each month to receive their bribes. In addition, the police received large quantities of alcohol at wholesale prices.

To show his contempt for the Gennas and to emphasize his dissatisfaction with Torrio's leadership, O'Banion hijacked a Genna truck loaded with thirty thousand dollars' worth of whisky. The Gennas immediately polished up their armament and started on the warpath, but were restrained by Torrio and by Mike Merlo, president of the Unione Siciliana, an important figure in the Nineteenth Ward, and the most powerful Sicilian or Italian in Chicago. Among his countrymen Merlo's word was law. He was intimately associated with Torrio, Capone, and other Italian and Sicilian gangsters and tolerated much lawlessness, but took no part in gang wars and was strongly opposed to murder. Both he and Torrio believed that peace with O'Banion could be arranged without recourse to the pistol and the shotgun. At that time, incidentally, the machine-gun had not yet appeared as an instrument of gang warfare.

But O'Banion refused to listen to Torrio's overtures, and relations between the North Side chieftain and the leaders of the Sicilian gangs were strained throughout the winter of 1923–4, although no shootings occurred. The

347

breaking-point was reached in the spring of 1924, when O'Banion double-crossed Torrio and swindled him out of several hundred thousand dollars. In partnership with Torrio and Capone, O'Banion owned the Sieben Brewery on the North Side, one of the largest breweries to operate during prohibition. About the middle of May 1924 O'Banion called Torrio and Capone into conference and told them he had decided to wind up his affairs and retire to Louis Alterie's ranch in Colorado. To make the story more plausible he intimated that he was afraid of the Gennas. Torrio and Capone bought O'Banion's share of the brewery for a price said to have been half a million dollars, and the property was transferred immediately. O'Banion agreed to assist in the dispatch and protection of one more convoy of beer from the plant and suggested May 19 as the best date for making the shipment.

On the night of May 19 the Sieben Brewery was raided by a strong force of policemen under the command of Chief of Police Morgan Collins and Captain Matthew Zimmer. Thirteen trucks piled high with beer barrels were confiscated, and twenty-eight gangsters and beer-runners arrested, including Torrio, Hymie Weiss, Louis Alterie, and O'Banion. Instead of taking his prisoners to a police station, Chief Collins turned them over to the Federal authorities. When asked why he had thus taken the case out of the hands of the State's Attorney, Chief Collins replied that the United States District Attorney " has promised us prompt co-operation." Johnny Torrio dipped into his well-lined pockets and brought up cash bail for himself and his half-dozen gunmen, but declined to furnish bonds for O'Banion, Weiss, and Alterie, none of whom had the necessary money on hand. They were compelled to await the arrival of Billy Skidmore, a professional bondsman and gambler, whose name is still frequently mentioned in connection with the Chicago underworld.

348

As soon as the police appeared at the brewery, Johnny Torrio suspected treachery. Later he obtained proof that O'Banion had double-crossed him. Through his political connections the North Sider had learned of the raid and had taken advantage of the knowledge to unload his share of the brewery upon Torrio and Capone. O'Banion also knew that the prosecution would be handled by the United States District Attorney, and that Torrio's influence did not extend to the Federal court. He was well aware that he might himself be fined, but he anticipated that Torrio, as one of the owners of the brewery and as a second offender — Torrio had been fined two thousand dollars in 1923 for operating a brewery — would be much more severely punished. In the main, events occurred as O'Banion had expected. He paid no fine himself because he was dead by the time the brewery case came into court, but Torrio, one of eleven defendants who pleaded guilty, was fined five thousand dollars and sentenced to nine months in jail. He remained free on bail, however, for nearly a year.

Among Johnny Torrio's dominant traits, and accounting in large measure for his greatness as a criminal, were patience and the ability to hold his passions in check. Unquestionably he hated O'Banion as much as he had ever hated anyone, but he went about his business as if nothing had happened, realizing that war with the fierce North Sider would disrupt his system of liquor distribution, and throw gangland into chaos, as, eventually, it did. But O'Banion soon made a bad matter worse. Advised by the shrewd Hymie Weiss to make peace with Torrio and the Gennas, O'Banion said with huge contempt: " Oh, to hell with them Sicilians." This phrase, repeated by O'Banion gunmen as a choice bit of gangland repartee, was really the gangster florist's death warrant, for to Sicilians and Italians alike it was a deadly insult. Several times during the summer of 1924 the murder of O'Banion was planned by Torrio, Capone,

349

and the Gennas, but each time they were stopped by Mike Merlo, who still hoped for a peaceful settlement. But Merlo died on November 8, 1924, to be succeeded by Angelo Genna as president of the Unione Siciliana, and two days later Dion O'Banion lay dead among his flowers.

Merlo's funeral was an imposing ceremony. A hundred thousand dollars' worth of flowers were sent to his home by friends; they filled not only the house but the lawn outside as well. The most impressive of these pieces was a statue of the dead man twelve feet high, made entirely of flowers, and said to have been a recognizable likeness. In the funeral cortege it was carried in a car preceding the hearse. Many of the flowers came from O'Banion's shop; he filled a ten-thousand-dollar order for Torrio, and an eight-thousand-dollar order for Al Capone. Even one of the Gennas, Jim, called at O'Banion's place and paid seven hundred and fifty dollars for a floral tribute. But, as developed later, Genna's visit was really for the purpose of familiarizing himself with the interior of the shop. All day Sunday, November 9, O'Banion and his partner, Schofield, worked hard arranging floral designs and sending them to the Merlo residence. That night, after O'Banion had gone, a man called by telephone and ordered a wreath. He said it would be called for next morning.

About noon on November 10 three men entered O'Banion's flower shop and walked abreast toward the gangster, who was clipping the stems of a bunch of chrysanthemums in the rear of the front room. He was alone in the place except for a Negro porter, mopping the floor in the back room. Over the top of a swinging wicker door, the porter saw O'Banion advance to meet the callers, heard him say: " Hello, boys, you want Merlo's flowers? " and saw him extend a hand in greeting. Ordinarily when O'Banion talked to anyone, particularly to strangers, he kept one hand in a pistol pocket. But this time he was off guard; his right hand was outstretched, and the left, holding a pair of shears, was at his side. The center man of the three simply grasped O'Banion's hand and suddenly jerked him forward, and before the gangster could recover his equilibrium and snatch a pistol, the men on either side of him had fired five bullets into his body, and a sixth — the grace shot to make death certain — into his head.

The Negro porter said that two of O'Banion's murderers were Italians, and that the third might have been a Greek or a Jew, but he could give no better description of their appearance. The police were never able to obtain sufficient evidence even to justify an arrest, and the crime is still officially unsolved. But O'Banion's gunmen learned, to their own satisfaction at least, that the killing was planned by Torrio and Capone, and that the man who seized O'Banion's hand was Mike Genna. The death shots were fired by John Scalisi and Albert Anselmi, each of whom received ten thousand dollars in cash and a three-thousand-dollar diamond ring. Scalisi sent his ring to his sweetheart in Sicily.

The funeral of O'Banion was the gaudiest of all gangland's burials. His casket cost ten thousand dollars, and was shipped from Philadelphia to Chicago in a special express car. Forty thousand persons viewed the body as it "lay in state," as the *Tribune* put it, in an undertaker's chapel. The funeral procession was a mile long, led by three bands and a police escort from Stickney, Chief Collins having refused to allow Chicago policemen to participate in the ceremonies. Twenty-five trucks and cars were required to carry the flowers. Ten thousand persons followed the hearse, and ten thousand more waited at the grave. Cardinal Mundelein had refused to allow funeral services to be held over the dead gangster, but at Mount Carmel Cemetery a priest who had known O'Banion since childhood recited a litany, a Hail Mary, and the Lord's Prayer. The gangster was buried in unconsecrated ground, but five months after his death the body was disinterred and reburied in a plot which had been bought by Mrs. O'Banion. It was thus placed in consecrated ground, a circumstance which led Captain John Stege, an honest policeman who fought the gangsters with great vigor, to remark:

"O'Banion was a thief and a murderer, but look at him now, buried eighty feet from a bishop."[1]

10

Hymie Weiss, who was the second of the Big Shots to die and the third to vanish from the Chicago scene, was born in Poland. His real name was Wajciechowski, a jawbreaker which was changed to Weiss soon after his family arrived in the United States. Chicago police records give his first name as Earl, but in the underworld he was known as Hymie the Polack, Little Hymie, and Hymie, most often the last. Before prohibition he was a burglar, a safe-blower, and an automobile-thief, and occasionally a hired slugger and killer for labor unions. His disposition was ugly and savage, although, as his gangster friends often pointed out, he was kind to his mother. Like so many gangland murderers, he was religious; he carried crucifixes and rosaries in his pockets and was a regular attendant at Mass. He was a great deal more prudent and far-seeing than O'Banion, who was impulsive and headstrong, and the pair made an excellent criminal combination. The Chicago police always said that it was Weiss who really built up O'Banion's booze business to such huge proportions; he was always ready to adjust complaints of the saloon-keepers, and slugged them only when he was unable to keep them in line by peaceful means.

Weiss assumed the leadership of the North Side gang

---

[1] This was true. About that distance away from O'Banion's grave is the mausoleum in which lie the bodies of Archbishops Feehan and Quigley and Bishop Porter.

THE BIGGEST OF THE BIG SHOTS—JOHNNY TORRIO AND AL CAPONE

upon the death of O'Banion and immediately declared war upon Torrio, Capone, and the six Genna brothers. He struck first at Capone. On January 12, 1925, while Capone's car was parked in front of a restaurant at State and Fifty-fifth Streets, Weiss, Schemer Drucci, and Bugs Moran drove slowly by and raked the machine with a fusillade of bullets from shotguns and automatic pistols. Capone's chauffeur was wounded, but two of the gangster's bodyguard, sitting in the rear seat, dropped to the floor and were not hurt. Capone was not in the car; he had stepped into the restaurant a few moments before the assailants appeared.

Johnny Torrio attended Dion O'Banion's wake, which under the circumstances required considerable courage, but the ceremonies had scarcely ended before he was in flight. Trailed by O'Banion gunmen, who were never more than a few jumps behind him, Torrio went to Hot Springs, to New Orleans, to Havana and the Bahamas, and to Palm Beach and St. Petersburg in Florida. He returned to Chicago some eight or nine days after the attempt upon Capone, and on the afternoon of January 24, 1925 went shopping in the Loop with his wife. About half past four o'clock they drove up to their home at No. 7011 Clyde Avenue, in the Jackson Park section of the South Side. It was growing dark, and Torrio failed to see the automobile parked around the corner in Seventieth Street. Mrs. Torrio got out of the car and walked toward her front door, and Torrio followed, his arms filled with parcels. He had taken no more than half a dozen steps when two men, armed with a shotgun and automatic pistols, rushed across the street. They fired first at Torrio's car, shattering the windshield and wounding the chauffeur. Then they turned their guns on Torrio, and the master of the booze traffic fell with five bullets in his jaw, right arm, abdomen, and chest.

For three weeks Torrio lay in the Jackson Park Hospital, closely guarded by two policemen and a band of gunmen under the personal command of Al Capone. On February 9, 1925, heavily bandaged, Torrio appeared in the United States Court, paid the fine imposed upon him in the Sieben Brewery case, and was sent to the Lake County Jail at Waukegan to serve his sentence of nine months. The kind-hearted Sheriff allowed the gangster many privileges. He fitted up his cell with rugs, chairs, and a comfortable bed, installed bullet-proof steel-mesh blinds at the windows, and hired two deputy sheriffs to patrol the corridor outside the cell. Some time in March 1925 Torrio summoned Al Capone and his lawyers and transferred to Capone all his brothels, cabarets, gambling-houses, breweries, and distilleries and all right and title to his high estate in gangland, transactions which are said to have involved several million dollars. When he was released from jail in the fall of 1925, three automobiles filled with gunmen waited for him at the gates and he was rushed through Chicago to Gary, Indiana, where he took a train for New York. There he boarded a steamer for Italy. Unless he returned unbeknown to the police, Torrio was never again in Chicago, although he was back in the United States within a few years. At last reports he was living in Brooklyn. Estimates of his wealth when he left Chicago ranged from ten to thirty million dollars.

II

THE attacks upon Al Capone and Johnny Torrio marked the beginning of the gang wars which spread Chicago's evil renown to the far corners of the earth. Coupled with the increased activity of Chief of Police Morgan Collins under the direct order of Mayor Dever, the flight of Torrio and the efforts of Hymie Weiss to exact vengeance for the murder of O'Banion threw gangland into a turmoil and completely disrupted the system of booze distribution and control of vice and gambling which Torrio had so carefully

354

organized. Old alliances were broken, and gang chieftains who had worked amicably together since the dawn of prohibition became deadly enemies. Myles and Klondike O'Donnell joined forces with Weiss, and so did Joe Saltis and Frank McErlane and various other outfits composed mainly of Americans and Irishmen. Ralph Sheldon and Danny Stanton remained loyal to Capone, as did the Gennas and the lesser Sicilian gangs. In general, a gangster was either a "Capone guy" or a "Weiss guy." Territorial claims were ignored, trucks were hi-jacked, breweries and distilleries robbed, and Chicago's streets echoed to the roar of shotguns, the crack of automatic pistols, and the rattle of machine-guns. The speakeasy-owner, caught in the middle, was slugged and terrorized by all factions. Except for a brief breathing spell late in 1926 and early in 1927, the wars continued for five years. Including those who fell in the taking of Cicero and in the fighting between Torrio and Spike O'Donnell, more than five hundred men died. Just how many of these killings Al Capone was responsible for was never known, but estimates ranged from twenty to sixty. The Chicago *Tribune* once listed thirty-three persons who were described as "Capone's Victims," and appended to the list this significant statement: "and many others about whom definite information is not available." Here are some of the more important entries in the five-year catalogue of murder:

Three of the Gennas were killed. The first was Angelo. On May 26, 1925, three men, said to have been Weiss, Bugs Moran, and Schemer Drucci, came up behind him in a touring car on Ogden Avenue and blasted him to death with sawed-off shotguns. Mike Genna was next. On June 13, 1925, together with Scalisi and Anselmi, he exchanged volleys with Moran and Drucci, who were seriously hurt but managed to escape. Pursued and overtaken by a police car, the three Genna gangsters opened fire with shotguns upon

Detectives Michael J. Conway, William Sweeney, Charles B. Walsh, and Harold F. Olson. In the battle that followed, Mike Genna and Detectives Walsh and Olson were killed and Conway was wounded. Scalisi and Anselmi escaped, but were later arrested. At their third trial for the murder of Walsh and Olson, more than two years after the crime was committed, they were acquitted upon the remarkable ground that they had only resisted unwarranted police aggression. A defense fund of a hundred thousand dollars was expended on behalf of the two gunmen, and several Italians, among them Henry Spingola, were murdered because they refused to contribute more than once. The third of the Gennas to die was Tony the Gentleman; he was slain from ambush by Joseph Nerone, the Cavalier. Less than a year later Nerone was shot by a Capone gunman. The successive deaths of Angelo, Mike, and Tony broke up the gang. Sam and Pete went into hiding, and Jim fled to Italy, where he remained five years. Part of that time he was in an Italian jail.

Sam Smoots Amatuna was shot to death as he sat in a barber's chair, by two men who were believed to have been Schemer Drucci and Jim Doherty, the latter one of Myles O'Donnell's most efficient killers. Amatuna had succeeded Angelo Genna as president of the Unione Siciliana and was trying to rally the depleted forces of the Sicilians. Before the summer of 1929 three more Unione presidents — Antonio Lombardo, Pasquale Lolordo, and Joseph Guinta — were slain as the result of Capone's efforts to control the organization. Lombardo was killed in a rush-hour crowd at State and Madison Streets, one of the busiest corners in the world. In 1928 Frankie Uale, national head of the Unione, was murdered in Brooklyn, supposedly by Capone's orders.

Jim Doherty and Tom Duffy, the latter also an O'Donnell gunman, were killed on the night of April 27, 1926, less than two months after the death of Amatuna, in front of the Pony Inn on Roosevelt Road in Cicero. In this murder the machine-gun appeared for the first time in gang warfare, and Al Capone himself is said to have handled the weapon. Slain in the same burst of fire was William H. McSwiggin, a policeman's son and an Assistant State's Attorney. Myles and Klondike O'Donnell escaped by throwing themselves to the ground and shamming death. Why McSwiggin was killed, and why he was in the company of such notorious criminals, have never been explained; the State's Attorney's office said vaguely that he was trying to obtain information. The police theory was that he was killed simply because he chanced to be with the O'Donnells. At first McSwiggin was regarded as a martyr, but investigation disclosed that he had long been friendly with the O'Donnells and with Doherty and Duffy, that he had often " played around " with gangsters, and that ten days before the murder he had held a long conference with Capone at the latter's headquarters in Cicero. Capone vanished after the killing and remained in hiding for four months. When he returned to Chicago he found that the police had no evidence whatever connecting him with the crime.

The North Side gangsters made a dozen attempts to kill Capone, and nearly succeeded on September 20, 1926. At noon on that day, while Twenty-second Street in Cicero was filled with shoppers and lunch-hour promenaders, eleven automobiles filled with Weiss gangsters drove slowly past the Hawthorne Inn and poured into the building more than a thousand bullets and slugs from machine-guns, automatic pistols, and shotguns. After the roar of the attack had subsided, bullet-holes were found in thirty-five automobiles parked at the curb. Inside the hotel, woodwork and doors had been splintered, windows shattered, plaster ripped from walls, and furniture wrecked in the office and lobby. Capone, lunching in a restaurant next door, escaped injury, although bullets snapped above his head as he lay on the floor. One of his gunmen, Louis Barko, was shot in the shoulder. Mrs. Clyde Freeman, sitting with her infant son in a car that was struck thirty times, was hit by a bullet that plowed a furrow across her forehead and injured her eyes. Another creased the skull of her son. Capone is said to have paid physicians five thousand dollars to save Mrs. Freeman's sight.

Hymie Weiss lived just twenty days after his attack upon Al Capone in Cicero. At four o'clock on the afternoon of October 11, 1926, Weiss drove up to his headquarters above O'Banion's flower shop at No. 738 North State Street, accompanied by Paddy Murray, his bodyguard; Sam Peller, his chauffeur; W. W. O'Brien, a lawyer; and Benny Jacobs, an investigator employed by O'Brien. They had spent the afternoon at the Criminal Court Building, where Joe Saltis and his right-hand man, Lefty Koncil, were on trial for the murder of Mitters Foley of the Sheldon gang. Incidentally, Saltis and Koncil were acquitted. As Weiss and his four companions walked slowly across the sidewalk, the two gunmen opened fire upon them with a shotgun and a machine-gun from a window on the third floor of a boarding-house next door, where, as was afterward learned, they had lain in wait for three days. Weiss was killed almost instantly by ten machine-gun bullets. Murray, hit fifteen times, fell dead beside him. Peller, Jacobs, and O'Brien were wounded, but eventually recovered. Weiss was twenty-eight years old when he died, and possessed a fortune conservatively estimated at one million three hundred thousand dollars.

Schemer Drucci, who succeeded Weiss as chief of the O'Banion gang, died ingloriously, according to gangland standards, at the hands of a policeman. Arrested for creating a disturbance at a polling place on April 4, 1927, Drucci was being taken to a police station when he became enraged and tried to snatch Detective Dan Healy's revolver. Healy shot him four times. Drucci left an estate appraised at five hundred thousand dollars. With Drucci gone, Bugs Moran became leader of the North Side gang and transferred his headquarters to a garage at No. 2122 North Clark Street.

Seven men were killed in this garage in the famous St. Valentine's Day massacre of February 14, 1929. One of the victims was a young optometrist, Dr. Reinhart H. Schwimmer, who was an old-time friend of Moran's and, like McSwiggin, enjoyed "playing around" with gangsters. The others were members of Moran's gang — Frank Gusenberg; his brother Peter, who had served three years in a Federal prison for a mail-truck robbery in 1921; James Clark, Moran's brother-in-law, whose real name was Kashellek; John May, safe-blower and mechanic; Adam Hyer, ex-convict and expert accountant; and Alfred Weinshank, an official of the Central Cleaners' and Dyers' Association, who had only recently joined the gang. All of these men, waiting at the garage for a truckload of booze which they supposed was being run into Chicago by the Purple gang of Detroit, were disarmed and lined up against the wall by three gangsters wearing police uniforms. Then two other men, in plain clothing, stepped forward and raked the line with machine-guns. The police arrested Jack McGurn, John Scalisi, and Joseph Guinta, all of the Capone gang, but McGurn proved an alibi and Scalisi and Guinta were killed before they could be tried. Capone himself had the best alibi of all; at the moment the crime was committed he was talking to the District Attorney of Miami, Florida. Nevertheless, the police were certain, though unable to prove, that he had planned the massacre, and that the machine-guns were operated by Scalisi and Anselmi. Bugs Moran said: "Only the Capone gang kills like that."

The bodies of Guinta, Scalisi, and Anselmi were found on May 8, 1929, huddled on the floor of an automobile parked near Gray's Lake in Douglas Park. Each of the men had been shot several times, and their bodies beaten almost to a pulp. The crime was never solved, but the police advanced three theories, all plausible. One was that Moran and his gang had killed the fearsome Sicilians. Another was that Capone had put them on the spot in order to make peace with Moran. The third, which the police believed to be most likely, was that Capone had ordered them killed because they were becoming too important, especially Scalisi. That brutal thug had become chief bodyguard to Capone after the collapse of the Genna gang, and had amassed a fortune of two hundred and fifty thousand dollars. He had also been appointed assistant to Guinta as president of the Unione Siciliana and had quickly relegated Guinta to the background and himself taken over the conduct of the organization's affairs. Moreover, he had been heard to remark, soon after the slaughter of the Moran gangsters: " I am the most powerful man in Chicago." Evidence gathered by the police indicated that Capone believed Scalisi, Anselmi, and Guinta to be plotting against him, and that the three were bludgeoned and shot while attending a gangland banquet given to celebrate the victory over the Morans.

Jake Lingle was killed on June 9, 1930, in a pedestrian underpass at Randolph Street and Michigan Avenue. Ostensibly Lingle was a police reporter on the *Tribune* earning sixty-five dollars a week, but death revealed him as possessing an income of more than sixty thousand dollars a year. He drove a big car, owned an eighteen-thousand-dollar summer home, plunged in the stock market, bet heavily on the races, and maintained an elaborate suite of rooms at one of Chicago's most expensive hotels. He was also disclosed as an intimate friend of Al Capone, as an occasional visitor at Capone's estate in Florida, as the proud owner of a diamond-studded belt given to him by Capone, as the friend of other gang leaders, as a fixer for gambling-houses and other shady enterprises, as the " unofficial chief of police," and as the man who, by his own admission, " fixed the price of beer in Chicago." But the full extent of his underworld connections, and the secret of his political power, were never divulged. Leo Brothers, a St. Louis gunman, was convicted of the killing and sentenced to prison for fourteen years, of which he served ten.

Jack Zuta, believed by the police to have planned the murder of Jake Lingle, was killed on August 1, 1930, at the Lake View Hotel on Lake Nemahbin near Delafield, Wisconsin. As Zuta stood in the hotel's dance pavilion feeding nickels into an electric piano, five men entered, walking in single file and carrying a machine-gun, a rifle, two shotguns, and pistols. They lined up behind Zuta, and when he turned to face them, a smile on his face, they riddled his body with sixteen slugs and bullets. Zuta had occupied the same position in Moran's gang as Harry Cusick and Mike de Pike Heitler did in Capone's — he was general manager of brothels and immoral cabarets. As far as prostitution was concerned, Drucci, Weiss, and Moran had not seen eye to eye with Dion O'Banion. In safety-deposit boxes owned by Zuta the police found ledgers, canceled checks, and memoranda which Zuta had carefully preserved over a period of several years. They showed that Moran's gross income, even after the St. Valentine Day massacre had left him, as was popularly supposed, with few followers, amounted to more than four hundred thousand dollars a week. Zuta's records also showed payment of more than a hundred thousand dollars a week to " M. K.," identified by the police as Matt Kolb, politician and gambler, who apparently handled the gang's protection money. They also showed that Zuta had given or loaned money to many judges, state senators, and other men high in public and private life. But nothing came of these disclosures.

Joseph Aiello died in a burst of machine-gun fire as he stepped into the street from an apartment house on North Kolmar Avenue on October 23, 1930. He was struck by

361

fifty-nine bullets, weighing all together more than a pound. Aiello was the leader of an Italian gang which had arisen after the downfall of the Gennas, and was allied with Bugs Moran. He had been fighting Al Capone for control of the Unione Siciliana and had tried several times to have the gangster king killed, once by bribing a restaurant chef to put prussic acid in Capone's soup, and again by offering a reward of fifty thousand dollars.

Al Capone attempted to arrange a truce with the embattled North Siders after Hymie Weiss and his cohorts had invaded Cicero and bombarded the Hawthorne Inn, and late in September 1926 representatives of both gangs met in conference at the Hotel Sherman. They discussed their differences for several hours, but all prospect of peace vanished when Weiss insisted that Scalisi and Anselmi be "put on the spot" for the murder of Dion O'Banion. When Capone was told of this ultimatum, he sent word to Moran: "I wouldn't do that to a yellow dog," a statement which, when repeated in the newspapers, drew this comment from Police Captain John Stege: "There is no one on earth Capone wouldn't send to death if he thought his interests would be served." Another meeting of gangsters was held at the Hotel Morrison on October 21, 1926, which was attended by delegations from all of the principal gangs, with Maxie Eisen, who had embarked upon a private career as a racketeer levying tribute from pushcart peddlers, present as peacemaker. New territorial allotments were agreed upon, and peace of a sort arranged, but it lasted only a few months. Moran and Capone finally composed their differences after Scalisi and Anselmi had been slain, and the agreement was ratified by some thirty Chicago gang leaders who met in Atlantic City, New Jersey. "We agreed to forget the past and begin all over again," said Capone, "and we drew up a written agreement, and each man signed on the dotted line."

There were many gang killings in Chicago after that, but most of them were disciplinary or protective in character. Such old-timers as Capone, Bugs Moran, and the O'Donnells fought each other no more. They had at last realized the truth of Maxie Eisen's remark: "We're a bunch of saps, killing each other this way and giving the cops a laugh."

12

ABOVE the carnage of the gang wars waved the bloody banner of Al Capone. By the late winter of 1927, despite the fierce enmity of Bugs Moran and the frequent outbreaks of dissatisfaction in the ranks of the Sicilians, the one-time lowly hoodlum from Brooklyn was by far the dominant figure of the Chicago underworld. Moreover, so well had publicity done its work, the famous seven-ton armored car, with the pudgy gangster lolling on silken cushions in its darkened recesses, a big cigar in his fat face, and a fifty-thousand-dollar diamond ring blazing from his left hand, was one of the sights of the city; the average tourist felt that his trip to Chicago was a failure unless it included a view of Capone out for a spin. The mere whisper: " Here comes Al," was sufficient to stop traffic and to set thousands of curious citizens craning their necks along the curbing. In Cicero the conductors of sightseeing buses pointed out the Hawthorne Inn as " Capone Castle."

During the three or four years in which he was the criminal boss of America's second city, Capone's fame spread to the far corners of the earth. European journalists traveled four thousand miles to see and interview him; he received fan mail from the Orient, from Africa, from Australia, and from virtually every country in Europe; once a woman wrote from London offering to pay his passage to England if he would run over and kill some neighbors with whom she had quarreled. He was probably the most talked-of and most written-about man in the world, and was certainly the most shot-at. He was the subject of a greater literature, much of it maudlin and most of it untrustworthy, than any other criminal who ever lived, with the possible exception of Jesse James. Novels, biographies, historical and psychological studies, magazine and newspaper articles, even poems, all dealing with various phases of Capone's career, poured from the presses; plays and moving pictures acquainted millions with his talk and mannerisms.

There were stories of his prodigal spending — he had sunk half a million dollars in his palatial estate near Miami, Florida; his armored car had cost twenty thousand dollars; he never gave a hat-check girl less than ten dollars, nor a newsboy less than five, and a hundred was his minimum tip to a waiter; he carried a roll of fifty thousand dollars in his pocket and threw it away on whatever caught his fancy. There were stories of his unparalleled generosity — his annual expenditure for Christmas gifts exceeded a hundred thousand dollars; to his intimates, at all times of the year, he presented diamond-studded belts and solid-gold cigarette cases encrusted with precious stones; he entertained his political henchmen at elaborate banquets and kept their cellars filled with the finest champagne; he was an easy mark for any one with a hard-luck story; and every winter the big-hearted crook gave Cicero coal yards and department stores carte-blanche orders to supply all of the city's poor families with coal, clothing, and groceries. There were stories of his love of gambling — he shot craps for fifty thousand and a hundred thousand a throw, and never for less than one thousand unless he was playing with friends not "up in the bucks"; he bet a hundred thousand dollars at a crack on a horse-race; at Hawthorne he won three hundred and fifty thousand dollars in two days, but at New Orleans he lost six hundred thousand in a single afternoon. In 1928 he said himself that since his arrival in Chicago in 1920 he had " fooled away " seven million dollars.

But Capone could afford his extravagances, for his private fortune was estimated at forty million dollars, and he was overlord of a criminal empire which operated on a gross income of more than a hundred million dollars a year — sixty millions from beer, liquor, and alky-cooking; twenty-five millions from gambling-houses and dog-tracks; and ten millions from brothels, roadhouses, cabarets, and other immoral resorts. Another ten millions came from racketeering, a form of extortion with which American business men have become all too familiar during the past twenty years, and which was succinctly described by the Illinois Crime Survey as " the exploitation for personal profit, by means of violence of a business association or employees' organization." Perhaps the best of all definitions of " racketeer " was that published in the Chicago *Journal of Commerce* on December 17, 1927:

> " A racketeer may be the boss of a supposedly legitimate business association; he may be a labor union organizer; he may pretend to be one or the other, or both; or he may be just a journeyman thug. Whether he is a gunman who has imposed himself upon some union as its leader, or whether he is a business association organizer, his methods are the same; by throwing bricks into a few windows, and incidental and perhaps accidental murder, he succeeds in organizing a group of smaller business men into what he calls a protective association. He then proceeds to collect what fees and dues he likes, to impose what fines suit him, regulates prices and hours of work, and in various ways undertakes to boss the outfit to his own profit. Any merchant who doesn't come in, or who comes in and doesn't stay in and continue to pay tribute, is bombed, slugged or otherwise intimidated."

Racketeering in one form or another has been practiced in the large cities in the world for more than two thousand years, but nowhere else was the system ever developed to such perfection as in Chicago during the overlordship of Al Capone. The Employers' Association of Chicago published a report late in 1927 listing twenty-three separate lines of business which racketeers either controlled or were attempting to control — window-cleaning, machinery-moving, paper stock, cleaning and dyeing, laundries, candy jobbers, dental laboratories, ash- and rubbish-hauling, grocery and delicatessen stores, garages, physicians, drug stores, milk-dealers, glaziers, photographers, florists, boot-blacks, restaurants, shoe-repairers, fish and poultry markets, butchers, bakers, and window-shades. This list was admittedly incomplete, and probably included no more than half of the businesses which had been brought under the domination of the racketeers. Within another two years the number had been more than tripled, and hundreds of Chicago business men had learned that the report had spoken truth when it said: " Conditions are becoming such that any man who dares to oppose certain kinds of racketeers or refuses to pay tribute to them is in actual physical danger."

All of the leaders of Chicago's big gangs maintained their own racketeering departments, and there were also numerous independents who preyed upon industries too small to interest a Big Shot. But at least seventy per cent of the rackets from 1926 to 1931 were controlled by Al Capone, or by subsidiary racketeers closely allied to him and working under his general direction. He controlled a score of labor unions, most of them officered by ex-convicts, and as many protective associations. To build up this phase of the Capone syndicate operations, and to hold in line the business already conquered, bands of gunmen and sluggers hi-jacked and destroyed truckloads of merchandise, bombed stores and manufacturing plants or wrecked them with axes and crowbars,

366

put acid into laundry vats, poured corrosives onto clothing hanging in cleaning and dyeing shops, blackjacked both workers and employers, and killed when necessary to enforce their demands or break down opposition. In some instances Capone became a partner in a legitimate business enterprise in order to protect it from the inroads of rival racketeers. One notable incident of this description occurred during the fight to control the cleaning and dyeing industry. Morris Becker, president of a company which operated a cleaning plant and a chain of stores, was unable to obtain protection from the police or the Employers' Association, so he reorganized his business, gave a full partnership to Capone, and then issued this announcement:

"I have no need of the police or of the Employers' Association. I now have the best protection in the world."

13

AL CAPONE maintained for more than seven years the headquarters which he had established at the Hawthorne Inn upon the capture of Cicero in 1924, but after the departure of Johnny Torrio the Inn was used principally for quiet conferences with politicians and with police, city, and county officials. The general offices of the syndicate remained at the Four Deuces until that dive was closed by order of Mayor William E. Dever, and were then transferred to the Hotel Metropole at No. 2300 South Michigan Avenue. When the Metropole was invaded by the police during Mayor Dever's energetic but futile attempt to smash the power of gangland, Capone and his staff moved to the Lexington Hotel at State and Twenty-second Streets, on the fringe of the old South Side Levee. In the raid on the Metropole the police seized ledgers and documents which comprised a part of the syndicate's bookkeeping system, and Mayor Dever said with great satisfaction: "We've got the goods this time." From the Mayor's office it was announced that damning proof of wholesale corruption had been obtained, and that the records would be turned over to the Federal authorities. Before this could be done they were impounded by Judge Howard Hayes of the Municipal Court, and were returned to Capone after a special hearing of which the city received no formal notification. Edwin A. Olson, United States District Attorney, denounced Judge Hayes's action as a direct refusal to co-operate with the government.

At both the Metropole and the Lexington Capone's organization occupied between fifty and sixty rooms on two floors, the hallways of which were patrolled constantly by heavily armed gunmen. "They operated their own private elevators and maintained their own service bars," said a contemporary description of the gangster stronghold. "Gambling went on openly and women visited the floors at all hours of the day and night. Nearly every hotel rule and regulation were violated daily. On Sunday mornings especially the lobby was a beehive of activity. Prominent criminal lawyers and high officials of the police department, along with politicians and dive-keepers, waited their turn to consult with the Big Shot. Policemen in uniform streamed in and out. A blind pig operated in the lobby by a semi-public official did a land office business. In an underground vault, especially constructed, were stored $150,000 worth of wines and liquors. The stock was constantly replenished. It was for the gang's private use."

Capone himself occupied two rooms. In one, sitting at the head of a long mahogany table under the framed portraits of George Washington, Abraham Lincoln, and Big Bill Thompson, the gangster king held daily conferences with his subordinates, planning sluggings and murders, arranging hi-jacking forays, formulating instructions for rum-runners and smugglers, and transacting the manifold details of his extraordinary business. The guns of Bugs Moran and other

368

enemies caused frequent changes in the personnel of Capone's board of directors, but among those who were active during the greater part of his regime were Frank Nitti, second in command, who handled most of the protection money; Jack Cusick, also called Guzik, the business manager of the syndicate, and his brother Harry, in charge of prostitution, with Mike de Pike Heitler; Jimmy Mondi, Mops Volpi, and Frankie Pope, head of the gambling interests; Hymie Levine, chief collector; Johnny Genaro and Jim Belcastro, leaders of the bombing squads; Capone's brother Ralph, also known as Bottles; Dago Lawrence Mangano and Charley Fischetti, managers of beer and liquor distribution; Jack McGurn, whose real name was Demora, head of the machine-gun squad and chief hi-jacker; Frankie Rio and Frankie Diamond, captains of the bodyguard; and Johnny Patton, brewery operator and political fixer, who as the Mayor of Burnham had invited Johnny Torrio to establish brothels in that pleasant suburban village.

14

THE most important of the many factors which combined to rid Chicago of Al Capone and disrupt the working of his evil machine was the Chicago Crime Commission; it has brought about more improvements in the administration of criminal justice than any other reform organization in the history of the city. With the co-operation of the newspapers, the Commission hammered away without ceasing at gangland and the conditions which had made gangland possible. Though essentially a fact-finding body with no authority to prosecute nor power to enforce its recommendations, the Commission could and did initiate prosecutions, make investigations, and engage in crusades. Some of the accomplishments of the Commission since it was organized on January 1, 1919 are:

It helped eliminate the rings of crooked bondsmen, and compelled the establishment of a bond department in the State's Attorney's office.

It procured a special appropriation for a thousand additional patrolmen, and caused the virtual drafting of eleven of Chicago's best lawyers as special prosecutors.

It made a thorough and careful survey of the Police Department, on the basis of which the force was reorganized.

It was principally responsible for the anti-crime mass meeting of the Illinois Manufacturers' Association, the formation of the Evanston Crime Commission, and the decision of the Industrial Club of Chicago to finance a statewide survey of crime and the administration of justice.

It made public the records of judges, with regard to time spent on the bench, disposition of cases, and jury trials. As a result the average of time on the bench rose from two and a half to four hours a day, with a corresponding increase in the number of jury trials and dispositions.

It sponsored a drastic concealed-weapons and vagrancy act.

It crusaded against automobile thieves and handlers of stolen cars, and theft-insurance rates in Illinois dropped twenty-six per cent.

Under the management of Colonel Henry Barrett Chamberlin, Operating Director for the past twenty years, the Crime Commission has become one of America's principal clearing houses for information about crime. Its files contain complete records of more than sixty thousand criminals. It keeps a docket on which is recorded the progress of every case on trial in the criminal courts. Every parole asked for in Cook County is submitted to the Commission for a report. It receives daily reports from the Police Department on the previous day's crimes. In the automobile court and in every branch of the criminal court is stationed an observer who reports daily to the Commission on the evidence and the conduct of judges, bailiffs, prosecutors and policemen.

In 1930 the Crime Commission struck directly at the principal figures of gangland, making a public list of twenty-eight leading gangsters, headed by Al Capone, and branding them as public enemies. Copies of this list were sent to judges, to the State's Attorney, the Sheriff of Cook County, and the Commissioner of Police, together with a letter from Frank J. Loesch, president of the Commission, recommending that the gangsters be relentlessly pursued in every legal way as aliens, tax-evaders, inmates of gambling and disorderly houses, and vagrants. "The purpose," said Mr. Loesch, "is to keep the light of publicity shining on Chicago's most prominent well known and notorious gangsters to the end that they may be under constant observation by the enforcing authorities and law-abiding citizens apprised of the hazards to be encountered in dealing with those who are constantly in conflict with the law."

The response to the Commission's attempt to keep "the light of publicity shining on notorious gangsters" was extraordinary. The phrase "public enemies" caught the popular fancy at once; editorial writers in newspapers all over the United States discussed its implications, columnists took it up, books and moving pictures bearing the two simple words as titles were rushed into print and on the screen, and it quickly became a catch-phrase throughout the country. Probably no other single action ever undertaken against criminals received such widespread publicity. And it was bad publicity for the gangsters. As a Crime Commission report put it, "this move stirred the entire nation to action, and gangdom began to feel the lash of an aroused citizenry." Even Chicago police officials made big talk about what they would do to the gangsters, and what's more, actually did it! By the beginning of 1934 the Crime Commission was able to announce that since 1930 fifteen public enemies had been convicted, nine had died, one was awaiting deportation, the cases of eight were awaiting disposition in the courts, and the rest were "on the run and in hideouts because of the existence of various warrants against them."

15

AL CAPONE and his chief bodyguard, Frankie Rio, went to Philadelphia after the peace conference with other Chicago gangsters at Atlantic City in 1929, and on the night of May 16 they were picked up by the Philadelphia police on a charge of carrying concealed weapons. In less than seventeen hours they had been arraigned in court, found guilty, and sentenced to one year's imprisonment in the Holmesburg County Jail. Later they were transferred to the Eastern Penitentiary. There has always been considerable mystery attached to Capone's presence in Philadelphia at this particular time. One theory was that he had gone there to confer with Maxie Boo-Boo Hoff, the boss of the Philadelphia underworld. Another was that he was seeking a hide-away as far as possible from Chicago, and had courted arrest and imprisonment through fear of gangsters who had not attended the Atlantic City meeting and with whom he had not been able to make peace. On the night of his arrest Capone told Major Lemuel B. Schofield, Philadelphia's Director of Public Safety, that he had been trying to retire for two years. "But once in the racket," he said, "you're always in. I haven't had peace of mind for years. I never know when I'm going to get it. Even when I'm on a peace errand I must take a chance on the light going suddenly out. I have a wife and an eleven-year-old boy I idolize, at Palm Island, Florida. If I could go there and forget it all, I would be the happiest man in the world. I want peace, and I'm willing to live and let live. I'm tired of gang murders and gang shootings."

Nevertheless Capone continued to transact his business from the Eastern Penitentiary; he was given a private cell, allowed to make long-distance calls, and to use the Warden's office for conferences with his lawyers and with Frank Nitti, Jack Cusick, and his brother Ralph, who made frequent trips to Philadelphia. With two months off for good behavior, Capone was released on March 17, 1930, to find himself branded as Public Enemy Number One. In Chicago Captain John Stege had posted a guard of twenty-five policemen in front of the Capone home on Prairie Avenue, once the finest residential thoroughfare in Chicago, with orders to arrest the gangster as soon as he appeared. But Capone slipped quietly into the city and went to the Hawthorne Inn at Cicero, where he spent four days answering his mail and attending to business affairs. Then, in company with his lawyer, he called upon Captain Stege, the State's Attorney, and the United States District Attorney, to find that none held a warrant for his arrest, and that no charges whatever had been made against him. There was no law under which he could be held, but also there was no law to prevent Captain Stege from keeping him under surveillance as a suspected crook. So two uniformed policemen were assigned to follow Capone, and for weeks they dogged his footsteps day and night.

The gang chieftain was visibly annoyed by these attentions, although he made no complaint. He could easily have had the policemen killed, but he was smart enough to realize that such a crime, with public opinion now so generally arrayed against him, would in all likelihood send him to the gallows. After a few months in Chicago Capone began to travel about the country, apparently seeking a place where he could retire and re-establish himself as a private citizen. But he was not wanted anywhere. He went to Los Angeles, and the police ordered him to leave within twenty-four hours. He tried the Black Hills of South Dakota, but the Governor of the state said that the National Guard would be called out if necessary to chase him away. He was barred from the Bahama Islands, and warned not to tarry in Havana. He started for Florida, and the Governor of that state notified the sixty-seven Florida sheriffs to arrest the gangster and escort him to the border. But there Capone fought back; his lawyers obtained an injunction restraining the Florida authorities from molesting him, and he was finally able to reach his estate near Miami.

In the late summer of 1931 Capone returned to Chicago, and on October 6 was arrested by Federal agents who had been investigating the sources of his income. He was indicted, and on October 17, 1931, in Federal court, he was found guilty on five counts, three of evading payment of taxes from 1925 to 1928 on an income of six hundred and seventy thousand dollars, and two of failing to make tax returns for 1928 and 1929. He was sentenced to serve eight years in Alcatraz Prison in San Francisco Bay. Several of his most faithful henchmen, including his brother Ralph and Jack Cusick, had already been convicted of similar offenses.

Chicago was through with Capone when he went to Alcatraz, but it was not through with the conditions that Capone had fostered. The city is still struggling to erase the imprint of his fine Italian hand.

Curiously enough, during the decade in which Chicago was overrun by gangsters and was a synonym for crime and corruption everywhere in the world, the population of the city increased by nearly seven hundred thousand.

BIBLIOGRAPHY

A GREAT DEAL of the material in this book was procured from the files of various magazines and the Chicago newspapers, from police and court records and the reports of the Chicago Crime Commission, and from talks with old-time policemen and politicians. Following are a few of the other sources consulted:

AHERN, M. L.: *The Political History of Chicago, Covering the Period from 1837 to 1887.* Chicago, 1886.

ANDREAS, A. T.: *History of Chicago.* Three volumes. Chicago, 1884.

ANONYMOUS: " Chicago as Seen by Herself "; in *McClure's Magazine,* May 1907.

BENNETT, JAMES O'DONNELL: *Chicago Gangland, the True Story of Chicago Crime.* Chicago, 1929.

BRIGHT, JOHN: *Hizzoner Big Bill Thompson, an Idyll of Chicago.* New York, 1930.

BURNS, WALTER NOBLE: *The One-Way Ride.* New York, 1931.

BYRNES, THOMAS: *Professional Criminals of America.* New York, 1886. New and Revised Edition, New York, 1895.

CATON, JOHN D.: *Miscellanies.* Boston, 1880.

CHRISTISON, J. SANDERSON, M.D.: *Crime and Criminals.* Chicago, 1897.

COLBERT, ELIAS, and CHAMBERLIN, EVERETT: *Chicago and the Great Conflagration.* Cincinnati and New York, 1872.

COOK, FREDERICK FRANCIS: *Bygone Days in Chicago. Recollections of the Garden City of the Sixties.* Chicago, 1910.

CRESSY, PAUL G.: *The Taxi-Dance Hall, a Sociological Study in Commercialized Recreation and City Life.* Chicago, 1932.

DOBYNS, FLETCHER: *The Underworld of American Politics.* New York, 1932.

ERBSTEIN, CHARLES E.: *The Show-Up. Stories before the Bar*. Chicago, 1926.

FARLEY, PHIL: *Criminals of America*. New York, 1876.

FLEXNER, BERNARD, and BALDWIN, ROGER N.: *Juvenile Courts and Probation*. New York, 1916.

FLINN, JOHN J.: *Chicago, the Marvelous City of the West; a History, an Encyclopedia, and a Guide*. Chicago, 1891.

——, assisted by JOHN E. WILKIE: *History of the Chicago Police from the Settlement of the Community to the Present Time*. Chicago, 1887.

FLYNT, JOSIAH: " In the World of Graft — Chi, an Honest City "; in *McClure's Magazine*, February 1901.

GALE, EDWIN O.: *Reminiscences of Early Chicago and Vicinity*. New York and Chicago, 1902.

HANRAHAN, JAMES: *The Thrilling Story of James Hanrahan, alias James D. Burton, Auctioneer; Fifty Years a Fugitive*. 1912.

HARRISON, CARTER H.: *Stormy Years, the Autobiography of*. Indianapolis, 1935.

HUNTER, ROBERT: *Tenement Conditions in Chicago*. Report by the Investigating Committee of the City Homes Association. Chicago, 1901.

JOHNSON, CLAUDIUS O.: *Carter Henry Harrison I, Political Leader*. Chicago, 1928.

KIRKLAND, JOSEPH: "Among the Poor of Chicago "; in *Scribner's Magazine*, July 1892.

LANDESCO, JOHN: *Organized Crime in Chicago*. Part III, Illinois Crime Survey. Chicago, 1929.

——: " The Criminal Underworld of Chicago in the 80's and 90's "; in the *Journal of the American Institute of Criminal Law and Criminology*, May–June 1934, March–April 1935.

——: " The Woman and the Underworld "; in the *Journal of the American Institute of Criminal Law and Criminology*, March 1936.

LEHMAN, REV. F. M.: *The White Slave Hell, or With Christ at Midnight in the Slums of Chicago*. Chicago, 1910.

LEWIS, LLOYD, and SMITH, HENRY JUSTIN: *Chicago, the History of Its Reputation*. New York, 1929.

Marquis' Handbook of Chicago, a Complete History, Reference Book and Guide to the City. Chicago, 1885.

McCONAUGHY, JOHN: *From Cain to Capone, or, Racketeering Down the Ages*. New York, 1931.

McILVAINE, MABEL, editor: *Reminiscences of Chicago during the Forties and Fifties*, by William Bross, Charles Cleaver, Joseph Jefferson, and Capt. A. T. Andreas. Chicago, 1913.

376

McKenna, John J.: *Reminiscences of the Chicago Fire of 1871*. Chicago, 1933.

O'Sullivan, F. Dalton: *Crime Detection*. Chicago, 1928.

Owen, Collinson: *King Crime, an English Study of America's Greatest Problem*. New York, 1932.

Pasley, Fred D.: *Al Capone, the Biography of a Self-Made Man*. New York, 1930.

Pierce, Bessie Louise, editor: *As Others See Chicago; Impressions of Visitors, 1673–1933*. Chicago, 1933.

Reckless, Walter C.: *Vice in Chicago*. Chicago, 1933.

Report of Senate Vice Committee, State of Illinois. Chicago, 1916.

Roe, Clifford G.: *The Girl Who Disappeared*. Chicago, 1914.

Rowan, Richard Wilmer: *The Pinkertons, a Detective Dynasty*. Boston, 1931.

Salisbury, William: *The Career of a Journalist*. New York, 1908.

Shackleton, Robert: *The Book of Chicago*. Philadelphia, 1920.

Shaw, Clifford R., in collaboration with Maurice E. Moore: *The Natural History of a Delinquent Career*. Chicago, 1931.

Social Evil in Chicago, The. A Study of Existing Conditions with Recommendations by the Vice Commission of Chicago. Chicago, 1911.

Stead, William T.: *If Christ Came to Chicago! A Plea for the Union of All Who Love in the Service of All Who Suffer*. Chicago and London, 1894.

Stuart, William H.: *The Twenty Incredible Years*. New York, 1930.

Sullivan, Edward D.: *Rattling the Cup on Chicago Crime*. New York, 1929.

Sutherland, Edwin H., editor: *The Professional Thief, by a Professional Thief*. Chicago, 1937.

Thrasher, Frederic M., Ph.D.: *The Gang, a Study of 1,313 Gangs in Chicago*. Chicago, 1927.

Turner, George Kibbe: "The City of Chicago, a Study of the Great Immoralities"; in *McClure's Magazine*, April 1907.

Washburn, Charles: *Come into My Parlor, a Biography of the Aristocratic Everleigh Sisters of Chicago*. New York, 1936.

Wilson, Samuel Paynter: *Chicago by Gaslight*. Chicago, n.d.

———: *Chicago and Its Cess-Pools of Infamy*. Chicago, n.d.

Wooldridge, Clifton R.: *Hands Up! In the World of Crime, or Twelve Years a Detective*. Chicago, 1906.

———: *The Devil and the Grafter, and How They Work Together to Deceive, Swindle and Destroy Men, Women, Society and Religion*. Chicago, n.d.

INDEX

i

ii

iii

iv

vii

viii

x

xii

xiv

xvi

xviii